the
PACIFICWAR

the
PACIFICWAR

THE STRATEGY, POLITICS, AND PLAYERS THAT WON THE WAR

William B. Hopkins

ZENITH PRESS

I dedicate this book to my wife of more than sixty years, Virginia G. Hopkins.

First published in 2008 by Zenith Press, an imprint of MBI Publishing Company, 400 First Avenue North, Suite 300, Minneapolis, MN 55401 USA

Copyright © 2008, 2010 by William B. Hopkins
Hardcover edition published 2008. Softcover edition 2010

Zenith Press titles are also available at discounts in bulk quantity for industrial or sales-promotional use. For details write to Special Sales Manager at MBI Publishing Company, 400 First Avenue North, Suite 300, Minneapolis, MN 55401 USA.

To find out more about our books, visit us online at www.zenithpress.com.

ISBN-13: 978-0-7603-3975-6

Library of Congress Cataloging-in-Publication Data

Hopkins, William B., 1922-
    The Pacific War : the strategy, politics, and players that won the war / William B. Hopkins.
       p. cm.
    Includes bibliographical references.
    ISBN 978-0-7603-3435-5 (hb w/ jkt)
1. World War, 1939-1945--Pacific Area. 2. United States--Military policy--20th century. 3. Strategy. 4. United States--Politics and government--1933-1945. I. Title.
       D767.H592 2008
       940.54'26--dc22
                         2008038157

Design Manager: Brenda C. Canales
Cover designed by: Andrew Brozyna, AJB Design, Inc.
Maps by: Paul Stump, Postscript Art Studios

About the Author:
William B. Hopkins, a native of Rocky Mount, Virginia, graduated from Washington & Lee University and then served with the 3rd Marine Division in the South Pacific in World War II. He graduated from the University of Virginia Law School in the fall of 1947 and began practicing law in Roanoke, Virginia. In 1951 he was called to active duty in the Korean War, where he was wounded later that year and sent back to the United States for hospitalization. After being honorably discharged as a major in the Marine Corps Reserve, he returned to practicing law in Roanoke. He served for twenty years in the Virginia State Senate, four as majority leader. He is married to Virginia G. Hopkins and has five children—two sons and three daughters. Hopkins' critically acclaimed first book, *One Bugle, No Drums: The Marines at Chosin Reservoir*, related his Korean War service.

On the cover: *Top:* B-29s based in the Mariana Islands. *USAAF photo*
Bottom: The USS Idaho fires on Okinawa prior to the landing of the Tenth Army. *U.S. Navy photo*

On the back cover: General Douglas MacArthur, President Franklin Roosevelt, and Admiral Chester W. Nimitz aboard the heavy cruiser USS *Baltimore* in Pearl Harbor on 26 July 1944. *U.S. Navy photo*

Printed in the United States of America

Contents

Acknowledgments

I wish to thank Amy O'Neil for her assistance in the preparation of my first rough draft. Special thanks are due to Lucy Glenn, Research Librarian at the Roanoke Library, who acquired many of the books listed in the bibliography and the newspaper articles quoted herein. Thanks are due to my three daughters, Dabney Hopkins, Sarah Hopkins Finley, and Marshall Hopkins Martin, who travelled with me to acquire pictures and information from the U.S. Naval Institute at Annapolis, Maryland; the U.S. Archives at College Park, Maryland; the Franklin Delano Roosevelt Library at Hyde Park, New York; and Duke University Library at Durham, North Carolina. Thanks also to Don Wallace and Paul Stump for the maps contained throughout the book. Above all, I wish to thank Anita Firebaugh who had the patience to make the many revisions of the original manuscript and to provide the proper footnotes.

Introduction
My View: Then and Now

*H*AVING SERVED AS A JUNIOR OFFICER with the 3rd Marine Division in the South Pacific during World War II, I have always had a deep-felt interest in the Pacific War. As a participant and avid reader of the daily happenings, I, along with the American public, formed one view of events. The reader of this book will be presented with facts unknown to the American public while war was being waged, how battles were won or lost, and—above all—why they were fought. My view changed considerably during the past decade as I discovered a factual picture of the war against Japan. This book attempts to portray both views.

I was surprised to find that two U.S. Marine Corps officers, Lt. Gen. John A. Lejeune and Lt. Col. Earl H. Ellis, made significant contributions to the winning strategy, though neither served during World War II. In the early 1990s, I had the pleasure of reading and making copies of the minutes of the Joint Chiefs of Staff (American) and the Combined Chiefs of Staff (British and American) meetings as they pertained to the war in the Pacific. Fortunately, they were all then declassified and available at the George C. Marshall Museum on the grounds of Virginia Military Institute in Lexington, Virginia, just fifty miles from my home in Roanoke. Anyone expecting to get a clear picture of the Pacific War by reading these minutes will be greatly disappointed. However, they did create a desire to delve much deeper.

From the very start, the British handed over to the Americans the responsibility for the war against Japan in the Pacific theater. Did those at the top argue and disagree over the moves our military should make? Yes, they did, but somehow they arrived at a consensus, putting discord aside. For many years prior to the war's beginning, the U.S. military had developed the strategy of encirclement of the Japanese home islands by the U.S. Fleet. This strategy was called Plan Orange and was the most expeditious method to defeat Japan.

The success of the Nazi war machine prior to the U.S. entry into World War II, coupled with the threat of the Japanese attack from the west, persuaded

1

American military planners to adopt a series of five plans labeled Rainbow. Rainbow Five was the plan adopted for World War II. It called for the defeat of Germany, beginning with a holding action in the Pacific before implementing Plan Orange, which was the method designed for the defeat of Japan. Regardless of prewar strategy, successive Japanese victories during the first five months of the war compelled the United States to adopt a defensive role in the Pacific.

As the war progressed, opinions changed among the U.S. Joint Chiefs, usually for the best. Before the end, most of the prewar strategy had again been adopted. It is interesting to note that at war's end most of Germany's fleet lay at the bottom of the Atlantic Ocean, while her armies were thoroughly defeated in North Africa, Sicily, Italy, and the European continent. In contrast, Japan lost what it now calls the Pacific War, but the great mass of its army was still intact and lay undefeated in China, southeastern Asia, the Netherlands East Indies, and the bypassed islands of the Pacific. Yet, with the loss of its navy, its merchant fleet, and its manufacturing facilities, Japan was a thoroughly defeated nation, the same as Germany.

President Franklin D. Roosevelt; Secretary of War Henry Stimson; Secretaries of the Navy Frank Knox and James Forrestal; and the Joint Chiefs of Staff, namely Adm. William D. Leahy (special aide to the president), Gen. George C. Marshall, Adm. Ernest J. King, and air force Gen. H. H. "Hap" Arnold all played vital roles. Marshall seemed to have a superior global view over the other members of the American Joint Chiefs. Yet, from a strategic standpoint, King stood out as the architect of victory in the Pacific. He—above all others—kept the United States on the right track for Japan's defeat at the least cost in men and materials. But credit for implementation of the winning strategy goes primarily to Adm. Chester W. Nimitz.

The Pacific War was predominantly a navy war. From the start, most military leaders in Japan and the United States recognized this; however, U.S. news releases at the time did not portray it as such. Most focused on Gen. Douglas MacArthur and the U.S. Marine and Army ground troops. Although Japanese losses caused by the U.S. Navy and U.S. Air Force were frequently mentioned, strict censorship prevented the U.S. Navy's role in those losses from being reported to—and fully understood by—the American public. Very few news articles recounted the role of the U.S. submarine fleet, whose performance in cutting Japanese supply lines excelled that of all other branches of service.

The United States was blessed with dedicated and courageous fighting men, a winning strategy, and above all, a unified home front, essential for a nation at war. After the Japanese struck at Pearl Harbor, Congress passed two War Powers acts, which placed in the hands of the commander in chief of the U.S. forces the full responsibility for the pursuit of military objectives. Thereafter, Congress could no longer interfere with President Roosevelt's judicial role as commander in chief of the U.S. armed services.

In the presentation of the U.S. Navy's part in the Pacific, military scholars are indebted to Samuel Eliot Morison, who shortly after the war oversaw the writing of *The History of United States Naval Operations in World War II*. His writings give a comprehensive view of U.S. Navy operations, although he admitted that at the time of his writing he lacked information from the Japanese side, and any attempt to describe battles from one side only is fatally handicapped. He said:

> I do not claim omniscience. As fresh data appear, mistakes will be found and later writers will make new interpretations. It is the fate of all historians, especially those who take the risk of writing shortly after the event, to be superseded. Far safer to write about an era long past, in which all the actors are long since dead! But my warm contact with the United States Navy in action has given me the opportunity to see events for myself, to obtain oral information while men's memories are still fresh, and to correct mistakes in the written record.[1]

Morison also recognized that there were numerous items of information that had not been declassified and thus were unavailable to him and his staff. In fact, for many years after the war, historians failed to learn about the value to the U.S. military of the breaking of Japanese secret codes.

The Allies prosecuted the ground war in the Pacific on two fronts: primarily the drive across the Central Pacific, which followed the strategy of the prewar Plan Orange, and secondarily the thrust from the South and southwest Pacific. Although Rainbow Five envisioned a holding action against Japan as the Allies first fought to defeat Germany, the United States took the offensive in the Pacific earlier than expected. Admiral Nimitz began his drive across the Central Pacific in late 1943. Afterward, his command moved quickly to its main objective: the encirclement of the Japanese home islands. General Douglas MacArthur pressed forward from his base in Australia through New Guinea to his main objective: the liberation of the Philippines. The turning points in the Pacific War occurred the first year, with the U.S. naval victory at Midway and the successful campaign for Guadalcanal conducted by the U.S. Navy, Marines, and Army.

More than six decades since the close of the Pacific War, both Japanese and American historians have thoroughly examined most aspects of that war. Accordingly, this book relies heavily on the expertise of the scholars listed in the bibliography for factual information. The United States Army published eleven books on the war in the Pacific. The Australian War Memorial dedicated four volumes to battles in the southwest and western Pacific. Australian histories paint a somewhat different picture than that of the U.S. Army during the first two years of the war. The chapters on Papua and Australian New Guinea emphasize the fact that it supplied most of the ground troops involved. United States Army history does not disagree, yet it does not portray the true worth of the Australians and to a lesser degree the New Zealanders. During the war and for many years thereafter, neither we in the military nor the American public recognized the true value of our down-under Allies.

For the sake of clarity, chronological order has been set aside in many cases in this book in favor of a region-by-region approach to events. Except for the day the Japanese attacked Pearl Harbor, I do not personally appear in the picture.

A comprehensive view of each major battle as depicted by Samuel Eliot Morison or U.S. Marines and U.S. Army history is not intended here. Instead, this book attempts to present to the non-specialist reader a condensed account of the fighting highlights with emphasis on the personalities, politics, and strategy that caused each to take place. To those veterans of the Pacific War still living, the following pages should serve as a refresher course.

Chapter 1
Plan Orange

*T*HE UNITED STATES AND JAPAN both planned for the Pacific War years ahead of the actual event. After acquiring the Philippines as a protectorate at the end of the Spanish-American War of 1898, it did not take long for military planners to recognize that United States' interests might collide with those of Japan in the western Pacific. Japan was clearly a war-like nation. It had acquired the island of Formosa as a result of its victory over China in the war of 1894–1895. It established a protectorate over Korea, which became a Japanese colony in 1910. It destroyed most of Russia's naval power in 1905 in the Battle of Tsushima. This victory caused other countries to acknowledge Japan as a world power. Japan's military leaders also recognized the potential for future conflict. As early as 1908, "the Japanese Navy was considering the problem of fighting the United States Navy in Pacific waters; by 1910 it was studying the question of attacking the Philippines." [1]

In November 1904, the United States Joint Army-Navy Board approved for planning purposes a series of color designations for various nations of the world. They assigned the code color orange to Japan and the code color blue to the United States. In 1906, the U.S. Joint Army-Navy Board arrived at the first Plan Orange. It decided that Japan could be defeated by simply taking advantage of geography. The Japanese homeland was a heavily populated island kingdom with insufficient natural resources to support its people. Placing a naval blockade around the islands to prevent men and materials from moving in and out of the homeland would make Japan incapable of conducting an offensive war. Through the ensuing years until World War II, the U.S. Joint Army-Navy Board would adopt many variations of Plan Orange, yet "the siege remained the commonly understood American policy." [2]

To counter American influence, Japan determined to build a fleet capable of defeating the United States Navy or at least fighting it on equal terms. In 1914, during World War I, Japan took a giant step in extending its influence eastward across the Pacific. After declaring war against Germany, she occupied the numerous German Pacific possessions north of the equator, namely the Mariana, Caroline, and Marshall islands. Australia staked claims on the

German possessions of New Guinea, the Solomon Islands, and the Bismarck Archipelago, as did New Zealand on Samoa. This move gave Japan a vast new empire in the Central Pacific after Germany's defeat. When the League of Nations mandated ownership of this area to Japan in 1919, it greatly transformed the strategic situation in the western and Central Pacific. On some of the islands Japan could—and did—build a spider web of air bases capable of interdicting the U.S. Navy's move west.

Emboldened by this recent acquisition, in 1920 Japan formulated the original basic strategic concept of war against America. It provided:

a. To control the command of the sea in the Orient in order to secure the traffic between the Asia continent and the southern district.
b. To invade the Guam Island at the beginning of the war, thus laying patrol lines from the Benin Island, extending south to the Marianas.
c. To invade the Philippines.
d. To have the fleet wait at Amamioshima, expecting to have the decisive sea battle somewhere from the Nansei Islands down to east of the Philippines.[3]

In the summer of 1921, Rear Adm. Clarence Stewart Williams took command of the U.S. Navy's War Plans Division. During his tenure from July 1921 to September 1922, Plan Orange was recast to an advance through the mandated islands. Yet, if the U.S. Fleet could not move across the Pacific without being constantly attacked from ground-based enemy planes, was it possible to achieve the envisioned success, that is, encirclement of the Japanese homeland? A little-known U.S. Marine Corps lieutenant colonel would make a huge contribution on how best to "bell the cat."

On 21 May 1923, the American embassy in Tokyo cabled the State Department in Washington that Earl H. Ellis, a representative of Hughes Trading Company of 2 Rector Street, New York, had died at Parao, Caroline Island, on 12 May. It said that the Japanese government awaited instructions as to his remains and effects in their possession.[4]

The Hughes Company president, a retired Marine Corps colonel, after considerable questioning, acknowledged that Earl Hancock Ellis was not his employee but an active Marine Corps lieutenant colonel on an intelligence mission. His company had been used as a cover for Ellis.

Major General John A. Lejeune, commandant of the Marine Corps, when finally forced to comment, said Ellis had been a patient at the Naval Hospital Yokohama and was last seen 6 October 1922. He had been on leave touring the Orient. Leave had been revoked before Ellis vanished. The official records backed up Lejeune's statement.[5]

Newsmen would have been startled had they known the whole of the Ellis story. None of it became public until well after the close of World War II.

Born on a Kansas farm in mid-December 1880, Earl Hancock "Pete" Ellis spent his youth as a typical midwestern farm boy. After graduating from high school at age eighteen, he worked two years on his father's farm. Three months before his twentieth birthday he enlisted as a private in the Marine Corps. Before finishing his first enlistment, he was commissioned a second lieutenant. In 1911, Captain Ellis attended Naval War College at Newport, Rhode Island. There he advocated amphibious operations to seize key islands as advance bases for the U.S. Navy. Prior to World War I, he established a strong friendship with a future commandant of the Marine Corps, John A. Lejeune.

In 1914, he was sent to Guam to prepare that island's defense plan. There, in 1915, wrote biographer Dirk Anthony Ballendorf, Ellis led a small group of men in hauling a 3-inch gun across the reef at Orote Point, demonstrating for the first time that artillery could be landed from boats. However, it was not until the advent of World War II that the United States began producing landing craft suitable for amphibious operations. While Ellis was stationed at Guam, his problem with depression came to the forefront, causing him to be hospitalized for several months.

When Colonel Lejeune became assistant commandant in 1915, he had Ellis transferred to Washington. With Lejeune's promotion to major general in 1918, he took command of the 2nd Division, composed of the 4th Marine Brigade and the U.S. Army's 3rd Infantry Brigade. Ellis, promoted to temporary lieutenant colonel, became his adjutant.

In early October 1918, when the French army stalled on Mont Blanc Ridge, a key German strongpoint on the Hindenburg Line, Lejeune offered the services of his 2nd Division. French Gen. Henri Gouraud requested that Lejeune's troops be used as replacements for three of his divisions. Lejeune refused, then counteroffered: Leave the 2nd Division intact, and the Americans would take the Mont Blanc heights. He directed Ellis to prepare the assault plan that captured Mont Blanc Ridge after days of heavy fighting. General Gouraud gratefully presented Ellis with the Croix de Guerre and the Legion d'Honour. His American superiors recommended him for the Distinguished Service Medal and the Navy Cross. The citation mentioned ". . . his imperviousness to fatigue and his alertness under strain and sleeplessness, words which indicate that the nervousness and physical disorders diagnosed under headings such as neurasthenia and psychasthenia were becoming much more frequent and serious." [6]

From 1918 on, entries of hospitalization and sick leave in his record indicated a rapid nervous and physical decline. He took to drinking with increasing regularity. In January 1920, navy doctors prescribed three months' sick leave for Pete Ellis.

When Lejeune became the thirteenth commandant of the Marine Corps in July 1920, he ordered Ellis to Washington for a special assignment. The next year, Lejeune sent Maj. Holland M. Smith, USMC, to the Navy War Plans Division and Col. Ben H. Fuller, USMC, to the planning staff of the Naval War College. Both Smith and Fuller advised Lejeune that the navy was making detailed plans of a war against Japan. They both urged the commandant to develop a role for the Marine Corps. Lejeune had already assigned Ellis to this task.

For years, Ellis had believed that war between the United States and Japan was inevitable. After World War I, when the League of Nations awarded the widely separated island groups of Micronesia—the Marianas, the Carolines, and the Marshalls—to Japan, Ellis said the U.S. delegates who had agreed to Japan's request had cast their vote for the next war.[7] His outspoken criticism of America's foreign policy landed him in hot water but did not shut him up.

As Ellis saw it, the numerous islands stretching from Japan to the equator formed a protective cover for imperialistic Japan to carry out its long-cherished dream of expansion. "Anyone who could not see the danger in giving Japan control over these Pacific islands had no business deciding the issue," Ellis said whenever and wherever the opportunity presented itself.[8] Although Ellis had little support in Washington outside of Lejeune, he had a vocal soul mate in the person of Prime Minister W. M. Hughes of Australia.

The dilemma in which Australia became increasingly involved had been clearly stated in the House of Representatives by Prime Minister Hughes, upon his return from the Imperial Conference of 1921:

> For us the Pacific problem is for all practical purposes the problem of Japan. Here is a nation of nearly 70 millions of people, crowded together in narrow islands; its population is increasing rapidly, and is already pressing on the margin of subsistence. She wants both room for her increasing millions of population, and markets for her manufactured goods. And she wants these very badly indeed. America and Australia say to her millions "Ye cannot enter in." Japan, then, is faced with the great problem which has bred wars since time began. For when the tribes and nations of the past outgrew the resources of their own territory they moved on and on, hacking their way to the fertile pastures of their neighbors. But where are the overflowing millions of Japanese to find room? Not in Australia; not in America. Well, where, then? . . .
>
> These 70,000,000 Japanese cannot possibly live, except as a manufacturing nation. Their position is analogous to that of Great Britain. To a manufacturing nation, overseas markets are essential to its very existence. Japan sees across a narrow strip of water 400,000,000 Chinese gradually awakening to an appreciation of Western methods, and she sees in China the natural market for her goods. She feels that her geographical circumstances give her a special right to the exploitation of the Chinese markets. But other countries want the market too, and so comes the demand for the "Open Door" . . . .
>
> This is the problem of the Pacific—the modern riddle of the Sphinx, for which we must find an answer . . . Talk about disarmament is idle unless the causes of naval armaments are removed. [9]

Another statesman at the conference made a prophecy. "Our temptation is still to look upon the European stage as of the first importance," said the South African prime minister, J. C. Smuts. "It is no longer so . . . these are not really first-rate events any more . . . Undoubtedly the scene has shifted away from Europe to the Far East and to the Pacific. The problems of the Pacific are to my mind the world problems of the next fifty years or more." [10]

After Commandant Lejeune ordered Ellis to Washington, he was seldom seen. Almost a year later, Ellis emerged from seclusion with the product of his labor: a 30,000-word document entitled "Advanced Base Operations in Micronesia." On 23 July 1921, Lejeune approved this top-secret document as Operation Plan 712-H, which was passed on to the U.S. Navy Department. In this document Ellis wrote, "Japan is a World Power, and her army and navy will doubtless be up to date as to training and material. Considering our consistent policy of non-aggression, she will probably initiate the war, which will indicate that, in her own mind, she believes that, considering her natural defensive position, she has sufficient military strength to defeat our fleet."

With prophetic insight, Ellis listed the objectives against which Japan would launch her attack: Hawaii, Wake, Midway, Guam, and the Philippines. Ellis' plan called for U.S. seizure of key islands in the Marshalls and Carolines. Eniwetok was identified as a needed forward naval base. The eventual advance on the Japanese homeland would remain flexible.

Other U.S. Navy military planners recognized that Japan's bases in the Central Pacific could thwart the U.S. Fleet's move west. This called for a new concept in offensive warfare, one that Ellis had espoused years before, namely amphibious warfare. Ellis' detailed blueprint of how this mode of battle should be conducted did not readily meet with approval. The generals and admirals were cognizant of the military disaster, for both naval attacks and after ground forces landed, at Gallipoli in 1915, where sixteen Allied divisions, predominantly British, suffered more than 200,000 casualties before being withdrawn from the peninsula. Winston Churchill, first lord of the admiralty at that time, was forced to resign from the government as a result.

The long hours of overwork and intensity took their toll on Ellis. A week after submitting his plan to Lejeune, doctors admitted Ellis to the naval hospital, where he stayed for the next three months. Two weeks after his discharge, he asked for and was given a ninety-day leave, ostensibly to visit Europe. This began his tour of the Japanese mandated islands in the Pacific. Prior to his departure, Ellis called at the commandant's office to say goodbye. It has been said that during the apparently normal conversation Lejeune's secretary noticed Ellis pass a sealed envelope to the general. Lejeune unobtrusively slipped it into his desk drawer. Ellis was never seen again at U.S. Marine Corps Headquarters. [11]

During his non-productive sojourn around the Pacific, Ellis was in and out of hospitals. Although a brilliant strategist, he was an amateur spy at best. To Ellis' chagrin, the Japanese had not yet begun to develop their newly acquired mandated islands into strong military bases, which would come later. Thus, he was unable to learn any additional information about Japanese intentions that would prove valuable to the U.S. military. The cause of his death has never been established fully, yet the best evidence points to death by natural causes.

After Ellis' death, it has been written that Lejeune took from the drawer of his desk the sealed envelope that Ellis had left behind, placed it in an ashtray, struck a match, and watched burn Ellis' undated resignation from the Marine Corps.[12] Thus ended the final chapter of Ellis' life, and America's successful adoption of the island-hopping campaign for the Pacific War.

Prior to Ellis' tour of the Pacific, five nations held a major naval conference in Washington, D.C. There, they agreed to the following limits on naval strength in ships of the larger classes: United States, 525,000 tons; Britain and her dominions, 525,000; Japan, 315,000; France and Italy, each 175,000. Japan, at first, was unwilling to accept naval inferiority. She reluctantly agreed upon the condition that the United States would not further develop any naval base west of Hawaii, nor would Britain east of Singapore.

In August 1924 the Joint Army-Navy Board adopted a Joint War Plan Orange. After approval by the cabinet secretaries, the nation had its official Joint Plan Orange "endorsed at the highest seat of civil authority save the presidency." [13] The first objective, after blocking Japanese expansion, was to establish U.S. sea power in the western Pacific superior to that of Japan. This meant occupying or controlling the Japanese mandated islands and holding or retaking Manila Bay. Ellis had recommended that the U.S. Navy create an engineering and construction force to build piers, airfields, roads, and necessary buildings for the troops after occupation of a hostile island. The navy had no such force at the time. Its construction unit achieved its goals through private contractors.

In 1924, the war against Japan was expected to be long, preceded by a period of mobilization. Fifty-thousand troops would be transferred to Oahu on D-day plus 10, then leave the Hawaiian Islands for Manila Bay four days later. This was more than a third of the current 132,000 strength of the U.S. Army. The lack of military strength showed the plan to be unrealistic.

The drafters of this 1924 Plan Orange were insistent that all forces should be under the immediate command of an officer of their respective services, but that it was essential to have a single overall commander with a joint staff to control each phase of the operations. Through the period of isolation and harassment, this would be the commander in chief, U.S. Fleet; the president would designate the commander for any subsequent operations. The Joint Board objected to the provision for unified command. Both army and navy could not readily agree to serve under the direction of the other. This interservice rivalry would continue through the end of World War II. Before the board approved the plan, it insisted upon the principle of mutual cooperation between the services.

World War I was supposed to have been the war to end all wars; so thought the president, the Congress, and the nation as a whole. Inside the

United States, the military services fared poorly in this atmosphere of disarmament and isolationism. Between 1923 and 1935 the total strength of the army ranged between 131,000 and 141,000 men. The navy received somewhat better support from Congress, but it, too, was maintained below the limits of international agreements. For years, service personnel were saddled with low pay and almost no promotions.

In the U.S. Army, it took thirteen years to go from first lieutenant to captain and some captains remained in grade for seventeen years.[14] Obviously many officers stagnated under such conditions and were wholly unfit for combat at the beginning of World War II.

In accepting Ellis' ideas, Lejeune adopted the amphibious assault as the Marine Corps' primary mission with the U.S. Navy. In this type of operation the risks of failure are so great that the attacker needs every possible advantage in his favor—control of the sea and air, superior combat power to overwhelm the defending enemy, and secure lines of communication. Lejeune further stressed that marine aviation belonged to the assault force. Nevertheless, he could not readily change the thinking inside the Marine Corps and the U.S. Navy.

At the Marine Corps schools, for example, the curriculum stressed land combat, and in 1924 and 1925 the advanced students spent only a few hours on landing operations. Not until 1926 did the curriculum at the Marine Corps schools include forty-nine hours of instruction, and escalated to more than one hundred hours a year later. However, tight budgets prevented the U.S. Navy and the Marine Corps from conducting enough in-depth practice drills or from acquiring the right type of small landing craft.

Unlike the Americans, the Japanese coupled preparations with planning. Its army began providing for a war on the Asian continent, while its navy trained for the defense of the homeland and the maintenance of sea lanes of communication with the continent north of Formosa Straits. This meant targeting the U.S. Navy. The Japanese determined to avoid war with the United States until it developed military facilities on its mandated islands: the Marshalls, the Marianas, and the Carolines. With these naval and air bases they could block American trans-Pacific routes to Asia. The Japanese could not view the United States as a friendly nation after Congress passed the Immigration Act of 1924, which effectively eliminated all Asian immigration until after World War II.

In 1925, Japan's Army Minister Ugaki posted active-duty officers in Japan's middle schools and universities to provide military training, a move that was unpopular with the professional educators. With the death of his father at 1:25 A.M. on 25 December 1926, Prince Hirohito succeeded immediately to the throne. At age twenty-five, he became by right of blood, training, and the authority of the constitution the so-called 124th Emperor of Japan. Article I of the Meiji Constitution, which he inherited, stipulated that "the Empire of Japan shall be reigned over and governed by a line of emperors unbroken for ages eternal."[15]

At an early age, Hirohito came under the tutelage of Gen. Nogi Maresuke, the intellectual war hero who defeated the Russians in 1905, and Adm. Togo Heihachiro, the victor in the decisive battle of Tsushima in the Russo-Japanese War. Because he also had good science tutors, Hirohito took a special interest in the natural sciences. A person's heroes say a lot about the person himself. Three portraits graced the walls in Hirohito's study—Napoleon Bonaparte, Abraham Lincoln, and Charles Darwin. Following ancient custom, Hirohito chose "Showa" as the name by which he was to be officially remembered. The word means "enlightened peace," although from 1926 onward, education was militarized even at the elementary level. Emperor worship, aimed at the institution as the source of all legitimacy rather than a person, was nurtured.

Hirohito encouraged the role of the Japanese military. Many army leaders claimed their emperor to be a direct descendant of the gods, ruling the state as a living god. He originally dwelt with the gods and was inherently different from his subjects. To which Hirohito himself observed " . . . I am not sure whether it was Honjo or Usami (Okiie) who held that I am a living god. I told him it disturbs me to be called that because I have the same bodily structure as an ordinary human being." [16] Nevertheless, the Japanese people's worship of the emperor and respect for the military seemed to grow in tandem as the years rolled by.

In 1927, at the urging of General Lejeune, the Joint Army-Navy Board gave the Marine Corps its new justification by awarding it the mission of amphibious assault in support of naval operations. The board assumed that, in the event of war with Japan, the marines would be responsible for seizing Japanese-held islands in the Pacific. By 1934, the Marine Corps published its developed doctrine for amphibious warfare as *The Tentative Manual for Landing Operations*. Continued study by both the Marine Corps and U.S. Navy proved invaluable to all services during World War II.

Late in 1928 the Secretary of War and Secretary of the Navy approved a detailed revision of the Joint War Plan Orange that did provide initially for unified command under the navy, in accordance with the principle of paramount interest. The strategic concept was approximately the same as the earlier one, with the added point that large army forces might be employed in major land operations in the western Pacific. The plan was more realistic than the 1924 version, for it allowed more time for a smaller number of troops to be ready to leave the West Coast and it provided for the establishment of secure lines of communications before U.S. Army troops would move to the western Pacific.

Although this Plan Orange had the approval of the Secretary of War and Secretary of the Navy, the U.S. State Department was moving in a different direction. Secretary of State Frank B. Kellogg insisted on the signing of a multilateral treaty for the renunciation of war known as the Kellogg-Briand Pact or the Pact of Paris. The treaty condemned recourse to war for the solution of international controversies and renounced it as an instrument of national policy in their relations with one another. Having been formally proclaimed on 24 July 1929, the treaty was subsequently ratified by sixty-three nations, including the United States and Japan.

With war outlawed and U.S. military forces reduced in size and pinched for cash, one wonders why anyone wanted to remain a professional soldier with such obvious lack of appreciation from the president, Congress, and the American citizenry. Yet, some in the military had a more realistic view of the future. They had world history on their side.

While many army and navy regulars stagnated, a cadre of military professionals would emerge as the great leaders of World War II.

Chapter 2
Political Stalemate

*D*URING THE DECADE OF THE 1930S, Americans watched the accumulation of ominous war clouds. Unfortunately, they preferred the role of spectator rather than prepare for the gathering storm.

President Herbert Hoover's Secretary of State, Henry L. Stimson, claimed that World War II actually began in 1931. That year Japanese militarists invaded and conquered Manchuria and changed the name of the province to Manchukuo. Eighteen months of diplomatic crisis followed. With no support from the United States or the large powers in the League of Nations, the League satisfied itself with a commission of inquiry. Stimson later contended that World War II resulted from the events that began in Manchuria.

Born in New York City on 21 September 1867, Stimson was the son of a successful and socially prominent banker and physician. Educated at Yale University and Harvard School of Law, he was admitted to the New York Bar in 1891. As a lawyer he distinguished himself in the trust-busting policies of his friend and mentor, President Theodore Roosevelt. From 1911 through 1913 he was Secretary of War in the cabinet of President William Howard Taft. He rose to the rank of colonel in the 31st Field Artillery in France during World War I.

Hoover, Congress, and the American public did not share Stimson's concern about happenings in China. All were too much involved in the continuing economic deterioration throughout the country. From 1929 to 1932, the gross national product of the United States was reduced by half, with a 1932 unemployment rate of 25 percent. Literally thousands became homeless every day. The misery index was the worst ever for American citizens.

Although an outstanding public servant throughout his career, Stimson made a mistake while serving as Hoover's Secretary of State. In 1929, Stimson failed to appreciate the value of cryptanalysis. Herbert Yardley, a cryptanalyst, would cause Stimson to err.

In New York City, Yardley operated a code-breaking organization called the Black Chamber for the U.S. State and War departments. One of Yardley's first tasks was to break the Japanese diplomatic codes. When the 1921–1922 Washington Naval Conference convened to set limits on the tonnage of capital ships in the navies of Great Britain, the United States, France, Japan, and Italy, Yardley's Black Chamber was able to decipher Japan's diplomatic code. Although the Japanese ambassador demanded a 10:7 ratio, he was authorized to accept 10:6. The Black Chamber promptly relayed the contents of this message to Secretary of State Charles Evans Hughes, who held out for 10:6. On 10 December Japan gave in.

In early May 1929, Yardley sent a series of decrypts from the Black Chamber for payment by the Secretary of State. This shocked Stimson. He considered it highly unethical and ordered the operation to shut down at once. "Gentlemen do not read other's mail," he said.[1]

Spying is as old as civilization itself. Although in modern times, code breaking has played a major role in detecting the secrets of other nations, the United States immediately took a backseat to others in this all-important function of military intelligence.

The U.S. Department of the Navy had a small cryptanalysis unit that was not under the jurisdiction of the Secretary of State. In 1924, the U.S. Navy established the Coded Signal Section (CSS) as part of the Office of Naval Communications under Lt. Laurence L. Safford. Originally, Safford had one cryptanalyst, Mrs. Agnes Meyer Driscoll, and two typists to work on the Red Book. This was a two-volume copy with translations of the Japanese Consular Code bound in red cloth by the Americans, hence the name. In October 1925, Lt. j.g. Joseph J. Rochefort, USNR, a former World War I enlisted man, joined Safford and Driscoll. He later went to Tokyo for three years to learn Japanese. The three would play a major role in deciphering Japanese codes used by its diplomats and navy prior to and during World War II.[2]

With the closing of the Black Chamber, the War Department was left with one cryptanalyst, William F. Friedman, the son of Russian-Jewish immigrants. Born in Kishinev, Russia, in 1891, he had arrived in the United States at the age of one. As a member of the Army Signal Corps, Friedman's main job was to devise codes for use by the U.S. Army. In April 1930, Friedman employed three junior cryptanalysts at $2,000 each per year, namely schoolteachers Frank Rowlett, a high school math teacher from the small town of Rocky Mount, Virginia, and Abraham Sinkov and Solomon Kullback from New York City. This staff would remain intact and increase in size slightly each year from 1934 through 1939, in spite of the passage of the Federal Communications Act of 1934. This legislation prohibited all U.S. government agencies from intercepting messages between foreign countries and the United States. To circumvent this law, the cryptanalysts claimed that intercepted messages were being decrypted for purposes of training, not intelligence. Under this ruse, the select few pressed their attack on foreign codes and ciphers.

The year 1930 witnessed the London Naval Conference. Japan, Great Britain, and the United States signed a treaty on 22 April that restricted the number of capital ships, cruisers, and other auxiliary ships that each signatory could build. Japan agreed to accept a 6:9 ratio plus parity with the United States in submarine tonnage. All parties agreed to renegotiate the treaty after six years.

The same year, Gen. Douglas A. MacArthur assumed the post as chief of staff of the United States Army in November. He had no chance of making a superior contribution in this role, as pacifism and the Great Depression compelled severe cuts in military spending, already dangerously low. As a student at West Point, he graduated with the highest honors, number one in his class of 1903. He made a distinguished record as brigadier general with the Rainbow Division in World War I for which he received the Distinguished Service Medal, seven Silver Stars, two Purple Hearts, plus nineteen foreign honors awarded by various governments.[3] In 1919 he became superintendent of the Military Academy at West Point. Indeed, up to this point, MacArthur had achieved a most enviable record.

The most significant event during MacArthur's tenure came in 1932. In June of that year, 22,000 veterans of World War I tramped to Washington demanding payment of a $1,000 bonus promised by Congress in earlier legislation. Impoverished veterans peacefully lobbied Congress to pass a bill introduced by Wright Patman granting them immediately the promised pension bonus. The House passed this bill in mid-June, but President Hoover promised a veto should it pass the Senate. On 17 June the Senate defeated the measure. As a sop, the legislative body offered to buy tickets home for the protesters. About 6,000 accepted the offer while others drifted away. By July, however, the city fathers and President Hoover decided to disperse the remaining 10,000 bonus marchers.

On 28 July, after imposing restrictions on demonstrations, the district police with U.S. Army backing began to disperse the remaining marchers. After a panicked policeman shot and killed two veterans, Hoover ordered the army to clear the protesters from the center of the city. MacArthur assembled nearly 1,000 troops from infantry, cavalry, and mechanized units. When his aide, Maj. Dwight D. Eisenhower, questioned whether the chief of staff should be involved personally, the general responded that there was incipient revolution in the air. MacArthur told a late-night press conference that he had suppressed a mob animated by the essence of revolution. He claimed the protesters were plotting to seize power and in another week the whole government would have been severely threatened.[4] Thereafter, Hoover and MacArthur remained lifelong friends and political allies, even though MacArthur's handling of the bonus marchers did not enhance the president's re-election chances in the fall.

Near the end of his term Hoover made a very wise choice in the appointment of Joseph Clark Grew as ambassador to Japan. Grew was the first career foreign service officer to become ambassador to a major nation. He had married Alice de Vermandois Perry, a descendant of Commodore Oliver Perry. She had spent her youth in Japan, knew the language, and provided entrees to Japanese society unusual for a western diplomat. Although Grew was unable to turn Japan away from its course of conquest, he was able to provide the U.S. State Department with invaluable information concerning happenings in that country.

In the summer of 1932, the Democrats nominated Franklin D. Roosevelt, the governor of New York, to run for president. Although Hoover repeatedly claimed that prosperity was just around the corner, the nation's economy continued to worsen on a daily basis. On 8 November 1932, Roosevelt won election by a landslide.

Taking office on 4 March 1933, Roosevelt declared:

> So first of all let me assert my firm belief that the only thing we have to fear is fear itself—nameless, unreasoning, unjustified terror which paralyzes needed efforts to convert retreat into advance. In every dark hour of our national life a leadership of frankness and vigor has met with that understanding and support of the people themselves which is essential to victory. I am convinced that you will again give that support to leadership in these critical days.[5]

He said the trouble lay in material things. "Plenty is at our doorstep, but a generous use of it languishes in the very sight of the supply." [6]

In the next hundred days, Roosevelt embarked upon an impressive legislative program unmatched by any administration in the nation's history. He placed the federal government squarely into the act of putting people to work. He labeled his program "The New Deal." The future of the armed services remained dismal. However, at his second cabinet meeting Roosevelt discussed the ultimate possibility of a war with Japan, whose troops were swarming toward the Great Wall of China. Still, his first budget showed a decline in the already depressed outlays for the army and navy.

Roosevelt established the Civilian Conservation Corps (CCC) as a temporary project to put young men to work. By midsummer, a quarter of a million young men began building dams, draining marshlands, fighting forest fires, planting trees, instituting soil erosion prevention measures, and developing state and national parks. Roosevelt called upon Gen. Douglas MacArthur to use army personnel as administrators for the many CCC camps around the nation. MacArthur agreed, but, to add insult to injury, the young CCC boys received $30 a month as pay—$5 to keep and $25 to be sent home to parents—whereas an army private received only $17 per month. However, in these dark days of the Depression, thousands would gladly enlist for the food and shelter provided, if the army or navy had a vacancy.

Because of the isolationist atmosphere in Congress and throughout the nation, Roosevelt specifically prohibited the army from making the CCC camps a military project. In the second year of its existence, the War Department called up some 9,300 reserve officers to active duty to relieve the regulars so that they could return to their units. Many of these reservists remained on active duty until the United States entered World War II.[7] "Experience in the mobilization of large numbers of men, training the reserve officers, and a disciplined routine for hundreds of thousands of young Americans were unintended benefits of the CCC program." [8]

By the end of his first year in office, Roosevelt realized the need to increase funding for the armed services. Although he and MacArthur distrusted each other, Roosevelt asked the general to continue as chief of staff for an additional year. Roosevelt knew he needed help in reaching the most conservative members of Congress, with whom MacArthur had rapport.

In February 1933, the League of Nations Assembly passed a resolution condemning Japan and asking for restoration of Manchuria to Chinese sovereignty. Japan responded by walking out of the League. The war rumblings in Europe and Asia failed to increase the size of the United States armed services, but it did make the military realize the impracticability of mobilizing troops in the existing Plan Orange. The U.S. Army revised its part for a slower schedule for the embarkation of forces to the western Pacific. The plan as changed provided for U.S. forces in the early stages of the war to eject the Japanese from their bases in the Marshall and Caroline islands in order to reach the Philippines.

Throughout 1934 the president, the Congress, and the nation were consumed with digging out of the Depression. To build up the military in peacetime, Roosevelt had to face the simple truth as chief executive of a democracy. He must convince and persuade rather than command. He had to face the fact that the main weakness of a democracy is that it seldom rises above the mores of the people. Most of the nation's print media, controlled largely by its owners, opposed Roosevelt and his policies, including increased military spending. He managed to neutralize the media with his so-called "fireside chats," which he periodically delivered over the radio. With an exceptional radio voice, he spoke in terms his listeners could easily understand.

With war clouds piling up in Europe, millions of Americans reflected on World War I and vowed "never again." Isolationism was especially strong in the Midwest, Northwest, and the Rockies. With all of his popularity, Roosevelt became powerless to fight this mobilization of public opinion toward isolation that shackled his ability to make foreign policy.

Yet, at the U.S. Army War College there was concern that the United States would become involved in another war with more than one country at the same time. Accordingly, its membership began a study in 1934 under the heading "Participation with Allies." Captain William F. Halsey, USN, one of the few navy members of the class, was asked to do an estimate of the allied situation in relation to a war with Japan. He said, "in the first place the navy cannot win a war. The war has to be decided on land." [9] While a student at the War College, he had apparently adopted the traditional army view that wars are won by defeating the opposing military forces and/or by occupying its home territory. The U.S. Navy had a different view as to a war with Japan in that defeat of the Japanese armies and occupation of the home islands was not necessary. Later, Halsey would assume the navy opinion. Studies at this time at both the army and navy war colleges seemed to reflect the fact that the United States would not go to war unless there was a violation of the Monroe Doctrine or an attack by a foreign government, namely Japan against U.S. possessions in the Pacific, especially the Philippines.

In the early days of 1935, the isolationists pressed for legislation requiring the president in the event of war abroad to embargo export of arms to all belligerents. Roosevelt and his Secretary of State, Cordell Hull, favored such embargo authority, but they wanted to empower the president to discriminate between aggressor and victim by embargoing exports of arms only to the former. They reasoned that such discretionary power would help deter aggressors. The isolationists claimed such discretion meant entanglement in foreign quarrels. Senator Key Pittman of Nevada, the chief sponsor of the legislation, agreed to introduce such a discretionary provision, but vowed the president's amendment would fail, which it did. Mandatory arms embargo legislation passed both chambers by almost unanimous votes.

Seeing that a veto would be overridden, Roosevelt signed the Neutrality Act at the end of August 1935. After two and a half years in office, events abroad drew Roosevelt's focus to foreign affairs. "I am very much more worried about the world situation than the domestic," Roosevelt wrote to Senator Josiah Bailey shortly thereafter.[10] Nevertheless, while dictators girded for war in Europe and Asia, the U.S. Congress stripped the president of any power to throw his country's weight against the aggressors.

Although by 1935 War Department expenditures for national defense began a slow upward climb, Hanson W. Baldwin of the *New York Times* noted that "the growth of our military and naval forces in these years did not equal the rapid deterioration in the world situation . . . The progress in quantity was not matched by the progress in quality." [11]

One of MacArthur's last acts as U.S. Army chief of staff was the approval by the Joint Army-Navy Board of a revised Plan Orange submitted by the U.S. Navy War Plans Division in January 1935 and approved in May of that year. This plan called for a thrust across the Central Pacific through the Marshalls to Truk, where the navy would establish its main fleet base in a war against Japan. As always, the ultimate objective would be a blockade around the home islands.

The next year, 1936, Col. Walter Krueger, the director of the Army War Plans Division and later leader of the Sixth Army under MacArthur, proposed an amendment to Plan Orange. After reaching Truk, U.S. forces would advance on the Marianas, namely Saipan and Guam. He considered the Marianas as a part of the Japanese main line of resistance in the Pacific, and that to reach any position in the Far East, American forces would have to punch through the Japanese mail line of resistance (MLR).

The Tydings-McDuffie Act, which became law in 1935, granted independence to the Philippines in 1946. Manuel Quezon, the Philippine president-elect, requested that MacArthur be assigned to advise him since it was known that the latter was about to retire as army chief of staff. MacArthur was especially popular with the Filipinos, as he had served there prior to becoming army chief of staff. He accepted Quezon's offer and "asked—practically demanded—that Ike (Maj. Dwight D. Eisenhower) go with him as chief of staff of the military mission." [12] Two other officers, namely Capt. Thomas Jefferson "T. J." Davis and Maj. James

B. Ord, would also serve with Ike. Eisenhower "greatly admired MacArthur's extraordinary mind, and he was impressed by MacArthur's moral courage in fighting for greater U.S. Army appropriations in Congress, at considerable risk to his own position. Moreover, Ike was acutely conscious of MacArthur's value as a symbol of American military prowess, an almost intangible asset to the army standing and morale." [13] But during his four years of service in the Philippines, Ike became very much aware of the general's shortcomings.

MacArthur's reports to the U.S. War Department contained glowing plus wildly optimistic descriptions of the standard of training of Filipino troops. In his formal report on national defense of the Philippines submitted in April 1936, MacArthur called for organizing a vast reserve of citizen soldiers led by a small regular army. The Philippine army would begin training in primary school and be stationed throughout the archipelago. A flotilla of torpedo boats and an air force would augment the army, which MacArthur maintained could deter or destroy any invader. Over the objection of Eisenhower and Ord, he claimed that progress toward the goal had already exceeded anticipation.[14] The Philippine government did not agree with MacArthur, as it had unmet domestic needs that took priority over the implementation of such a program. "The fledgling Philippine government while needing an army for prestige purposes and for internal security was unwilling to pay for it." [15]

In 1936, after considerable protest from the local commanders in the Philippines, the Joint Army-Navy Board finally accepted the fact that the small garrisons there could not hold the islands against a strong Japanese attack. The Joint Board reduced the mission of forces in the Philippines from holding the Manila Bay area to holding the entrance to Manila Bay, which called for the Americans to occupy the Bataan Peninsula and the island of Corregidor. The Asiatic Fleet was assigned the task of furthering the advance of the military and naval forces from the United States, particularly by attacking Japanese commerce and diverting the Japanese fleet.

Japanese planners were also thinking ahead about war with the United States. In 1936, its army and navy agreed on a statement of Fundamental Principles of National Security. Their army was committed to achieving enough strength to contain the Soviet Union while the Japanese navy, after acquiring dominance in the South Seas, should have the ability to "secure command of the western Pacific against the U.S. Navy." [16]

In November 1936 President Roosevelt scored a landslide victory for a second term by receiving 61 percent of the popular vote. Shortly after his inauguration he made the worst political blunder of his career. The Supreme Court had previously declared unconstitutional much of his New Deal legislation. Six of the justices who had voted against his program were over seventy years of age. He proposed that for every Supreme Court justice who failed to resign the bench within six months after reaching seventy, the president could appoint a new justice up to a total of six.

Congress overwhelmingly refused to support Roosevelt. This episode curtailed the president's influence with the legislative body for the remainder of his second term. Although he was well ahead of Congress and the public in seeing the need to substantially increase the size of the nation's military, he was unable to do so until the last year of his second term.

By 1937, the year when Japan started its undeclared war with China, realization had grown in Washington that U.S. forces in the Philippines could not hold long enough against a serious Japanese attack for the U.S. Fleet to reach the area. Increasing the defenses there was out of the question, for appropriations were still low and other demands had held priority on limited resources. Army officers asserted that the United States should no longer plan to push westward across the Pacific but should concentrate on maintaining a defense line in the eastern Pacific, then seek by economic pressure to accomplish Japan's collapse.

Late in 1937, the Joint Board directed its Joint Planning Committee to prepare a new Plan Orange that provided for holding an initial "position of readiness" on the general line Alaska-Oahu-Panama and offer practicable alternative courses of subsequent action. Army members of the committee disagreed strongly with naval members, who insisted that the war should be fought offensively. The new plan when finally adopted called for the use of military and economic pressure, primarily naval operations.

The navy insisted on a more aggressive policy. The Joint Board finally agreed that command of the area would be extended westward as rapidly as secure lines of communication could be built. But for the army to agree, it could not be left out of the action. The final draft called for a large army force to be provided, but failed to say how they would be used.

For the remainder of the decade until the advent of World War II, the navy took the lead in strategic planning for the war with Japan, for it was evident that the U.S. Fleet would have to defend U.S. interests in the Far East or fight its way back across the Pacific, should the Japanese attack. Class after class at the Naval War College at Newport, Rhode Island, studied the strategy for defeating Japan. Many of the top-ranking naval officers of World War II fought the war on the game boards at Newport and became convinced that Japan could be defeated by a blockade around its home islands.

On 5 October 1937, Roosevelt created a sensation with his quarantine speech made in Chicago. Referring indirectly to hostilities in Spain and China, he said that the very foundations of civilization were threatened by the current reign of terror and international lawlessness. If conditions got worse, America could not expect mercy; the Western Hemisphere could not avoid attack. He said:

> The peace-loving nations must make a concerted effort in opposition to those violations of treaties and those ignorings of humane instincts which today are creating a state of international anarchy and instability from which there is no escape through mere isolation or neutrality . . . The peace, the freedom and the security of ninety per cent of the population of the world is being jeopardized by the remaining ten per cent who are threatening a breakdown of all international order and law.

When an epidemic of physical disease starts to spread, the community approves and joins in a quarantine of the patients in order to protect the health of the community against the spread of the disease . . . We are adopting such measures as will minimize our risk of involvement, but we cannot have complete protection in a world of disorder in which confidence and security have broken down.[17]

Back in Washington, stunned Democratic Party leaders remained silent while the opposition spoke out vigorously. Pacifists charged the president with starting the people down the road to war. Some isolationist congressmen even threatened him with impeachment. To top things off, the American Federation of Labor passed a resolution against involvement in foreign wars.

"It's a terrible thing," Roosevelt said later to his friend Samuel I. Rosenman, "to look over your shoulder when you are trying to lead—and to find no one there."[18] A few days later, the president pulled in his horns. He announced the United States would participate in a conference of the parties to the Treaty of Washington over the Far Eastern situation, a clear indication since Japan and China had both signed the treaty so that sanctions against aggressor nations were out of the question—for now.

Meanwhile, as soon as the naval treaties agreed upon by the United States, Great Britain, and Japan at the 1930 London Naval Disarmament Conference expired, Tokyo laid down two super battleships, *Yamato* and *Musashi*. In 1934, Japan had already denounced the agreement reached at London. When launched, *Yamato* and *Musashi* would be the largest and most heavily armored warships in the world. Each displaced 63,700 tons with an overall length of 866 feet and an 18.1-inch main battery. By 1940, Japan had a navy much stronger than the U.S. Pacific Fleet.

Recognizing that he was unable to expand and improve the armed services, as he would like, Roosevelt determined to promote the best men possible to run the show. On 28 September 1938, President Roosevelt called Henry H. "Hap" Arnold to the White House. The president asked Arnold for an assessment of foreign aircraft strength, which Arnold gave in detail as to France, England, Italy, and Germany; however, he pressed home the point that a large number of airplanes did not necessarily indicate air power. "The strength of an air force cannot be measured in terms of airplanes only," he said. "Other things are essential—productive capacity of airplanes, of pilots, of mechanics, and bases from which to operate. A sound training program is essential to provide replacements." And there would have to be a large, continuous flow of replacements, both machines and men.[19] On the day after that crucial White House meeting, Arnold was named chief of the Army Air Corps.

At this point, top officials in the United States had an altruistic view on how to wage war. "In 1938, the U.S. Department of State announced that aerial bombardment of civilians was 'in violation of the most elementary principles of those standards of humane conduct which have been developed as an essential part of modern civilization.' " And Secretary Hull had particularly condemned air attacks using incendiaries which "inevitably and ruthlessly jeopardize non-military persons and property." [20]

The 1938 fall elections sealed the fate for any meaningful build-up of the U.S. armed services in spite of war rumblings in Europe. The Republicans gained eighty-one members in the House and seven in the Senate. Even though the Republicans were still heavily outnumbered, isolationism was the overwhelming view of the new congressional membership.

On 14 November 1938, Roosevelt called a conference at the White House of members of his cabinet and his military advisors at which he proposed a program for the building of 10,000 warplanes. Ostensibly these planes would be used to bolster the strength of the U.S. Army Air Corps, and that was what George C. Marshall, the deputy chief of staff, understood would be their purpose. In reality Roosevelt intended to ship the planes, once they were built, to Britain and France to strengthen their air arms. But he did not say that; he could not, since isolationists in and out of Congress would have immediately attacked him. He let it be assumed that they would be part of the U.S. armed forces.

Marshall wondered how the president possibly could ask for new factories to be opened and 10,000 planes to be built and not at the same time also lay out a program for recruiting the pilots and crews and service personnel who would be needed to man those planes. It was not the first time Marshall had met the president; but it was his first conference with Roosevelt, and he was shocked by what he considered loose thinking.

Most of those present at the conference seemed to agree with everything the president had said. After Roosevelt finished making his case, he came among his listeners and stopped in front of Marshall and asked, "Don't you think so?" Marshall looked at him stonily and replied, "I am sorry, Mr. President, but I don't agree with you at all."

A startled expression crossed Roosevelt's face. He seemed about to ask why and then thought better of it. After the meeting broke up, those who had been silent came by Marshall to shake his hand. "Well, it's been nice knowing you," said Secretary of the Treasury Henry Morgenthau. Like the rest of them, he made it obvious he thought that Marshall had just ruined his career and that his tour in Washington was over.[21]

A year later, Roosevelt selected Marshall as U.S. Army chief of staff. The day Marshall was sworn in, 1 September 1939, Germany invaded Poland. Thus began World War II. On Sunday, 3 September, Roosevelt spoke to the nation in one of his fireside chats:

> It is easy for you and for me to shrug our shoulders and say that conflicts taking place thousands of miles from the continental United States, and indeed thousands of miles from the whole American hemisphere, do not seriously affect the Americas—and that all the United States has to do is to ignore them and go about its own business. . . .
> Passionately though we may desire detachment, we are forced to realize

that every word that comes through the air, every ship that sails the sea, every battle that is fought, does affect the American future.[22]

In spite of this admonition, Congress saw no need to accelerate the build-up of America's military. There was a feeling among some that if you have a large army, you will certainly use it.

In reference to Marshall, the press reported he had been selected over thirty-five others senior in grade or rank. He had served in the U.S. Army since his graduation from Virginia Military Institute in 1901.

In 1929, Lt. Col. George C. Marshall had become assistant commandant at the army infantry school at Fort Benning, Georgia. Placed in charge of instruction, he was credited with raising the school to a higher plane of professionalism:

> During his tenure Marshall tried to inculcate the idea that war was uncertain and did not lend itself to textbook rigidity. He lessened the importance of the once almighty school solution (the only answer accepted as correct for tactical problems) and forced faculty to look at each student's work on its own merits. He attempted to simulate "how little information you actually have in war" by making students use imperfect maps and by adding surprise events to field exercises. Night maneuvers, previously unheard of, became a staple of the course.[23]

Marshall led in the redesign of army doctrine and organization for a triangular structure where each level of command had three subordinate maneuver units and a fire support unit. His work came to be known in the army as the Benning Revolution.[24]

Lieutenant General Lewis B. "Chesty" Puller, USMC, when retired, often told of an incident about Marshall when First Lieutenant Puller was enrolled as a Fort Benning student in 1931 and 1932. Like Marshall, Puller had attended Virginia Military Institute, but then he had enlisted in the U.S. Marine Corps. Marshall asked Puller why he had made the choice of marines over army.

Puller replied, "In addition to being a part of the military, you have adventure and travel in the peace-time Marine Corps which is not available in the army."

Marshall said, ". . .and that's not fair." He repeated, "And that's not fair. And if I ever get to the point that I can make a change, I'm going to do so." [25]

Above all, Marshall could never forget he was an army man. Later, Gen. Mathew B. Ridgway would label him "the greatest of them all." Now he headed a force of 242,648 officers and men in the regular army along with 251,000 National Guardsmen, which placed the United States military on par with Portugal, nineteenth in size among the nations of the Earth.

In addition to Marshall's appointment as chief of staff, the army made another significant step forward. Army cryptanalysts under Friedman's direction made a significant breakthrough in deciphering the Japanese diplomatic codes by the use of the specially designed "Purple Machine." Its product was known as MAGIC. Shortly thereafter, navy cryptanalysts learned to decipher the latest Japanese naval code, JN-25. Unfortunately, the U.S. Navy lacked the staff necessary to deal with the huge volume of intercepted traffic. However, some Japanese diplomatic messages could be read soon after their receipt. Thereafter, through the expansion and training of personnel, cryptography would play a major role in winning the Pacific War.

The year 1939 witnessed another event that foreshadowed the establishment of the Manhattan Project (atomic bomb) in 1942. Alexander Sachs, a well-known economist and an intimate of Roosevelt, was prevailed upon to take a message to the White House written and signed by scientist Albert Einstein. The letter began:

> Sir: Some recent work by E. Fermi and L. Szilard, which has been communicated to me in manuscript, leads me to expect that the element uranium may be turned into a new and important source of energy in the immediate future. Certain aspects of the situation seem to call for watchfulness and, if necessary, quick action on the part of the administration . . .
>
> . . . that it may become possible to set up nuclear chain reactions in a large mass of uranium, by which vast amounts of power and large quantities of new radium-like elements would be generated. Now it appears almost certain that this could be achieved in the immediate future . . .
>
> The United States has only very poor ores of uranium in moderate quantities. There is some good ore in Canada and the former Czechoslovakia, while the most important source of uranium is the Belgian Congo.
>
> In view of this situation you may think it desirable to have some permanent contact maintained between the administration and the group of physicists working on chain reaction in America . . .
>
> I understand that Germany has actually stopped the sale of uranium from the Czechoslovakian mines which she has taken over. That she should have taken such early action might perhaps be understood on the ground that the son of the German Undersecretary of State, von Weizsaker, is attached to the Kaiser Wilhelm Institute of Berlin, where some of the American work on uranium is now being repeated.
>
> Yours very truly,
> A. Einstein[26]

At his meeting with Roosevelt, Sachs read aloud his covering letter, which emphasized the same ideas as the Einstein communication but stressed the need for funds. When Sachs finished, Roosevelt remarked, "Alex, what you are after is to see that the Nazis don't blow us up." He then called "Pa" Watson (Gen. Edwin M. Watson, the president's secretary) and announced, "This requires action." [27]
By evening, the Briggs committee had been established, chaired by Dr. Lyman

J. Briggs, director of the U.S. Bureau of Standards. This committee was charged with investigating the potentiality of nuclear fission.

As the year 1940 approached, Germany and Japan had prepared well for World War II. The United Kingdom had only partially prepared for the fight ahead. France had prepared extremely well for World War I. The United States had plans but was not prepared for any war. By the spring of 1940, it became apparent to the class at the U.S. Army War College that the United States might be involved with the Axis powers—Germany, Italy, and Japan—all at the same time. Study groups were assigned to develop a plan called Rainbow X.[28] Five different Rainbow plans would be developed during the next year and a half. All would include Plan Orange as envisioned primarily by the U.S. Navy.

Chapter 3
The Build-up for War

*I*T WAS NOT UNTIL 10 JUNE 1940 that the United States' mobilization for war began in earnest. With the Germans nearing Paris, on this day Italy declared war on France and England. That evening President Roosevelt spoke to the graduating class of the University of Virginia at Charlottesville. The Associated Press covered the president's speech, which made front-page headlines throughout the country. Roosevelt accused Italy of plunging a dagger into the back of its neighbor. He said that America faced a hopeless nightmare if the Germans and Italians won. The press reported that the president received cheers and rebel yells from his audience every time he expressed sympathy with Great Britain and France.

Roosevelt announced a policy to save Britain and at the same time prepare America for a national emergency. He said:

> In our American unity, we will pursue two obvious and simultaneous courses: we will extend to the opponents of force the material resources of this nation; and, at the same time, we will harness and speed up the use of those resources in order that we ourselves in the Americas may have equipment and training equal to the task of any emergency and every defense.[1]

Four days later, 14 June 1940, the Germans occupied Paris. Simultaneously the president signed a naval expansion bill that had been debated for months. In effect, it gave the U.S. Navy the green light to build a "two-ocean" navy, which previously had been only lip service. By the end of the fiscal year, federal expenditures for the U.S. Army and U.S. Navy rose from $1.8 billion for the fiscal year 1940 to $6.3 billion for the fiscal year 1941.

The next day, 15 June, the president appointed a group of eminent civilian scientists to a new National Defense Research Committee. Vannevar Bush, president of the Carnegie Institute of Washington, was the chairman. From this committee stemmed most of the scientific research done for the armed forces during the war.

In July 1940 Roosevelt appointed two Republicans, Frank Knox and Henry Stimson, as Secretary of the Navy and Secretary of War, respectively. Both men were in their seventies. These appointments created a political uproar. Knox had been the Republican vice presidential candidate in 1936, and his newspaper, the Chicago *Daily News*, had consistently opposed the New Deal. Henry Stimson had long-term Republican credentials. He broke with the strong isolationist movement in his party in the spring of 1940. His speech at Yale University created banner headlines because he came out in support of President Roosevelt's program for a draft to build up the American military and to aid Great Britain in her fight against Germany. Roosevelt announced both appointments just before the Republican National Convention met to select a presidential candidate for the fall election. The convention delegates labeled both Knox and Stimson as defectors; however, Roosevelt had his coalition cabinet.

A man of wide and varied interests, Knox had become wealthy both as an industrialist and as a publisher. He patterned his behavior after Theodore Roosevelt, with whom he had served in the Spanish-American War. He was addressed as "colonel" because of his service in World War I and as a reservist. Roosevelt reasoned that Knox would support his foreign policy and military preparedness programs. Knox's political experience would help in dealing with Congress, one of the primary functions of the Secretary of the Navy. He forced concessions from the president before taking the job. The most important was that Knox would run the Navy Department without interference from Roosevelt.

The political conventions and the presidential campaigns that followed did not prepare the American public for the war that was sure to come. The anti-war covenants of the Democratic Party were clear-cut: "We will not participate in foreign wars, and we will not send our army, naval, or air forces to fight in foreign lands outside of the Americas, except in case of attack . . . The direction and aim of our foreign policy has been, and will continue to be, the security and defense of our own land and the maintenance of its peace." [2]

Wendell Willkie, the Republican presidential candidate, also knew that the sentiment of the country was almost solidly against the United States going to war, so that during the campaign there was little difference between the candidates on this issue.

In supplementing the pledges of the Democratic platform, President Roosevelt had also been unequivocal in his personal declarations. At Philadelphia, 23 October 1940, he had branded as false a Republican charge that "this Administration wishes to lead this country into war," and proclaimed that he was "following the road to peace." In Boston on 30 October he was even more emphatic, for there he declared: "I have said this before, but I shall say it again and again and again: Your boys are not going to be sent into any foreign wars . . . The purpose of our defense is defense." [3]

However, before the beginning of the year, U.S. military leaders agreed that the country might well be involved simultaneously in a war with the Axis powers. A series of five plans labeled "Rainbow" evolved as a result. The early plans were more concerned that the Axis powers might establish bases in the Western Hemisphere upon the defeat of France and England. After France fell, twenty-one nations met in Havana, Cuba, in late July 1940 and on 30 July signed the Act of Havana Treaty claiming collective security against Germany coming into the hemisphere. Each Rainbow plan included Plan Orange. Rainbow Five gave first priority to the defeat of Germany and Italy, and with its adoption, the preceding four plans were voided.

In September 1940, Congress established the first peacetime compulsory military service program with the Selective Training and Service Act, which called for the registration of all men age twenty-one to thirty-five. Reflecting the country's attitude not to be engaged in any foreign war unless specifically attacked, draftees were prohibited from being sent to any foreign country. A private's pay had been increased to $21 per month. Many draftees had good jobs prior to enlistment in the armed services. They proudly proclaimed they were being paid $21 per day—once a month.

In November Roosevelt was re-elected president for a third term by a comfortable margin but less than in his two previous elections.

Near the end of the year, the president established the Office of Production Management under William S. Knudsen, former president of General Motors, to coordinate defense production.

For months, Ambassador Joseph Grew in Tokyo had been reporting that Japan's public pronouncements were not bluster, that she was committed to her "Greater East Asia Co-Prosperity Sphere," which in plain terms meant the expulsion of all Western interests and influence from the Orient. It was clear that Japan had further expansion in mind when it signed the tripartite pact with Germany and Italy in September 1940.

Previously, in November 1936, Japan had signed an anti-Comintern pact with Germany, and later with Italy. In this latest treaty, Germany and Italy recognized Japan as a leader of a new order for Asia. The three nations further agreed to assist one another if any one were attacked by a power not then at war. In April 1941, Japan signed a neutrality pact with the Soviet Union. Diplomatically, this cleared the way for her to move south.

On 16 January 1941, Roosevelt discussed the possibilities of sudden and simultaneous action on the part of Germany and Japan against the United States at a conference attended by the Secretaries of State, War, and Navy; chief of naval operations Adm. Harold Stark; and General Marshall. The president felt there was one chance out of five of such an eventuality and that it might occur any day.[4]

On 27 January 1941, Grew cabled to Hull that there was talk in Tokyo that the Japanese military forces planned a surprise mass attack on Pearl Harbor in case of trouble between the United States and Japan. This report was passed on to the War and Navy departments.[5] Three days prior on 24 January, Secretary of the Navy Frank Knox wrote Secretary of War Stimson, "If war eventuates with Japan, it is believed easily possible that hostilities would be initiated by a surprise attack upon the Fleet or the Naval Base at Pearl Harbor. . . . The dangers envisaged, in their order of importance and probability, are considered to be 1) air bombing attack; 2) air torpedo-plane attack; 3) sabotage; 4) submarine attack; 5) mining; 6) bombardment by gunfire. Defense against all but the first two of these dangers appears to have been provided for satisfactorily." [6]

In early 1941, the president's Lend-Lease Bill caused a huge political fight in Congress. After prolonged debates and several amendments, large majorities in both houses of Congress finally passed the bill. Although there were some defections from party ranks, the main support for the measure came from Democrats, while Republicans supplied the major portion of the opposition votes. In the House of Representatives the vote was 260 for and 165 against; in the Senate it was 60 for and 31 against. With the signature of President Roosevelt, the bill, entitled "An Act to Promote the Defense of the United States," became law on 11 March 1941. The president's critics claimed it authorized the president to wage undeclared wars. Senator Tom Connally of Texas declared it was "intended to keep [the nation] out of war."

With an eye on the West, Admiral Stark, chief of naval operations, discussed the possibility of a Japanese attack on Hawaii with Admiral Kimmel, the fleet commander. He twice warned that a surprise attack on Pearl Harbor prior to the declaration of war was a "possibility." On 31 March two senior officers, namely Maj. Gen. Fredrick Martin, commander of the U.S. Army Air Force in Hawaii, and Rear Adm. Patrick Bellinger, both serving under General Short and Admiral King, respectively, issued a secret report for a joint action if Oahu or the Pacific Fleet were attacked. The report called attention to the fact that Japan had begun its war with Russia in 1905 with a successful surprise attack on the Russian fleet at Port Arthur. Japan's attack on north China in 1937 had not been preceded by a declaration of war.[7] The report added that, "the most likely and dangerous form of attack on Oahu would be an air attack launched from carriers." Additionally, in a dawn attack, "there is a high probability that it could be delivered as a complete surprise in spite of any patrols we might be using." [8]

On 1 April all naval districts, including the Hawaiian Islands, were urged by Admiral Stark to take special precautions against sudden attacks on weekends. Ever since the highly successful British bombing attacks on ships in the port of Taranto, Italy, both War and Navy departments focused on strengthening Pearl Harbor defenses.

In early 1941, discussions in Washington among British and American military planners resulted in the ABC-1 plan. Generally speaking, this was a blueprint for mutual defense in the Far East between the British, Americans, and Chinese in case of Japanese attack. Although only a contingency arrangement, the discussions continued throughout World War II. In April, American naval officers conferred with their Dutch and British counterparts in Singapore to consider committing greater resources to Southeast Asia in case of a Pacific war. Both U.S. Army and Navy rejected placing more American resources in the Far East. At this time, American war planners rightfully discounted the effectiveness of Filipino war forces.

For most of 1941, War Plan Orange Three envisioned only the defense of Manila Bay, the understanding between the army and navy being that the Philippines had been written off as indefensible in a war with Japan. Staff talks with the British led in March 1941 to the adoption of "Rainbow Five." This plan envisaged the main enemy as Germany; until Hitler was defeated, the Pacific would be a secondary theater, with war there being defensive. War Plan Orange remained intact as a part of Rainbow Five, but it implicitly accepted the loss of the Philippines, Wake, and Guam.

Japan's ambassador to the United States, Kichisaburo Nomura, arrived in Washington in February 1941 to settle issues concerning Japan's intended expansion. Secretary of State Hull defined the American position as:

1) Respect for the territorial integrity and the sovereignty of each and all nations.
2) Support of the principle of non-interference in the internal affairs of other countries.
3) Support of the principle of equality, including equality of commercial opportunity.
4) Non-disturbance of the status quo in the Pacific except as the status quo may be altered by peaceful means.[9]

No progress in negotiations had been made by early summer. The German invasion of the Soviet Union on 22 June 1941 had a profound effect on Japan. It caused the Japanese to re-examine their previously established policies. The die was cast on 2 July 1941. On that date, the Japanese Imperial Conference adopted a report entitled "Outline of the Empire's National Policies in View of the Changing Situation."

This document, as approved by Emperor Hirohito and the conference, specifically called for the establishment of the "Greater East Asia Co-Prosperity Sphere." It endorsed the continuance of the China war and the advance to the south to establish a solid basis for Japan's preservation and security. It further stipulated: ". . . In order to achieve the above objectives, preparations for war with Great Britain and the United States will be made . . . [and] our empire will not be deterred by the possibility of being involved in a war with Great Britain and the United States."[10]

Near the end of July 1941 the Japanese Planning Board prepared a study called "Requirements for the Mobilization of Commodities for the Prosecution of War." Such a war, the board said, must be regarded as a war of resources. The board asserted that if Japan were to continue her course of relying for her requirements on Britain and America, she "would undoubtedly collapse and be unable to rise again." She must make a final decision promptly. If she decided upon war, she must capture the rich natural resources of the southern area at the outset. Unless command of the air and sea was immediately secured, the minimum requirements of the mobilization of supplies could not be fulfilled.[11]

On this basis, the supreme commands of the Japanese army and navy studied four alternative proposals:

1) To capture the Netherlands East Indies first and then attack Malaya and the Philippines.
2) To carry out operations against the Philippines, Borneo, Java, Sumatra and Malaya in that order.
3) To carry out operations in the order Malaya, Sumatra, Borneo, Java and the Philippines to delay for as long as possible the entry into the war of the United States.
4) To start operations against the Philippines and Malaya simultaneously and proceed southward promptly and at length assault Java from both east and west.

The [Japanese] Army favored the third course, which insofar as it might delay America's entry into the war fitted in with German wishes. It would, however, involve serious risk to the Japanese lines of communication, over which the Americans might in time exert a stranglehold if they could muster sufficient strength in the Philippines.[12]

Plan number four was adopted as the final decision for the attack.

In essence, the Japanese Imperial Conference decided on expansion southward, even if it meant war with the United States and Great Britain. On 21 July France announced its acceptance of Japanese demands for military control of French Indochina. Four days later, America declared economic warfare on Japan, freezing all Japanese assets in the United States and stopping all trading with Japan. Diplomatically, the remaining months of 1941 were concerned with talks between Japan and the United States about resuming trade and the American demand for Japan to get out of China and French Indochina. Yet, to the American public, war did not seem imminent during diplomatic discussions.

At his conference with congressional leaders on 18 August, the president referred to the possibility of "shooting" troubles in the Far East, but he told them that no "new commitments" had been made at the Atlantic Conference in Argentia, Newfoundland, attended by both himself and Churchill. Roosevelt failed to say that relations with Japan were at, or approaching, a danger point. On the contrary, the New York Times, in its account (19 August 1941) said: "The result of the President's report to the Congressional group was a lifting of spirits among some of them, who had thought that the Roosevelt-Churchill conference meant early steps that would take this country near to the brink of war." In the same edition a dispatch from Tokyo reported: "Relations with Japan were reported to be near the breaking point after a long conference between Ambassador Grew and Foreign Minister Toyoda; for Mr. Grew warned Mr. Toyoda that unless Japan made fundamental alterations in her foreign policy, American pressure on Japan would be intensified."

Earl Ellis had predicted that Japan would strike first if it thought it could win over the United States. From the vantage point of Japan's military leaders, the time now looked ripe for war with America. The Axis powers in Europe appeared unstoppable. Clearly, the United States was a divided country. There were numerous labor strikes across the country. In August, Congress divided deeply on the extension of the draft; after a lengthy and acrimonious debate in the House, the margin to extend the draft succeeded by only one vote. Japan now had a larger navy, a better-trained army, and a screen of outlying islands with airdromes that could prevent the U.S. Navy from proceeding west.

The Japanese felt they needed to wage war in a desperate race against time. Circumstances decreed that the home islands must import nearly all its strategic war materials, among them, rubber, tin, iron, copper, bauxite, some rice, and, most critically, oil. Before the war, some 80 percent of Japan's oil came from the United States or from Venezuela, which had to utilize the Panama Canal for shipment. The Japanese planners, in recognition of this deficiency, had stockpiled more than 43 million barrels of oil—enough to meet wartime and domestic needs for only little more than a year.

In September 1941, about forty of Japan's top navy officers met for a two-week conference at Tokyo's Naval War College to plan for the seizure of Southeast Asia. The Japanese officers foresaw that the Pacific War could be decided by a single great naval battle. Japanese Adm. Isoroku Yamamoto declared, "Our best course of action is to deliver a knockout blow to the American fleet at the very start." [13] He had already conceived the surprise attack on Pearl Harbor. He intended to damage the American fleet in the beginning so that when later brought to battle, "We can destroy it completely." [14] Yamamoto's strategy made sense provided he could accomplish his intended purpose of eliminating the U.S. Pacific Fleet at the outset. A spokesman in a discussion period at the Army War College in 1938 repeated that "the Navy believes it can defeat Japan. He concluded by saying 'I admit if the Japs beat our fleet the war is over.' " [15]

Isoroku Yamamoto was born in 1884 at Nagaoka. He graduated from the Japanese naval academy in 1904 just in time to participate in the war with Russia. He was badly wounded at the battle of Tsushima. This Japanese victory over the Russian navy influenced the Japanese hierarchy into thinking that they could win again with a major decisive victory over the U.S. Fleet.

In 1918, Yamamoto married his wife, Reizo, eventually fathering two sons and two daughters. In April 1919, he came to America, where he enrolled at Harvard University. He undertook studies in English and petroleum resources, the latter a matter of great importance to the Imperial Navy. He found time to read Carl Sandburg's biography of Abraham Lincoln, which he recommended to others. While in this country, he had the opportunity to travel to the industrial heartland, including the cities of Chicago and Detroit, which convinced him that Japan should never engage in war with the United States. He liked Scotch and cigars and became an expert at poker and bridge, where he is said to have won money on most occasions when so engaged.

In 1924, at age forty, he switched his professional specialty from gunnery to aviation. Thereafter, he took the leading role in educating the Japanese navy in the importance of the new seaborne air power. He was appointed commander in chief of the Japanese Combined Fleet on 30 August 1939, attaining the rank of full admiral in 1940 at the age of fifty-six.

In 1940, he told Prime Minister Konoe, "If we are ordered to go to war with America, then I can guarantee to put up a tough fight for the first six months, but I have absolutely no confidence about what would happen if it went on for two or three years . . . I hope you will make every effort to avoid war with America." [16] As late as October 1941, he told a friend privately that war with America was exactly the opposite of his personal view.

But Japan's leaders, with a few exceptions, did not recognize the tremendous economic and military potential of the United States. Equally gross miscalculations were taking place in the Philippines.

On 26 July 1941, Gen. Douglas MacArthur was called back to active duty as commanding general, United States Forces, Far East Asia. He had long claimed that if he were given a substantial force of long-range bombers and the modern fighter aircraft to protect them, then there was no need to retreat to the Bataan Peninsula and Corregidor as envisioned in the latest Plan Orange for the protection of Manila Bay. He claimed that his newly created army was capable of denying the whole of the islands to the Japanese, and he wrote long and detailed reports seeking the acceptance of this theory. He claimed that his forces should be so deployed that they would meet any Japanese attack on the beaches and throw it back into the sea, no matter where it might occur. Since the length of the Philippine shoreline exceeded that of the United States, such a strategy should have seemed impossible. The lack of training and equipment of Filipino troops was readily apparent to the professional soldier in the field. Major General Jonathan M. Wainwright wrote his daughter-in-law on 17 August 1941 that "The P.A. [Philippine army] troops are not well trained so I will have a job getting them ready to fight." [17] Later in the year Brig. Gen. Bradford Grethen Chynoweth, who took over command of the 61st Infantry Division of the Philippine army, wrote of the appalling conditions of his troops who were without supplies, organization, or training. After the war he criticized MacArthur as being:

> Lazy, almost shiftless, frivolous, uncommunicative, uncooperative. He never visited his troops. His tactical judgment was nil. He was the poorest judge of subordinates that I *ever* knew! Yet, he achieved GREATNESS! After deep thought, in retrospect, I stumbled on the *answer*. He was a great Work of Art—like an impressionist masterpiece. If you stood close, you could see nothing but glaring defects. If you stood far off, you suddenly perceived the *Whole Man*. He was a SUPREME

EMOTIONAL ACTOR—and he was an unshakeable STATUE OF *VICTORY!* [emphasis his][18]

Nevertheless, MacArthur communicated his optimism to others both on and off the scene. Many in the U.S. Army—including both Gen. George Marshall and Gen. "Hap" Arnold—were carried along at least partway by the flood tide of MacArthur's strongly stated beliefs that the Philippines could and would be held.

For years U.S. military leaders recognized that the Philippine archipelago was a defensive liability. The 8,000 islands are almost 7,000 miles from the continental base of supplies. They are positioned behind a screen of Japanese-dominated islands and they were entirely dependent upon the United States for war equipment. They were also geographically unnecessary for the defense of the North American continent. In 1941, the Philippines lacked the facilities necessary for maintenance of a large fleet. Above all, the islands produced no supplies needed by the military other than food.

Although ill-suited for defensive operations, a strong Philippines base could offer one certain strategic advantage to the offensive: it could assist in cutting Japan's supply lines to the Netherlands East Indies. But this advantage would be minimized if the Japanese controlled the air and sea lanes of Eastern Asia from China through Singapore. Because of MacArthur's urging, fortifying the Philippines held top priority in the shipments of war materials to the Pacific for the remainder of the year.

MacArthur had the phenomenal ability to convince others of his point of view. In the fall of 1941, Sir Earl Page of Australia visited the general in Manila. MacArthur told Page that after five years of intermittent war in China, Japan had become over-extended and needed a long period of recuperation before she could undertake another major struggle. He insisted that Japan had gone to the limit of her southward expansion, and under present conditions further expansion could be successfully resisted. When Page reached Washington, he found MacArthur had convinced General Marshall that the Philippines had already reached a high state of preparedness. Marshall told Page that by early 1942 the American forces would "constitute such a serious menace to Japan that she would be forced out of the Axis." [19]

On 1 October 1941, MacArthur sent to the adjutant general of the War Department his amendment to the Rainbow Five Plan as it pertained to the Philippines. Paragraph three said, in part:

> The Philippine Islands are now being organized into a potential Theatre of Operations, with a force of from eleven to thirteen divisions with corresponding Air, Corps and Army Troops. The total force will soon be equivalent to an army of approximately 200,000 men. The strategic mission, as formerly visualized, of defending merely the entrance to Manila Bay by a citadel type defense with a small token force, should be broadened to include the Defense of the Philippine Islands. There can

be no adequate defense of Manila Bay nor of the Island of Luzon if an enemy is permitted to seize and operate from land bases on the islands immediately south thereof. The wide scope of possible enemy operations, especially aviation, now makes imperative the broadening of the concept of Philippine defense, and the strength and composition of the defense forces projected here are believed to be sufficient to accomplish such a mission . . .

Paragraph 4: In the revision of the Operations Plan, the extent of the Philippine Coastal Frontier should be defined as the land and sea areas necessary for the defense of the Philippine Archipelago, and the Joint mission and the Army mission should be changed accordingly. The Commander designated should be the Commanding General, United States Army Forces in the Far East, instead of the Commanding General, Philippine Department.[20]

By memorandum dated 18 October 1941, Marshall approved of MacArthur's revision. With the advantage of hindsight, it seems incredible that anyone could persuade Marshall and the War Department to adopt this scattering-of-forces strategy with the numbers available.

With Japan having been fully prepared for war by the end of October 1941, the British and Dutch kept a watchful eye on the area, waiting for the attack they knew was coming. The only question was when it would be launched.

Chapter 4
Pearl Harbor

*T*HE JAPANESE ATTACK ON PEARL HARBOR came as a tremendous shock to the American public. Most believed that if war came it would be against Germany and Italy, and most Americans failed to recognize that the United States was unprepared to fight an aggressive war. Most believed the nation was much stronger militarily than was the case and that no nation would dare attack. War became inevitable with the change of command in Tokyo on 16 October 1941. With Emperor Hirohito's blessing, Gen. Hideki Tojo, the Japanese army's strongest advocate of war and the main opponent of withdrawal from China, became the prime minister. He relieved Prince Fuminaro Konoe. In his letter of resignation, Konoe pointed out that on four separate occasions he had sought to withdraw troops in order to preserve peace with the United States, while Tojo had opposed both the action and its purpose. "With the China incident unresolved, he, as a loyal subject of the emperor, could not take on the responsibilities of entering into a huge new war whose outcome could not be foreseen." [1]

On 16 October, Otto Tolischus, in reporting to the *New York Times*, said that the director of Japanese naval intelligence had declared that the relations of the United States and Japan were "now approaching the final parting of the ways." From Shanghai on the same day came a dispatch stating that the Central China *Daily News*, organ of the Japanese-sponsored regime in Nanking, had asserted that war between Japan and the United States "is inevitable." [2]

As negotiations between the United States and Japan continued to worsen, on 27 November General Marshall warned MacArthur:

> Negotiations with Japan appear to be terminated to all practical purposes with only the barest possibilities that the Japanese government might come back and offer to continue. Japanese future action unpredictable but hostile action possible at any moment. If hostilities cannot, repeat cannot, be avoided the United States desires that Japan commit the first overt act. This policy should not, repeat not, be construed as restricting you to a course of action that might jeopardize your defense.

<u>Prior to hostile Japanese action you are directed to undertake such</u> <u>reconnaissance and other measures as you deem necessary</u> but report measures taken to defend the Philippines. Should hostilities occur you will carry out the tasks assigned in Rainbow 5 so far as they pertain to Japan. Limit dissemination of this highly secret information to minimum essential officers.[3]

Similar warnings were dispatched to other top commanders in the Pacific, especially those at Pearl Harbor. Shortly after General Marshall's warning, Admiral Stark sent a dispatch to Admirals Hart and Kimmel. His message said:

This dispatch is to be considered a war warning. Negotiations with Japan looking toward stabilization of conditions in the Pacific have ceased and an aggressive move by Japan is expected within the next few days.

The number and equipment of Japanese troops and the organization of naval task forces indicate an amphibious expedition against either the Philippines, Thai, or Kra Peninsula or possibly Borneo.

Execute an appropriate defense deployment preparatory to carrying out the tasks assigned in War Plan 46 (Rainbow T). Inform District and army authorities. A similar warning is being sent by War Department. SPENAVO [Special Naval Observer in London, Vice Adm. Ghormley] inform British. Continental districts, Guam, Samoa directed to take appropriate measures against sabotage.[4]

Both before and after the Pearl Harbor attack, the best information on the whereabouts of the Japanese fleet as well as merchant ships derived from the Fourteenth Naval District's Combat Intelligence Unit on Oahu, called Station Hypo. Lieutenant Commander Joseph J. Rochefort was the chief cryptanalyst; Lt. Cmdr. Edwin T. Layton, the intelligence chief. On 2 December, Layton informed Adm. Husband Kimmel that, "As there had been no radio traffic from four Japanese carriers for fully fifteen and possibly twenty-five days, their location was unknown."[5]

On the night of 3 December, British intelligence in Manila sent an urgent cable to British intelligence in Hawaii, saying:

We have received considerable intelligence confirming following developments in Indochina.

1. Accelerated Japanese preparation of airfields and railways.

2. Arrival since Nov. 10 of additional 100,000 repeat 100,000 troops and considerable quantities fighters, medium bombers, tanks and guns (75mm).

Estimate of specific quantities have already been telegraphed Washington Nov. 21 by American military intelligence here.

Our considered opinion concludes that Japan envisages early hostilities with Britain and U.S. Japan does not repeat not intend to attack Russia at present but will act in South.

You may inform Chiefs of American Military and Naval Intelligence Honolulu.[6]

Again, on 3 December, Admiral Stark sent another dispatch to Hart, Kimmel, and the naval district commandants in Manila and Honolulu. He informed them that Japanese diplomatic and consular posts at Hong Kong, Singapore, Batavia, Manila, Washington, and London had been ordered to destroy their codes. Stark thought this urgent order by the Japanese to demolish their codes, ciphers, and secret documents to be "one of the most telling items of information we had received and our dispatch . . . was one of the most important dispatches we ever sent." War was obviously near.[7]

On 6 December, Joseph C. Harsch, the correspondent for the *Christian Science Monitor*, met with Admiral Kimmel and his staff at fleet headquarters. Those present recall the following exchange:

Harsch: Admiral, now that the Japanese have moved into Indochina
. . . what do you think they will do next?
Kimmel: I don't know. What do you think?
Harsch: Well, do you think they will attack us?
Kimmel: No, young man, I don't think they'd be such
damned fools.[8]

Kimmel's hubris was like that of most Americans at the time.

On the night of 6 December, thirteen parts of a fourteen-paragraph message from Tokyo were decrypted and delivered to President Roosevelt. These showed Japan intended to break off diplomatic relations. Roosevelt instinctively knew this meant war. He now knew Japan was going to strike, but he didn't know where. The fourteenth part of the decrypted message gave the time of delivery to Secretary of State Hull as 1:00 P.M. Washington, D.C., time, which was 7:00 A.M. in Honolulu. Although this information was known in Washington some hours prior to 7:00 A.M. in Hawaii, through a series of errors, the warning did not reach Honolulu in time to prevent disaster.

No American old enough to remember can forget where he was and what he was doing that Sunday, 7 December 1941, when he first heard over the radio that Pearl Harbor had been bombed. All knew this meant war and that great damage had been done, the full extent of which was not revealed to the American public until months later.

I had finished midday dinner at the KA (Kappa Alpha) House in Lexington, Virginia, when I first heard the news. There were eighteen fraternity brothers in my senior year class at Washington and Lee University. A couple had already been drafted. Everyone knew that each would soon be going into some branch of the U.S. armed services. Having completed two platoon leader's classes in the previous summers, I would soon be called up for marine officer's training at Indiantown, Pennsylvania. All afternoon, we listened attentively to the radio news in the hope of getting an assessment of the full extent of the damage. Of course, this was not to be.

Virginia law forbade the Sunday sale of alcoholic beverages in any form, including beer. Someone got the idea of purchasing some white lightnin' from a bootlegger located a few blocks away. We obtained ice and fruit juices from the kitchen and mixed them in a huge bowl with the whiskey. In a somewhat somber mood, we speculated on our future as we listened to the radio and sipped drinks into the wee hours of the morning.

Although the radio did not report the full damage, eight American battleships had been hit, along with three destroyers and three light cruisers. After the Japanese planes completed their final run, more than 2,400 soldiers, sailors, and civilians had lost their lives.

President Roosevelt was sitting in his study with Harry Hopkins when Secretary Knox called to say, "It looks like the Japanese have attacked Pearl Harbor." [9] Hopkins thought the news was a mistake, as the Japanese would never attack Pearl Harbor. All doubt was settled a few minutes later when Admiral Stark called to confirm the attack.

Winston Churchill called the White House. "Mr. President, what's this about Japan?"

"It's quite true," Roosevelt replied. "They have attacked us at Pearl Harbour. We are all in the same boat now."

Churchill later wrote, "To have the United States at our side was to me the greatest joy." Churchill thought of a remark British politician Sir Edward Grey had made more than thirty years earlier. He said the United States was like "a gigantic boiler. Once the fire is lighted under it there is no limit to the power it can generate." [10]

At a cabinet meeting at 8:30 P.M. that Sunday night, Roosevelt said, "I'm thankful you all got here," after which he described the devastation at Pearl Harbor. Twice he turned to Knox, "Find out, for God's sake, why the ships were tied up in rows."

Knox replied, "That's the way they berth them!"

After again describing the damage to the fleet, Roosevelt then said half the planes in Hawaii had been destroyed "on the ground, by God, on the ground." [11]

At 10:00 P.M. congressional leaders joined the gathering. Roosevelt again told what was known of the damage to the U.S. Army and Navy in Honolulu. Senator Tom Connally, chairman of the Senate Foreign Relations Committee, posed the question that some Americans still ask: "How did it happen that our warships were caught like tame ducks in Pearl Harbor?" [12] Secretary Knox explained to the president that both Gen. Walter Short and Adm. Husband Kimmel felt certain that such an attack would take place nearer Japan's base of operations—that is, in the Far East. He had not planned on the ingenuity of Admiral Yamamoto.

In February 1941, Yamamoto ordered Cmdr. Genda Minoru, an air staff officer of the Japanese 1st Air Fleet, to make an investigation on the feasibility of the Pearl Harbor attack. Thorough studies and meticulous planning followed. In October, the liner *Taiyo Maru* sailed the chosen route for the Japanese attack fleet without sighting a single ship.[13]

In November, Yamamoto addressed about a hundred officers on the flight deck of the *Akagi*:

> Although we hope to achieve surprise, everyone should be prepared for terrific American resistance to this operation . . . [Kimmel is] no ordinary or average man. . . . We can expect him to put up a courageous fight. . . . Moreover, he is said to be farsighted and cautious, so it is quite possible that he has instituted very close measures to cope with any emergency. Therefore, you must take into careful consideration the possibility that the attack may not be a surprise after all. *You may have to fight your way in to the target.* [emphasis his][14]

On 22 November 1941, the Japanese fleet assembled at Hitokappu Bay in the Kurile Islands, immediately northeast of Japan proper. This attack force set sail four days later, running slowly eastward through fog and gales while always maintaining radio silence.

The core of this mobile fleet was based on six carriers in three divisions with a total of more than four hundred planes. A light cruiser led a screen of nine destroyers, two battleships, two heavy cruisers, plus a train of eight tankers and supply ships. Three submarines provided reconnaissance together with two extra destroyers to watch out for American planes based on Midway Island. However, the route selected was outside the pattern of America's patrol planes at Midway. Vice Admiral Nagumo Chuichi was in overall command.

On 3 December the formation reached a point 900 miles north of Midway, then turned south. On 7 December it proceeded due south, after parting company with the tankers. All warships put on speed until the carriers reached the designated point of launch 275 miles due north of Pearl Harbor just before 6:00 A.M. Hawaiian time. Execution of Yamamoto's well-planned attack on Pearl Harbor then followed. It crippled the U.S. Fleet to the point it could not move west to interdict the Japanese main thrust southward to the Netherlands East Indies. Yamamoto envisioned that his submarine fleet would play a major role as his chief of staff noted that he "expected that more damage would be inflicted by submarine attacks which would be continued over a longer period, than by the air attacks, which would be of comparatively short duration."[15]

The twenty-five Japanese regular submarines plus five midgets in Hawaiian waters did only minimal damage on 7 December and the following few weeks. At 6:30 A.M. Hawaiian time, the net in Oahu opened to admit the USS *Antares*, an old freighter. Casually watching *Antares* pass, a helmsman on the nearby destroyer *Ward* noticed a strange object that appeared to be a buoy. The *Ward* captain immediately identified the object as the conning tower of a submarine.

Ward opened fire with 4-inch guns, followed by depth charges. The midget expired at the bottom of Pearl Harbor.

Ward sent a message to headquarters of the Fourteenth Naval District: WE HAVE ATTACKED, FIRED UPON AND DROPPED DEPTH CHARGES ON A SUBMARINE OPERATING IN THE DEFENSIVE SEA AREA. Admiral Kimmel was immediately notified, but it was already too late to avert disaster. By 7:30 A.M. Japanese planes roared over Pearl Harbor. The U.S. Navy put the other four midget submarines out of action without damage to any American ship. On the afternoon of 10 December planes from *Enterprise* sank the Japanese *I-170* with all hands. The Japanese submarine's failure to live up to expectations greatly disappointed the high command.

In spite of previous warnings, lack of readiness characterized every aspect of the base at Pearl Harbor. On the same day, the Japanese attacked the Philippines, Malaya, Wake Island, Guam, and Hong Kong. On the bright side, all four U.S. aircraft carriers plus five cruisers as well as most destroyers assigned to the Pacific were on missions away from Pearl Harbor. The Japanese attack proved to be a blessing in disguise. For the remainder of the war, U.S. naval planners elevated the aircraft carrier above the battleship as the best offensive weapon for the Pacific Fleet.

At noon on 8 December, Roosevelt addressed a joint session of Congress where he declared that 7 December was a day that would "live in infamy" and that "this form of treachery shall never endanger us again. The American people in their righteous might will win through to absolute victory." [16] He was greeted with deafening applause. Both chambers approved a declaration of war against Japan with only one dissenting vote, that of Representative Jeanette Rankin of Montana. Roosevelt did not request, nor did Congress approve, a declaration of war against the other Axis powers. Four days later, Germany and Italy declared war on the United States. Japan had succeeded in doing what the president up to this point had been unable to do: it unified the American people as they had never been before or since.

The news media reported Guam as having fallen the first day, and only on Wake Island and the Philippines were American fighting men opposing Japanese invaders. The Japanese added to the Pacific defense perimeter by capturing the cluster of British islands known as the Gilberts on 10 December 1941.

The Greek poet Aeschylus observed that "When war begins, truth is the first casualty." Although he wrote the words 500 years before the time of Christ, they still held true in 1941. In the world of politics there is often a gap between the perception of the public and the reality of events, yet a false perception usually shifts under the examination of the free press. In war, especially World War II, strict censorship under the guise of national security prevented the public from learning the truth in a timely fashion. Nowhere is this better illustrated than the flow of communiqués from the Philippines in the aftermath of Pearl Harbor.

Near Manila, the U.S. Navy at Cavite received the first word that the war had started. Admiral Kimmel had announced to all ships at sea and to all U.S. Navy bases: RAID ON PEARL HARBOR. THIS IS NOT A DRILL.

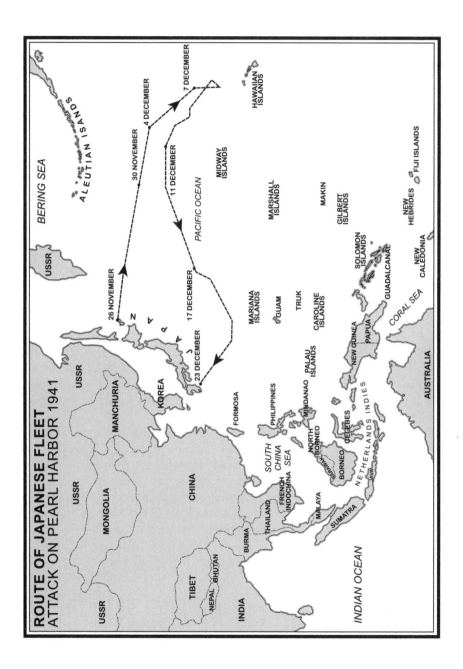

ROUTE OF JAPANESE FLEET
ATTACK ON PEARL HARBOR 1941

No one at Cavite bothered to tell the U.S. Army. Major General Sutherland, MacArthur's chief of staff, had attended a party given for Maj. Gen. Lewis H. Brereton, commander of U.S. Air Force Far East, at the Manila Hotel. MacArthur and his family occupied a penthouse atop the hotel's roof. When Sutherland arrived home he learned of the disaster at Pearl Harbor from a radio news broadcast at 3:40 A.M. He contacted MacArthur immediately, but the United States of America had been at war for almost two hours.

Ten hours after the attack on Pearl Harbor, almost eight hours after MacArthur had been informed that the country was at war, disaster struck at Clark Field. Some historians place full blame on MacArthur, while others have him sharing it with Brereton or Sutherland. In the early morning, Brereton had tried to reach MacArthur for a decision but was prevented from doing so by Sutherland. Eighteen of the thirty-five B-17 Flying Fortresses had previously been sent to Del Monte Field in Mindanao, out of range of the Japanese bombers at Formosa. The remaining B-17s plus numerous other aircraft were sitting in the open in neat lines waiting to be serviced. MacArthur appeared to be frozen in thought while Brereton and Sutherland failed to take the initiative in removing the planes from harm's way. At this point in time, MacArthur had a totally unrealistic view of Japanese air capabilities. On 5 December, just three days before the Japanese attack, he told British Vice Adm. Tom Phillips: "The inability of an enemy to launch his attack on these islands is our greatest security," which "leaves me with a sense of complete security." [17]

At 12:25 P.M., most airmen had finished lunch and were awaiting orders when the Japanese planes arrived. No American fighters rose to meet them. The anti-aircraft guns were either unattended or silent as fifty-four Japanese bombers and thirty-six Zero fighters moved into the attack. The parked bombers and fighters were easily destroyed. At Iba, forty miles north of Clark Field, Japanese aircraft destroyed all but two of a squadron of P-40s, which had just returned from patrol. By 1:30 P.M., MacArthur's air force had ceased to exist as an effective element of defense. With eight hours' warning, the Philippines was even less prepared than Pearl Harbor, which had no warning at all. Twenty-nine enemy planes were shot down at Pearl.

Fortunately for MacArthur, the American public and press focused on the debacle at Hawaii. Secretary Frank Knox was immediately sent to Hawaii on a fact-finding mission. There he talked to Adm. Husband E. Kimmel, commander in chief of the Pacific Fleet, and Lt. Gen. Walter C. Short, commander of the U.S. Army, Hawaiian Department. He delivered his report to President Roosevelt on 14 December. In it, he said:

> There was no attempt by either Admiral Kimmel or General Short to alibi the lack of a state of readiness for the air attack. Both admitted that they did not expect it, and had taken no adequate measures to meet one if it came. Both Kimmel and Short evidently regarded an air attack as extremely unlikely. . . . Both felt that if any surprise attack was attempted it would be made in the Far East.[18]

On 16 December, both Kimmel and Short were relieved of their commands.

The Pearl Harbor disaster brought into the open the inadequacies of command by mutual cooperation with divided responsibility. It defied the maxim of Gen. Ulysses S. Grant, who declared "two commanders on the same field are always one too many." [19] As early as February 1941, General Marshall complained that old army and navy feuds in Hawaii were becoming confused with questions of national defense. Both the U.S. Army and the U.S. Navy objected violently to being placed under the jurisdiction of the other service. Different training, years of competing for its share of inadequate funds in the defense budget, and the annual Army-Navy football game caused jealousies and rivalries to run deep.

Recognizing the dangers of divided command, on 12 December 1941, President Roosevelt ordered his military and naval advisors to establish a unified command in Panama under the U.S. Army, much to the chagrin of high-ranking naval officers. On 17 December the U.S. Navy was given command in Hawaii. Marshall explained to the U.S. Army commander in Hawaii that "the Secretary of War and the Secretary of the Navy were determined there would be no question of future confusion as to responsibility . . . Both Stark and I were struggling to the same end." [20]

Although fixing responsibility under one commander at Pearl Harbor for most of the Pacific theater was a giant step forward, inter-service rivalry did not disappear, either there or in Washington, D.C.

Chapter 5
The Arcadia Conference

*F*RANKLIN D. ROOSEVELT AND WINSTON CHURCHILL recognized immediately that to win battles a nation must have the requisite military power. Equally important, if not more so, it must have the means to deliver that power. The Japanese raid on Pearl Harbor eliminated the U.S. Navy's ability to implement the prewar Plan Orange for the present and immediate future. As commander in chief, U.S. forces, Roosevelt knew he had to rebuild the Pacific Fleet.

Within twenty-four hours of the Pearl Harbor attack, Winston Churchill secured cabinet approval for an immediate visit to meet Franklin D. Roosevelt, noting that, "we are in the same boat . . . It would also be a great pleasure for me to meet you again, and the sooner the better." [1] Initially Roosevelt leaned toward putting Churchill off. Both Gen. George Marshall and Admiral Stark believed that Churchill and his war chiefs should visit Washington after the United States had settled its basic war strategy. [2] After careful thought, Roosevelt wired Churchill:

> Delighted to have you here at the White House. . . . I know that you will bear in mind that the production and allocation problems can and will be worked out with complete understanding and accord. . . . Details of production and allocation can be handled at long range. Naval situation and other matters of strategy require discussion. [3]

On 12 December 1941, Winston Churchill's special train left London to meet the battleship *Duke of York*, which would take him and his entourage across the Atlantic. On 13 December, Churchill's party, thirty-eight in all, from his chiefs of staff to private secretaries, official photographers, and newsreel cameramen, arrived in Gourock, Scotland, where they boarded the *Duke of York*. Pending the British arrival on 22 December, Washington, D.C., was a beehive of activity as Allied prospects in the Pacific theater went steadily downhill.

One week after the Japanese attack, Roosevelt and Secretary Frank Knox decided to make Adm. Ernest J. King commander in chief of the U.S. Fleet. Later, when Roosevelt sent Adm. Harold Stark to command U.S. naval forces in Europe, he gave King the additional duties of chief of naval operations (CNO). King impressed Roosevelt and Secretary Frank Knox in August 1941 when he personally escorted Roosevelt to his first meeting with Churchill at Argentia, Newfoundland, as they sailed together in the heavy cruiser *Augusta*. He was on hand when Roosevelt and Knox needed naval advice in talks with the British. King's grasp of strategy and phenomenal knowledge of detail made an abiding impression. Because he had studied the numerous versions of Plan Orange developed primarily by the U.S. Navy over a period of years, King would prove to be America's most knowledgeable strategist of the Pacific War.

King was born in Lorain, Ohio, in 1878, shortly after his Scottish father migrated to America to become a foreman in a railroad repair shop. He graduated fourth in the class of 1901 at Annapolis Naval Academy. In 1917, as a staff member in the U.S. Atlantic Fleet, he learned to dislike the British, especially the English ruling class so heavily represented in the Royal Navy. He finished World War I as a youthful captain, age thirty-nine, with the Navy Cross.

In 1925, he won fame by salvaging a sunken submarine off Rhode Island. As naval aviation began to develop, King gained his wings in 1928, just short of age fifty. He took command of the aircraft carrier *Lexington* and in war games made a successful mock attack on Pearl Harbor. Like Yamamoto, King was a prime mover behind the development of maritime air power during the prewar years, although congressional budget restraints prevented him from getting the carriers he deemed sorely needed.

In early 1941, he commanded the newly re-created U.S. Atlantic Fleet, which brought him his fourth star as a full admiral. He was a known heavy drinker and womanizer, which caused him to be passed over on one occasion in his climb to full admiral. He disliked incompetence and the media, along with Englishmen. Throughout the war, his dislike of the press caused him to play second fiddle to other officers of his rank in the eyes of the American public, especially MacArthur.

Recognizing that he shouldered much, if not all, of the blame for the destruction of his air force without a fight, MacArthur immediately initiated a cover-up. On 10 December he sent Gen. Hap Arnold an effusive radiogram about the gallantry of the aircrews in the Philippines. "Their losses were due entirely to the overwhelming superiority of enemy force," he said. "No unit could have done better . . . No item of loss can properly be attributed to neglect or lack of care . . . You may take pride in their conduct." [4] But he did not explain why, despite adequate knowledge of what had happened in Hawaii ten hours earlier, he had allowed so many planes to be sitting in tidy rows on the airfields when the Japanese attackers arrived.

During the period of 10 December through 12 December, the Japanese landed a total of 6,500 troops on Luzon, 2,000 each at Aparri and Vigan, and 2,500 at Legaspi in South Luzon. [5]

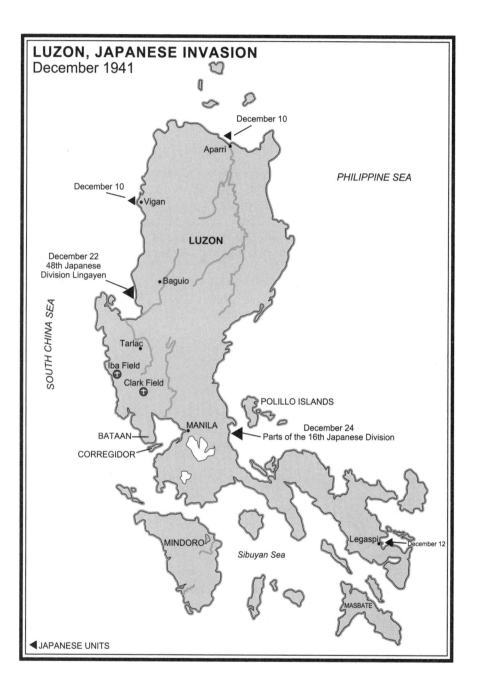

LUZON, JAPANESE INVASION
December 1941

December 10

Aparri

PHILIPPINE SEA

December 10

•Vigan

LUZON

December 22
48th Japanese
Division Lingayen

•Baguio

SOUTH CHINA SEA

Tarlac•

Iba Field

Clark Field

POLILLO ISLANDS

MANILA

December 24
Parts of the 16th Japanese Division

BATAAN

CORREGIDOR

MINDORO

Sibuyan Sea

Legaspi

December 12

MASBATE

◀ JAPANESE UNITS

On 12 December 1941, MacArthur created the war's first American hero, other than himself. His communiqué announced "with great sorrow the death of Captain Colin P. Kelly Jr., who distinguished himself by scoring three direct hits on the Japanese capital battleship *Haruna*, leaving her in flames and in distress." [6] The War Department in Washington announced that the 29,330-ton ship was sunk north of Luzon. Kelly, a twenty-five-year-old West Point graduate, was supposedly looking for an enemy aircraft carrier when he came upon the *Haruna*. Some versions of the story even had Kelly piloting his shot-up B-17 into the *Haruna* on a suicide run to finish off the battleship.

The Colin Kelly episode made a great story, except no Japanese battleship had been attacked or sunk. The *Haruna* was not even in the area. Kelly and his crew bombed the *Ashigira*, but the Japanese cruiser was not sunk. Nevertheless, Kelly did die heroically that day. As the B-17 flew back to Clark Field, Zeros attacked, badly damaging the aircraft. Kelly stayed at the controls, giving his surviving crew time to bail out, and he died in the crash. The exaggerated version, however, told the American public what it wanted to hear and provided the country with its first full-fledged war hero. President Roosevelt made an immediate posthumous award of the Distinguished Service Cross in his honor. Days later, Roosevelt wrote a letter to the future president of the United States in 1956 on behalf of Captain Kelly's infant son:

> I am writing this letter as an act of faith in the destiny of our country. My request is that you consider the merit of a young American youth of goodly heritage, Colin P. Kelly III for appointment as a Cadet in the United States Military Academy at West Point. I make this appeal in behalf of this youth as a token of the nation's appreciation of the heroic service of his father.[7] [In 1956 President Eisenhower honored the letter, and Colin P. Kelly III entered West Point.]

On paper, MacArthur commanded a force that should have defeated the Japanese troops committed to the occupation of the Philippines. His command consisted of about 31,000 Americans, 12,000 Filipino scouts, and 100,000 conscripts of the Philippine army, a force more than three times the size of the Japanese troops that landed in December 1941 and January 1942, numbering a total of 42,000. In reality, "MacArthur's army was mostly a political myth," as claimed by Brig. Gen. Bradford Grethen Chynoweth in his memoirs.

The available fleet at hand should have deterred the enemy's invasion forces but failed to do so. Admiral Thomas E. Hart, commander of the U.S. Asiatic Fleet, had one heavy cruiser, two light cruisers, four destroyers, twenty-nine submarines, thirty-two patrol bombers, and a number of auxiliaries.

The twenty-nine submarines in the Philippines, the United States' largest concentration, were completely ineffective. They were equipped with the U.S. Navy's Mark 14 torpedo with a magnetic exploder designed to erupt under a ship's keel. Prior to the war, the navy Bureau of Ordnance never properly

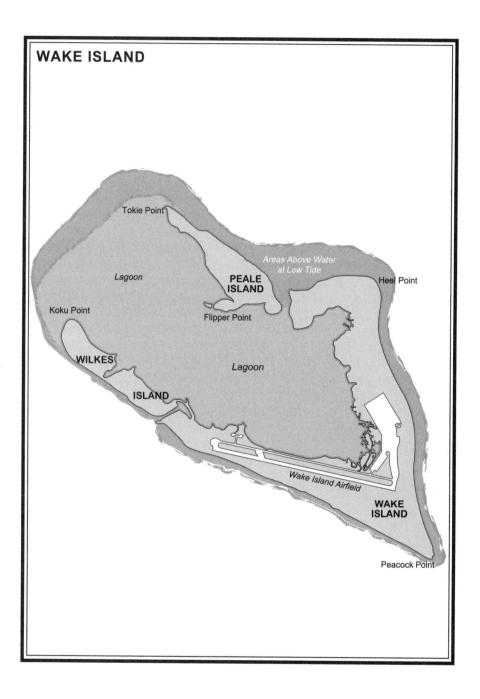

WAKE ISLAND

Tokie Point

Lagoon

Areas Above Water at Low Tide

PEALE ISLAND

Heel Point

Koku Point

Flipper Point

WILKES

Lagoon

ISLAND

Wake Island Airfield

WAKE ISLAND

Peacock Point

tested the Mark 14 warhead, costing $10,000 each. Instead, exercise warheads filled with water were used. This failing was not corrected until many months later. With the Japanese in control of the air, Hart ordered his navy south to prevent destruction.

For the first two weeks of the war, the Japanese made only minor unopposed landings, at Aparri on the north coast on 10 December, at Vigan on the northwest coast the same day, and at Legaspi to the southeast on 12 December. Each day following these landings the U.S. news media focused on the U.S. Marines defending Wake Island and General MacArthur's heroic stand in the Philippines.

Wake Island had no indigenous population when annexed by the United States in 1899. In 1935, Pan American Airways established a refueling station there for its trans-Pacific clippers. Passenger service began the following year and facilities were expanded to include a forty-eight-room hotel. Travel time on the San Francisco-to-Manila route was six days, which included overnight stops in Honolulu, Midway, Wake, and Guam. In January 1941, the U.S. Navy authorized the building of an air station scheduled for completion by the summer of 1942. Wake Island's land area of only 4.5 square miles was located 2,000 miles west of Hawaii, across the International Date Line.

Beginning at 11:58 A.M. on 8 December, the small U.S. Marine garrison came under constant attack by Japanese navy bombers from Roi in the Marshalls. The daily bombings and the defense by the marines made front-page news across the United States. Because a cable connected Wake with Pearl Harbor, accurate information could be transmitted in a timely fashion.

On 11 December the Japanese attempted an amphibious landing. Marine Maj. James P. S. Devereux ordered his troops to hold fire until the Japanese came within close range. The Japanese suffered two destroyers sunk, seven damaged—some seriously—with 700 casualties, most of them deaths, before Rear Admiral Kajioka decided to retire to Kwajalein. Naval historian Samuel Eliot Morison said, "December 11, 1941, should always be a proud day in the history of the Corps. Never again, in this Pacific war, did coast defense guns beat off an amphibious landing." [8]

Each day Americans received news of Japanese bombings and the U.S. Marines' refusal to surrender. A detachment of reinforcements was sent from Pearl Harbor to Wake Island but turned back upon reaching a point about 500 miles from the island.

On 21 December, Kajioka set out from the Marshalls for a second attempt at Wake. His forces included the same ships that had survived the first attack plus four heavy cruisers, a seaplane carrier, and 1,500 amphibious troops. In addition, the Japanese High Command gave Kajioka two aircraft carriers, *Sorva* and *Hiryu*, together with a covered force of destroyers that were on the way back to Japan from the attack on Pearl Harbor.

In the early morning of 23 December the Japanese began landing troops. By 3:00 A.M., a thin line of marines on Wake battled the Japanese invaders. With daylight came the Japanese air armada. The marines sent a message: "Enemy on island. Issue in doubt." Thus Pearl Harbor received its last message from the Wake Island defenders.

While the American public took for granted the loss of Wake, it was encouraged by news from the Philippines. Strict censorship of the facts enabled numerous fictitious or exaggerated communiqués to go unchallenged and uncorrected. On 13 December Manila reported: "Attempted Japanese Landing Off Luzon's West Coast Pushed Back Into the Sea." [9] Each day the Manila communiqués reported sporadic to heavy fighting in the Philippines, including many enemy ships being sunk. In reality, there was no attempted Japanese landing on the west coast, no significant fighting, and no record of any enemy ships sunk.

The 20 December communiqué reported "the Americans have taken a heavy toll of Japanese ships, planes and men, but have made no concerted effort thus far to drive these invaders out by land assault." [10] The report said Gen. Douglas MacArthur's headquarters "announced yesterday afternoon that land forces long prepared for just such an attempt opposing the invasion. Doubtless these forces were strongly supported by American planes." [11] Yet, the Japanese had not invaded any part of the Philippine archipelago in division strength.

The 21 December communiqué reported the defenders were opposing numerically superior Japanese forces as MacArthur personally took to the field along with his staff.[12] In reality, on this date only 6,500 Japanese troops had landed on Luzon.

On Monday, 22 December, the *Duke of York* landed safely in the United States with Churchill's contingent. They journeyed to Washington, D.C., where Churchill along with his personal physician, Dr. Charles Wilson, stayed in the White House as guests of Roosevelt. This same day, MacArthur's communiqué reported a flotilla of eighty enemy transports sighted off Lingayen Gulf. (The Port of Lingayen, 110 miles northwest of Manila, lies in the sheltered waters of the gulf of the same name.) This statement was accurate, except the communiqué added: "The Japanese tried one landing there last week but were pushed back into the sea by Philippines land forces. General Douglas MacArthur's headquarters had anticipated an attempted landing there and preparations have long been completed there to meet just such an eventuality." [13] There is no record of a Japanese landing or attempted landing at Lingayen Gulf prior to 22 December 1941.

On Tuesday, 23 December, the Manila communiqué reported, "A heavy force of Japanese sea-borne troops supported by airplanes landed yesterday at Santo Tomas on the Gulf of Lingayen northwest of here, but Gen. Douglas MacArthur's headquarters announced that American defenders had the situation 'well in hand.' " [14] The Japanese did land a division at the Gulf of Lingayen, but the American defenders did not have the situation well in hand. In fact, when ground fighting began, much of the Philippine army was revealed to be an ill-trained, ill-equipped mob.

On this same day, 23 December 1941, the conference labeled "Arcadia" by Churchill began in the afternoon at the White House. Churchill brought with him Chief of War Production Lord Beaverbrook; Admiral of the Fleet Sir

Dudley Pound; the First Sea Lord, Field Marshal Sir John Dill; and Air Chief Marshal Sir Charles Portal. Besides the president, the American contingent included Harry Hopkins, civilian advisor to the president; Secretary of War Henry Stimson; Secretary of Navy Frank Knox; Gen. George Marshall; Lt. Gen. Henry H. Arnold; and Adms. Harold Stark and Ernest King.

Initially the British worried about the effect on the Americans of the rapid Japanese conquests during December. They thought that the United States might reverse the Rainbow Five Plan, which gave the defeat of Germany first priority. Information from the Far East was all bad, and the American public was especially angered by the Japanese sneak attack on Pearl Harbor.

Roosevelt put Churchill's mind at ease by assuring him that he intended to abide by the Rainbow Five Plan, which gave the European war first priority. Early on, Churchill informed Roosevelt privately of England's atomic energy research program and Britain's most closely guarded secret, ULTRA, the code breakers at Bletchley Park.

Christmas Day headlines in U.S. newspapers announced: Battle for Manila is Launched While Heroic Saga of Wake's Marines Ends. In Washington, the U.S. Navy reported that fewer than 400 marines repulsed fourteen attacks before losing the island. Wake Island would remain in Japanese hands for the remainder of the war. It had little, if any, strategic value to either side. Yet the courageous stand of the marines was a needed morale builder to all in the United States.

By Christmas Day, the Japanese had captured Hong Kong, sunk the British ships *Prince of Wales* and *Repulse*, occupied Wake Island, Guam, and the Gilbert Islands, and were moving steadily down the Malay Peninsula. A report of MacArthur's magnificent stand in the Philippines was the only bright spot on the horizon.

MacArthur himself was now a hero of unbounded proportions to all Americans, including the military establishment in Washington, many of whom had been previous doubters. Because of his previous association, Dwight D. Eisenhower still remained a disbeliever. A few days after the news of Pearl Harbor, Marshall brought Ike to Washington to serve in the War Plans Division under Brig. Gen. Leonard T. Gerow. "Ike was known to be the one available officer who was familiar with MacArthur's plan for the defense of the Philippines." [15] Moreover he had distinguished himself as chief of staff in Gen. Walter Krueger's Third Army during the Louisiana Maneuvers in the summer of 1941. He was promoted to brigadier general shortly after his arrival. A month later he was promoted to major general to lead the War Plans Division in the place and stead of Gerow.

Marshall determined to have the best men possible regardless of seniority to serve in the key military positions. Yet public opinion influenced some strictly military decisions. In a democracy, where power at the top derives from the people, MacArthur's popularity would impact the strategy of the Joint Chiefs of Staff and Roosevelt, the commander in chief, until the end of the war. However, Admiral King recognized that the U.S. Navy shouldered the heaviest burden for the defeat of Japan. Indeed, the campaign that ensued would be the largest naval conflict in history.

Much to the dismay of King, Roosevelt and Knox decided that Adm. Chester W. Nimitz was the right man for the job to replace Kimmel. King might have made the same decision upon reflection, but there were twenty-eight admirals senior to Nimitz when he became commander in chief of the U.S. Pacific Fleet. Nimitz came to the attention of Roosevelt and Knox in his position as chief of the Bureau of Navigation—that is, personnel. As such, it was his responsibility to advise the president and Secretary of the Navy on senior naval appointments.

Nimitz descended from German stock on both sides. He was a second-generation American born in Fredericksburg, Texas, in 1885. Lacking the money to go to college, he applied to the Military Academy at West Point. When told there was no vacancy, he tried for the Naval Academy at Annapolis and was accepted, graduating seventh in his class of 114 in 1905.

He was only twenty-two and still an ensign on being given command of an old destroyer. The next year, his career almost sank when he ran his ship aground. After receiving a reprimand from his court-martial, his overall record still permitted him to be promoted that same year.

He next moved into submarines and, at age twenty-six, commanded a division of boats, becoming a technical expert on diesel engines. He invented a system of refueling on the move as well as the circular formation for the battle group at sea. He helped develop ways of integrating the new carriers into the fleet. In World War I, he served as engineering staff officer with the submarine force of the U.S. Atlantic Fleet in British and Mediterranean waters. Afterward, he oversaw the building of the submarine base at Pearl Harbor in 1922. He rose to the rank of rear admiral in 1937 and was assigned command of the 1st Battleship Division.

When he arrived at Pearl Harbor on 31 December, he sympathized with Kimmel by saying, "The same thing could have happened to anybody." [16] He calmed nerves by keeping nearly all of Kimmel's staff. Though Kimmel may have acquitted himself with distinction by remaining in his post as commander in chief of the Pacific Fleet, the fact remains no one could have done a better job than Nimitz for the ensuing three and a half years plus.

Back in Washington at the Arcadia Conference, the Allies tackled two immediate problems in the Pacific theater. Five different countries—the United States, Great Britain, the Netherlands, Australia, and New Zealand—were fighting individually for want of a common commander. More importantly, the Allies faced an acute shipping shortage that severely limited the movement of supplies and forces to any war zone, Atlantic or Pacific.

The British had a solution, which the Americans accepted. British Gen. Sir Archibald Wavell was selected as supreme commander for Allied forces opposing the Japanese in the area comprising the South China Sea, the Netherlands East Indies, and the Indian Ocean; however, his scope of duties was not fully articulated or to whom he would answer.

British and American officials agreed to utilize existing machinery to get rapid decisions in lieu of creating a special body to supervise Wavell. Other governments would be excluded from the Chiefs of Staff Committee, composed of only the British and American Chiefs of Staff. This committee alone, argued the British, with approval from the president and prime minister, would determine Allied strategy and direct the Allied supreme commanders. In effect the American and British Chiefs of Staff would run the war with the lesser countries following orders. The Combined Chiefs of Staff thus came into being on 31 December 1941.

The conference centered on the defense of island bases between Hawaii and Australia, as there was unanimous agreement that Australia must be held. To do so the sea lanes of communication leading to Australia had to be safeguarded. King insisted the key bases—New Caledonia, Fiji, and American Samoa—had to be reinforced. Land, air, and navy forces needed to protect convoys all the way to Australia. As a first step, U.S. Marines landed at Samoa by late January. Throughout the conference Winston Churchill stressed that Singapore could withstand all Japanese assaults against it.

While the Combined Chiefs of Staff haggled over sending troops and convoys to New Caledonia at the expense of the Atlantic theater, Japan declared war against the Dutch on 11 January and invaded the Netherlands East Indies. Admiral King became more convinced than ever that the war against Japan had to take first priority; however, the British were unwilling to shift their emphasis from the European theater.

On 12 January Marshall temporarily came to King's side and proposed sending 10,000 American troops to New Caledonia. Aircraft, gasoline, and war material had to be sent as well. American garrisons in Iceland and Northern Ireland were reduced to provide for the needed personnel and shipping.

Near the end of Arcadia, the participants after much wrangling agreed that Allied headquarters would be in Washington. The U.S. Joint Chiefs of Staff consisted of King, Marshall, Stark, and Arnold, the equivalent to the British Chiefs: Field Marshal Alan Brooke, Pound, and Portal. The British agreed to maintain a liaison group in Washington headed by Dill, who would work directly with the American Joint Chiefs of Staff on day-to-day matters. Periodically, the Joint Chiefs of Staff and the British Chiefs of Staff together with Roosevelt and Churchill would meet to decide grand strategy and other crucial matters affecting the war.

The extensive staff work performed by the British in contemplation of this meeting impressed General Marshall, as this staff work had not been met in kind by the Americans. This caused Field Marshal Sir John Dill to say, the United States "has not—repeat not—the slightest conception of what the war means, and their armed forces are more unready for war than it is possible to imagine." [17] Dill based his harsh judgment on the observation that there were no regular meetings between the service Chiefs of Staff, no joint secretariat, no system for regular consultation between the president and his military advisors, and such consultations as the president had with his military leaders were haphazard. Marshall remedied this situation in short order.

Next to the last day of meetings, the conference came to an impasse over the allocation of munitions. The British had proposed two parallel allocation committees not responsible to the Combined Chiefs of Staff (CCS) committee. Marshall insisted that the allocation of war materials had to be subservient to the CCS committee in Washington. Marshall made it clear that munitions allocated by a politically appointed body directed by Roosevelt and Churchill were wrong because the military would ultimately use the munitions. Roosevelt after consulting with Harry Hopkins came to Marshall's side and in turn the Munitions Assignment Board as established came into being under the direction of the Combined Chiefs of Staff.

The Arcadia Conference established a framework for British and American cooperation for the remainder of the war. Many historians say this was the most successful coalition in the history of warfare. General George Marshall's performance throughout validated Roosevelt's judgment when he selected the general as U.S. Army Chief of Staff over the heads of thirty-five others senior in grade or rank.

Indeed, Winston Churchill's personal physician, an unbiased observer, Dr. Charles Wilson, noted in his diary:

> The Prime Minister . . . "wanted to show the President how to run the war. It has not worked out quite like that." Instead, George Marshall, "in his quiet, unprovocative way" had taken charge of the meetings. "Marshall remains the key to the situation," Wilson presciently observed. Neither Churchill nor Franklin Roosevelt "can contemplate going forward without Marshall." [18]

Chapter 6
The Lean Months

T HE JAPANESE WAR MACHINE CONTINUED to experience phenomenal success during the months of January through May 1942. These were clearly the lean months for the Allies in the Pacific War. The Japanese cut off further supply to America's ally, China. Roosevelt and Churchill took different views on the need to send tons of weapons to Chiang Kai-shek's Nationalist army. Roosevelt considered it very important to keep China in the war, while Churchill viewed China's role as much less essential.

In Roosevelt's message to Congress on 6 January 1942, he listed the Allies whom the United States had joined in war. When he referred to the brave people of China, members gave a loud and spontaneous applause. "Those millions," the president said, "who for four and a half years have withstood bombs and starvation and have whipped the invaders time and again in spite of superior Japanese equipment and arms," added to the mystique of the enduring courage of the Chinese.[1]

On 15 December 1941, a Chinese communiqué reported that the Nationalists had dispatched two armies against the rear of the Japanese attacking Hong Kong, had engaged the enemy, and had inflicted 15,000 casualties. No such battle had occurred. In January, Chiang Kai-shek informed the American government of his intention to launch an offensive to drive the Japanese out of Indochina. America's top military advisor in China, Brig. Gen. John Magruder, observed that the Chinese are "great believers in the world of make believe. They shut their eyes to actualities, preferring flattering but fictitious symbols which they regard as more real than cold facts." [2] These press releases caused widespread misconceptions about China with the American public.

After the British returned home from the Arcadia Conference, an analysis of American naval forces in the Pacific showed the impracticality of aiding the Philippines. The Japanese had ten carriers; the Americans, three. All American battleships were sunk, damaged, or otherwise unavailable; the Japanese had twelve. Twenty-five Japanese cruisers outnumbered the fifteen remaining cruisers of the Pacific Fleet. There were similar disparities in destroyers and submarines. In addition, the Japanese occupied numerous air bases in the islands on the ocean highway between Pearl Harbor and Manila Bay. After *Prince of Wales* and *Repulse* were sunk off Malaya, no one doubted that airplanes could sink a moving ship.

Although the American public had received fictitious reports almost daily during the month of December about battles in the Philippines, no serious fighting had occurred until mid-January 1942. The first landings by the enemy in division strength came on 22 December when the 48th Japanese Division landed in Lingayen Gulf north of Manila. Part of the Japanese 16th Division beached in Lamon Bay southeast of Manila on 23 and 24 December.

MacArthur belatedly withdrew his forces on Luzon into the Bataan Peninsula as he moved his headquarters to the island fortress of Corregidor on 24 December, the same day he ordered a military evacuation and declared Manila an open city. Having previously scorned Plan Orange (WPO-3) as defeatist, he failed to invoke it until he had no other choice. On 2 January the Japanese entered Manila.

After capturing the city, the Japanese made a very wise move. Their military authorities called upon Filipino officials to remain in their jobs. They promised early independence as a reward for collaboration. Leading members of the oligarchy organized a Japanese-approved administration council, the nucleus of a puppet regime.

President Quezon reportedly told subordinates that he and MacArthur agreed that they might cooperate with the Japanese so long as they did not formally pledge allegiance to Tokyo. Later, MacArthur denied this. To cement their friendship, President Quezon issued a secret executive order on 3 January 1942 awarding $645,000 in commonwealth funds on deposit in the United States to General MacArthur and his staff. To MacArthur, he gave $500,000; to Richard Sutherland, $75,000; to Richard J. Marshall, $45,000; and to Sidney Huff, $25,000.[3] The American commander waited almost six weeks before accepting the award, which violated U.S. Army regulations.

By early January, about 80,000 soldiers plus 26,000 civilians and some material reached Bataan Peninsula, which is about thirty miles long and twenty miles wide. The troops formed a line across the neck of the peninsula. Unfortunately for the Americans and Filipinos, the move into the Bataan Peninsula was made too late to recover the great quantities of food, medicines, ammunition, and other supplies that remained in U.S. depots around the islands. This costly failure remains unexplained.

After only a short time on the peninsula, MacArthur on 5 January 1942 ordered all troops on Bataan and Corregidor placed on half rations.[4] The dismal diet—barely 1,000 calories a day near the end—the humidity, and the lack of clothing suitable to protect against insects combined to cause 80 percent to become ill from malaria and intestinal and nutritional diseases. In the opinion of Harold K. Johnson, then a lieutenant in the 57th Infantry and later a member of the Joint Chiefs of Staff, MacArthur should have been supervising the shipment of supplies, which would be desperately needed later on Bataan. MacArthur's

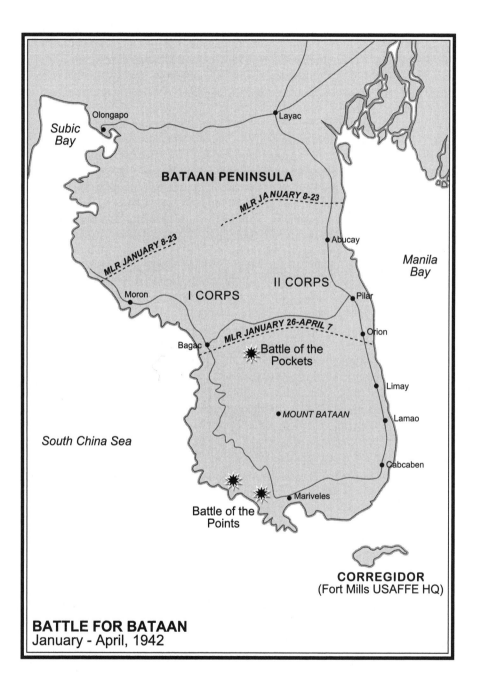

Subic
Bay

Olongapo

Layac

BATAAN PENINSULA

MLR JANUARY 8-23

MLR JANUARY 8-23

Abucay

Manila
Bay

I CORPS

II CORPS

Moron

Pilar

MLR JANUARY 26-APRIL 7

Orion

Bagac

Battle of the
Pockets

Limay

MOUNT BATAAN

Lamao

South China Sea

Cabcaben

Battle of the
Points

Mariveles

CORREGIDOR
(Fort Mills USAFFE HQ)

BATTLE FOR BATAAN
January - April, 1942

beach defense plan "was a tragic error," he said. "The supplies that could have been moved in the two-week period probably meant the difference between another three or four weeks on Bataan. It wasn't the enemy that licked us. It was the disease and the absence of food that really licked us." Johnson claimed one depot alone at Cabanatuan in central Luzon held 50 million bushels of rice, enough to feed U.S. and Filipino troops for more than four years.[5] Chynoweth in his memoirs claimed there were large stockpiles of food and ammunition left on the docks of Manila.

In mid-January, the Japanese attacked the Bataan line. By then, American and Filipino troops suffered more from disease and hunger than from battle. Some Filipinos began melting away. Morale deteriorated further after 24 January when MacArthur ordered Brig. Gen. George F. Moore, the harbor defense commander, to maintain a reserve on Corregidor large enough to feed 20,000 men, twice the number on the island, through 30 June 1942.[6] Obviously, this food supply had to be extracted from the meager diet of the Bataan defenders. When fighting slowed down during February and March, disease and malnutrition continued to exact a heavy toll.

In his ten weeks on Corregidor, MacArthur's headquarters released more than 140 press releases, many of which he wrote himself. A large majority referred to the general exclusively. The releases frequently reported victories in imaginary battles. "Single handedly, it seemed, he was frustrating Tokyo's war plan," although only once did he leave the sanctuary of the Corregidor fortress to visit his commanders at the front.[7] On 9 January 1942, he met with his leaders on Bataan before the Japanese had attacked the Allies' main defense line.

To the American public, MacArthur was now a hero unequaled by any other, although irate soldiers in the front lines on Bataan had a different opinion. They composed derisive songs about Dugout Doug, an epithet that stayed with him for the rest of the war. To the War Department in Washington, Stimson complained that messages from the Far Eastern commander were of a "most harassing and agonizing character." [8]

Yet in Washington Eisenhower was the only high-ranking military officer who became completely disgusted with MacArthur. He considered MacArthur "as big a baby as ever." [9] This is shown by entries in Eisenhower's diary, which consistently criticized the general.

However, MacArthur told the American public what it wanted to hear. Strict censorship rules prevented pesky reporters from refuting his claims. General Marshall recommended MacArthur for the Medal of Honor. He

> saw it as a way to "offset any propaganda by the enemy" about the disaster in the Philippines, and as a way to boost morale in the United States. Roosevelt clearly did not think the medal was awarded for heroism. On the contrary, Roosevelt viewed MacArthur's performance in Corregidor and Bataan as "more a rout than a military achievement" and told Supreme Court Justice Frank Murphy that his actions in approving the award were "pure yielding to Congressional and public opinion." [10]

The Army Air Force gained a measure of new prestige on 9 February 1942, when Lt. Gen. "Hap" Arnold took his place as a member at the first formal meeting of the Joint Chiefs of Staff, which included Adm. Ernest King, General Marshall, and General Arnold and which thereafter constituted the American High Command.

The concept of the Joint Chiefs was born at the Argentia Conference in August 1941, when the Americans felt the need for an agency to parallel the British command structure. President Roosevelt had invited Arnold to the Argentia Conference at the request of Marshall and the insistence of Harry Hopkins, who continued to support, within the White House, both Arnold and air power.

Admiral King and his aides never wholeheartedly accepted him. Marshall was eager to have Arnold because he felt that the army air wing deserved representation. At the behest of General Marshall, Adm. William D. Leahy would later be brought back from Vichy France to be chief of staff of the Joint Chiefs. By letter dated 20 July 1942, Leahy would be so appointed by President Franklin D. Roosevelt.[11]

Leahy had already retired after a term as chief of naval operations. Afterward, he had become American ambassador to the Vichy French government. Marshall suggested that Roosevelt bring him home to head the Joint Chiefs because "I thought the Navy couldn't resist this, and from what I had learned, I was willing to trust Leahy to be a neutral chairman."[12]

Marshall worried he would have trouble with Admiral King, who had replaced Adm. Harold Stark as chief of naval operations. King had a reputation of being difficult and he seemed determined to live up to his reputation. One morning during the early days of the war, King came to Marshall's office for a talk. Marshall couldn't see him immediately because he was engaged in a delicate conversation with someone else. After waiting a few minutes, King left in obvious indignation. When Marshall heard about it, he hurried to King's office to explain and apologize.

"I think this is important," Marshall said to King, "because if you or I begin fighting at the very start of the war, what in the world will the public have to say about us. We can't afford to fight. So we ought to find a way to get along together."

King replied, "We'll see if we can get along, and I think we can."[13]

But King was an unbending man. On 23 February 1942, two weeks after the first formal meeting of the Joint Chiefs, Eisenhower wrote: "Admiral King is an arbitrary, stubborn type with too much brain and a tendency toward bullying his juniors. But I think he wants to fight, which is vastly encouraging."[14]

King did indeed want to fight. The great fighting record of the U.S. Navy in the Pacific reflects his insistent personality. But to Marshall and Arnold's chagrin, he was so eager to fight the Japanese that he sometimes seemed unable to understand or accept the Allied grand strategy to hold off Japan while concentrating on the defeat of Germany. Later, when King took the view that the

U.S. Marines should take the essential islands and be relieved by army troops, Eisenhower, the U.S. Army's chief Pacific planner, wrote in his diary, "One thing that might help win this war is to get someone to shoot King." [15] As a West Point graduate, Eisenhower never had an affinity for the marines.

King became increasingly more petulant as the Japanese advanced down the Malay Peninsula toward Singapore during January and early February. The Malay states produced copious supplies of tin and rubber, which made Singapore one of the great ports in the world. The Japanese conquered the peninsula by 30 January 1942 and had reached a point opposite the island of Singapore. On 8 February they landed on the one coastal spot that was concealed by a mangrove belt. They could now cut off the island's water supply from the hills of Johore. On 15 February Lt. Gen. Sir Arthur Percival ignominiously surrendered 80,000 British and Australian troops to Lt. Gen. Tomoyuki Yamashita, who commanded 30,000 Japanese. This greatly shocked Winston Churchill.

The Japanese continued their advance into the islands of the Netherlands East Indies; then, on 19 February 1942, they swung eastward to launch a surprise air raid on Darwin, Australia. Here, they destroyed twenty aircraft while sinking eleven ships, demolishing the airfield, and killing almost 250 military and civilian personnel.

A last-ditch effort by the Allies to send fighter planes to Java ended with disaster on 27 February. Japanese planes sank the U.S. tender *Langley*, once a carrier, and its deck load of aircraft. Another ship accompanying *Langley* reached Java, but its cargo of crated planes was destroyed to keep it from falling into enemy hands.

On 22 February Roosevelt instructed MacArthur to go to Australia to command the newly defined Southwest Pacific Area. Eisenhower composed the message that sent by the president. His 23 February 1942 diary entry reflects his true feeling about this decision:

> Message sent to MacArthur was approved by president and dispatched. I'm dubious about the thing. I cannot help believing that we are disturbed by editorials and reacting to "public opinion" rather than to military logic. "Pa" Watson is certain we must get MacArthur out, as being worth "five army corps." [16]

At first MacArthur protested but then obeyed. He departed from Manila Bay by motor torpedo boat on 12 March, the day of the final capitulation in Java.

Eisenhower personally objected to the move, as he readily saw the potential for politics to triumph over strategy in the Pacific War. He expressed his fears about establishing the Southwest Pacific Area Command in his diary entry of 19 March 1942:

> MacArthur is out of Philippine Islands. Now supreme commander of "Southwest Pacific Area." The newspapers acclaim the move—the public has built itself a hero out of its own imagination. I hope he can do the

miracles expected and predicted; we could use a few now. Strange that no one sees the dangers. Some apply to MacArthur, who could be ruined by it. But this I minimize; I know him too well. The other danger is that we will move too heavily in the Southwest. Urging us in that direction now will be: Australians, New Zealanders, and our public (wanting support for the hero), and MacArthur. If we tie up our shipping for the SW Pacific, we'll lose this war . . .[17]

Australia is more distant from the U.S. West Coast than any part of the Philippines. At this early stage, Eisenhower recognized that from a logistical standpoint a move northward from Australia would be far more costly in men and materials than a thrust across the Central Pacific.

Admiral King insisted that all cryptanalysts and anyone involved with code breaking should be removed from Corregidor by submarine. He reasoned that even though the machines and codebooks could be destroyed, the American code breakers could not withstand the torture to which they would be subjected without giving up vital information.

On 9 March 1942, President Roosevelt cabled Winston Churchill, "The Pacific situation is now very grave." [18] Java had surrendered the day before, although some sporadic fighting continued. Only in Japan was there cause for optimism. In the Pacific, the Japanese now controlled all lands and waters between the Solomons and Burma, China and everything north of Australia (except doomed Bataan, where the Japanese were closing in), and the southern coast of New Guinea (their next objective).

On 17 March 1942, Roosevelt and Churchill agreed that the United States would assume responsibility for the defense of the entire Pacific, including New Zealand and Australia. The British would undertake defense of the Indian Ocean and the Middle East. They confirmed the basic strategy to "beat Hitler first." This meant that the United States was committed to a strategic defense in the Pacific. But while forces were being trained and materials accumulated for an offensive in Europe or Africa, the Pacific theater would have highest immediate priority for ships, planes, and troops in order to hold vital positions and protect communications.

Meanwhile, additional troops were sent to Lt. Gen. Masaharu Homma on Bataan, bringing to 57,000 the number of Japanese troops involved in the capture of the Philippines. It was erroneously stated at the time that General Yamashita, the conqueror of Malaya and Singapore, had come to Homma's aid. Indeed, he did not arrive in the Philippines until 1944.

By the end of March, the plight of the defenders had become desperate. Lieutenant General Jonathan Wainwright notified Washington that the meager food supplies would be completely exhausted by 15 April. By early April, the weak, hungry, demoralized American and Filipino troops had no fight left. By one source, 75 percent had malaria, while all suffered from malnutrition, all horses and water buffalo having been consumed.[19] On 8 April, Maj. Gen. Edward P. King, commander of Bataan forces, made the anguished decision to surrender. As he rode forward to meet Homma on 9 April, he remembered that Gen. Robert E. Lee had surrendered at Appomattox on the same date, concluding, "Then there is nothing to do but to go and see General Grant, and I would rather die a thousand deaths." [20]

Many more than a thousand deaths awaited the surrendering forces as the Japanese marched them off to a prison camp. The four-day, sixty-three-mile march in ninety-five degree weather would not have been difficult for well-nourished soldiers; but for malaria-ridden, ill-fed troops, the march was brutal. The Japanese killed many prisoners who were unable to move forward. It has been estimated that upwards of 14,000 died along the way. Survivors aptly named the journey the Bataan Death March. Upon reaching the prison camp, untold more thousands perished for lack of food, water, and medical supplies.

Under the impact of defeat after defeat in the Pacific, unbalanced by anything hopeful, many Americans regarded the Japanese as endowed with fabulous fighting virtue, a feeling also shared by the Japanese public. Japan based its initial plan on the assumption that it would take about six months to conquer the Philippines and Malaya, including the Netherlands East Indies. Logistics experts wanted six months more to get the oil fields operating again with production sufficient for war purposes. Now, the schedule of conquest had been shortened, especially since the scorched-earth policy in the oil fields had failed; the oil rigs had not been disabled before the Japanese took over. Japanese planners determined to accelerate their next moves.

Their marvelous conquests had come very cheap. Through May 1942, the Japanese had experienced only minimal losses. With Wainwright's surrender at Corregidor on 6 May 1942, the Japanese had killed or captured more than a quarter million Allied troops and had committed only eleven divisions in so doing. Because the Corregidor troops were much better supplied with food and medicines than the Bataan defenders, historians do not write about a Corregidor Death March.

Again, Eisenhower wrote in his diary:

> Corregidor surrendered last night. Poor Wainwright! He did the fighting in the Philippine Islands, another got such glory as the public could find in the operation. Resistance elsewhere in the P.I. will quickly close, so it lasted five months.
>
> General MacArthur's tirades, to which TJ and I so often listened in Manila, would now sound as silly to the public as they then did to us. But he's a hero! Yah.[21]

Easy success and "victory disease" did not alter the basic Japanese strategy but speeded it up. Their conquests encouraged the Japanese to extend their defensive perimeter rather than wait for the Greater East Asia Co-Prosperity Sphere consolidation. They planned three new, successive conquests: 1) Tulagi and Moresby, in order to secure air mastery of the Coral Sea and its shores; 2) Midway Atoll and the Western Aleutians, in order to strengthen the defensive perimeter and bring the remainder of the United States Pacific Fleet to a decisive engagement; and 3) New Caledonia, Fiji, and Samoa, in order to cut lines of communication between the United States and Australia.[22]

In Washington the Joint Chiefs of Staff formed the structure to block these next enemy moves. Soon after MacArthur's arrival at Melbourne, the Australian and New Zealand governments were informed of the detailed proposals for the division of the world into three Allied strategic theaters and the proposals for the subdivision of the Pacific.

In anticipation of the 17 March agreement between Roosevelt and Churchill, the Joint Chiefs of Staff planned the subdivision of the Pacific area. On 8 March after studying the Australian and New Zealand proposals, they accepted instead the view that the U.S. Navy was primarily concerned with protecting the Pacific lines of communication and that New Zealand belonged within those lines; they regarded the Australian continent and the direct enemy approaches there as a separate strategic entity. They defined Australia and the areas to the north and northeast as far as and including the Philippines as the Southwest Pacific Area (SWPA), which would be an army responsibility under General MacArthur as supreme commander, and designated the rest of the Pacific as the Pacific Ocean Area for which the U.S. Navy would be responsible and in which Adm. Chester W. Nimitz would be supreme commander.

Both Australia and New Zealand protested, as they saw themselves and their adjacent islands as one strategic whole. They were overruled on the grounds that the division was one of convenience only and did not mean that there would be any absence of joint planning and cooperation.

On 1 April, the new Pacific War Council came into being as a consultative and advisory board to the Chiefs of Staff. As planned by President Roosevelt, the group consisted of representatives from Great Britain, Australia, New Zealand, Canada, China, and the Netherlands. On 3 April, Dr. H. V. Evatt, the Australian representative, cabled to Prime Minister John Curtin the full text of the directives that had been framed for issue to General MacArthur and Admiral Nimitz and asked for formal approval to be given as soon as possible. All countries of the Pacific War Council agreed to the partition of authority as established by the Joint Chiefs. These defined the Pacific theater and, within it, the Southwest Pacific Area, the Southeast Pacific Area, and the Pacific Ocean Area (which also included the North Pacific, Central Pacific, and South Pacific areas).

The Joint Chiefs now had in place a command infrastructure designed to curtail the disasters of the first five months. They would direct the strategy of the war in the Pacific until Japan had been defeated. A large military bureaucracy would be established in Washington housed in the Pentagon and Naval Annex buildings that included the War Plans committee, the Joint Intelligence Committee, and groupings in "the fields of transportation, communications, new weapons and equipment, logistics, production surveys, post-war plans, civil affairs, meteorological data, security control, munitions allocation and the Army-Navy Petroleum Board." [23] Position papers on approximately 1,457 separate subjects were supplied for consideration by the Joint Chiefs during the period of the war; "in addition the Combined Chiefs of Staff considered some 902 subjects." [24] Needless to say, top Allied military leaders were well informed.

Marshall recognized that he had a greater need for Eisenhower in the European theater where foot soldiers would play a much greater role than in the Pacific War. In late June, Ike would be sent to London, where he was soon made a lieutenant general and named commanding general, U.S. Army in Europe.

Chapter 7
The Home Front

*T*HE PACIFIC WAR WAS WAGED across the Earth's largest body of water. After Pearl Harbor, the Japanese had the upper hand by virtue of a larger navy, more and better airplanes, and better-trained soldiers. Both countries had a unity of purpose, with a citizenry dedicated to winning. The manpower pool gave the United States a slight edge. Japan proper had a population of 71.9 million. Together with its colonies of 59.8 million, it governed 131.7 million inhabitants.[1] The 1940 census shows the United States with 130,962,661, together with the Philippines population of 16,356,000, for a combined total of 147,318,661. But wars are often won by the home front, and herein lay the huge mismatch.

Previously, Japanese Adm. Isoroku Yamamoto had said, "It is a mistake to regard Americans as luxury loving and weak. I can tell you that they are full of spirit, adventure, fight, and justice. Their thinking is scientific and well advanced. Lindbergh's solo flight across the Atlantic was an act characteristic of Americans—adventuresome but scientifically based. Remember that American industry is much more developed than ours, and—unlike us—they have all the oil they want. Japan cannot vanquish the United States. Therefore we should not fight the United States."[2]

Japan's military controlled all aspects of its government. In contrast, the United States had a system that enabled the civilian authority to mobilize its superior assets to support its military in time of war. Clause 1, Section 2, Article 2 of the Constitution of the United States states, "The president shall be commander in chief of the Army and Navy of the United States, and of the militia of the several states, when called into the actual service of the United States. . . ."

Throughout the history of the United States, military officers have recognized and studiously abided by this section of the Constitution even though the president may not have had any prior military service. In most cases, the president has served the country well in the exercise of this constitutional authority. Abraham Lincoln and Franklin D. Roosevelt stand out as prime examples. Some historians claim that Abraham Lincoln had to search long and hard to find a general in the form of Ulysses S. Grant while others argue that he consistently had "to educate his generals about the purposes of the war and remind them of its fundamental political characteristics." [3] Lincoln was a hands-on commander in dealing with his top army generals, while Roosevelt relied heavily on his Secretaries of War and Navy and his Joint Chiefs of Staff. Roosevelt excelled by giving his admirals and generals the all-out support they needed in personnel, materials, and advanced technology. At war's beginning, he, as commander in chief of the armed forces, had the duty to marshal the assets of the United States to defeat the Axis powers, a task he performed exceptionally well.

Both Lincoln and Roosevelt knew war was coming but wanted the moral as well as propaganda advantage of having the enemy strike the first blow. Lincoln made capital of the South's firing on Fort Sumter. In the Pacific War, "Remember Pearl Harbor" became the battle cry, adopted by the armed services, and emblazoned on billboards, recruiting posters, newspaper advertisements, and other media. The slogan was repeated over and over until war's end.

On 18 December 1941, Congress passed the First War Powers Act, which gave the president virtually complete authority to reorganize the Executive Branch, the independent government agencies, and government corporations as he deemed appropriate to expedite prosecution of the war. These powers were to remain in force until six months after war's end. Congress granted the president additional powers by the Second War Powers Act on 27 March 1942. This combined legislation enabled Roosevelt to create forty-four new governmental agencies, some with great sweeping power, others with only minimal authority. Although a majority of Americans admired the president, a vocal significant minority disliked Roosevelt, mainly because of his domestic policies. However, the president called upon this latter group, mainly top business leaders, to implement the power granted the Executive Branch by the War Powers acts. These business executives set aside previous antagonisms towards Roosevelt in mobilizing the home front for all-out war.

On 6 January 1942, in his State of the Union message, Roosevelt told Congress, "We must raise our sights all along the production line. Let no man say it cannot be done." He then outlined a set of production goals for 1942: 60,000 planes, 45,000 tanks, 20,000 anti-aircraft guns, and 6 million tons of merchant shipping. When advisor Harry Hopkins questioned the wisdom of reaching so high, Roosevelt replied, "Oh—the production people can do it, if they really try."

"The figures," Roosevelt told a cheering Congress, "will give the Japanese and the Nazis a little idea of just what they accomplished at Pearl Harbor." Roosevelt said workers must be prepared to work long and hard to turn out weapons twenty-four hours a day, seven days a week. Every available tool, whether in the auto industry or the village machine shop, must be devoted to the production of munitions. "The militarists of Berlin and Tokyo started the war," he said. "But the massed, angered forces of common humanity will finish it." [4]

From the very start it became evident that the Japanese were going south through Southeast Asia, where they would take charge of the rubber plantations in Malaya and the Netherlands East Indies. The United States had only a limited amount of natural rubber from South America, and the manufacture of synthetic rubber was still many months distant. All retail and wholesale stocks of rubber tires were put into a stringent ration system. It could not be sold unless essential for national defense, medical personnel, public transportation, or other compelling need.

John Kenneth Galbraith was charged with implementing the nation's rationing program. When Roosevelt heard the specifics of the rubber edict, he questioned what "congenital idiot" had supposed that ministers of the gospel were not essential; particularly, he asked Galbraith, had he never heard of the Southern Baptists and their political impact in Roosevelt's strongest base of support? Within a day or two, ministers became essential.[5]

Throughout the war, the average citizen could not purchase an automobile tire. When a tire became slick from wear, the owner appeared before the ration board to get his tire retreaded. A committee led by Bernard Baruch and Harvard President James B. Conant recommended a speed limit of thirty-five miles per hour on all the nation's highways to conserve rubber. The governors of all states except Texas agreed to enforce the thirty-five-miles-per-hour speed limit. When Galbraith called on Governor Coke R. Stevenson of Texas in an effort to persuade him, Stevenson responded, "Doctor, here in the state of Texas, when you drive thirty-five miles an hour, you don't get there." [6]

In June 1942, Roosevelt held a press conference to promote a nationwide campaign to collect scrap rubber. A governmental study showed that "from a worn out tire enough rubber can be reclaimed to recap two or possibly three others, with the use of only about two ounces of virgin product as a binder." [7] Roosevelt gave a fireside chat to initiate a nationwide rubber drive. The response was overwhelming. The average contribution was almost seven pounds for each man, woman, or child.[8]

Rationing of gasoline followed rationing of tires. This began on the eastern seaboard on 15 May 1942. Though gasoline was not in short supply, the government needed gas rationing to save rubber. The decision was made to start with the seventeen eastern states and then extend the gas rationing westward. Consumers of gas were divided into different classes: the majority of drivers were granted A cards, which entitled them to five gallons a week; B cards were given to war workers, doctors, and others whose vocations required supplemental mileage; X cards were granted to those whose occupations required unlimited mileage.

The first step in developing the rationing system was the creation of a list of essential items in short supply. Each item was then given a price in points, and each man, woman, and child in the country was given a book of stamps. The stamps in each ration book—worth forty-eight points each month and good for six months—could be spent on any combination of goods, from meat, butter, and canned vegetables to sugar and shoes. The retailer used the expended stamps to replenish his stocks. To augment the daily diet, Roosevelt encouraged the civilian population to plant Victory gardens. The growing of vegetables in backyards and former flowerbeds became commonplace.

The automobile industry became the first to feel the force of the president's powers. A complete ban was imposed on the retail sale of new passenger autos plus light and heavy trucks. The order froze all stock in the hands of dealers until 15 January 1942. The entire manufacturing facilities of the auto industries were thereby brought into the national armaments program. The nation's auto dealers and their employees were confined to the sale and repair of used cars until well after war's end.

On 13 January 1942, Roosevelt announced that former Sears, Roebuck executive Donald Nelson would head a powerful new organization, the War Production Board, which would have "final" decisions on procurement and production. Prior thereto, William Knudsen left the presidency of General Motors in 1940 to become director of industrial production for the National Defense Research Committee. He continued to direct production of war material as head of the U.S. Office of Production Management and as lieutenant general in charge of production for the War Department.

On 30 January, the president signed an Emergency Price Control Bill, which gave Leon Henderson, director of the Office of Price Administration, power to keep prices down. Under the new legislation, Henderson could impose ceilings on a selective range of consumer items from raw materials to finished goods, and he could fix maximum rents in defense areas.

General Hap Arnold pointed out the necessity for ground crews to service the planes. Accordingly, the mechanics from the domestic air service industry were conscripted into the U.S. Army Air Force. Private air service was reduced to one-third its previous size, with the transport of mail its major function.

At an early meeting of the Joint Chiefs, General Marshall observed that the U.S. Army was training numerous men to fight, but there was insufficient shipping (meaning transports and cargo vessels) to take them to the war zone and keep them supplied. If deployment of the U.S. Army depended upon American shipping, Roosevelt determined that more ships had to be built. In his State of the Union message, Roosevelt set an incredibly high goal. Yet, in the wake of the alarming sinking of ships in the Atlantic during the first few months of 1942, he raised his sights to 24 million tons for 1942 and 1943.

The crisis in shipping could not have occurred at a worse time. From building fewer than 100 ships a year, the U.S. Maritime Commission was now charged with building 2,900 ships right away; from dealing with 46 shipways, it was now responsible for nearly 300; from thinking in terms of 100,000 men, it could soon count on more than 700,000. In peacetime, ship fitters had to serve a four-year apprenticeship; the training period was now reduced to seven weeks. "It gives you a feeling like holding a hand grenade after removing the pin," Adm. H. L. Vickery admitted.[9]

The government turned to Henry Kaiser, a sixty-year-old industrialist who had been involved in the building of Boulder Dam, Grand Coulee

Dam, and the Oakland-San Francisco Bridge. Though new to the shipping business, Kaiser was a master in the field of industrial productions. He sent bulldozers to build his first shipyard in Richmond, California, across the bay from San Francisco on 20 January 1941. Eighty-five working days later, he laid his first keel.

Kaiser built ships as fast as steel could be found. Under his leadership, the average time to deliver a ship was cut from 355 days in 1940 to 194 days in 1941 to 60 days in early 1942. With six new yards in operation after only one year in the business, he had become the pacesetter for the entire shipbuilding industry. The Maritime Commission translated each new record he set into a schedule for shipyards across the nation.

Kaiser's Liberty ship fell short of traditional shipbuilding standards; nevertheless, each could carry a heavy load across the Pacific. Because of its slow speed, military servicemen disliked traveling the vast distances across the Pacific in a Liberty ship. But, in time, it would get you there.

On 13 November 1942, to the amazement of the press and public, Rear Adm. Emory S. Land, chairman of the U.S. Maritime Commission and head of the War Shipping Administration, announced that the goal in ships of 24 million tons set by the president would be met by the end of 1943. Included in the report published 14 November 1942 in the *New York Times* is the statement:

> At Richmond, Calif., yesterday, 4 days 15 hours and 25 minutes after the first section of the keel had been laid, the 10,500-ton cargo ship Robert E. Peary was launched at one of Henry J. Kaisers West Coast shipbuilding plants, Richmond Yard No. 2.[10]

Being at war greatly increased productivity among American workers. It enhanced the values of most citizens toward their country, although it was not an unalloyed patriotism, especially on the West Coast. Irrational fear of possible Japanese attack resulted in the denial of civil rights to a large number of loyal Americans, which in hindsight was Roosevelt's most controversial decision of the war.

Directly after the Pearl Harbor attack, U.S. Navy Secretary Frank Knox made an inspection visit to Hawaii. Upon his return on 15 December, he told reporters, "I think the most effective Fifth Column work of the entire war was done in Hawaii with the possible exception of Norway." [11] At a cabinet meeting, he said that local Japanese fishing boats had furnished information on the location of warships, and the Japanese consulate had engaged in espionage. He then recommended to the president that the Secretary of War take all aliens out of Hawaii and send them to another island. Roosevelt diplomatically praised Knox but refused to approve any such removal.

Misinformation about imagined happenings caused excessive fear on the West Coast. On 9 December, local newspapers in big headlines reported Japanese planes off the coast of San Francisco. Brigadier General William Ord Ryan said a large number of unidentified aircraft were turned back at the Golden Gate.

He said the invading planes vanished to the southwest. The papers reported that the general's statement came after three hours of uncertainty in which San Francisco was partially blacked out. A Japanese submarine reinforced the credibility of the many stories based on fantasy. On 14 December, it sank one U.S. merchant ship and caused another to go aground when it went into the mouth of the Columbia River.

Afterward, the entire coast became dark at night. The annual Rose Bowl game was canceled. Oregon State, the Pacific Coast Conference candidate, traveled to Durham, North Carolina, to play Duke University on New Year's Day 1942. The final score: Oregon State 20, Duke 16.

On 16 December, Gen. John L. DeWitt, the West Coast defense commander, recommended that a one-hundred-mile-wide coastal strip be designated a military area and that all persons deemed undesirable by the military be removed. Three days later, he recommended to the War Department that all enemy aliens over the age of fourteen be removed inland. The Japanese community consisted of the Issei—those born outside the country, therefore non-citizens—and the Nisei—those of Japanese ancestry born in the United States, thus American citizens. In contrast to DeWitt's opinion, Roosevelt appeared to be in agreement with his attorney general, Francis Biddle, who opposed a broad-scale removal. Biddle had the support of Federal Bureau of Investigation Director J. Edgar Hoover, who reported that the control of this volatile situation could be made without transporting the Issei and Nisei from their homes.

Both local press and politicians formed an almost unanimous chorus for the evacuation from the West Coast of persons of Japanese ancestry, regardless of citizenship. California newspaper reporters were especially vicious. California Attorney General Earl Warren, later to become Chief Justice of the U.S. Supreme Court, publicly advocated evacuation.

President Roosevelt called upon writer Louis Adamic, a champion of ethnic minorities, to conduct a propaganda campaign to counter the anti-Asian hysteria. Eleanor Roosevelt, the president's wife, was present. Adamic was taken aback when she remarked, "But some of the Japanese on the Coast have been caught as spies of the Japanese government." [12] She had publicly spoken in support of both Issei and Nisei loyalty only two days before.

On 31 January, the *Los Angeles Times* reported that all West Coast members of Congress from Washington, Oregon, and California had called upon President Roosevelt the day before asking for speedy exercise of authority "to clear the vital defense areas of enemy aliens at once." [13] Starting 1 February through 24 February 1942, the need to remove Japanese Americans from the West Coast was reported daily in front-page stories of the *Los Angeles Times*. No such emphasis appeared in the East Coast news media. Roosevelt appeared inclined to follow the recommendations of his attorney general, Francis Biddle.

The *et tu Brute* came when Walter Lippmann joined the ranks of the evacuation movement. Relying on information from Earl Warren and others, on 13 February he wrote the first of two columns stating that the Japanese Americans were planning acts of sabotage. At age fifty-two and a former supporter of Roosevelt, he was a syndicated U.S. columnist of tremendous respect. On 14 February, gunners on the deck of the Japanese sub *I-17* fired at tanks at Elwood Oil Field, twelve miles north of Santa Barbara, California. Although it caused only slight damage, the incident increased the growing tension on the West Coast.

On 15 February, the *New York Times* published an article whereby Thomas C. Clark, the enemy alien control coordinator for the western defense command, challenged the factual information upon which Walter Lippmann based his opinion. He said, "I wish Mr. Lippmann would give us the names and places, if anybody is signaling back and forth along this coast." In the news article, Clark said he would recommend to Attorney General Francis Biddle on Monday emergency methods for handling Japanese citizens as well as aliens in the coast combat zone. He further said, "I intend to recommend that all persons regarded as inimical to defense efforts be removed from vital areas already designated and from such additional ones as are designated by the War and Navy Departments. This will include citizens as well as aliens." [14]

Faced with the recommendation of Secretary of War Henry L. Stimson in support of Lieutenant General DeWitt, which recommendation was still opposed by Attorney General Francis Biddle, Roosevelt sided with his Secretary of War. On 19 February, the president issued Executive Order 9066, which authorized the Secretary of War and military commanders to prescribe military areas " 'from which any or all persons may be excluded, and with respect to which, the right of any person to enter, remain in, or leave shall be subject to whatever restriction' they cared to impose. It further authorized the military to provide transportation and accommodations for any excluded people and to accept assistance from state and local authorities." [15]

The *Los Angeles Times* commented in the 21 February editorial page:

> Yesterday's Presidential order directing the establishment of military zones in the United States—meaning, in particular, the West Coast—from which any person can be excluded, will be welcomed here with relief as meeting at least the menace of enemy sabotage. Already delayed beyond all reason, the order, it is to be hoped, will be put into full effect without delay.[16]

Shortly thereafter, Congress passed a law making it a crime for anyone to disobey the president's executive order.

The War Relocation Authority was formed on 18 March 1942 with Milton Eisenhower, General Ike's brother, as director. After only three months in office and having no stomach for the job at hand, Milton resigned. In his report to the president, he reported that, "the initial idea of voluntary evacuation was not a feasible solution. Public opinion in the inter-mountain states . . . was bitterly antagonistic to the influx of Japanese from coastal areas." [17] Accordingly, the 110,000 Japanese Americans were forced into ten detainment camps, so-called relocation centers. Milton Eisenhower further wrote:

> Yet in leaving the War Relocation Authority after a few extremely crowded weeks, I cannot help expressing the hope that the American people will grow toward a broader appreciation of the essential Americanism of a great majority of the evacuees and of the difficult sacrifice they are making.
>
> Only when the prevailing attitudes of unreasoning bitterness have been replaced by tolerance and understanding will it be possible to carry forward a genuinely satisfactory relocation program and to plan intelligently for the reassimilation of the evacuees into American life when the war is over.
>
> I wish to give you my considered judgment that fully 80 to 85 percent of the Nisei are loyal to the United States; perhaps 50 percent of the Issei are passively loyal; but a large portion of the Kibei (American citizens educated in Japan and about 9,000 in number) feel a strong cultural attachment to Japan.[18]

The action taken was legal though not necessarily right in that the Constitution provides that the right of habeas corpus may be suspended in time of rebellion or invasion or when the public safety may require it. During the American Civil War, Abraham Lincoln approved the arrest of former congressman Clement Vanlandingham without benefit of habeas corpus for speaking out against the North's position in the Civil War. Military tribunals were established whereby citizens arrested by the military ranged from 13,000 to 38,000,[19] "and according to one estimate some 300 newspapers were suspended for at least a brief period." [20] Again, during World War I, many abuses against those of German descent were approved through the Espionage Act of 1917 and the Sedition Act of 1918.

A young Nisei, Fred Korematsu, refused to obey the military curfew and orders that followed Roosevelt's edict. He claimed as a loyal American citizen his only crime was one of "looking like the enemy." His criminal conviction for disobedience was upheld by the U.S. Supreme Court in 1943 and 1944. The whole episode concerning citizens of Japanese descent was a classic case where nationalism won out over patriotism, a common occurrence in time of war.

On 23 February 1942, at 10:00 P.M. eastern standard time, in celebration of George Washington's 210th birthday, Roosevelt made a fireside chat to one of his largest radio audiences ever. Prior to his address, he had asked the nation to purchase world maps to have on hand as he talked. The war was obviously not going well, and Roosevelt told the American people they must be prepared to suffer more losses before the turn of the tide. But, he said, "Your government has unmistakable confidence in your ability to hear the worst without flinching or losing heart. You must in turn have complete confidence that your government is keeping nothing from you except information that will help the enemy." [21]

He pointed out that:

> The broad oceans which have been heralded in the past as our protection from attack have become endless battlefields on which we are constantly being challenged by our enemies. . . . On Jan. 6 of this year I set certain definite goals of production for airplanes, tanks, guns and ships. The Axis propagandists called them fantastic. Tonight, nearly two months later, and after a careful survey of progress by Donald Nelson and others charged with responsibility for our production, I can tell you that these goals will be obtained. [22]

In reference to the Philippines, he said:

> Immediately after this war started the Japanese forces moved down on either side of the Philippines to numerous points south of them, thereby completely encircling the islands from north, south, east, and west. It is that complete encirclement, with control of the air by Japanese land-based aircraft, which has prevented us from sending substantial reinforcements of men and material to the gallant defenders of the Philippines.[23]

Roosevelt obviously knew the history of the prewar Plan Orange, as he continued, "For forty years it has always been our strategy—a strategy born of necessity—that in the event of a full-scale attack on the Islands by Japan, we should fight a delaying action, attempting to retire slowly into Bataan Peninsula and Corregidor." [24]

He said that the first job at the home front was "to build up production— *uninterrupted production*—so that the United Nations can maintain control of the seas and attain control of the air—not merely a slight superiority, but an overwhelming superiority."[25] In the *New York Times*, the editorial page commented: "The President spoke last night in one of the great crises of our history, and his words were both a warning that a long war lies ahead and a reassurance of his faith in final victory." [26]

The first six months of the war brought on two revolutions: one in East Asia, where the Japanese had driven out the British, French, Dutch, and Americans to the point that Western Colonialism would never again have the same status; and the other in the United States, where women and minorities took on a standing never before achieved.

An otherwise little-known incident condoned legal discrimination against people of color for more than half a century. In 1895, African-American Homer Plessy was arrested for sitting down in a train car reserved for whites. A year later, the U.S. Supreme Court held that the equal protection declaration in the Fourteenth Amendment "could not have intended to abolish distinctions based upon color . . . or commingling of the races." In his dissent, Justice John Marshall Holland said:

> In the eye of the law, there is in this country no superior, dominant ruling class of citizens. There is no caste here. Our Constitution is color blind . . . the destinies of the two races in this country are indissolubly linked together, and the interests of both require that the common government of all shall not permit the seeds of hate to be planted under the direction of law.[27]

As a result of the majority opinion of the Court, twenty-one states passed segregation laws and the U.S. armed services followed suit.

In early 1942, because of pressure from the Fair Employment Practices Commission, a majority of defense industry companies committed to the principle of employing African-American labor. In hundreds of cases, blacks worked in firms that had formerly banned them. The gains were significant, though much less than their percentage of the overall population. Roosevelt told the Fraternal Council of Negro Churches, "I look for an acceleration of this improvement as the demand for labor in our war industries increases." [28] The numbers did increase substantially as the president had predicted.

On 9 December 1941, the National Association for the Advancement of Colored People sent a telegram to U.S. Navy Secretary Frank Knox asking whether "in view of the intensive recruiting campaign then under way, the Navy would accept colored recruits for other than the messman's branch." The Bureau of Navigation replied that "there has been no change in policy and that none was contemplated." [29] Black leaders complained to the White House, which in turn called upon Secretary Knox. Knox asked the General Board to submit a plan for taking 5,000 African Americans for billets other than as messman. When the General Board refused to accept blacks in branches other than messman, Roosevelt told Knox that the report was unsatisfactory and insufficient. He said:

> Officers of the U.S. Navy are not officers only but are American citizens . . . They should, therefore, be expected to recognize social and economic problems which are related to national welfare . . . It is incumbent on all officers to recognize the fact that about 1/10th of the population of the United States is composed of members of the Negro race who are American citizens . . . It is my considered opinion that there are additional tasks in the Naval establishment to which we could properly assign an additional number of enlisted men who are members of the Negro race . . . I [ask] you to return the recommendations of the General Board to that Board for further study and report. [30]

The General Board had to capitulate. It issued a second report to Knox agreeing that blacks could enlist for other general service, such as gunners, clerks, signalmen, radio operators, and ammunition handlers, as long as the training and the units remained segregated. "Navy Broke Down A Historic Barrier," the *New York Times* reported. Numerous legal barriers would remain as long as the U.S. Supreme Court condoned segregation; however, African Americans had made a forward move for social change that would accelerate after the war.

A more significant social change came about as a result of the defense industry's acute demand for more workers. Across the country, factories big and small turned to recruiting female employees for the assembly lines. The recruiting posters showed an attractive female in work clothes with the caption "Rosie the Riveter" with the implication "the nation needs you." A large segment of the female population became emancipated from housework-only duty as they flooded workplaces heretofore forbidden. By the end of the war, women constituted 37 percent of the nation's workforce.

Roosevelt was at his best in involving all citizens to pay for the huge cost of the war and at the same time to maintain a stable economy. On 27 April, he set forth his goals and plan of action to Congress, in which he noted:

> Organized labor has voluntarily given up its right to strike during the war. Therefore all stabilization or adjustment of wages will be settled by the War Labor Board machinery which has been generally accepted by industry and labor for the settlement of all disputes.[31]

Next day Roosevelt followed his speech to Congress with a fireside chat to the American public. He told his radio audience:

> There is one front and one battle where everyone in the United States—every man, woman and child—is in this action, and will be privileged to remain in action throughout the war. That front is right here at home, in our daily lives, (and) in our daily tasks. Here at home everyone will have the privilege of making whatever self-denial is necessary, not only to supply our fighting men, but to keep the economic structure of our country fortified and secure by during the war and after the war.[32]

He then set forth the seven-point program, which he had previously spelled out to Congress in more detail:

> First, we must, through heavier taxes, keep personal and corporate profits at a low reasonable rate.
> Second, we must fix ceilings on prices and rents.
> Third, we must stabilize wages.
> Fourth, we must stabilize farm prices.
> Fifth, we must put more billions into war bonds.
> Sixth, we must ration all essential commodities which are scarce.
> Seventh, we must discourage installment buying, and encourage paying off debt and mortgages.[33]

To raise money, individual and corporate taxes were raised across the board. A reasonable rate of return was placed on corporate profits with everything above that decreed reasonable paid to the U.S. Treasury as excess profit taxes. The president's taxing policy on individuals required that no one should receive a net yearly income of more than $25,000. Annual federal deficits still ran high, in spite of full employment and an economy running at full throttle. To finance the deficits, war bond rallies were held periodically throughout the country. Numerous movie stars volunteered to participate in the war bond drives held in the larger cities. In rural America, these rallies took on the air of patriotic social events, with speeches by local politicians and refreshments served. By war's end, the federal deficit had escalated to $247 billion. To minimize the adverse impact of the deficit on the federal government, the war bonds had an interest rate of less than 3 percent.

Still, at the home front, the man in uniform held the most admired ranking. There was a universal desire to serve in some branch of the armed services even by those of celebrity or privileged status: Clark Gable, Jimmy Stewart, and Tyrone Power among the many movie stars; Ted Williams, Joe DiMaggio, and Joe Lewis were some of the many professional athletes. Each of President Roosevelt's four sons joined a branch of the armed services, as did the sons and daughters of other high-ranking politicians across the country. The notion that "Nothing's too good for our boys in service" prevailed throughout. Many times when a serviceman on leave visited a bar or restaurant, an older person would come over and ask to pick up the tab. When a soldier came home from extended or overseas duty, the rationing board willingly awarded additional gasoline and restricted food items—especially meat—to the family for use by the serviceman while on leave.

Within months of the attack on Pearl Harbor, America's spiritual strength and material resources had been marshaled for total war. In spite of the privations placed upon the civilian population, most cheerfully accepted the necessary sacrifices and agreed with Roosevelt, who in an address to the home front said:

> Some have called this an "economy of sacrifice". Some interpret it in terms that are more accurate—the "equality of sacrifice". I have never been able to bring myself, however, to full acceptance of the word "sacrifice", because free men and women, bred in the concepts of democracy and wedded to the principles of democracy, deem it a privilege rather than a sacrifice to work and to fight for the perpetuation of the democratic ideal. It is, therefore, more true to call this total effort of the American people an "equality of privilege." [34]

Chapter 8
Midway

MIDWAY ISLAND ACTS AS A SENTRY FOR HAWAII," said Japanese Vice Adm. Chuichi Nagumo in his report on the great battle.[1] Situated 1,135 miles west-northwest of Pearl Harbor, Midway is the farthest outpost of the Hawaiian chain, excepting the small, unoccupied Kure Atoll, sixty miles beyond. Smaller even than Wake, the entire atoll is but six miles in diameter, and only a small portion of that is dry land.

Admiral Isoroku Yamamoto wanted to take Midway and the Western Aleutians island of Kiska. They would serve as key points in a new outer perimeter, Kiska-Midway-Wake-Marshalls-Gilberts-Guadalcanal-Port Moresby. Midway-based patrol planes, in conjunction with others flying out of Kiska and Wake, would be able to detect any task force attempting to raid Japan's inner defense.

Yamamoto's chief of staff, Rear Adm. Matome Ugaki, was even more ambitious. He believed, "that the Japanese Armed Forces, instead of reverting to a defensive strategy which would yield the initiative to the enemy, must remain vigorously on the offensive."[2] According to his diary, Ugaki favored

> seizure of Hawaii and destruction of American fleet strength consti-
> tuted the most damaging blows which could be inflicted upon the
> United States . . . Despite the apparent risks involved in the invasion
> attempt and in fighting a decisive fleet engagement in waters close to
> Hawaii [he argued] the chances of success appeared preponderant since
> the Japanese Fleet had a three-to-one advantage in aircraft carriers in
> addition to overwhelming superiority in battleships.[3]

United States submarines from Hawaii used Midway as an important forward fueling point. Most important from Yamamoto's point of view, Midway would draw out Adm. Chester W. Nimitz's fleet. The commander in chief of the Japanese Combined Fleet knew he had to annihilate the United States Pacific

Fleet in 1942 or lose the war. He argued that Japan must get the U.S. Pacific Fleet into a position where it could be wiped out. What could be better bait than Midway? The naval staff in Tokyo hesitated to adopt Yamamoto's plan but did not refuse him. An unforeseen event would give the go-ahead signal.

Success in China and the unbroken triumphs to the south during the first months of war convinced the Japanese people that Tokyo would not be bombed. On the evening of 17 April 1942, Japanese Foreign Minister Shigenori Togo's German-born wife told the spouse of a neutral diplomat at dinner that she need not "worry about sending her furs and jewels and wines out of Tokyo or go to the expense of building an air-raid shelter, since the Americans could never bomb Tokyo." [4]

The next day, 18 April 1942, General Tojo was returning to Tokyo from an inspection tour when his plane had to avoid a twin-engine aircraft he did not recognize. The general became incredulous when told that it was an American army-type bomber. More American planes approached the Japanese island of Honshu. They came from a task force of two aircraft carriers. Vice Admiral William F. Halsey flew his flag on USS *Hornet*, upon whose flight deck rested sixteen B-25 medium bombers. The USS *Enterprise* went along to provide a combat air patrol—reconnaissance and fighter cover to protect the *Hornet*. A screen of cruisers and destroyers commanded by Rear Adm. Raymond Spruance covered as escorts.

This operation grew from a suggestion by Lt. Col. James Doolittle of the U.S. Army Air Corps, who believed that a B-25 bomber could take off from a carrier deck. With the aid of a group of young Army Air Corps pilots, he proved that it could be done on test runs in the States. Flying with maximum fuel loads, the operation began from a greater distance than land-based Japanese planes could threaten the ships. Since it was quite impossible for an aircraft that size to return to the aircraft carrier, after target bombing Doolittle planned for his planes to fly to friendly airfields in northern China.

Nine aircraft, including Doolittle's, bombed the Japanese capital, Tokyo. Three flew over Yokohama, three more over Nagoya, while a lone aircraft bombed Kobe and Kyoto. The plan called for the launching of the planes from a range of 400 miles. However, early on 18 April while more than 600 miles east of Tokyo (720 miles according to Japanese sources), lookouts aboard an escort cruiser sighted *Nitto Maru*, a former Japanese fishing boat now on picket duty. [5] Halsey's radiomen heard it send out a wireless signal before his cruisers sank it with gunfire. Halsey decided to launch immediately, thus the whole squadron became airborne by 8:24 A.M. Upon receiving *Nitto Maru*'s warning, Japanese Combined Fleet Headquarters acted immediately. Vice Admiral Kondo's 2nd Fleet, which had just returned to Yokosuka, was ordered to attack the American fleet, believed to have had three aircraft carriers. [6]

"There was no fuel margin which would enable [Doolittle's aircraft] to maneuver and form up as a squadron after take off." [7] The first aircraft flew over Tokyo at noon. The B-25s arrived over their targets singly and from widely varying direction. Despite the early warning given by the *Nitto Maru*, none of the crews met any significant opposition from anti-aircraft fire and none whatever from fighter aircraft. Doolittle dropped:

> . . . incendiary bombs in downtown Tokyo. Other aircraft bombed defense plants and wharves. In all, a number of factories were burned and considerable damage was done to an oil tank farm and an aircraft factory at Kobe. Each aircraft dropped its bomb load, then continued west to China, where [fifteen] of the sixteen planes crash-landed. A [sixteenth] landed in Vladivostok, where the Russians interned the crew. None of the crews found a friendly airfield, but most fell into friendly Chinese hands. Of the eighty brave souls who manned the sixteen bombers, seventy-one survived. [8]

The Japanese beheaded two of the unfortunate airmen who landed in their territory.

This air raid was a tremendous morale booster in America. The Japanese press claimed nine planes were shot down, when in reality there was only one. When President Roosevelt was questioned, he claimed the planes came from Shangri-La, a mythical land made popular in a recent movie made from the novel *Lost Horizon*. This air raid made front-page news in the American press for five days. The headlines in the 21 April newspapers said, "Japs Try To Minimize Attacks But Indications Show Damage Severe." A Berlin broadcast said the Japanese government had provided funds to rebuild the factories, dwellings, and one cinema that were burned down in the Tokyo area.

Later, when the Japanese learned who commanded the raid, a headquarters spokesman sarcastically claimed that "the attack is not even a 'do little' but rather a do-nothing raid." [9] Indeed, the physical results of this raid did little to diminish Japan's military capacity, but the psychological impact upon the Japanese government, its people, and its military was so strong that it crystallized Yamamoto's plan to attack Midway Island. Vice Admiral Kondo's ship failed to locate the American force that had launched the Doolittle raid. Halsey's task force retired uneventfully and re-entered Pearl Harbor on 25 April.

Imperial General Headquarters approved Yamamoto's plan to take Port Moresby prior to Midway. He would then seize Samoa, Fiji, and New Caledonia, thus isolating New Zealand plus severing the U.S. supply line to Australia. The Japanese planned to assemble a force of 5,000 marines of the Special Naval Landing Forces to sail around the eastern tip of New Guinea to assault Port Moresby. D-day for the landing at Moresby was set for early May. Admiral Takeo Takagi, with carriers Zuikaku and Shokaku, and light carrier Shoho, would support the invasion force, while the remainder of the fleet prepared for Midway.

Yamamoto had an abundance of ships available compared to the Allies, but Nimitz had one potent weapon unknown to the Japanese: Shortly after Nimitz arrived at Pearl Harbor, he was introduced to Lt. Cmdr. Joseph Rochefort, officer in charge of the Fourteenth Naval District's Combat Intelligence Unit, called Station Hypo. Rochefort worried that he might be dismissed for failure to detect the whereabouts of the Japanese fleet on 7 December 1941. Fortunately, Nimitz kept him at his job. Later, he informed Nimitz that his code breakers could read all or at least a part of the coded Japanese radio traffic. This pertinent information on major Japanese fleet movements became known as ULTRA, short for ultra secret. "Originally, ULTRA was the name the British gave to information obtained from breaking German wireless traffic enciphered on the Enigma machine. However, distinct nomenclature broke down, and by 1943 the term 'Japanese ULTRA' was commonly used by Americans for information obtained from reading Japanese navy, army, and air systems." [10] For the remainder of the war, ULTRA became an important offensive tool in the hands of the U.S. Pacific Fleet.

Before the Japanese invasion convoy left Truk and Rabaul, Nimitz knew the timetable, names, and locations of the ships involved. This knowledge enabled Adm. Frank Jack Fletcher to sail from Pearl Harbor in time for aircraft carrier Lexington to make a record-breaking high-speed run to rendezvous with carrier Yorktown. Together, they were dispatched to intercept the Japanese armada. The Southwest Pacific Navy also joined Fletcher's command. This consisted of the Australian cruisers Australia and Hobart, the American cruiser Chicago, and a few destroyers. They were under the command of Rear Adm. J. G. Crace of the Royal Navy.

These ships would engage the Japanese in the Battle of the Coral Sea, a sea battle unique in world history. For the first time, a major naval battle took place in which the ships involved never sighted one another. On 7 May, Admiral Fletcher detached Admiral Crace's cruisers and sent them to find the Moresby attack force. His ships came under attack from Japanese land-based bombers, which were repulsed without casualty. At 8:15 that same morning, search planes from Yorktown reported they had found the Japanese main battle fleet, two carriers and four heavy cruisers, about 170 miles northwest of the American force.[11] They had mistakenly found only two cruisers and a destroyer. Upon returning, they came upon the light aircraft carrier Shoho. American dive-bombers promptly sank her.

Toward evening, Admiral Takagi sent out search-and-destroy missions to seek Yorktown and Lexington. His planes did not find the ships but did find a squadron of Admiral Fletcher's Wildcat fighters. The Americans shot down nine of the Japanese aircraft. Later, in the dark, six of the enemy survivors tried to land on Lexington, having mistaken her for their own carrier. Ten other Japanese aircraft were damaged while landing on their own ships in the dark.[12]

On 8 May, battle was joined in earnest, with aircraft from both task forces finding their opponents' carriers. Both Shokaku and Zuikaku were larger than the American carriers and normally carried more aircraft. The Japanese losses on the previous day created parity. As the battle opened, the Japanese ships had 123 aircraft; the Americans, 122. Yorktown planes scored two bomb hits on Shokaku. One damaged her flight deck, disabling her ability to launch aircraft. Ordered out of battle by Admiral Takagi, she steamed back to the Japanese

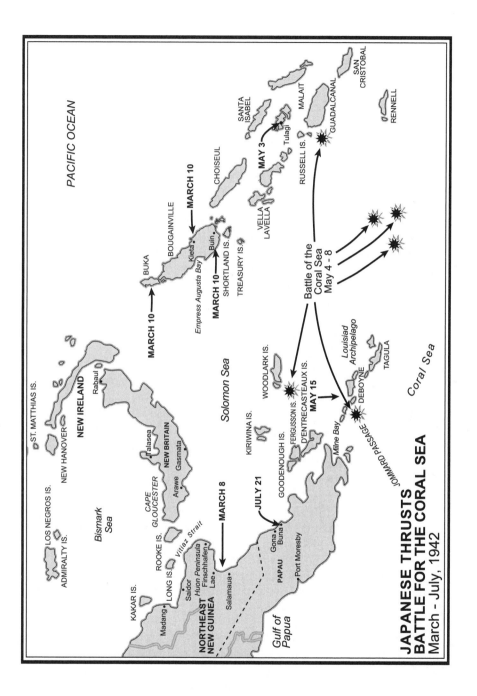

JAPANESE THRUSTS
BATTLE FOR THE CORAL SEA
March – July, 1942

PACIFIC OCEAN

ST. MATTHIAS IS.

NEW HANOVER

LOS NEGROS IS.

ADMIRALTY IS.

NEW IRELAND

Rabaul

Bismark
Sea

KAKAR IS.

LONG IS.

ROOKE IS.

Vitiaz Strait

CAPE
GLOUCESTER

Arawe

Gasmata

Talasea

NEW BRITAIN

Madang

Saidor

Huon Peninsula

Finschhafen

Lae

Salamaua

MARCH 8

NORTHEAST
NEW GUINEA

Gulf of
Papua

PAPAU

Gona

Buna

JULY 21

Port Moresby

Solomon Sea

WOODLARK IS.

KIRIWINA IS.

GOODENOUGH IS.

FERGUSSON IS.

D'ENTRECASTEAUX IS.

MAY 15

Milne Bay

JOMMARD PASSAGE

Louisiad
Archipelago

DEBOYNE

TAGULA

Coral Sea

Battle of the
Coral Sea
May 4 - 8

BUKA

BOUGAINVILLE

Empress Augusta Bay

Kieta

Buin

MARCH 10

MARCH 10

SHORTLAND IS.

TREASURY IS.

CHOISEUL

MARCH 10

VELLA
LAVELLA

MAY 3

Tulagi

RUSSELL IS.

SANTA
ISABEL

MALAIT

GUADALCANAL

SAN
CRISTOBAL

RENNELL

base at Truk. Meanwhile, seventy Japanese aircraft from Zuikaku found the two American carriers in plain view. Yorktown lost sixty-six men killed when a bomb struck an elevator. Two torpedoes plus several other bombs hit Lexington. Inside explosions caused an order to abandon ship. Afterward, American destroyers sank her.[13]

Both the United States and Japan claimed victory. The Japanese lost light carrier Shoho, destroyer Kikuziki, plus three small naval units sunk, carrier Shokaku damaged, seventy-seven planes lost, and 1,074 men killed or wounded. The Americans lost the carrier Lexington, oiler Neosho, and destroyer Sims, in addition to Yorktown damaged, sixty-six planes downed, and 543 killed or wounded.[14]

Based on the tonnage lost by both sides, the Japanese held a slight advantage. But what of the amphibious force? The 5,000 Japanese marines returned to Rabaul. The plan to seize Port Moresby had failed. The enemy never again tried to take her by sea. The Coral Sea battle made a major contribution to the American victory in the upcoming Battle of Midway in that neither the carriers Shokaku nor Zuikaku was available to aid the Japanese cause. After the battle, Nimitz ordered Yorktown to return immediately to Pearl Harbor. This "left the balance of carriers in the two Pacific navies as follows: Japan, Zuikaku, Shokaku, Hiryu, Soryu, Kaga, Akagi, and the small carriers Ryujo and Zuiho; the United States, Saratoga, Wasp, Ranger, Enterprise, Yorktown, and Hornet." [15] The Japanese carrier Shokaku retired to Truk for repair. Zuikaku lost so many aircraft at the Coral Sea battle, it had to be withdrawn to refit. The American carriers Wasp and Ranger were absent as they were being used in the Mediterranean to ferry fighters to the besieged island of Malta. Saratoga was on the West Coast receiving repairs as a result of being torpedoed by a Japanese submarine in January.

On 26 May Admiral Halsey's task force returned to Pearl Harbor from the Solomon Islands in the South Pacific. Halsey suffered greatly from a severe case of dermatitis, a torturing skin eruption. Navy doctors immediately ordered him to the hospital. Because he constantly experienced excruciating pain, arrangements were made to place him in care of the foremost allergist in the United States, Dr. Warren T. Vaughn, at the Johnston-Willis Hospital in Richmond, Virginia. Halsey could not return to active duty until early September.

Rear Admiral Raymond Spruance took temporary command of Halsey's Task Force 16. On 27 May, Admiral Fletcher's Task Force 17 arrived at Oahu, with Yorktown trailing an oil slick ten miles long. Nimitz, a marine engineer, led an inspection party in an examination of Yorktown's hull. He had received radio reports that it would take ninety days to make all necessary repairs. As it would take much less time to make her battle-worthy, Nimitz told his inspection party, "We must have this ship back in three days." [16] Within an hour, welding equipment, steel plates, and other materials were assembled so that repairs could continue around the clock.

Commander Joseph J. Rochefort had previously warned Nimitz that a Japanese attack in Midway was imminent. Rochefort told Nimitz that Japan had no plans to attack Australia and that, following the move to seize the eastern end of New Guinea, the Japanese would move with a much larger operation in the Pacific involving most of the Combined Fleet. Rochefort concluded that the Japanese next intended to capture Midway. Nimitz tentatively accepted Rochefort's analysis, but he could not disregard conclusions reached elsewhere. The Army Air Force expected a raid on San Francisco. MacArthur's headquarters opined that the Japanese would resume their drive in the New Guinea-Solomons area. British army planners argued that Japan's next move would be into the Indian Ocean.

Rochefort noted that the Japanese made repeated references to "AF." Unable to convince all parties, Rochefort and Cmdr. Edwin T. Layton, conceived a scheme to make sure. They suggested that Admiral Nimitz order Midway to "send out a fake radio message stating that their distillation plant had broken down," causing a serious problem for fresh water.

Nimitz agreed. A cable line stretched between Oahu and Midway so that the enemy could not overhear communications between the two. Midway made the radio report. "Two days later, Hypo decrypted a Japanese intercept reporting that " 'AF' has a shortage of fresh water." [17]

Nimitz demanded specific information from Hypo. In response, he was told that Japanese carriers would probably attack Midway on the morning of 4 June. They would come in from the northwest on bearing 325 degrees. They would be sighted about 175 miles from Midway about 6:00 A.M. Midway time. Nimitz laid plans to eliminate the carriers in Vice Admiral Nagumo's command based on this Hypo information. [18]

Midway actually consists of two islands, Eastern Island with 328 acres and Sand Island with 850 acres. It derived its name from its geographical location: the center in the Pacific Ocean. Prior to battle, the 6th Marine Defense Battalion was reinforced so that approximately 3,000 troops occupied the island in June 1942.

On 25 May, the Midway and Aleutians operations were rehearsed in tabletop maneuvers aboard Admiral Yamamoto's flagship, Yamato. [19] Vice Admiral Nagumo commanded the first carrier striking force, which included the carriers Akagi, Kaga, Hiryu, and Soryu among the number of battleships, cruisers, and destroyers. One-third of Nagumo's striking force, namely Shokaku and Zuikaku, were not available. Vice Admiral Nobutake Kondo commanded the large invasion force. Vice Admiral Mushiro Hosogayo commanded the large Aleutian force, which included the light carrier Ryugo and the carrier Junyo. Yamamoto commanded the main force.

Although the Japanese held overwhelming strength in combat ships, this advantage was somewhat offset by Nimitz's superior intelligence. Another disadvantage for the Japanese was the fact "that Nagumo had been assigned two tactical missions which were essentially incompatible. The assignment to attack Midway on 5 June in preparation for the landing operation put his force under rigid limitations of movement. The other mission—to contact and destroy enemy naval forces." [20] Had Zuikaku and Shokaku been available,

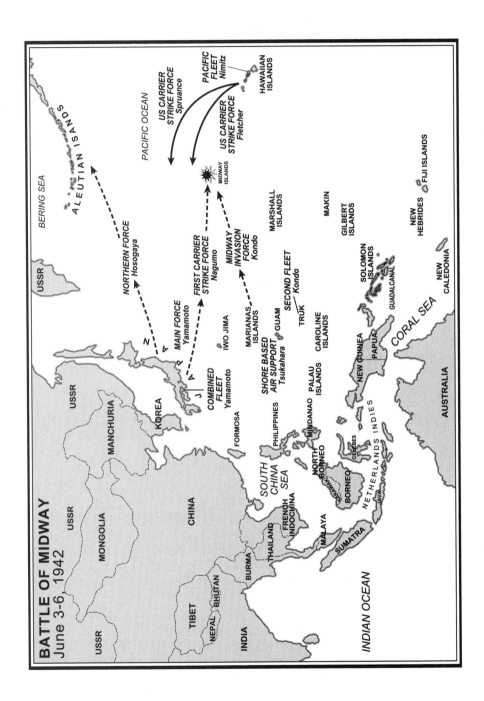

BATTLE OF MIDWAY
June 3-6, 1942

Nagumo, in all probability, would have had the strength to carry forward both missions simultaneously.

On 28 May, Task Force 16, commanded by Admiral Spruance with the carriers *Enterprise* and *Hornet*, moved north from Pearl Harbor to take positions east and northeast of Midway. Task Force 17, commanded by Adm. Jack Fletcher, with the hastily repaired *Yorktown*, departed Hawaii on 30 May. Not until the morning of 3 June did Catalinas, patrolling 700 miles westward from Midway, report: "Main Body . . . bearing 262, distance 700 . . . eleven ships, course 090, speed 19." [21] Nimitz notified Fletcher that the "main body" referred to was in fact the invasion force rather than the enemy striking force. At dawn on 4 June, Nagumo launched 108 aircraft against Midway from more than 180 miles out.[22] He did so completely oblivious to the American carriers on his flank. The Japanese planes inflicted widespread damage on Midway facilities, but unlike the raids on Pearl Harbor and the Philippines, the Japanese found no enemy planes on the ground. This should have advised them that the Americans had been forewarned.

More than sixty bombers and torpedo planes from Midway attacked the Japanese in five separate waves. The Americans suffered severe losses, mainly from the agile Zero fighters, and made not a single hit on any Japanese ship. At this stage in the war, the Zero was superior to any American fighter aircraft. Next came three separate attacks by torpedo planes from *Hornet*, *Enterprise*, and *Yorktown*. All these were shot down without inflicting any damage upon the enemy.

The Japanese ships had come unscathed through eight successive attacks. But the strikes by the American planes were not entirely fruitless. Their disastrous showing caused Nagumo to relax caution, and the low-flying torpedo planes drew the airborne Zeros—and Japanese attention—down to low altitude. Furthermore, Nagumo recognized that to complete his mission to prepare for the landing operation, he needed to make a second attack on Midway. However, he had lost thirty-eight planes to anti-aircraft fire, plus twenty-nine more damaged so as to be inoperable.[23]

At 8:30 A.M., Rear Adm. Tamon Yamaguchi, commanding Carrier Division 2 in *Hiryu*, upon learning of the American carrier force to the northeast, advised Nagumo to launch an immediate attack on it with his reserve planes. Nagumo disregarded this advice. He began replacing the instant-contact bombs, with which his reserve planes were armed in anticipation of a second strike on Midway, with armor-piercing bombs and torpedoes. He recovered his combat air patrol of Zeros and also his planes returning from the initial raid on Midway. Most of these operations were carried out while under attack, which delayed Nagumo two hours.

By 10:00 A.M., no one with knowledge of the situation at Midway could have predicted that the Americans had the slightest chance for victory. The four Japanese carriers had on their flight decks a strike force armed, fueled, and ready to take off, and a second strike force being readied below. Few of the American Midway-based aircraft, except the B-17s, were fit for further service.

Then the Americans' luck changed. Lieutenant Commander Clarence McClusky of the *Enterprise* had under his command two squadrons of dauntless dive-bombers, thirty-seven planes including his own. At 7:52 A.M., he launched with no fighter plane protection. An hour and a half later, as he reached the point where he expected to meet the Japanese, only empty ocean could be seen. He continued in the same direction for another thirty-five miles, then turned north. At 9:35 A.M., he sighted a Japanese destroyer moving northeastward at its maximum speed. Correctly assuming that she was trying to catch up with Nagumo's strike force, McClusky took his course from the enemy destroyer.

At 10:00 A.M., the presence and course of half the Japanese strike force reached Fletcher. Minutes later, McClusky heard the shouts over the radio-telephone: "Attack! Attack!" at which he replied, "Wilco, as soon as I find the bastards!"[24] Shortly thereafter, he could see all four Japanese carriers rapidly maneuvering to escape the torpedo-plane attacks not yet over. Approaching from a different direction, *Yorktown* planes arrived over the enemy force at the same time as McClusky's, unobserved by the Japanese and both unaware of each other's presence.

When the last of the American torpedo-planes had been wiped out, Nagumo finally ordered his counterattack. He had armed and fueled planes spotted on their flight decks about to take off and other planes on their hangar decks arming and fueling. Discarded instant-contact bombs were still lying on the hangar decks awaiting return to the magazines. His force stood in the ultimate state of vulnerability. Before a Japanese strike could be launched, bombers from *Yorktown* and *Enterprise* dove from 15,000 feet and, in seconds, changed the whole course of the battle. They released bombs that hit *Soryu*, *Kaga*, and Nagumo's flagship *Akagi*, setting off lethal fires and explosions in all three.[25]

The carrier *Hiryu*, escaping unscathed to the north with some of the Japanese surface vessels, first launched bombers, then torpedo planes, which found and disabled *Yorktown*. *Yorktown* later sank as a result of being torpedoed by a Japanese submarine; however, most of her crew was saved, and her planes were able to land on the decks of the *Hornet* and *Enterprise*. At 5:00 P.M., dive-bombers from the *Enterprise* located *Hiryu* just as she was about to launch an attack on the other American carriers.[26] They scored four direct hits on the Japanese carrier, setting off explosions and uncontrollable fires. A dozen B-17s from Midway participated in the attack on *Hiryu*, none of whose bombs hit the target. One army bomber did succeed in strafing the burning carrier before she sank. At 2:55 A.M. on 5 June, Admiral Yamamoto concluded that his eastbound ships were less likely to be victors of a night battle than victims of a dawn air attack.[27] Accordingly, he canceled the Midway operation by ordering a general retreat.

The Japanese 2nd Fleet's four-cruiser bombardment group, then nearing Midway, reversed course after sighting the U.S. submarine *Tambor*. In maneuvering to avoid torpedoes that they mistakenly supposed *Tambor* had fired,

Mogami and *Mikuma* collided. The other two cruisers sped away, leaving the damaged vessels with the two escorting destroyers to make what speed they could. By 9:00 A.M. on 5 June, all four of Nagumo's carriers had gone down. That morning B-17s and Marine Corps planes from Midway attacked *Mogami* and *Mikuma*. All their bombs missed, but marine Capt. Richard Fleming crashed his flaming plane into *Mikuma*'s after turret, starting fires that caused numerous casualties and widespread damage. On 6 June, Task Force 16 attacked the battered cruisers with dive-bombers, sinking *Mikuma* and damaging *Mogami* so badly that it took almost a year for repairs.[28]

Directly following the battle and for several days thereafter, U.S. air- and surface craft searched the seas north and west of Midway, picking up downed airmen and other survivors, Japanese and American. On 7 June, the Japanese landed without opposition on the Aleutian Islands of Attu and Kiska.

This American victory cost one carrier and one destroyer sunk, 307 men killed, 147 aircraft lost, extensive damage to installations at Midway, moderate damage to installations at Dutch Harbor, and Attu and Kiska lost. Although Japanese losses were not as severe as U.S. wartime estimates indicated, they sustained four carriers and one heavy cruiser sunk; another heavy cruiser wrecked; one battleship, one oiler, and three destroyers damaged; 322 aircraft lost, and 2,500 men killed, including many experienced pilots.[29]

Even more than at Coral Sea, the Battle of Midway emphasized the vital role of carrier-borne air power in modern naval warfare. Yamamoto had to abandon his mission despite the possession of vastly superior gun power because Fletcher and Spruance had destroyed the Japanese air component while preserving most of their own. In addition to the brave airplane pilots, a major credit for this naval victory goes to Nimitz, who had the fortitude to take a tremendous risk with his remaining fleet. He commented, "Had we lacked early information of the Japanese movements, and had we been caught with carrier forces dispersed, . . . the Battle of Midway would have ended differently." [30]

The American public was never told the true story about the Battle of Midway until some time after the end of World War II. Accordingly, U.S. Army bombers stationed on the island itself took credit for sinking the Japanese ships. *Time* magazine in its 15 June 1942 issue said:

> The U.S.—not Japan—is stronger, now and potentially in the long ranged, heavy-loaded land based army bombers of the kind which sent the Japs reeling back from Midway and it was in this fact rather than in the actual comparative losses at Midway that the U.S. saw the face of victory.[31]

Because of fear that the Japanese would suspect that the United States was reading their secret codes, Admiral King was quoted in the same article as saying the U.S. "knew the Japanese had assembled for a major blow—the question was: where? They had to apply what Admiral King called his doctrine of 'calculated risk,' placing the bulk of what they had where the Japs seemed most likely to strike—they calculated the risk and chose Midway." [32] *Time*'s 22 June 1942 issue gave some minimal credit to the navy:

The Japs were hit with everything Midway could throw at them. Marine Corps dive bombers struck the leading cruisers and destroyers. Colonel Sweeney's heavy bombers went for the carriers, left one blazing. Four converted bombers, the first Army torpedo-planes ever recorded in action, hit the other carriers . . . The Navy had some land-based bombers and torpedo planes on Midway, and these also joined the battle.[33]

The true significance of the battle was not spelled out to the American public, mainly because of Admiral King, who was the despair of the press. King acknowledged that the public had a right to know as long as this knowledge did not give aid and comfort to the enemy. He strongly believed that military considerations outweighed satisfying the natural curiosity of the public. King said that small bits of information could be used by the Japanese to piece together the bigger picture, the same as each missing piece in a jigsaw puzzle helps provide a better view of the whole picture.[34] As a result, at no time during the war did the U.S. Navy receive the credit it deserved for winning the Pacific War.

Shortly after the Midway defeat, Imperial General Headquarters reversed its decision to seize Samoa, Fiji, and New Caledonia, but again turned its attention to the capture of Port Moresby. Samuel Eliot Morison characterizes the United States' victory at Midway as a victory of intelligence. Japanese authors Mitsuo Fuchida and Masatake Okumiya fully concur, writing, "For it is beyond the slightest possibility of doubt that the advance discovery of the Japanese plan to attack was the foremost single and immediate cause of Japan's defeat." [35] These authors further claim that by the time of the Midway battle, "arrogance had reached a point where it had permeated the thinking and actions of officers and men in the fighting services. This malady of overconfidence has been aptly called 'Victory Disease' and the spread of the virus was so great that its effects may be found on every level of the planning and execution of the Midway operation." [36]

Chapter 9
Defense of Australia

MANY TIMES AFTER FIRST BEING ELECTED PRESIDENT, Roosevelt insisted that we must put first things first. In the spring of 1942, preventing further encroachment by the Japanese throughout the Pacific took first priority. Already, at the Arcadia Conference, the Combined Chiefs of Staff had agreed that the defense of Australia and New Zealand and the sea lanes to them were essential.

In area, Australia is only slightly smaller than the lower forty-eight states. Its large area and small population made it highly vulnerable to a Japanese invasion. In 1942, it had a population of approximately 7 million, most of it concentrated along the east coast from Brisbane to Melbourne. No nation on Earth had a longer coastline.

After World War I, Australians recognized that their continent presented large areas especially along the country's northwest and northern coast where an enemy might move in without anyone in government being aware of it. The Australian navy decided to designate some civilians in the remote coastal areas as coast watchers. Each coast watcher was supplied with printed instructions on what and how to report. The pedal radio gave them a link with the outside world. Naval intelligence enrolled scattered missionaries and cattlemen. During the 1930s the coast watchers adopted the name "Ferdinand" to describe their society.[1] Like Disney's *Ferdinand the Bull*, which preferred smelling the flowers rather than fighting, it was their duty to gather information rather than fight.

Australian administrative offices at coastal stations in Papua, New Guinea, and the Solomon Islands were enrolled as coast watchers. Thus by September 1939 the Ferdinand Society numbered approximately 800 members. In the months ahead, especially during landings in the Solomon Islands, Australian coast watchers gave vital information to American fighting forces. Many lost their lives when captured by the Japanese.

By the end of February 1942, the Japanese were on Australia's doorstep. There was great fear of invasion by the enemy, and with good reason. Australia's finest troops were serving the British cause in the Middle East, and the Japanese had sunk a large portion of the American fleet at Pearl Harbor. After the sinking of *Prince of Wales* and *Repulse* together with numerous other British and Dutch ships in the Netherlands East Indies, it had to depend upon its own resources and those of the United States for any meaningful help.

On 27 December 1942, Australia's prime minister, John Curtin, shocked and angered Winston Churchill with his assessment of where Australia's greatest support lay. Melbourne's *Herald* newspaper published an article over Curtin's byline, which outlined the situation as he saw it and which concluded:

> Without any inhibitions of any kind, I make it quite clear that Australia looks to America, free of any pangs as to our traditional links or kinship with the United Kingdom. We know ... that Australia can go and Britain can still hold on. We are, therefore, determined that Australia shall not go, and shall exert all of our energies toward the shaping of a plan, with the United States as its keystone, which will give to our country some confidence of being able to hold out until the tide of battle turns against the enemy.[2]

The fall of Singapore saw the loss of more than 20,000 highly trained volunteers of the Australian Imperial Force, when most of Australia's 8th Division was taken prisoner of war in Malaya. Dutch forces in Java and Sumatra offered only token resistance, and by 20 February 1942, the Japanese had captured airfields within bombing range of Darwin on the Australian mainland.

Having declared his intention to rely on aid from the United States, Prime Minister Curtin pressed Roosevelt for the appointment of an American general to take command in the South Pacific Area. The urgency of his plea heightened when on 22 February Japan made an air raid on Darwin. Earlier, American troops and material diverted from the Philippines arrived to raise hopes that more men and materials would be coming from America.

The Japanese held a strategy meeting on Australia on 15 March 1942 at which the general staffs of both the army and navy were represented. The army staff estimated that an invasion would require ten divisions, which they were unwilling to commit at this time.[3]

Admiral Yamamoto disagreed with the generals. His plan called for the establishment of a naval base on the east coast, there to land five divisions close to the large population centers in the Sydney-New Castle area. Yamashita, the Tiger of Malaya, preferred an Australian campaign similar to the one the Japanese undertook in Burma:

> With even Sydney and Brisbane in my hands, it would have been comparatively simple to subdue Australia . . . Although the Japanese General Staff felt my supply lines would have been too long, so would the American or British lines. We could have been safe there forever.[4]

The strategy adopted called for taking Port Moresby plus isolating Australia and New Zealand from the United States by the capture of Fiji, Samoa, and New Caledonia. Yamamoto had to settle for the subjugation of New Guinea, although he did not forget the Australian venture.

After the war, Japanese Prime Minister Gen. Tojo stated that the Japanese never intended to invade Australia.[5] Nevertheless, had the Japanese been successful in taking Port Moresby, plus the capture of Fiji, Samoa, and New Caledonia, how could they have resisted going after such a large landmass that was inhabited by so few people?

In response to Curtin's plea, President Roosevelt and the Joint Chiefs agreed to send General MacArthur to Australia. After an exciting evacuation by fast PT boat from Corregidor, two B-17s were sent to Del Monte Air Field in Mindanao to pick up MacArthur, his wife and child, and a group of officers who had served on his staff in the Philippines. In *Reminiscences*, MacArthur described his exciting flight:

> Over Timor, we were spotted and they came up after us. But we changed course from Darwin . . . and came in at Batchelor Field just as they hit the Darwin field. They discovered their mistake too late, and their dive-bombers and fighters roared in at Batchelor ten minutes after I had left in another plane for Alice Springs in the south.
>
> "It was close," I remarked to Dick Sutherland when we landed, "but that's the way it is in war. You win or lose, live or die—and the difference is just an eyelash." [6]

In contrast to the general's version, Master Sgt. Dick Graf, the wireless operator aboard one of the aircraft, said:

> The flight to and from the Philippines was purely routine. We collected General MacArthur and his party and took off from Del Monte around 2130 on the night of the 16th and the flight to Batchelor was uneventful. There was never any intention to land at Darwin, so we were certainly not diverted to Batchelor. Batchelor was the base from which all B-17 flights to the Philippines were made. We didn't go anywhere near Timor and certainly no fighters rose from there to intercept us.[7]

From Alice Springs the group traveled by rail to Adelaide, where reporters met them. MacArthur stated that he had been ordered by President Roosevelt to proceed to Australia ". . . for the purpose, as I understand it, of organizing the American offensive against Japan, a primary object of which is the relief of the Philippines . . ." He concluded with the famous line, "I came through, and I SHALL RETURN." [8] For the remainder of the war, the liberation of the Philippines dominated MacArthur's war plans.

He continued on to Melbourne, where he established his initial headquarters. A picture in the *Melbourne Herald* showed MacArthur and his staff upon their arrival. The caption under the photograph in *The Odd Couple* said, "Despite claims that they had existed on the same starvation rations as the troops fighting on Bataan, MacArthur, General Willoughby and public relations officer Lt. Col. "Pik" Diller all looked remarkably well fed." [9]

The Australians welcomed MacArthur with open arms. According to news releases, Prime Minister Curtin had obtained the services of the most experienced, most decorated, most competent, and most courageous soldier in the American army. Shortly after his arrival, MacArthur received a rude awakening. He learned that he had an unbalanced assortment of fewer than 26,000 of all ranks and arms of American forces. There was a mixture of Dutch and American aircraft, refugees from lost battles in the Netherlands Indies and the Philippines. The American contingent included field artillery units, U.S. Army Air Corps ground staff, two battalions of anti-aircraft gunners, but no infantry. Fortunately a substantial submarine fleet harbored on the east and west coasts of Australia. Those boats formerly stationed at Cavite were now at Fremantle. Admiral King on 28 February ordered six "S" boats to depart from the Panama Canal and proceed to Brisbane. These were old boats with a limited range of 5,000 nautical miles, sailing from Balboa on the Pacific side of the Panama Canal. They refueled at Bora Bora, 4,652 nautical miles' distance from Panama, before traveling on to Brisbane, arriving 15 April.[10]

After some delay because of the necessity of getting all nations involved to accept his authority as supreme commander, Southwest Pacific Area, MacArthur established headquarters in Melbourne, more than 2,000 miles from the nearest fighting front. He immediately importuned the Joint Chiefs for more troops, more ships, more aircraft, more of everything. When troops and supplies from the United States did not arrive in the desired quantities, he complained bitterly to anyone who would listen of his lack of support from Washington.

While in Melbourne, MacArthur denounced Franklin D. Roosevelt and George Marshall for this lack of support. He downgraded the U.S. Navy to *Time* correspondent Theodore H. White. MacArthur said, "The best navy in the world is the Japanese Navy. A first-class navy. Then comes the British Navy. The U.S. Navy is a fourth-class navy, not even as good as the Italian Navy." [11] MacArthur's attitude mellowed somewhat after his association with Halsey and Nimitz, but at no time was he prepared to give the U.S. Navy its just due.

Six days after MacArthur's arrival in Australia, Gen. Thomas Blamey arrived in Fremantle as a passenger aboard the *Queen Mary* in transit from North Africa, where he commanded the Australian Imperial Force and served as deputy to the British commanding officer, Gen. Claude Auchinleck. While aboard ship he learned that he had been appointed commander in chief, Allied armies in the Australian area. He would serve directly under General MacArthur.

Blamey was the seventh child of Richard and Margaret Blamey of Lake Albert in the Rivana district of New South Wales. Determined to be a soldier, young Blamey entered the Australian permanent army as a lieutenant through competitive examination. After more than thirty years' service, the last thirteen of which were part-time, he was chosen to raise the Australian 6th Infantry

Division at the outbreak of war in 1939 and was promoted to the rank of lieutenant general. Before he returned to Australia, he was promoted to full general as deputy commander in chief, Middle East, under Gen. Claude Auchinleck, who described him as "a tough old boy with plenty of common sense." [12]

On 18 April, General MacArthur received a directive from the Joint Chiefs of Staff that instructed him to "hold the key military regions of Australia as bases for future offensive action against Japan, and in order to check the Japanese conquest of the South West Pacific area to check the enemy advance toward Australia and its essential lines of communication and to prepare to take the offensive." [13]

On 9 April, General Marshall had suggested to MacArthur that all the participating governments should be represented on his staff. Marshall directed that a number of the higher positions on the staff should go to Dutch and Australian officers—particularly to Australians. On 19 April, the day after MacArthur assumed command, he announced the heads of the branches of his staff. All were Americans; eight had served with him in the Philippines.

Marshall again pressed MacArthur to include Allied officers in his staff in senior appointments, but MacArthur failed to do so. On 15 June, he informed Marshall that the Australians did not have enough staff officers to meet their own needs. "There is no prospect," he said, "of obtaining qualified senior staff officers from the Australians." Australian historian Dudley McCarthy disagreed:

> There is no record of MacArthur having asked Blamey to provide senior staff officers; yet there were in the Australian Army many senior specialists in each branch of staff work who were at least the equals of the Americans in military education and had the advantage of experience in recent operations in Africa, Europe and Asia. [14]

With few American ground troops available, MacArthur had to rely primarily on Australian soldiers commanded by Australian officers. When Japan entered the war, there were approximately 132,000 officers and men of the Australian militia on full-time duty, plus 35,000 Australian Imperial Force (AIF) available in the country itself. The AIF were volunteers who could be sent to any corner of the globe. The militia combined volunteers and conscripts, who, by law, were restricted to fighting only in Australia and its territories. By 5 February, the militia consisted of almost a quarter-million men on full-time duty. By the end of March, AIF troops available or in training exceeded 100,000. Two American infantry divisions were quick to arrive. The bulk of the U.S. 41st Infantry Division arrived in Australia on 6 April; the U.S. 32nd Infantry Division, plus the remainder of the 41st, on 14 May.

Initially, MacArthur accepted Blamey as commander in chief, Allied land forces, thus giving the Australian titular command of all land forces in the Southwest Pacific Area. In the spring and summer of 1942, while these forces were almost entirely Australian, Blamey did indeed exercise such command. The infantry defending Port Moresby, Milne Bay, and Papua were exclusively

Australian except for some units of U.S. Army engineers. When American troops came to Australia in significant numbers, MacArthur arranged to have an American army and an Australian army. Blamey's control over all ground troops was curtailed not by agreement but by MacArthur's determination to exercise operational command of American formations.

On 2 July the Joint Chiefs of Staff ordered MacArthur to seize and occupy those parts of eastern New Guinea not already held by the Allies. Four days after the Battle of Midway, MacArthur cabled Marshall suggesting that he attack New Britain and New Ireland in order to create a base from which he could destroy the stronghold of Rabaul. He asked the Joint Chiefs to provide him with a division of marines and a couple of aircraft carriers. Together with other forces, he said, he could drive the Japanese all the way back to Truk.[15] It did not take the Joint Chiefs much study to decide that MacArthur's plan was flawed, in that the U.S. Navy ships would have no protection from Japanese land-based aircraft.

On 24 July, Southwest Pacific headquarters moved to Brisbane, which was still more than 1,000 miles from the nearest fighting. Before leaving Melbourne, MacArthur issued an outline plan for the creation of airfields and other installations at the mission village of Buna, on the northern coast of New Guinea. This was to provide support for the planned recapture of New Britain. Australian infantry plus American engineers would advance across the Kokoda Trail from Port Moresby to the northern New Guinea coast to "seize an area suitable for the operation of all types of aircraft and secure a disembarkation point pending the arrival of sea parties." [16]

On 4 August, Maj. Gen. George Kenney replaced General Brett as air force commander because of Brett's inability to get along with MacArthur. Sutherland told Kenney that none of Brett's staff or senior commanders was any good. Also, he "thought the Australians were about as undisciplined, untrained, overadvertised and generally useless as the Air Force," but Brett held the Australian airmen in high esteem, carrying the Allied partnership so far as to require every American bomber pilot to have an Australian copilot and vice versa.[17] As time went on, MacArthur became more and more pleased with his new air force commander and they maintained a close relationship throughout the war.

Lieutenant General Robert L. Eichelberger arrived in late August as the American corps commander. Born 9 March 1886 in Urbana, Ohio, he graduated from the U.S. Military Academy at West Point in 1909. From 1918 to 1920 he served in Siberia with the American Expeditionary Force. From October 1940 to January 1942 he was superintendent of West Point.

After viewing the training of the U.S. 41st Infantry and 32nd Infantry Divisions, Eichelberger noted:

> In Washington I had read General MacArthur's estimates of his two infantry divisions, and these reports and our own inspections had convinced my staff and me that the American troops were in no sense ready for jungle warfare. It was true that we were newcomers, but I had

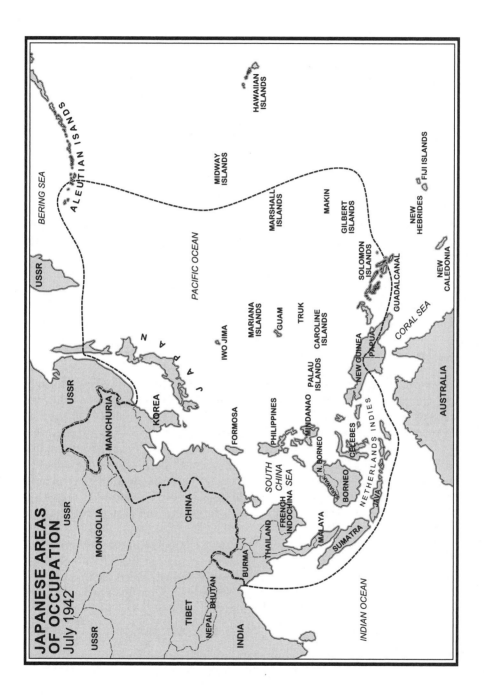

JAPANESE AREAS
OF OCCUPATION
July 1942

USSR

MONGOLIA

USSR

CHINA

MANCHURIA

KOREA

USSR

JAPAN

BERING SEA

ALEUTIAN ISLANDS

PACIFIC OCEAN

HAWAIIAN
ISLANDS

MIDWAY
ISLANDS

IWO JIMA

MARIANA
ISLANDS

GUAM

TRUK

CAROLINE
ISLANDS

PALAU
ISLANDS

MARSHALL
ISLANDS

GILBERT
ISLANDS

MAKIN

SOLOMON
ISLANDS

GUADALCANAL

NEW
HEBRIDES

FIJI ISLANDS

NEW
CALEDONIA

CORAL SEA

AUSTRALIA

NEW GUINEA

PAPUA

NETHERLANDS INDIES

CELEBES

MINDANAO

PHILIPPINES

FORMOSA

SOUTH
CHINA
SEA

FRENCH
INDOCHINA

THAILAND

BURMA

N. BORNEO

SARAWAK

BORNEO

JAVA

MALAYA

SUMATRA

INDIAN OCEAN

INDIA

NEPAL

BHUTAN

TIBET

expected to learn lessons in jungle training in Australia. And it seemed to me that our troops in training were just being given more of the same thing they had had back home . . . I told Generals MacArthur and Sutherland that I thought the 32nd Division was not sufficiently trained to meet Japanese veterans on equal terms. After an inspection . . . I gave the 32nd Division a "barely satisfactory" rating in combat efficiency . . . I was to lead these troops later, and I recall one soldier who told me that in twenty months of service he had had only one night problem. He asked how he could be expected to be proficient in night patrolling against the Japanese under those conditions.[18]

Unfortunately for the Australian troops, ignorance of local conditions in New Guinea at general headquarters (GHQ) in Brisbane caused excessive suffering and casualties throughout the year. The Owen Stanley Range in Papua towers to more than 12,000 feet at points, and there are no roads across it, only footpaths. Travel is measured in days instead of miles, a fact apparently unknown to MacArthur's staff.

By the time the marines invaded Guadalcanal, the Japanese were advancing rapidly along the Kokoda Trail, a footpath across the Owen Stanleys from Buna village to Port Moresby. On 29 July they entered the village of Kokoda, which is approximately fifty miles south of Buna and one hundred miles northwest of Port Moresby.[19] The Japanese, led by Maj. Gen. Tomitaro Horii, continued the march across the Owen Stanleys. MacArthur believed that Maj. Gen. Basil Morris had yielded Kokoda to a numerically inferior force, which was far from the truth. His small contingent of Australian troops had performed well before retreating; however, Morris differed strongly with the strategy involved. He considered the Kokoda Trail itself to be an obstacle that would defeat any attempt by the enemy to take Moresby. He believed the enemy could cross the Owen Stanleys, but it would suffer such attrition of men and equipment and would be so affected by disease and the nature of the country that it would be decimated before reaching Moresby.[20] Because MacArthur thought Morris had led poorly, he replaced him with Lt. Gen. Sydney F. Rowell, a distinguished Australian commander in the Middle East.

The Australians fought back on 8 August to briefly recapture the airstrip at Kokoda, but lost it again when the Japanese brought in fresh reinforcements from Buna. The Japanese continued to advance against savage Australian resistance, which finally stopped them on 17 September. They had reached a point on Imita Ridge only twenty-five miles from Port Moresby.[21]

Because the Japanese High Command shifted its priority to Guadalcanal, Horii received orders to take the defensive in Papua. At this time his supply line of food and military supplies had completely dried up.[22] General Morris' assessment of the enemy's problems had proved imminently correct. In Horii's announcement to his men on 20 September to withdraw, he said, "No pen or words can depict adequately the magnitude of the hardships suffered. From the

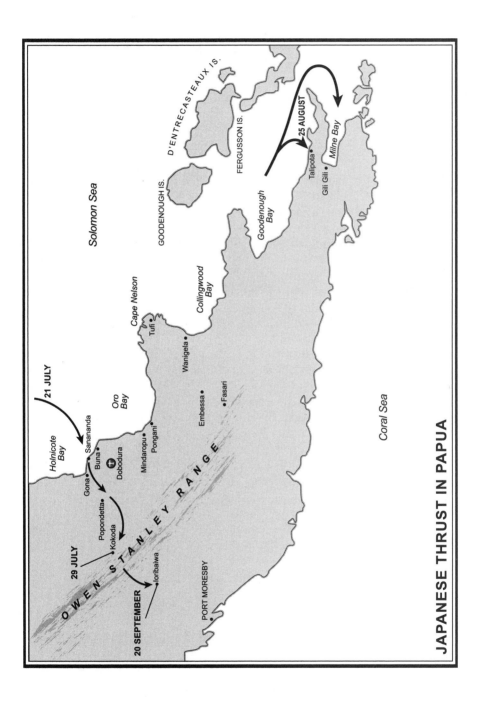

JAPANESE THRUST IN PAPUA

bottom of our hearts we appreciate these sacrifices and deeply sympathize with the great numbers killed and wounded." Horii's troops beat a hasty, disorganized retreat back over the Owens Stanleys while being pursued by the Australians. Numerous Japanese died along the way. Many drowned, along with General Horii himself, in an attempt to cross the Kumusi River.[23] The last threat to Port Moresby thus ended.

At the eastern end of New Guinea in the Milne Bay area, between 200 and 300 inches of rain falls each year. With malaria-bearing mosquitoes in abundance and mud ankle deep and up in most places, living conditions are oppressive where there are no Japanese. Three weeks prior to Horii's halted attack, about 2,000 Japanese marines landed east of Milne Bay. These numbers increased with more landings during the first few days thereafter. They moved toward the Allied base, where three partially completed airstrips were being built. Major General Cyril Clowes commanded a force at Milne Bay of "8,824 (Australian Army 7,459; United States Army 1,365); the infantry, however, numbered only about 4,500." [24] The American troops were primarily combat engineers. Two Royal Australian Air Force (RAAF) fighter squadrons plus an RAAF reconnaissance squadron also were stationed there. Clowes was a regular officer in the Australian army who had led the ANZAC Corps Artillery in the 1940 campaign in Greece prior to returning to Australia.[25]

After three days of heavy fighting, the Japanese began evacuating their troops on the night of 25 August. By 7 September all enemy troops had been withdrawn. "The victory at Milne Bay marked the first time a Japanese amphibious force had been defeated and dislodged after it had established a beachhead." [26]

In his 10 September communiqué, MacArthur took credit for the victory by saying, "With complete secrecy the position was occupied by our forces and converted into a strongpoint. The enemy fell into the trap with disastrous results to him." [27] Previously, on 30 August MacArthur told Marshall, "The enemy's defeat at Milne Bay must not be accepted as a measure of relative fighting capacity of the troops involved. The decisive factor was the complete surprise obtained over him by our preliminary concentration of superior forces." He deprecated Clowes' leadership, charging he should have "acted with great speed." [28]

General Rowell lashed back in defense of Clowes, "I'm sure that he was right. Inability to move except at a crawl, together with the constant threat of further landings, made it difficult for him to go fast or far." [29] MacArthur rendered his opinion while at Brisbane, more than 1,000 miles from Milne Bay, a place that neither he nor any member of his staff had ever seen. As historian Dudley McCarthy would comment, "In the beginning the lack of confidence undoubtedly arose from [MacArthur's] lack of knowledge of the nature of the country and of the problems of a form of warfare with which he was not familiar." [30] For reasons not fully explained, after the Milne Bay episode—maybe because of it—MacArthur became dissatisfied with General Rowell. He insisted to Curtin that Blamey take personal command in New Guinea. Blamey succeeded Rowell as commander of the New Guinea Force on 28 September.[31]

Throughout the months of September and October, MacArthur was convinced that the 1st Marine Division could not hold Guadalcanal. On 30 August he warned the Joint Chiefs of Staff that

> unless the strategic situation is constantly reviewed in light of current enemy potentialities in the Pacific and unless moves are made to meet the changing conditions, a disastrous outcome is bound to result shortly . . . It is no longer a question here of preparing a projected offensive. Without additional naval forces, either British or American, and unless steps are taken to match the heavy air and ground forces the enemy is assembling, I predict the development shortly of a situation similar to those that have successfully overwhelmed our forces in the Pacific since the beginning of the war.[32]

Again, on 16 October he warned Marshall, "It is now necessary to prepare for possible disaster in the Solomons. If we are defeated in the Solomons, as we must be unless the Navy accepts successfully the challenge of the enemy surface fleet, the entire SWPA will be in the greatest danger." [33]

MacArthur thought that if the U.S. Marines were defeated, Australia itself would be in danger of invasion by the Japanese. Accordingly, his headquarters developed a plan for redistribution of Allied forces in the event of Japanese success in the Solomon Islands. Labeled the Petersburg Plan, it was designed

> a. To defend the vital area of Continental Australia. . . .
> b. Protect sea and air communications with the United States and the United Kingdom, insofar as means permit.
> c. Prepare to take the offensive when necessary means are placed at the disposal of the Supreme Commander, Southwest Pacific Area.[34]

The Petersburg Plan observed that MacArthur's land forces available at this time included ten infantry divisions, two motorized divisions, one armored division, and one army tank brigade, which included 445,000 Australian personnel plus 45,000 U.S. Army, for a total Allied land force of 490,000. The Allied air force included 631 American planes of all types, 363 Royal Australian Air Force, and 18 of the Netherlands East Indies for a total of 1,012. Air force personnel including service elements totaled 51,250. The Allied naval force under Southwest Pacific Command included five cruisers, ten destroyers, twenty submarines, and seven other auxiliary ships. The thirty-three troop and cargo transports available could carry 18,000 troops plus 168,000 measured tons of cargo on any one voyage. In addition, the Southwest Pacific Command contained 31,000 communication and service personnel.[35]

Clearly, in October 1942 MacArthur commanded a much larger and stronger military force than he or any of his communiqués had admitted. He refused to recognize the quantity and excellent quality of his Australian troops. He had an adequate air force but did lack the needed navy ships to promote an aggressive amphibious offensive against the enemy.

The Petersburg Plan called for the protection of the Allied naval bases at Sydney, Brisbane, and Fremantle and air bases at Townsville, Brisbane, and Sydney-Melbourne; the denial of airdrome installations at Milne Bay and Port Moresby to the Japanese as long as possible; and "as a last resort, to hold the vicinity of Sydney to the limit of resistance, drawing major Japanese forces well to the South and affording a maximum opportunity for action by Allied sea and air forces against the Japanese homeland and extended lines of communication." [36]

No steps were made to implement the Petersburg Plan, for after the Japanese defeat on 24, 25, and 26 October, it became increasingly clear that they could not capture Guadalcanal. Blamey's Australian ground troops were now positioned to take the offensive in Papua, and for the first time with American infantry aid.

For the remainder of the war, the defense of the Australian continent was no longer an issue.

Chapter 10

Guadalcanal

*I*N LATE JUNE 1942, VICE ADM. ROBERT L. GHORMLEY, commander of the South Pacific Area and South Pacific Force headquartered at Noumea, New Caledonia, handed Maj. Gen. A. A. Vandegrift, USMC, a top-secret dispatch. It stated that the 1st Marine Division would attack the Japanese in the Tulagi-Guadalcanal region on 1 August. This would be the Allies' first offensive amphibious operation against the Japanese.

Vandegrift had just arrived in Wellington, New Zealand, with his 5th Marine Regiment. His 1st Marine Regiment was due to arrive two weeks later. His division would include the 2nd Marine Regiment, a part of the 2nd Marine Division then at San Diego. His landing force would consist of the 1st Marine Raider Battalion, then in New Caledonia; the 3rd Marine Defense Battalion, then at Pearl Harbor; plus the 1st Marine Parachute Battalion. One marine combat team, the 7th Regiment, was needed for the defense of Samoa and would remain there until well after the landing. Upon Vandegrift's arrival at Wellington, the striking New Zealand dockworkers refused to unload the marine's equipment. Doing the work of the dockworkers was good exercise for marines who had spent many days at sea.

Vandegrift had very little information, if any, on the area he was to attack. His intelligence officers searched for New Zealand residents who had formerly lived in the Solomons. His chief intelligence officer flew to Australia to interview Sydney and Melbourne residents who had knowledge of the Solomon Islands. Eight of those interviewed were subsequently attached to the marines as guides and advisors.

From information gained at Melbourne, the enemy strength was reported at 8,400 on the two islands as against Ghormley's estimate of 3,100. When he left the States, Vandegrift believed that the 1st Marine Division would be trained for action against the enemy in early 1943. With only one month to prepare and

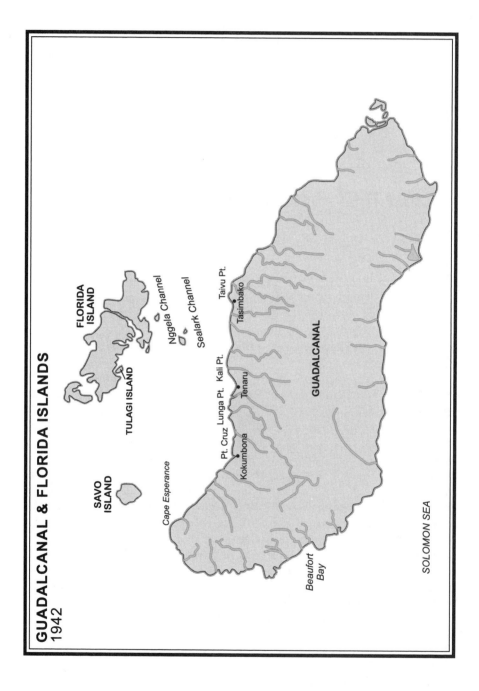

GUADALCANAL & FLORIDA ISLANDS
1942

FLORIDA ISLAND

TULAGI ISLAND

SAVO ISLAND

Cape Esperance

Kokumbona

Pt. Cruz Lunga Pt. Kali Pt.

Tenaru

Nggela Channel

Sealark Channel

Taivu Pt.

Tasimbako

GUADALCANAL

Beaufort Bay

SOLOMON SEA

placed in charge of troops he had never seen, he must have thought that this was one hell of a way to fight a war.

The Guadalcanal-Tulagi operation was the brainchild of Adm. Ernest J. King.[1] When Admiral King realized how badly beaten the Japanese had been at Midway, he insisted the American victory had to be exploited before the Japanese recovered their offensive momentum. On 8 June MacArthur proposed a grandiose offensive to seize Rabaul with himself in command. General Marshall "endorsed MacArthur's plan on the mistaken assumption that King would provide whatever ships and Marines MacArthur needed." [2]

On 23 June, King rebutted MacArthur's plan because Rabaul was too heavily defended. The U.S. Navy's alternative was an approach through the eastern Solomons where the Japanese were weaker. King then ordered Nimitz to prepare to seize Tulagi in the Solomons by amphibious assault using naval and marine forces. In early March, Roosevelt had approved King's memorandum for a limited offensive into the Solomons, which approval had never been canceled. The main problem was that Nimitz's amphibious assault would be in MacArthur's area.

On 25 June, King asked the Joint Chiefs of Staff to approve this plan. By now MacArthur had scrubbed his earlier plan of a bold direct assault against Rabaul. Marshall's mood worsened when he received an agitated dispatch from MacArthur, who was furious at King for ordering Nimitz into MacArthur's area. The navy, said MacArthur, was conspiring to reduce the army in the Pacific to no more than an occupation force. Marshall suggested on 29 June that Nimitz's South Pacific Area be enlarged to include the eastern Solomons, including Tulagi.

Final agreement came on 2 July when the Joint Chiefs of Staff issued their first directive governing strategy for the war in the Pacific:

> The objective of this directive is the seizure and occupation of the New Britain-New Ireland-New Guinea area, in order to deny those regions to Japan. Task I is the conquest and garrisoning of the Santa Cruz Islands, Tulagi and adjacent positions; Task II involves taking and retaining the remainder of the Solomons, Lae and Salamaua, and the north-eastern coast of New Guinea; and Task III is the seizure and occupation of Rabaul and adjacent positions in New Ireland-New Guinea area . . . Forces to be committed are ground, air and naval strength of SWPA, at least two aircraft carriers with accompanying cruisers and destroyers, the SOPAC (South Pacific) Amphibious Force with the necessary transport divisions, Marine air squadrons and land based air in SOPAC, and Army occupational forces in SOPAC for garrisoning Tulagi and adjacent island positions plus troops from Australia to garrison other zones . . .[3]

Both Ghormley and MacArthur protested that the date (early August) projected for the embarkation upon Task I did not allow them sufficient time for preparations. On 8 July they sent a joint dispatch to Admiral King and General Marshall:

> The opinion of the two commanders, independently arrived at, is that initiation of this operation, without assurance of air coverage during each phase, would be attended with the greatest risk (demonstrated by Japanese reverses in the Coral Sea and at Midway). The operation, once initiated, should be pushed to final conclusion, because partial attack leaving Rabaul still with the enemy, who has the ability to mass a heavy land supported concentration from Truk, might mean the destruction of our attacking elements. It is our considered opinion that the recently developed enemy positions, shortage of airfields and planes and lack of shipping make the successful accomplishment of the operation very doubtful.[4]

When it was learned through coast watchers and code breaking that the Japanese were building an airfield on Guadalcanal, it was determined that the American counteroffensive in the Pacific should proceed with all deliberate speed on 1 August 1942, with landings at Guadalcanal and Tulagi. On 28 July, Vandegrift's men from New Zealand arrived in Fiji; however, D-day had been pushed back to 7 August. There, they met the remainder of the force and rehearsed the landings. The leaders of the main components also met as a group for the first time. Vice Admiral Frank J. Fletcher commanded the entire expedition. Rear Admiral Richmond Kelly Turner commanded the amphibious force, with Rear Adm. Sir Victor Crutchley of Australia his second in command. Crutchley commanded the naval screening force, which included three Australian cruisers. Vandegrift would be in charge of troops once ashore. The meeting uncovered a basic misunderstanding between Vandegrift and the naval commanders. Vandegrift had based his plans upon the assumption that the Allies would firmly control the sea and air routes to the Solomons. This was not to be. The admirals were well aware that they were open to heavy Japanese air and sea attacks. They planned to get most of their ships well clear of the Solomons as soon as possible after landings were made.

With only light preliminary bombardment, landings took place on the morning of 7 August on Guadalcanal, Tulagi, and Gavutu. The latter two came close to the south coast of Florida, an island about twenty miles north of Guadalcanal. Tulagi was two miles long and half a mile wide. Tulagi Harbor stretched between Tulagi itself and Florida. In the harbor were the smaller islands of Gavutu and Tanambogo, connected by a causeway. In mid-May 1942, coast watchers had accurately informed the Allies that there were approximately 1,000 Japanese occupying Tulagi, together with the two small islands.

Lieutenant Colonel Merritt A. "Mike" Edson's 1st Marine Raider Battalion landed at exactly 8:00 A.M. on Tulagi Island followed by a battalion from the 5th Regiment. The attackers pushed straight across the island before turning southeast along the northern shore, where they met determined opposition. Fighting continued at nightfall.

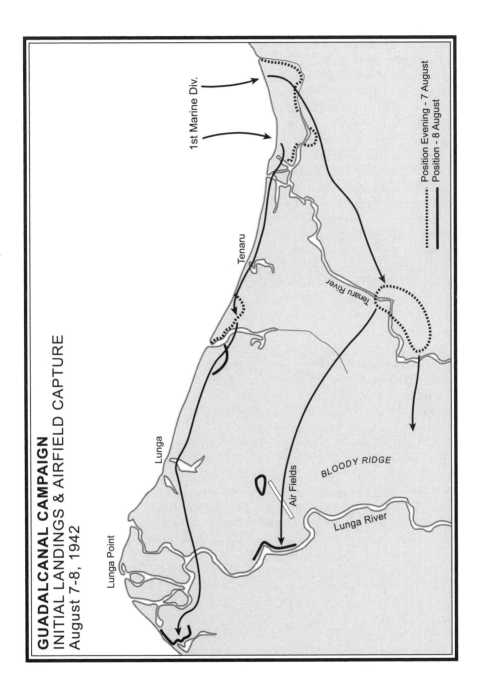

GUADALCANAL CAMPAIGN
INITIAL LANDINGS & AIRFIELD CAPTURE
August 7-8, 1942

Lunga Point

Lunga

Tenaru

1st Marine Div.

Tenaru River

Air Fields

BLOODY RIDGE

Lunga River

.... Position Evening - 7 August
———— Position - 8 August

On Gavutu, the 1st Parachute Battalion went ashore from small boats about noon and lost heavily during the actual landings, caught in a punishing fire from the shore. After they landed, fire from nearby Tanambogo harried them despite naval gunfire and bombing attacks. Reinforcements landed on 8 August as the fighting continued.

By nightfall of 8 August the harbor islands and Tulagi itself were in the U.S. Marines' hands. Tulagi cost 36 marines killed and 54 wounded, as against 200 Japanese killed, 3 surrendered, 40 escaped to Florida Island. On Gavutu and Tanambogo, the Americans lost 108 killed or missing and 140 wounded, while the whole garrison of some 500 Japanese was killed.

On Guadalcanal, the marines landed on the north coast to the east of Lunga Point and pushed cautiously westward on the first day. Japanese bombers appeared soon after noon. They paid little attention to the troops ashore because they were looking for the carriers, which they did not find. More aircraft came later in the afternoon and hit the destroyer *Mugford*. By this time, so much material had been landed at the beachhead, more supplies could not be unloaded. The marines bivouacked for the night, having suffered no casualties.

When the advance continued on 8 August, two prisoners were taken. Luckily, the marine intelligence section had on board the services of Capt. Sherwood F. Moran, a fifty-six-year-old Quaker who had previously served as headmaster for a school in Japan. From Japanese prisoners it became clear that the marines had overestimated the number of defenders. It seemed the Japanese force contained about 700 fighting men plus 1,200 to 1,500 service personnel who had fled westward when the first bombardment began. The marines quickly cleared some isolated resistance. During the afternoon they occupied the airfield, which they named Henderson in honor of Maj. Lofton B. Henderson, a marine dive-bombing squadron leader who had been killed in the Battle of Midway.

Vice Admiral Fletcher deployed his carriers southwest of Guadalcanal in support of the landings. Near nightfall, he had lost twenty-one of his ninety-nine carrier-borne planes. With fuel running low plus some Japanese aircraft still in the area, he requested from Ghormley permission to withdraw his carriers. Ghormley agreed. Rear Admiral Turner notified Vandegrift and Crutchley aboard the latter's flagship. Since the proposed withdrawal of the carriers would leave his ships without air protection, Turner said his fleet would withdraw at dawn next morning. Turner worried about a report that Japanese surface forces had been sighted approaching Guadalcanal.

Now it was Vandegrift's turn to be disturbed. He had 7,500 men ashore at or near Tulagi, 11,000 on Guadalcanal. He could not withdraw even if he wanted to. Much of his material had not been unloaded. He would soon be short of all essentials, including food and ammunition. He would be alone on a hostile shore whose surrounding waters would be under virtual command of his enemies. Counterinvasion seemed a certainty.

But, bad as the situation was, that same night saw matters drastically worsen. Just as the conference onboard Turner's flagship broke up, the first sounds of the Battle of Savo Island came rolling over the rain-drenched waters from the northwest. There, Crutchley's screening force was patrolling between Florida and Guadalcanal, where Savo Island lay midway between the western extremities of the two. A Japanese naval force surprised the screening ships. As a result, the American cruisers *Quincy*, *Vincennes*, and *Astoria* and the Australian cruiser *Canberra* were sunk; the heavy cruiser *Chicago* and the destroyers *Ralph Talbot* and *Patterson* were damaged. The Japanese lost no ships and, as was learned later, suffered hits by only two shells, which struck the flagship *Chokai*. But, fearing attack in the morning by American aircraft that they thought to be in the area, and *Chokai*'s charts having been destroyed by the two shells that struck her, the Japanese failed to engage the transports.[5]

The news of the disaster at Savo Island shocked Admiral King, so much so that weeks passed before he made public the loss. However, this was just the beginning of ship sinkings in the area. In the days and weeks ahead, so many ships of both sides were sunk north of Guadalcanal that the marines labeled the waters "Ironbottom Sound."

Vandegrift went into a defensive position. "He had only five battalions of infantry on Guadalcanal and, until he could provide air cover for the move, would not transfer any forces from Tulagi area to the larger island. He organized his defenses to extend from the Ilu River, east of Lunga Point, to the village of Kukum just west of the point." [6] His defense circled Henderson Field, which the marines now hurried to complete so that aircraft could be based on the island. Vandegrift worried that the Japanese would concentrate on his beachhead to destroy the stores piled there before he could get them inside his perimeter. He was pleased to find large quantities of rice and canned goods, which had been abandoned by the Japanese. This extra food supply enabled the marines to be fed twice a day until supply ships could again reach Guadalcanal. The Japanese also left behind significant engineering equipment.

About a week after the landings on Guadalcanal, the Australian district officer, Martin Clemens, reported in through the American lines. During the Japanese occupation he had remained on the island in accordance with the decision of the resident commissioner to maintain his administration despite the presence of the invaders. "From his position on the north coast, east of Lunga, Clemens had watched the initial American landings and hurried to contact the newcomers. He had with him a detachment of the Solomon Islands Defense Force—nearly 60 native volunteers—who had watched and patrolled extensively during the occupation and whom Clemens now placed at Vandegrift's disposal." [7]

Prior to the marine landing—that is, on 16 July 1942—the Japanese issued orders typed in English and distributed it to all the coastal villages:

JAPANESE OFFICIAL issued in 16th July 1942 to inhabitants of Guadalcanal.

Notice No. I. All of the inhabitants on this island must be ordered by Japanese Government to co-operate for Japan. Any inhabitant against it should be severely punished by Japanese martial law.

Order No. I. Men only of 14 years old or less than fifty years have to work for Japanese troops at some places on this island. After a month's labour they will be given the identity as a civilian on this island. During work for Japanese troops they will be given meal et cetera. [NO SIGNATURE][8]

Although some natives cooperated with the Japanese, Clemens' detachment proved very loyal to the Allies and was used extensively in the days and months ahead in patrolling outside the marine defense perimeter around Henderson Field. Clemens himself became an essential part of the 1st Marine Division "braintrust" that kept Vandegrift informed of Japanese intentions and movements. He was officially assigned to the division intelligence section headed by Lt. Col. Edmund J. Buckley, USMCR.[9]

The American landings in the Solomons caused a revision of the Japanese planning for the proposed attack on Port Moresby. Lieutenant General Hyakutake, commanding the Seventeenth Army headquartered at Rabaul, ordered recovery of Guadalcanal his primary mission. Hyakutake's formations were still widely scattered. However, he stayed in close touch with Admiral Yamamoto, who was stationed at Truk.

Hyakutake designated Col. Kiyono Ichiki to attack the American positions at Guadalcanal. Ichiki himself and his first echelon, about 1,000 strong, landed at Taivu Point (east of Lunga) 18 August at approximately the same time as some 500 men of the 5th Yokosuka Naval Landing Force landed at Kokumbona (west of Lunga). The rest of the Ichiki Force of 2,000 followed in slower transports. Hyakutake, however, under the misapprehension that the American forces on Guadalcanal were comparatively small, believed that Ichiki and his first echelon alone might be able to take the airfield. Ichiki agreed. His force confidently attacked across the mouth of the Ilu River on 21 August but encountered entrenched U.S. Marines. When he realized that the marines had destroyed his detachment, he burned his colors and killed himself on the battlefield.

On 17 August 1942, 221 marines of the 2nd Marine Raider Battalion under Lt. Col. Evans Carlson landed on Makin Island from the submarines *Nautilus* and *Argonaut*. The raid later made front-page news in the States, which reported that James Roosevelt, President Roosevelt's oldest son, was Carlson's executive officer, and was among the marines who landed on Makin. News articles did not say that the military value of the raid was paltry at best. The marines lost thirty men during the raid, nine of whom were inadvertently left behind during a disorganized nighttime withdrawal. The nine surrendered to the Japanese on 30 August and were later taken to Kwajalein and beheaded.

On 20 August, Cmdr. Joseph P. Blundon, a Seabee officer, reported to Gen. A. A. Vandegrift. Like many Seabees, Blundon had served in World War I with the army engineers. The marines had an engineering unit whose personnel were not as experienced in construction as the Seabees. Much of the time they occupied a place in the defense perimeter. Nevertheless, they reported Henderson Field fit to support an air operation on 19 August. The facilities were crude, but the base was ready for planes. The auxiliary carrier *Long Island* had left Efate on 18 August and joined with a covering force built around *Saratoga*. *Long Island* arrived off the southern tip of San Cristobal, 190 miles from Henderson Field, on 20 August and launched aircraft to the base.

A few days later, the 6th Seabees Battalion of 1,100 partially armed men arrived and was assigned the full responsibility for the completion and maintenance of Henderson Field. The Japanese had previously cleared an area 300 by 5,600 feet, none of it finished. Two 1,800-foot sections at the end of this area had been graded but were too rough for fighter operations.

The Seabees unit brought very little equipment: one carryall—the big, waddling machine that scoops up twelve cubic yards of earth—two bulldozers, and six dump trucks.[10] "Thanks to the Japanese, there were twenty-five flat-bottom trucks, one motor patrol grader, a Japanese tractor, plus a sheeps-foot roller. In addition, the Japanese had abandoned 10,000 barrels of cement, 18,000 feet of soil pipe, an abundance of creosote poles and lumber." [11] Blundon said the Japanese material and equipment made it possible to complete the airstrip.

The Seabees pitched camp at the edge of the field to save time, with foxholes dug alongside the landing area. As the Japanese were continually bombarding the airfield, crater filling became a constant duty. As Blundon put it:

> In addition to our crater-filling efforts, we fought the [Japanese] by working constantly to enlarge the operating surface of the field. Fighter planes can take off and land safely on a steel-matted area 75 by 2,500 feet. So, when we finished an area 150 by 2,500 feet, we had what amounted to *two* operating strips, since if we had craters on one side of this area we could rope off the damaged side and use the seventy-five-foot-wide strip that was not damaged. Then, when we finally completed an area 150 by 5,600 feet, we had *four* fighter strips. With the larger area we still had only one safe bomber strip, but bombers carry so much more fuel than fighters that they can give you more time to make repairs.
>
> Several times in the early days before we got the field lighted we had to land planes after dark. In such emergencies Seabees would hold flashlights and form a human boundary around the landing strip. Death would literally hover over these men, since the planes, often partially out of control, would come in feeling their way, and if they caught a little air pocket even the brush of a wingtip would sever the head of any man holding a light.[12]

The combination of Blundon's Seabees and Brig. Gen. Roy Geiger's Cactus Air Operation (Cactus being the code name for Guadalcanal) did a magnificent job of keeping an effective air arm in support of the U.S. Navy and ground troops. Yet, by early September, the Japanese on Guadalcanal had been heavily reinforced. Enemy ships dared not approach the island by day, but at night troop-carrying transports came down the Slot—the passage between the major Solomons—with such regularity that marines called them the "Tokyo Express."

Major General Kiyotaki Kawaguchi had six battalions for a total of 6,200 men in his command. He planned to move his men through the jungle to a ridge overlooking Henderson Field to attack on the moonless night of 12 September. In the meantime, the depleted 1st Marine Parachute Battalion had been attached to the 1st Raider Battalion, bringing Mike Edson's command up to a strength of 849 men. Two destroyer transports, *McKean* and *Manley*, carried the battalion from Tulagi to Guadalcanal on 9 September.

By nightfall of 12 September the Raiders and Parachutists had dug foxholes along the ridge south of Henderson Field, where Kawaguchi intended to make his main attack. Later in the evening, the Japanese made probing attacks along Edson's front. The next morning, 13 September, Edson said to his assembled officers, "They were testing, just testing. They'll be back . . . Today we dig, wire up tight, get some sleep. We'll all need it." [13] Darkness had barely settled over the ridge before the Japanese came lunging out of the nearby jungle. Heavy fighting continued until the morning of 14 September. Afterward, the Japanese attacked in small, uncoordinated groups. Kawaguchi admitted failure that afternoon and ordered the remnants of his brigade to retreat.

The 1st Raider Battalion lost 135 men; the 1st Parachute Battalion, another 128. Some 700 Japanese bodies littered the battlefield, and few of Kawaguchi's numerous wounded would survive their move back to the coast. Later, U.S. Marines referred to Edson's stand as the Battle of Bloody Ridge.

The Japanese lost because they still underestimated the American strength on Guadalcanal. The 6,200 Japanese on the island were pitted against 11,000 American marines, plus 5,000 on the islets to the north. Up to this point, the Japanese High Command had failed to observe a fundamental principle of warfare best expressed by Confederate Maj. Gen. Nathan Bedford Forrest: To win you must "git thar first with the most." In the meantime, American transports rushed the 7th Marine Regiment from Espiritu Santo to Guadalcanal. As the transports moved forward, enemy submarines got in among the escorting vessels. Within fifteen minutes, the Japanese torpedoed the *Wasp*, the *North Carolina*, and the destroyer *O'Brien*. The *Wasp* and *O'Brien* were sunk. Badly damaged, the *North Carolina* headed for repair at Pearl Harbor. The *Hornet* now became the lone operational U.S. carrier in the area. Having at last correctly estimated the American strength guarding Henderson Field, the Japanese command decided to go on the defensive in New Guinea in order to concentrate on the recapture of Guadalcanal.

The plight of the 1st Marine Division dominated news of the Pacific War in the United States. There was constant speculation and concern about whether or not the Japanese would push the marines off the island. On 12 September, Vandegrift was handed a copy of a memorandum from South Pacific headquarters, which reported the chances of holding Guadalcanal as nil. The memorandum expressed Ghormley's opinion, even though neither he nor any of his top-level subordinates had visited the island.[14] Information obtained through South Pacific headquarters caused the Joint Chiefs of Staff to have grave doubts for success on Guadalcanal. General Hap Arnold decided to make a fact-finding tour of the South Pacific.

On 20 September Arnold arrived at Pearl Harbor, where he met Lt. Gen. Delos Emmons, who had just returned from Southwest Pacific headquarters. Emmons said that both Ghormley and MacArthur believed that Guadalcanal could not be held. Nimitz felt that if the marines could hold out a little longer, the tide was bound to turn.

Arnold flew to New Caledonia and from there on to Australia, 750 miles west, where George Kenney met him and later introduced him to MacArthur. Arnold spent two hours with the general. His diary reported MacArthur as saying:

> The Japanese were better fighting men than the Germans. He didn't have enough troops to hold them. The Australians were not even good militiamen. The Japanese could take New Guinea and the Fijis any time they pleased, after which they would control the Pacific for a hundred years. And their move into the Aleutians was part of an eventual move into Siberia. As for the European war, no second front could be established from England because it would be impossible to build enough bases to provide air cover. And any move into North Africa was a waste of effort.[15]

Arnold was not surprised by MacArthur's comments because Emmons, who had previously visited the general, said MacArthur told him that the enemy "would take the Solomons, Fiji, New Guinea, Hawaii, then South America. And the United States was in greater danger of invasion by them than by the Germans because the U.S. Navy couldn't stop the Japanese."[16]

Again, in his diary, Arnold wrote that MacArthur

> gives me the impression of a brilliant mind—obsessed by a plan he can't carry out—dramatic to the extreme—much more nervous than when I formerly knew him. Hands twitch and tremble—shell-shocked.[17]

In spite of the diary entry, upon Arnold's return in October he recommended three officers for the post of unified commander for the South and southwest Pacific, namely General MacArthur, Lt. Gen. Joseph T. McNarney, and Lt. Gen. Lesley J. McNair. In a 6 October memo to General Marshall, he expressed the view that army aircraft under navy control were not being employed effectively. Only by establishing a single command for the entire theater and placing it under an army officer in charge could these problems be resolved.[18] Of course, the U.S. Navy took a different view.

Admiral Nimitz decided he had to see for himself if Guadalcanal could be held. On 25 September he departed Pearl Harbor accompanied by members of his staff.

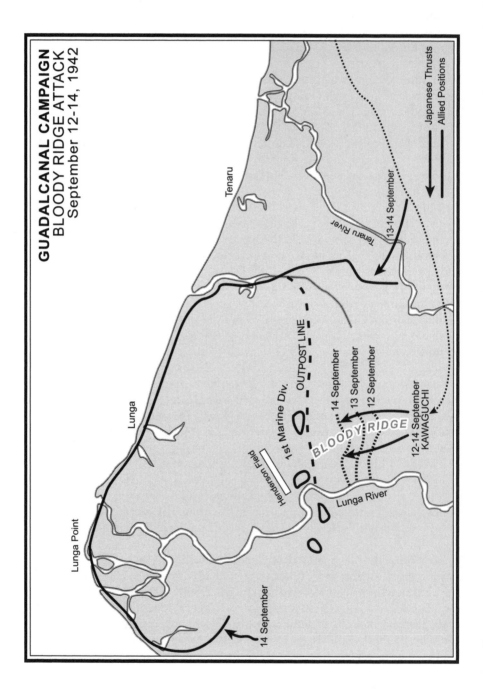

GUADALCANAL CAMPAIGN
BLOODY RIDGE ATTACK
September 12-14, 1942

Japanese Thrusts
Allied Positions

Tenaru

Tenaru River

13-14 September

Lunga

Lunga Point

Henderson Field

1st Marine Div.

OUTPOST LINE

14 September
13 September
12 September

BLOODY RIDGE

12-14 September
KAWAGUCHI

Lunga River

14 September

Nimitz radioed MacArthur to join him at a conference at Noumea. MacArthur declined, but sent two senior staff officers to Noumea to represent him.

When Nimitz arrived at Noumea, "he found Ghormley haggard with fatigue and anxiety. He occupied a small hotbox of an office in his headquarters ship, the *Argonne*, which had no air conditioning." [19] The conference began at 4:30 P.M. on 28 September and continued until 8:00 P.M. Present besides Nimitz and Ghormley and members of their staffs were Arnold and his assistant, who had just returned from Brisbane; Brig. Gen. St. Clair Street; MacArthur's chief of staff, Maj. Gen. Richard K. Sutherland, and his air commander, Lt. Gen. George C. Kenny; Rear Admiral Turner; and Maj. Gen. Millard F. Harmon, SOPAC army commander. Colonels De Witt Peck and Pfeiffer represented the Marine Corps. Nimitz asked numerous pointed questions about why there were doubts that the 1st Marine Division could hold Guadalcanal and why the army division in New Caledonia had not been sent to reinforce them.

Nimitz's party flew to Guadalcanal the next day in a B-17. Despite a heavy downpour, Nimitz inspected flight headquarters, Bloody Ridge, and points in the marines' defense perimeter. He visited the makeshift hospital, where he chatted with the sick and wounded. After dinner, Nimitz conferred with Vandegrift and his senior officers, then Vandegrift alone. Nimitz noted that the nearer one got to the combat zone, the more confidence he found. Defeatism seemed confined mainly to the headquarters at Noumea and Brisbane.[20]

Vandegrift explained his strategy. With his limited forces, he needed to maintain a defensive perimeter around Henderson Field, the key to the whole island. Whoever held the field held Guadalcanal, and the enemy indicated that it was building up strength to make another grab at the field. What Vandegrift needed, above all, were more men to hold the defense line and more fighter planes to beat back the bombers that persistently attacked the field. Nimitz left noncommittal, but his subsequent actions made clear that he agreed with Vandegrift.

When Nimitz got back to Noumea, he again conferred with Ghormley. In response to Nimitz's prodding, Ghormley dispatched a regiment of soldiers, the 164th Infantry, a unit of National Guardsmen from North Dakota and Minnesota, to Guadalcanal. Turner commanded the convoy; the *Hornet* and *Washington* forces covered its flanks; and a cruiser-destroyer force under Rear Adm. Norman Scott advanced to derail a Tokyo Express, which aviators had reported coming down the Slot. In the night of 11 and 12 October, Scott's force tangled with the Japanese northwest of Guadalcanal in the Battle of Cape Esperance. The Americans sank one cruiser and one destroyer and lost one destroyer.

The night of 12 October, four transports left Rabaul plus two from Short-lands bound for Guadalcanal. Support for the Japanese navy promised a major air attack on 13 October plus bombardment of the airfield by fleet elements the night of 14 October. Both sides now prepared for the next major ground fight.

American reinforcements reached Guadalcanal on 13 October and the convoy that carried them got safely away. The same night, two Japanese battleships in Ironbottom Sound destroyed half the planes on Henderson Field. Two bomber raids the next day and a cruiser bombardment the following night wrecked most of the remaining American aircraft.[21] In the early hours of 15 October, the six Japanese transports arrived at Guadalcanal and disembarked soldiers with impunity. Now there were as many Japanese as Americans on the island. In addition to equality in numbers, the Japanese possessed an elite group of well-trained English-speaking soldiers who could intercept U.S. communications, sabotage the message, or issue false commands to the American troops. In the early days of battle, marine leaders experienced the results of this enemy intrusion.

Sensitive messages had to be sent in code, yet officers complained that it took two hours and more to decode a single message, which when received was oftentimes too late for use. Near the end of September 1942, thirteen Navajo code talkers arrived on the island. They were ordered to report directly to General Vandegrift and no one else. Upon reporting, Vandegrift referred them to Lt. Sanford B. Hunt, his assistant division signal officer. Hunt immediately decided to give the Navajo code a trial. These thirteen were part of the first contingent of twenty-nine Navajo recruits who attended marine boot camp in May 1942.[22] Then, at Camp Elliott, California, they created the Navajo battle code, based largely on the unwritten Navajo language yet developed to include numerous military terms not a part of their original vocabulary.[23]

Hunt assigned the Navajos to radio jeeps and sent them in different directions. When the first messages hit the airwaves, chaos erupted. Marine radio operators were certain the Japanese had taken over their frequency. They immediately jammed the airwaves. Hunt delayed the test until all radio operators on Guadalcanal had been alerted. He recognized that in combat conditions an introductory phrase had to precede each message. Accordingly, Navajo messages were preceded by the words "Arizona" or "New Mexico." Later, when Hunt scheduled a competition trial between the code talkers and a code machine, the code talkers won hands down. In about two minutes the Navajos accurately sent and received a message that the machine needed four hours to decipher. From then on, messages sent from Vandegrift's command post with a "secret" or "urgent" status were sent in Navajo code.[24]

With the arrival of new replacements on both sides, the struggle for Guadalcanal was obviously approaching its crisis stage.

Having recovered from his debilitating dermatitis, Vice Adm. William F. Halsey reported to Adm. Chester W. Nimitz for active duty in mid-September. He stayed in Hawaii until 14 October while Nimitz contemplated his new assignment. On 18 October Halsey, accompanied by members of his staff, arrived at Noumea to assume his carrier command. Upon arrival he was handed a sealed envelope. He opened it, then tore open an envelope marked SECRET. Inside was a radio dispatch from Nimitz:

"Immediately upon your arrival at Noumea, you will relieve Vice Adm. Robert L. Ghormley of the duties of Commander South Pacific Area and South Pacific Force."

Halsey read the message again. "Jesus Christ and General Jackson!" he exploded. "This is the hottest potato they ever handed me!" [25]

Vice Admiral Ghormley greeted Halsey as the latter stepped onto the quarterdeck of the *Argonne*. Halsey recalled Ghormley as cordial and friendly, but both were ill at ease. Ghormley said, "This is a tough job they've given you, Bill."

"I damn well know it," replied Halsey.[26] Since no one on Ghormley's staff could give Halsey a first-hand description of the situation on Guadalcanal, Halsey radioed Maj. Gen. A. A. Vandegrift to report to Noumea as soon as possible. Vandegrift arrived on 23 October accompanied by Lt. Gen. Thomas Holcomb, commandant of the Marine Corps, who had been visiting Guadalcanal. As soon as dinner was over, Halsey settled down with his visitors for a conference. Among those present at the meeting were Maj. Gen. Alexander Patch, Major General Harmon, and Rear Adm. Kelly Turner.

Vandegrift reviewed the campaign to date and told what he suspected concerning the enemy's strength and intentions. He stressed the poor state of his own men, weakened by malaria, lack of food, and sleeplessness from night bombardment. He absolutely must have air and ground reinforcements without delay. Harmon and Holcomb strongly supported his statement. Halsey asked, "Can you hold?"

"Yes, I can hold," Vandegrift replied, "but I have to have more active support than I've been getting." [27] Turner protested that the U.S. Navy was losing transports and cargo ships at an alarming rate because there were not enough warships to protect them. Halsey then said, "You go on back there, Vandegrift. I promise to get you everything I have." [28]

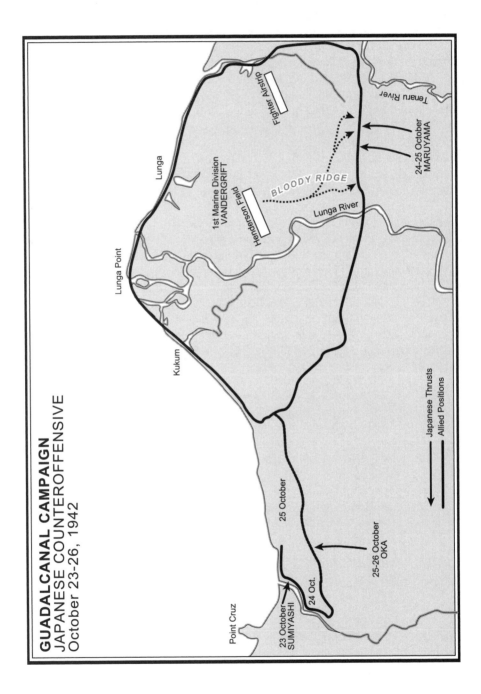

GUADALCANAL CAMPAIGN
JAPANESE COUNTEROFFENSIVE
October 23-26, 1942

Fighter Airstrip

Tenaru River

24-25 October
MARUYAMA

Lunga

1st Marine Division
VANDERGRIFT

BLOODY RIDGE

Henderson Field

Lunga River

Lunga Point

Kukum

Japanese Thrusts
Allied Positions

25 October

25-26 October
OKA

24 Oct.

Point Cruz

23 October
SUMIYASHI

Chapter 11
Halsey vs. Yamamoto

N EAR THE END OF OCTOBER, Japanese and American forces in the South Pacific were evenly matched. The Japanese had more warships available at Truk and more troops in reserve at Rabaul. But the Americans had land-based planes available at Henderson Field. The fight ahead was truly a test of wills between Halsey and Yamamoto.

On 24 October, President Roosevelt intervened. He wrote to the Joint Chiefs of Staff that he wanted every possible weapon sent to Guadalcanal and to the U.S. Army units scheduled to land in North Africa on 1 November, even at the expense of reducing strengths elsewhere. The battle for Guadalcanal had reached its most dangerous stage, which in effect was a battle to control Henderson Field. The Japanese Seventeenth Army had achieved frontline ground strength on the island equal to that of the 1st Marine Division as recently reinforced by the 164th National Guard Regiment. A command summary (U.S. Navy) put it succinctly:

> It now appears that we are unable to control the sea in the Guadal-
> canal area. Thus our supply of the positions will only be done at great
> expense to us. The situation is not hopeless, but it is certainly critical.[1]

Yamamoto had the same problem as the U.S. Navy in supplying his troops aimed at capturing Henderson Field, but try he must. On 24 October, the Japanese struck the U.S. Marines with a vengeance. All day Yamamoto's warships bombed Henderson Field as well as the marines in and around the perimeter. His planes controlled the airspace. The Japanese army planned a two-pronged attack with its largest force to date. With artillery support overlooking the airfield plus control of the sea and air, the Seventeenth Army commander was certain that Henderson Field would be taken the night of 24 and 25 October.

Yamamoto's staff was so confident of victory that they included instructions for the surrender ceremony as part of their planning. First Marine Division headquarters believed that the Japanese intended an all-out assault across the mouth of the Matanikau River. Three fresh rifle battalions including Lt. Col. Herman Hanneken's 2nd Battalion, 7th Marine Regiment, were dispatched to defend this area. The Japanese did make an initial thrust against Hanneken's front, which after heavy fighting was repulsed. However, the main point of attack came against Lt. Col. Lewis "Chesty" Puller's 1st Battalion, 7th Marines, which without support had the awesome task of covering a 2,500-yard line on and near Bloody Ridge.

"Chesty" Puller had achieved legendary status within the Marine Corps. A native of Saluda, Virginia, he had enlisted in the Marine Corps as a private during World War I where he experienced his first military action. Known as "El Tigre" in Nicaragua, he had earned two Navy Crosses before World War II. Puller's battalion mustered fewer than 700 effectives, less than the number that had defended Bloody Ridge under "Red" Mike Edson.

In the hope that the night would be clear and moonlit, the Japanese commanding officer, Maj. Gen. Yumio Nasu, ordered a narrow front assault just east of Bloody Ridge. Colonel Masajiro Furumiya's 29th Infantry would spearhead the assault, and Col. Yoshio Hiroyasu's 16th Infantry would exploit penetrations. To Nasu's chagrin, the attack had to be made through a heavy rain. Nevertheless, at approximately 10:00 P.M., the Japanese infantry sprang forward.

One of Puller's machine gun sections put out so much fire that during a lull its chief, platoon Sgt. John Basilone, had to send out a detail to flatten out the mound of Japanese corpses that obscured his field of fire. A native of Raritan, New Jersey, Basilone was known as "Manila John" because of his tour of duty with the U.S. Army in the Philippines. His machine guns, double the authorized number, were set up in the center of the battalion line, well protected in sandbag emplacements behind double apron barbed wire. For his exploits in keeping his machine guns blazing away throughout the night, Basilone would receive the Medal of Honor. It was recognized that on more than one occasion he was the man of the hour in preventing a Japanese penetration of the perimeter.

During a brief lull in fighting, Puller called Brig. Gen. Pedro A. del Valle, the commanding officer of the 11th Marine Regiment artillery:

"Give us all you've got. We're hanging on by our toenails," Puller said.

"I'll give you all you call for Puller," del Valle replied, "but God knows what'll happen when the ammo we have is gone."

"If we don't need it now, we'll never need it," Puller said. "If they get through here tonight, there won't be a tomorrow."

"She's yours as long as she lasts," del Valle answered.[2]

Marines pushed back by the constant Japanese assault waves regrouped to come forward to occupy former positions.

At 3:00 A.M. the 7th Marine regimental executive officer called to ask Puller if he needed reinforcements. "Sure we could use help, but if it's coming, for

God's sake, don't hold back. Send it on in," Puller said.[3] The only battalion left in reserve, Lt. Col. Bob Hall's 3rd Battalion, 164th Infantry, was sent to Puller's assistance. In this, its first fight, the 3rd Battalion's 164th Infantry acquitted itself extremely well. Although the Japanese re-formed and came forward time and again, they could no longer penetrate Puller's line of defense.

At 2:00 A.M., Yamamoto received the following message:

> 2100 BANZAI. THE KAWAGUCHI DETACHMENT CAPTURED THE AIRFIELD AND THE WESTERN FORCE IS FIGHTING TO THE WEST OF THE FIELD.[4]

The next morning, Yamamoto was told that the U.S. Marines still occupied the airfield. The second message—that Henderson Field had not been taken—did not reach Seventeenth Army headquarters. All during the day of 25 October at Rabaul, Rear Adm. R. Kusaka's 11th Air Fleet thought that the airfield on Guadalcanal was in Japanese hands. Wave after wave of fighters went south with orders to land at Guadalcanal. Not being able to land, they stayed over the field circling, waiting, and fighting American planes after they took off. At last, when seventeen of their number had been shot down, the rest limped back north, losing more by attrition on the way.

That night, Admiral Yamamoto issued a new order to all his fleet forces: Attack! The Japanese returned on the night of 25 October, each assault being far feebler than the first. The Japanese could make no headway and gave up the night of 25 and 26 October to haul away their wounded. They retreated back into the jungle, where they had to contend with another vicious enemy: the malaria-carrying mosquito.

The Japanese admiral went to bed hoping, even now, that the army would come through with the capture of Henderson Field. Before dawn of 26 October, Yamamoto was awakened. The report from the navy liaison station on Guadalcanal said, "The army had started its new attack at 10:00 P.M., but because the Nasu force had been decimated, there was no two-pronged attack. The Kawaguchi detachment now attacked frontally and the result was once again failure." [5]

Now the key message came from the chief of staff of the Seventeenth Army on Guadalcanal. It told Yamamoto what he already knew but hated to hear:

> In spite of the wholehearted cooperation of your fleet, our attempt to capture the enemy position at Guadalcanal airfield has failed, for which I am ashamed of myself. Under the present situation, we think we are forced to make a new offensive with more strength on a much larger scale . . . [6]

In response to Roosevelt's 24 October letter to the Joint Chiefs, Admiral King assured him that strong naval forces would meet his request. These included twelve submarines from MacArthur's area. General Marshall agreed to send more infantry but pointed out that the effectiveness of ground troops depended upon the ability to transport them to and maintain them in the combat area. This was the main problem for the Japanese as well. Like Vandegrift, Yamamoto considered Henderson Field the key to winning the battle for the island itself. To Yamamoto's disadvantage, the Cactus Air Force severely limited his ability to send reinforcements and supplies to his troops during daylight hours. This inability to supply the troops would cause the Japanese to refer to Guadalcanal as Starvation Island.

Total U.S. Army air strength in the South Pacific then consisted of 46 heavy bombers, 27 medium bombers, and 133 fighters; 23 heavy bombers were being flown and 53 fighters shipped from Hawaii to meet the emergency. Marshall directed MacArthur to furnish bomber reinforcements and P-38 replacement parts to the South Pacific.

At Truk, Yamamoto came under severe pressure. He had ordered a liaison mission back to Tokyo to tell Imperial General Headquarters his views on the seriousness of the Guadalcanal situation. He said the outcome of the war might depend on it. He claimed victory at the Battle of Santa Cruz, but on 29 October Emperor Hirohito indicated his strong feelings about the events on Guadalcanal so that the sailors and soldiers of Japan would know them:

> The Combined Fleet did great damage to the enemy fleet in the South Pacific. I commend this deeply. However, the situation in that area is still grave, so you shall make double efforts.
>
> What I would like to add on this occasion concerns the latter part of the Imperial Rescript. As Guadalcanal is the place of bitter struggle and is also an important base for the Navy, I wish you would make efforts to recapture it swiftly without being satisfied with the success at this time.[7]

Yamamoto replied, "We are deeply impressed with Your Majesty's gracious words. In view of the current grave situation, we, officers and men, will make further efforts and pledge ourselves to meet Your Majesty's wishes."[8]

To make matters worse, Nagumo's force picked up an American flyer who told them about the future. When asked about American carriers he named *Langley, Lexington, Saratoga, Ranger, Yorktown, Enterprise, Wasp, Hornet, Essex,* and *Bonhomme Richard.* Yamamoto had never heard of most of these. The American war machine was beginning to appear as another Hydra, the ancient mythical monster with twelve heads. Each time you cut off one head, two grew back in its place. Vice Admiral Matome Ugaki said in despair, "The enemy builds and christens second- and third-generation carriers as quickly as we destroy them."[9]

By November 1942, the American public—being unaware of the true situation—had become agitated with the progress of the war. The news media claimed the battle for Guadalcanal was still very much in doubt, and this was an island no American had heard of before the war. Ships were being sunk, and

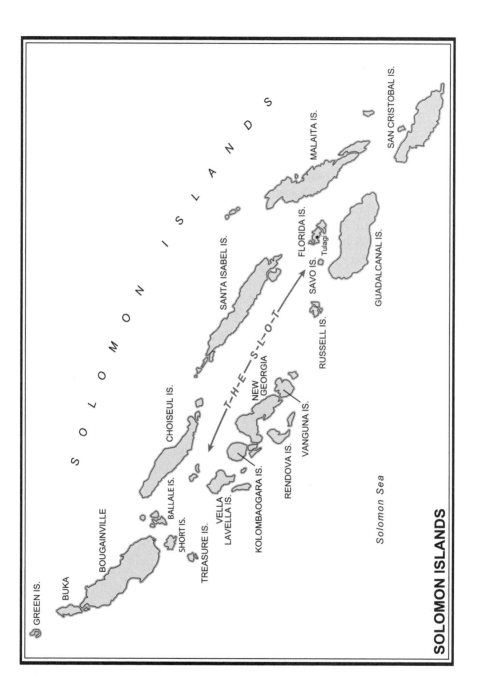

SOLOMON ISLANDS

men were being killed, which made the average citizen feel the United States was in for a long, costly, protracted war.

American soldiers had yet to face the Nazi enemy. Although the invasion of North Africa was scheduled for 1 November 1942, three days before Election Day, for pure military reasons, it was delayed until 8 November. Roosevelt was most anxious for this invasion to be made as scheduled, because he knew it would give his party a tremendous boost in the upcoming election. However, he did not complain to the Joint Chiefs for the change in timing. The public showed its antagonism when it went to the polls on 3 November. The result was disastrous for the Democrats and dangerous for the Roosevelt administration. The party lost fifty seats in the House and eight in the Senate.

The public did not realize that the Japanese, especially Admiral Yamamoto, considered the battle for Guadalcanal as the fork in the road in the Pacific War. Daily, Japanese ships and planes bombed Henderson Field. Under the tutelage of Cmdr. Joseph P. Blundon, the Seabees developed bomb damage repair into a science. "One hundred Seabees could repair the damage of a 500-pound bomb hit on the airstrip in forty minutes, including replacing the Marston mat. In other words, forty minutes after the bomb exploded, you couldn't tell the airstrip had ever been hit." [10]

Blundon claimed that in the twenty-four-hour period between 13 and 14 October, fifty-three bombs and shells hit Henderson airstrip. During one hour on 14 October the Seabees filled thirteen bomb craters while U.S. planes circled overhead waiting to land. "Because there were not enough shovels to go around, some men used their helmets to scoop up earth and carry it to the bomb craters. In the period from 1 September through 18 November there were 140 Japanese raids in which Henderson Field was hit at least once." [11]

According to Blundon, "Our worst moments were when the (Japanese) bomb or shell failed to explode when it hit. It still tore up our mat, and it had to come out. When you see men choke down their fear and dive in after an unexploded bomb so that our planes can land safely, a lump comes in your throat and you know why America wins wars." [12]

The Seabees built an emergency strip about two hundred feet from Henderson Field and running parallel to it. It was a rough strip with rolled-down grass and filled-in depressions, but it was one that could be used when holes were being filled on the main airstrip. [13]

On 8 November, Halsey paid a visit to Archie Vandegrift. The two toured the entire defensive perimeter and Halsey stopped several times to talk to the men. In a meeting at Vandegrift's headquarters, he was asked by war correspondents to explain his strategy. He replied, "To kill Japs, kill Japs, and keep on killing Japs." [14] That night a Japanese ship shelled Henderson Field. Having joined the men in a dugout, Halsey got a good idea about daily life for the marines on the island. Vandegrift acknowledged that Halsey's visit was "like a wonderful breath of fresh air." [15]

Halsey and Yamamoto each viewed the events of the week of 10 November through 14 November 1942 as crucial to both sides. Each knew that he needed to bring numerous fresh troops and supplies to Guadalcanal in order to win the land battle. Heretofore the Japanese had adopted a tactic of moving troops and barges by hiding during the day and traveling by night. Vandegrift knew that the enemy was building up forces against him, as Japanese ships were running along his shores almost every night shelling Henderson Field.

To tip the balance in favor of the Americans, Halsey ordered troops and supplies from Espiritu Santo and New Caledonia to be delivered to Guadalcanal under the command of Rear Admiral Turner. Turner divided his force again into three groups. One, a transport group under his own direct command, moving out of Noumea to Guadalcanal with reinforcements and supplies, was to be covered by a second, under Rear Adm. Daniel J. Callaghan, operating from Espiritu Santo. The third, under Rear Adm. Norman Scott, was to bring three transports from Espiritu Santo to Guadalcanal.

On 8 November, Turner's four transports, escorted by two of Callaghan's cruisers and three of his destroyers, stood out from Noumea and rendezvoused with the rest of Callaghan's warships off San Cristobal on 11 November. Meanwhile, closely guarding three transports, Scott arrived off Guadalcanal the morning of 12 November, where he linked with Callaghan and Turner. Dawn of that day found all transports busily unloading at Lunga Point guarded by warships offshore. Having received news that a fresh Japanese fleet was heading his way, Turner was anxious to get the seven transports emptied and away as soon as possible. Some twenty-five Japanese torpedo bombers interrupted the unloading near the middle of the afternoon. Callaghan's flagship—the cruiser *San Francisco*—and the destroyer *Buchanan* were both hit, but not sunk; yet no transport was damaged. Planes from Henderson Field, along with anti-aircraft weapons, shot down most of the enemy attackers. This allowed unloading to continue until near dusk.

Turner assessed the Japanese naval force as two battleships, two to four heavy cruisers, and ten to twelve destroyers. These were obviously intent on destroying ships, bombarding the airfield, or both. Turner, anxious not to be caught, cut short his unloading at the end of the day and sent his transports out of the danger area under a close escort. This left Callaghan and Scott to defend against the approaching Japanese fleet. Callaghan determined to protect the island from enemy bombardment by taking Scott, with the latter's flagship *Atlanta* and two of his destroyers, under his command. His force consisted of two heavy and three light cruisers and eight destroyers.

Headed toward Savo, Callaghan located the Japanese ships at 1:24 A.M. between Savo and Cape Esperance, but his radar was not strong enough to definitely find the position either of his own scattered forces or those of his enemies. Vice Admiral Nobutake Kondo, the Japanese overall commander of naval forces, opposed Callaghan. He had sent Vice Adm. Hiroaki Abe out from Truk on 9 November with the battleships *Hiyei* and *Kirishima* screened by light forces. Abe subsequently rendezvoused with more destroyers that put out from the Shortlands on 11 November. His mission was to shell Henderson Field. His fleet consisted of the two battleships, the light cruiser *Nagara*, and fourteen destroyers when he met Callaghan. The battle quickly became a naval free-for-all, with friend often not knowing foe across the dark waters. Both Callaghan and Scott were killed. Although the Americans were badly handled, Abe gave up his attempt to shell Henderson Field.

The new day exposed crippled ships of both sides between Savo and Guadalcanal. These still struck dying blows at one another. Among them was a stricken Japanese battleship. American airmen kept at her during the day and, when night came, her crew scuttled her. Limping away from the battle scene where she had been severely damaged, the American cruiser *Juneau* was again torpedoed about 11:00 A.M. by a Japanese submarine. She sank at the base of a great pillar of smoke with all but ten of her crew.

Five Sullivan brothers were lost with *Juneau*. Weeks later the American public was shocked and appalled to learn that the U.S. Navy had permitted five brothers to serve and die together on one ship. The U.S. Navy had adopted an advisory policy to prevent brothers from serving aboard the same ship, but the policy did not have the force and effect of a command. Hollywood made a movie of the Sullivans before the war ended.

Twelve of the thirteen American ships that had been engaged were sunk or damaged. The cruisers *Atlanta* and *Juneau* had gone down, together with four destroyers. The heavy cruisers *San Francisco* and *Portland*, with three destroyers, were seriously damaged. With two remaining ships, they made for Espiritu Santo after the battle. The Japanese lost the battleship *Hiyei* and two destroyers and had four destroyers damaged. Although numerically the Japanese fared better and lost far fewer men than the Americans, they failed in their objective to put Henderson Field out of action. More importantly, they failed to prevent the arrival of heavy reinforcements. Halsey's pledge to Vandegrift to give him everything he had in spite of the risk had paid big dividends for the Guadalcanal defenders.

Admiral Kondo had planned to follow up Abe's initial attack on Henderson Field with blows from Vice Adm. Gunichi Mikawa the following night. Mikawa commanded four heavy cruisers (*Chokai, Kinugasa, Suzuya,* and *Maya*), two light cruisers (*Isuzu* and *Tenryu*), and six destroyers. Admiral Kondo saw no reason to change his orders to Mikawa simply because Abe had failed. With Callaghan and Scott dead, their forces broken, and Kinkaid and Lee far to the south, there was little to hinder Mikawa when he arrived off Savo soon after midnight on 13 November. Peeling a patrol group off to westward under his own command, Mikawa sent Rear Adm. Shoji Nishimura to drench Henderson Field with high explosive. This lasted for thirty-seven minutes.

Back in Washington it was still the morning of Friday the thirteenth. Everyone hoped that Callaghan's sacrifice had stopped the enemy. They were shocked to hear that heavy Japanese surface forces were shelling Henderson Field. When, a few hours later, word came that Japanese transports were heading down the Slot unopposed, even President Roosevelt began to think that Guadalcanal might have to be evacuated. "The tension that I felt at that time," Secretary Forrestal wrote, "was matched only by the tension that pervaded Washington the night before the landing in Normandy." [16]

Early on 14 November, aircraft reported more fighting ships and some transports headed for Guadalcanal, with Mikawa's retiring support group some 140 miles northwest. American aircraft from Henderson Field then attacked Mikawa. They left *Kinugasa* burning and *Isuzu* smoking heavily. Shortly before ten o'clock, aircraft from *Enterprise* joined in to sink *Kinugasa*. Before Mikawa got clear, he also suffered damage to *Chokai*, *Maya*, and a destroyer.

Unwittingly Mikawa had served as a decoy to draw attention from Rear Adm. Raizo Tanaka's Reinforcement Group—eleven merchantmen escorted by eleven destroyers. Tanaka, obedient to Kondo's orders for the third phase of his plan, was bringing these down to Guadalcanal heavily laden with reinforcements. He had led them out from the Shortlands on 12 November. Sensibly, he had sheltered on 13 November in preparation for a dash on 14 November to enable him to discharge his troops under cover of darkness that night. But this was not to be. Henderson Field, despite all Kondo's planning, was still very much alive; Kinkaid's carrier-borne aircraft fanned in from the south, as aircraft from Espiritu Santo joined in. By the end of the day, seven of the eleven Japanese transports had been sunk, together with all personnel and supplies aboard. The four remaining transports arrived at Guadalcanal but were sunk by American planes after personnel came ashore but before the ships could be unloaded. This destroyed Yamamoto's dream of winning the Guadalcanal campaign. Halsey clearly held all the trump cards for any further land combat. The plight of the ill-supplied Japanese troops on the island caused the high command to make a very unwise decision. Submarines were ordered to bring food to Guadalcanal. This eliminated them as an attack weapon, and they were an inefficient means of supply.

On 19 November, a company of U.S. Marines patrolling eastward engaged a Japanese patrol. From examination of the well-fed Japanese dead, it was clear that they were newcomers to the island. Vandegrift decided that they were the spearhead of the counterattacking force he had been expecting. As he prepared on 20 November to meet the shock, he was cheered by the arrival at Henderson Field of marine aircraft—No. 223 Squadron (Wildcat fighters) and No. 232 Squadron (Douglas dive-bombers)—which had been catapulted in from an escort carrier. That night, concentrated enemy activity was reported from the perimeter at the Ilu. At 3:10 A.M. on 21 November, Japanese attacked across the sandbar at the river's mouth. By the time light came, however, the attacking force had been almost completely annihilated.

By the end of November, the Cactus Air Force was called upon less and less to defend Henderson Field and more and more to mount strikes against Japanese bases along the Slot. The 2nd Marine Division plus the U.S. Army's Americal Division (Infantry) had arrived. A third army division would come ashore in December, making it possible to relieve the 1st Marine Division on 9 December. With the beefing up of the Cactus Air Force, Yamamoto was faced with an almost impossible task of supplying his troops. The sea and air around Guadalcanal, day and night, had become Allied sea and air, and the Japanese risked everything when they came near. On 27 November 1942, Halsey was sworn in as a four-star admiral. Commenting in the 30 November 1942 issue of *Time* magazine, which carried Halsey's picture on the cover, Admiral Nimitz said:

Halsey's conduct of his present command leaves nothing to be desired. He is professionally competent and militarily aggressive without being reckless or foolhardy. He has that rare combination of intellectual capacity and operations when successful accomplishments will bring great returns. He possesses superb leadership qualities which have earned him a tremendous following of his men. His only enemies are Japs.[17]

By December, the Japanese situation on Guadalcanal was desperate. Only half were capable of fighting. The rest were suffering from beriberi or malaria, and men were dropping off at an alarming rate. Supplies came in by trickle, and many units had none at all. The commanders at Rabaul all agreed with Admiral Yamamoto and his staff that it was time to do something drastic. Yamamoto sent two staff officers to Tokyo to recommend most strongly that the Guadal-canal position be evacuated as quickly as possible and the whole operation in the South Pacific be turned to defense for the moment. Now all they could do was wait for the orders to come to the rescue of the troops left.

By the end of December, the Japanese commanders at Rabaul and Truk recognized that the situation on Guadalcanal was hopeless. Finally, on 3 January, Vice Admiral Shigeru Fukudome, chief of the operations bureau of the Naval General Staff, arrived at Truk. "General Imamura's people arrived from Rabaul. And there, on the flagship, the decision was made: Guadalcanal was to be evacuated and the major effort of army and navy was first the capture of Port Moresby and second the recapture of Guadalcanal. No timetable was set for the latter. Admiral Yamamoto assembled his destroyers and, on 1 February 1943, the evacuation of the troops from Guadalcanal began." [18]

During December 1942 and January and February 1943, Maj. Gen. Alexander Patch, U.S. Army, conducted an essentially offensive campaign to the inevitable conclusion, fighting a slow conventional battle of attrition, break-through, and pursuit, while in February the Japanese were intent on escaping from the island. By concealing his ships' movements to night only, Yamamoto managed to evacuate 13,000 of the more than 50,000 ground troops that Japan had committed to the Guadalcanal land battle. Approximately 25,000 Japanese soldiers had died on the island itself, 9,000 as a result of malaria, dengue, and starvation. Others died at sea en route to and from the island.[19]

Admiral Halsey's willingness to risk his ships gave the Americans control of land, sea, and air in the lower Solomons. In the six-month period beginning 7 August 1942, both navies lost twenty-six warships of about equal tonnage. Neither had the ships to lose, but the Japanese could not replace their losses, while the awakening American arsenals could. The

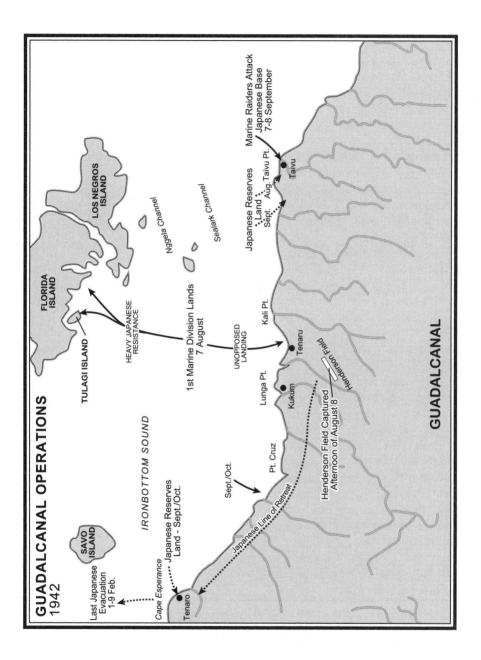

GUADALCANAL OPERATIONS
1942

SAVO ISLAND

IRONBOTTOM SOUND

Last Japanese
Evacuation
1-9 Feb.

Cape Esperance

Japanese Reserves
Land - Sept./Oct.

Tenaro

Japanese Line of Retreat

Sept./Oct.

Pt. Cruz

Lunga Pt.

Kukum

Henderson Field Captured
Afternoon of August 8

Henderson Field

Tenaru

Kali Pt.

UNOPPOSED
LANDING

1st Marine Division Lands
7 August

HEAVY JAPANESE
RESISTANCE

TULAGI ISLAND

FLORIDA
ISLAND

LOS NEGROS
ISLAND

Nggela Channel

Sealark Channel

Japanese Reserves
Land Aug. Taivu Pt.
Sept.

Taivu

Marine Raiders Attack
Japanese Base
7-8 September

GUADALCANAL

Japanese air arm lost 600 well-trained carrier and ground-based aircrews that could not be readily replaced.

For many reasons, during the remainder of the war, the U.S. Pacific Fleet would not lose or break even in any further encounters with the Japanese. United States Navy officers experienced an enhanced learning curve. American ships possessed better radar. The American air arm, both army and navy, would be superior to that of Japan. The United States' improvement in planes of all types made them superior to Japanese aircraft, and U.S. aircrews were far better trained. Numerous American air pilots became aces in short order. Due to the shortage of oil, Japan could not afford to give its aircrews nearly as much time in training as that received by the average American airman. "After Japan's stunning initial victories, its weaknesses in aircraft design and pilot output would lead quite quickly to a decline in its ability to wage carrier warfare on equal terms with the United States." [20] The combination of ULTRA and the addition to the Pacific Fleet of more and larger aircraft carriers of the Essex class placed the Japanese navy at a decided disadvantage in future encounters with the Americans.

The battle for Guadalcanal also became a proving stage for ground troops in future engagements with the Japanese. Marines learned better tactics, which weapons performed best, how to fight diseases little known in the States, and how to send secret messages under combat conditions. By June 1943, the commanding general of the 1st Marine Amphibious Corps recommended to the U.S. Marine Corps commandant that each division's table of organization should include 100 Navajo code talkers. In time, some 375 to 420 Navajo code talkers served in the six U.S. Marine divisions.[21]

When the 1st Marine Division retired to Australia, General Marshall made arrangements to have Lt. Col. "Chesty" Puller returned to the States for a speaking tour. He remembered Puller from Fort Benning days. Marshall knew he needed to dispel the myth of the invincible Japanese soldier created during the first few months of the Pacific War. Puller, with a few other veterans of Guadalcanal, made a six-week tour of U.S. Army reservations where divisions were being trained for Pacific duty. After the end of the tour, Marshall sent a letter to marine Commandant Thomas Holcomb: "I wanted you to know of the very excellent impression that [Puller] has made on all of the officers with whom he has come in contact." [22] Indeed, Marshall could not have picked a better man to inform the individual infantrymen heading for battle against the Japanese.

Veterans of Guadalcanal visited marines of the 3rd Marine Division being trained in New Zealand. In telling what to expect in jungle fighting in the Solomons, some warned:

> You've got to know how to read a map and rely on your compass when traveling in the jungle; otherwise, you'll travel in circles and get lost every time . . . Don't try to act brave at the expense of taking necessary caution . . . Dig a foxhole everywhere you go . . . In a foxhole, a shell won't kill you unless it lands right on top of you, and that's unlikely . . . Unless you

take your atabrine every day, you'll come down with malaria for sure . . . Don't worry about the rain. In the hot weather, you dry off quickly . . . In spite of the fact that the temperature stays in the mid 90s during the day, it cools off enough at night so that sleep comes easy . . . The Japanese are good at camouflage and like to come at you at night. The jungle is noisy at night with all sorts of sounds from tree frogs, crickets, or whatever. When these little creatures go silent, you know there is somebody out there. Stay in your foxhole. That way, even though the Jap is a much smaller man he's a much bigger target than you are . . . Stay in good shape physically. Chances of survival are much better . . . Remember, three times more are wounded and survive than those killed.[23]

This information came in handy in the days ahead.

As the Guadalcanal campaign ended, the United States and Japan experienced a role reversal from the early days of fighting. For the remainder of the Pacific War, Japan would be on the defensive. In General Marshall's Biennial Report to the Secretary of War, he said, "The highly prized airfield on Guadalcanal was held by the marines against a long series of heavy air, sea, and ground assaults by the enemy. The resolute defense of these marines under Major General (now Lieutenant General) Alexander A. Vandegrift and the desperate gallantry of our naval task forces marked the turning point in the Pacific." [24]

Had Admiral Yamamoto survived the war, he probably would have agreed with Marshall.

Chapter 12
Papua

*T*HE ISLAND OF NEW GUINEA is the second largest in the world, in area twice the size of California. Prior to the war, the Netherlands claimed the western half. Beginning in 1905, the commonwealth of Australia administered the territory of Papua, formerly known as British New Guinea. After World War I, the remainder of the eastern half of the island was mandated to Australia. As the crow flies, the island is approximately 1,500 miles long. In November 1942, the Japanese occupied strongpoints on the northern coast of Papua, together with a few along the northern coast to the Netherlands New Guinea.

Thick jungles plus the high mountains of the Owen Stanley Range kept development to a minimum. With no east-west or north-south roads, only foot trails; Australian mineral prospectors traveled in small planes before the Japanese arrived. Thus, there were numerous rudimentary landing strips throughout the land area administered by the Australians.

Most of the native population lived under primitive conditions. Education lay in the hands of a few scattered church missions. In 1942, Port Moresby, the largest town in Papua, had a non-indigenous population—other than military—of about 3,000. There were a few coconut plantations on the northern coast, plus about ten large plantations within easy reach of Port Moresby.

In the first year of the war, the Joint Chiefs of Staff determined to halt Japan's advance in the Pacific while developing the foundation for a counterattack. MacArthur never changed his focus for a return to the Philippines. But since the war in the Pacific was a war over water, no offensive could begin anywhere until the U.S. Navy had scored strategic victories in the Coral Sea and at Midway.

By July 1942, MacArthur turned his attention to Buna, a mission station on the northern coast of Papua. He proposed to seize the village and construct airfields as a first move toward the eventual capture of Rabaul. He ignored

137

warnings from naval intelligence that the Japanese also planned to take Buna as a base for an overland assault against Port Moresby. Accordingly, the Japanese got there first.

After the Australians blocked General Hori's Japanese forces, which were recalled back over the Owen Stanleys to Buna, the Australians pursued Hori's retreat. By the end of October 1942, American infantry had not been engaged in battle with the Japanese, although U.S. engineers under Maj. Gen. Hugh J. Casey had performed admirably in the preparation of airfields and other facilities in Papua, including those at Milne Bay.

Engineer/contractor Leif Sverdrup, also known as Jack Sverdrup, joined General Casey's command in Australia. Born in 1898 on the island of Outer Sellen off the coast of Norway, he came to America at age sixteen. He graduated from Augsburg College in Minnesota and, in 1918, he enlisted as a private in the U.S. Army, becoming a U.S. citizen in September of that year. In April 1942, he accepted an offer to become a colonel in the U.S. Army Corps of Engineers. Upon joining Maj. Gen. Hugh J. Casey's command, he was assigned the duty of constructing airfields in Papua capable of handling U.S. transport planes. While Australians did the ground fighting, American engineers contributed to their success by the construction of runways at Port Moresby, Milne Bay, and other key places in Papua.

To carry out his mission, Sverdrup made contact with two persons who proved to be valuable allies. One, a missionary named Cecil Abel, owned a plantation north of the Owen Stanleys. The other, a gold prospector named Michael J. Leahy, had hunted for ore in the jungle of New Guinea since the early 1930s, and knew the backcountry as no other white man did. Both men had long ties in dealing with the natives. With their help in recruitment, Sverdrup constructed suitable landing strips at Dobadura, Embessa, Pongani, and Fasari with hundreds of native laborers plus C Company of the U.S. 114th Engineer Battalion. The Dobadura airstrip became especially valuable since it lay only ten miles southeast of Buna and was used extensively after the Japanese had been removed from the area.

In his postwar book, *General Kenney Reports*, author George C. Kenney wrote:

> An engineer colonel by the name of Jack Sverdrup, a tall blond rein-carnation of Leif Ericson . . . was in charge of finding and preparing landing fields between Wanigela and Buna. He had already located and prepared six strips along that route and this had immensely facilitated the airborne movement. For some reason or other, Sverdrup had worked miracles with the natives, who seemed to be willing to work harder and longer hours for him than anyone else.[1]

For one thing, Sverdrup knew how to make in-kind payments that were most appreciated. For their services in building the airfields near Buna, Sverdrup paid the natives "1,500 lbs. of trading tobacco, 50 bolts of cloth, 1,000 Boy Scout knives, 50 cases of canned meat, 200 lbs. of salt, 1,000 tin-plate bowls, 1,000 spoons, and 1,000 packages of garden seed." [2]

In late October, Blamey proposed to fly elements of Maj. Gen. Edwin F. Harding's U.S. 32nd Division to Pongani Air Field on Papua's north coast, about twenty-five miles east of Buna. MacArthur turned him down. Some days after learning of the heavy losses sustained by the Japanese at Guadalcanal in late October, MacArthur reconsidered. However, the battle for Guadalcanal was still very much in doubt. In early November, MacArthur moved from the Lennox Hotel in Brisbane to Government House at Port Moresby, still 100 miles from the battlefront. His communiqué announced: "The Supreme Commander has taken to the field." [3] By mid-November, the battle to dislodge the enemy from the north coast of Papua began in earnest.

The Japanese occupied defensive positions along the northern coast at Buna village and mission, Sanananda, and Gona. Along the northern coast of New Guinea, all three concentrations of enemy forces were in easy range of naval gunfire, which was not used to reduce the strength of the Japanese. The attack plan called for the Australian 25th Brigade to advance on Gona, the 16th Infantry Brigade of the Australian 7th Division to descend upon Sanananda, and the U.S. 32nd Infantry Division to move on Buna. The troops of the 32nd were ill-prepared for the fight ahead.

The 32nd Infantry Division was formerly a Michigan and Wisconsin National Guard unit and, as late as December 1941, had been earmarked for duty in the European theater. Major General Edwin F. Harding joined as division commander in February 1942. The division was ordered to Fort Devens, Massachusetts, in late February with instructions to prepare for immediate movement to Northern Ireland. Orders were changed and, on 14 May, it reached Adelaide, Australia. Training had scarcely gotten under way when the division was ordered to move again, this time to Brisbane. The move was completed in mid-August and, before the training got into stride again, the first troops were moved to New Guinea. To make matters worse, the main emphasis of its training had been on the defense of Australia, primarily garrison duty. Before going into battle, the men had received very little instruction in jungle combat and, in this first taste of battle, few if any of the officers had experience.

As yet, the Allies had not broken the Japanese army codes, leaving intelligence information concerning enemy ground troops much less than desired. Brigadier General Charles Willoughby, MacArthur's G-2, prepared an estimate of the situation that caused Harding to expect only a small enemy force at the mission village. On 19 November the 32nd Infantry Division made its initial attack. The dug-in and well-camouflaged Japanese poured rifle and machine gun fire into American troops with impunity. The result was total disaster.

In the days that followed, Harding asked for Bren carriers with mounted guns. His request was denied. Airdrops supplying food and other supplies proved quite unsatisfactory. With no atabrine, only a little quinine, and inadequate food, sickness—especially malaria—became a more formidable enemy than the Japanese. Morale among the troops plummeted. Two weeks after the initial assault, the 32nd Infantry Division had not moved forward from its starting point.

Harding wrote that the troops were half starved. Most had been living on short rations for weeks and, since the fighting began, had averaged about a third of a C-ration per day, just enough to sustain life. Most of the men had very little tentage to protect themselves from the heavy rains. The majority became afflicted with malaria or dysentery. Most frustrating of all to Harding's command was the realization that he did not have the proper weapons to reduce the enemy bunkers that stood in his way—no tanks, grenade launchers, or flamethrowers and little heavy artillery.

General Blamey complained to MacArthur with justification that American troops were fighting badly and that some had even thrown away their machine guns and fled in panic. Thoroughly dissatisfied from these reports of the 32nd Infantry Division's performance, MacArthur blamed Harding. He called Lt. Gen. Robert L. Eichelberger forward to Port Moresby and ordered him to relieve Harding and take command at Buna. Upon the latter's arrival on 1 December MacArthur said, "Bob, I want you to go out there and take Buna or don't come back alive." [4] In so doing, he promised Eichelberger that he would make him a very prominent figure in the United States if he achieved victory.

Eichelberger met Harding at Dobadura Air Field. He found that disease and casualties had greatly thinned the Allied ranks. In Harding's defense, he had been expected to dislodge the enemy without the use of proper weapons, and the enemy numbered many times what he had been told. Eichelberger forthwith relieved Harding and most of his top-ranking officers of their commands. Nevertheless, it was impossible for Eichelberger to perform miracles overnight with the 32nd Infantry Division. He found it necessary to halt all attacks in order to effect an orderly chain of command. In the meantime, forty tons of much needed food, medicine, and ammunition arrived.

Maps with sufficient detail can be very important tools in the hands of a military commander. Eichelberger was given two maps, both lacking such detail as to be of any appreciable military value. One map showed footpaths, Jeep trails, and native villages with the disclaimer, "This map is based on the best available services but is not based on military surveys." A second map showed the texture of the landscape. The entire area is a combination of deep forest, dense jungles, mangrove swamps, swamps, and kunai grass, with no roads, only foot and Jeep tracks. This map had the same disclaimer as the first.[5]

On 5 December, Eichelberger ordered his first general assault, which produced heavy casualties with practically no gains. Being a quick learner, Eichelberger recognized that an assault against an unseen enemy, especially one against a well-entrenched foe, was tantamount to suicide. He realized you must first know the enemy's whereabouts and have the heavy weapons available to reduce its strength before moving in foot soldiers. After first making great improvements in the supply situation—including the arrival of the Bren carriers—Eichelberger began his campaign to eliminate the enemy. By the steady use of reconnaissance patrols, he pinpointed the primary enemy fortifications.

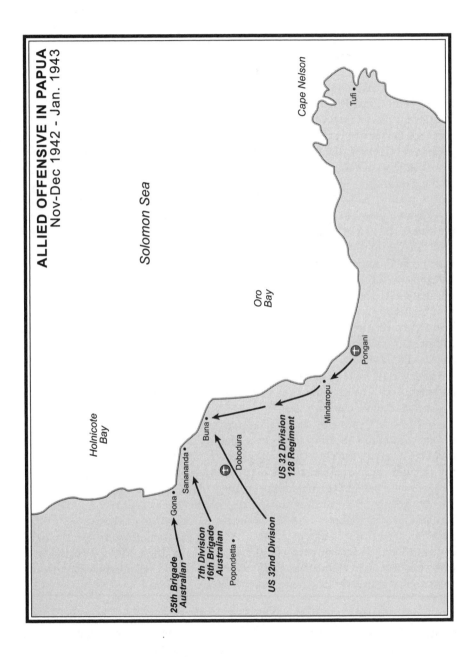

ALLIED OFFENSIVE IN PAPUA
Nov-Dec 1942 - Jan. 1943

Solomon Sea

Cape Nelson

Tufi

Oro
Bay

Pongani

Mindaropu

Holnicote
Bay

Gona

Sanananda

Buna

Dobodura

US 32 Division
128 Regiment

Popondetta

25th Brigade
Australian

7th Division
16th Brigade
Australian

US 32nd Division

He then concentrated mortar and artillery fire against them before moving in his infantry. Even so, dislodging the Japanese was a slow process.

Nearby, the Australians hammered at the defenses around Buna village, which caused the Japanese to evacuate the night of 13 and 14 December. By mid-December, Gona fell to the Australians, which allowed Brig. George Wootten's Australian 18th Brigade to come to the aid of the 32nd Infantry Division. On 27 December, the 163rd Infantry Regiment of the U.S. 41st Division arrived in Port Moresby. MacArthur conveyed orders to General Blamey that the regiment be sent to Buna rather than to the previously planned Sanananda front. Blamey immediately protested. He insisted that the Australian 21st Brigade be removed immediately if it was to continue as a fighting force. He expressed his regret that General MacArthur had taken it upon himself to interfere.

Blamey wrote that while he did not "for one moment question the right of the Commander-in-Chief to give such orders as he may think fit," he said nothing could be "more contrary to sound principles of command than that the Commander-in-Chief . . . should (personally) take over the direction of a portion of the battle." [6] MacArthur saw the point, although his communiqués to the United States would lead the reader to believe that he, rather than Blamey, was the field commander. The 163rd Infantry Division was flown to Dobadura and moved to the Sanananda front. A few days later, on 2 January 1943, Buna mission fell to the Allies.

MacArthur issued a communiqué announcing the Buna victory as if he had been there himself. He thereby embarked on an impressive public relations campaign that continued throughout the remainder of the war. His command could achieve victory with minimum casualties. He declared that "no campaign in history" had achieved such decisive results "with so low an expenditure of life and resources." [7] Yet, of the approximately 33,000 Allied troops in the Buna-Gona-Sanananda campaign, some 8,546 were combat casualties and 3,095 died. The death rate was three times greater than at Guadalcanal for ground troops, although U.S. Navy losses exceeded by far those for the Marines Corps and U.S. Army in the Guadalcanal campaign. The official U.S. Army history of the Papuan campaign concluded that "the victory there, proportionate to the forces engaged, had been one of the costliest of the Pacific war." [8]

MacArthur made no mention of the numerous casualties sustained as a result of malaria and other tropical diseases. Debilitating sickness caused more than twice the number of troops removed from the battlefront as did the listed dead and wounded. Fortunately for the Allies, the Japanese suffered much worse from malaria and malnutrition. In reference to the Buna-Gona-Sanananda campaign, Australian historian Dudley McCarthy noted:

> The Japanese at Sanananda performed a remarkable feat. Far in advance of their own main base, their line of supply never more than a thin and wavering one and for the last month almost non-existent, starving, sick, short of almost every physical and warlike need, the larger part of them exhausted from their struggles in the mountains, they held

the Australians and Americans in almost baffled impotence for some time and inflicted on them well over 2,000 casualties in battle.[9]

Eichelberger, in a letter to "Miss Em," his wife, bitterly resented the premature victory communiqué: "General MacArthur announced his return to Australia by saying that there was nothing left in Papua but some 'mopping up' at Sanananda. This was just an excuse to get home as at that time there was no indication of any crackup of the Japs at Sanananda." Biographer D. Clayton James observed, "that despite the fact that Allied casualties at Sanananda were nearly 3500, about 700 more than in the Buna operation, MacArthur's communiqué and subsequent press releases on the fall of the Buna area were more widely broadcast in the newspapers of Allied nations, and the Sanananda operation continued to be generally regarded as merely a mopping-up activity." [10]

"After the appearance of flattering articles about him in magazines such as *Life* and *Saturday Evening Post*, Eichelberger stated, General MacArthur sent for me . . . He said, 'Do you realize I could reduce you to the grade of colonel tomorrow and send you home?' Eichelberger answered, 'Of course you could.' MacArthur responded, 'Well, I won't do it.' " [11]

Later Eichelberger told his brother, "I went through many unhappy months because of the publicity that came out about me after Buna. I paid through the nose for every line of it . . . While I realize that publicity is the thing that brings one in the eyes of the people, it also may prove more dangerous than a Japanese bullet." [12]

With the assured defeat of the Japanese at Guadalcanal, and the forward progress of Australian and American troops in Papua, MacArthur's outlook brightened on his obsession of returning to the Philippines. On 27 December 1942, he used the Brisbane submarine *Gudeon* to transport Maj. Jesus Villamor plus six other Filipinos together with a ton of military supplies to aid guerrilla groups in the Philippines. Previously the Allied Intelligence Bureau had established a subsection to "aid and organize" guerrillas. Earlier in December, MacArthur had dispatched a group to the islands to set up an intelligence organization.[13]

In early January 1943, MacArthur made a personal relations faux pas in dealing with the location of the 1st Marine Division. Having been transferred to his Southwest Pacific Command during the month of December 1942, the marines were assigned to an abandoned camp forty-five miles from Brisbane. Vandegrift had been assured that the site was free of malaria. This fact was important because a large percentage of Vandegrift's marines were so infected. It was soon learned from the 1st Division surgeon that the camp was in the midst of the same kind of malaria-bearing mosquito as the men encountered on Guadalcanal. The director of Queensland Health Service concurred with the marine surgeon's findings.

Vandegrift dispatched officers to locate a more salubrious climate, which they found at Melbourne. Although he approved the move, MacArthur refused to provide transportation. He claimed that, "the already overburdened railroad facilities of Australia cannot cope with such a movement without jeopardizing operations upon which our forces are now engaged." [14]

Vandegrift prevailed upon Admiral Halsey to provide the ships to transport the division to a location thirty-five miles outside Melbourne where, upon arrival, almost 7,500 marines were hospital cases. In time, news of this incident spread to other marine divisions in the South Pacific. The marines did not believe that MacArthur's command lacked the facilities for the appropriate transportation, and most were upset that the health of the individual marine had such a low priority with the Southwest Pacific Command.

With the Dobadura Air Field in the hands of the Allies prior to the attack on Buna, and with the advantage of hindsight, the official Australian history observed that the "question arises as to the necessity for the Buna-Sanananda-Gona campaign—whether the Japanese garrison in that area could have been left to 'wither on the vine' as some island garrisons were left later in the war." [15]

At this stage of the war, and throughout the year 1943, the strategy of bypassing enemy strongpoints on the northern coast of New Guinea was apparently not envisioned by MacArthur's headquarters. Except for the Dobadura Air Field, which was never in the hands of the enemy, the Buna-Sanananda-Gona area had little or no strategic value in further battles with the Japanese.

No one in the United States questioned the feasibility of MacArthur's victory at Buna. His daily communiqués played well with the American public and the politicians in Washington. He particularly enthused Roosevelt's enemies. Senator Arthur Vandenberg of Michigan gradually and quietly assumed the unofficial leadership of a MacArthur for President movement, which already had support from many conservative leaders throughout the country. MacArthur continually declared that his Southwest Pacific Command was being starved at the expense of other theaters. His favorable press gave strong support to this claim.

MacArthur's command took a boost when Lt. Gen. Walter Krueger and the first echelon of his Sixth Army headquarters arrived at Brisbane in February. Previously on 11 January MacArthur wired Marshall:

> Experience indicates the necessity for a tactical organization of an American Army. In the absence of such an echelon the burden has been carried by General Headquarters. I recommend the U.S. Third Army under Lieutenant General Walter Krueger, which would provide an able commander and an efficient operating organization. I am especially anxious to have Krueger because of my long and intimate association with him. [16]

Krueger had been MacArthur's war plans chief when the latter was chief of staff. With the selection of Krueger, one questions Brigadier General Chenowyth's judgment when he wrote that MacArthur "was the poorest judge of subordinates I ever knew."

Krueger had a distinguished record. He was born in Flatow, West Prussia, on 28 January 1881, and came to the United States eight years later. He volunteered for duty as an enlisted man in 1898 during the Spanish-American War, becoming a second lieutenant in the regular U.S. Army in 1901. In World War I, he served as chief of the U.S. Tank Corps. In May 1941 until he was ordered to Australia, he was in charge of the Southern Defense Command. He was known throughout the U.S. Army as a skilled tactician and trainer of troops.

Instead of placing the Sixth Army under Blamey, MacArthur created an independent tactical organization, known as the New Britain Force, until July and, thereafter, as the Alamo Force. MacArthur did not give either Krueger or Blamey any reason for this designation.

With the completion of the Papuan campaign, Blamey and his New Guinea Force commander, E. F. Herring, emphasized the complementary nature of air and ground action in further campaign operations. They wrote, "Each forward move of air bases meant an increase in the range of our fighter planes and consequently an increase in the area in which transport planes supplying our troops could be operated. To get airfields further and further forward was thus the dominant aim of both land and air forces." [17] Blamey would next move Allied troops into Australian New Guinea.

With the Papuan campaign at an end, the time had come to relieve the worn-out troops of the Australian 7th and the U.S. 32nd Infantry Divisions. The latter was now a seasoned fighting force that had redeemed itself from its inauspicious beginnings, but the division had paid a heavy price. It is estimated that the division suffered a casualty rate of approximately 90 percent, including more than 7,000 sick.

In March 1943, a year after his arrival, General MacArthur publicly revealed that he no sooner reached Australia than he decided that the key to its defense lay not on the mainland but in New Guinea.

Prime Minister Curtin disagreed. He stated that not until a considerable time after MacArthur's arrival did the general transform his strategy from a defensive one on the mainland to a defense of the mainland from the line of the Owen Stanley Range.

MacArthur insisted, "It was never my intention to defend Australia on the mainland of Australia. That was the plan when I arrived, but to which I never subscribed, and which I immediately changed to a plan to defend Australia in New Guinea." [18] The paper trail seems to support Curtin's position, since it was MacArthur's headquarters' staff that formulated the Petersburg Plan. Nevertheless, from the date of his arrival in Australia to the final year of the war, MacArthur was a man with a mission, and his mission was the liberation of the Philippines. Each step westward along the northern coast of New Guinea carried him closer to his ultimate goal.

By the spring of 1943, the Allies had clearly met the initial objectives set forth by the Combined Chiefs at the Arcadia Conference—that is, contain and reverse the Japanese offensive and save Australia from a possible Japanese invasion. With all of Papua and the lower Solomons in Allied hands and having complete control of the air, the Japanese no longer presented a threat to Australia. With the logistical problem involved in supplying men and materials at such a great distance from the United States, one questions the need for American troops to advance further in this area.

Admiral King recognized that the time had arrived to implement the prewar Plan Orange, which could best be achieved with a unified command in the Pacific under the U.S. Navy. In late March, he, together with his war plans chief, Rear Adm. Charles M. Cooke, advocated placing all of the Solomon Islands under Halsey's jurisdiction. After Marshall strenuously objected, Cooke proposed, "that since the Pacific war 'is and will continue to be a Naval problem as a whole,' the entire Pacific Ocean should constitute a single theater with 'a unified Naval command' headed by Nimitz." [19] Although Cooke was eminently correct in his assessment, Marshall and Arnold were violently opposed to such a plan. In the interest of harmony, King did not press the issue again until 11 June 1943.

On that date, King submitted a proposal to the Joint Chiefs of Staff (JCS) containing three separate recommendations:

1) Invade the Marshalls by 1 November and establish dates for subsequent assaults.
2) Force MacArthur to specify his future operations, including "firm dates," so the JCS could allocate forces between Nimitz and MacArthur.
3) Authorize Nimitz to coordinate and schedule all offensive operations in the Pacific.[20]

The Joint Chiefs tentatively agreed to items 1 and 2, but tabled item 3. Had they adopted this proposal at this early date, it is doubtful that a move to the Philippines would later be deemed necessary. As long as the Joint Chiefs determined to maintain a dual thrust in the Pacific War, one advance across the Central Pacific and the other northwest from Australia to the Philippines, a divided command was militarily justified. President Roosevelt "pointed out that the logistics of the Pacific war represented the greatest single problem and because of the nature of Pacific geography, there could be no single command of all the Allied Forces." [21]

The Joint Chiefs did not seriously consider the issue of a unified command in the Pacific again until the last year of the war.

Chapter 13
Australian
New Guinea

BY THE SPRING OF 1943, American troops in the southwest Pacific were no longer needed to protect Australia, yet this did not change Allied strategy. The Australians were motivated to move west along the northern coast of New Guinea because it eliminated the Japanese from their territory. For MacArthur, the move bought him closer to his ultimate objective in the Pacific War. But at this stage, nothing came easy. The rugged, jungle-covered terrain made construction of landing strips essential for the movement of troops and supplies. The next suitable area for airfields was the valley of the Markham River, where the Vitiaz Strait between New Guinea and New Britain could be controlled. In anticipation of Blamey's move, Sverdrup and Michael Leahy flew from Port Moresby to Bena Bena, west of the entrenched Japanese garrison in the Lae-Salamaua area. They landed at a small, primitive airstrip Leahy had built a decade earlier as a base for his gold explorations. Sverdrup studied the nearby Markham Valley. Later, he constructed an air base on the site selected by the two men.

Blamey planned next to capture Lae and the Markham Valley. Lae would provide a land base to take supplies transported by sea, while the flat Markham Valley could provide an excellent base for an airfield. Once built, Kenney's air force already had the planes to bring in the troops and necessary supplies.

Thanks to ULTRA, during the three days from 2 to 5 March Kenney's air force struck a major blow against the enemy by the destruction of a convoy of eight destroyers and eight transports in the Bismarck Sea. Intelligence sources had given Kenney two weeks' advance notice of the Japanese convoy's route and destination.[1] The Japanese intended to reinforce the port of Lae with troops and materials from Rabaul. Except for four destroyers, which fled northward, by the night of 3 March all of the enemy ships were sunk, sinking, or badly damaged. Because the convoy traveled during daylight hours, the Japanese 51st Division lost almost 3,000 men and all supplies aboard the transports. Many PT boats roamed the waters attacking the remaining crippled ships and sending one to the bottom. Japanese submarines searched the area for survivors. The *I-17* picked up 156 soldiers while *I-26* rescued another 24.[2] Allied bombers returned to finish off two badly damaged destroyers. MacArthur's communiqué proclaimed:

> We have achieved a victory of such completeness as to assume the proportions of a major disaster to the enemy. His entire force has been practically destroyed. His naval component consisted of 22 vessels, comprising 12 transports and 10 warships—cruisers or destroyers. They represented a tonnage estimated at approximately 90,000 tons. They have all been sunk or are sinking. His air coverage for this naval force has been decimated or dispersed, 55 of his planes having been shot out of combat and many others damaged. His ground forces, estimated at probably 15,000, destined to attack in New Guinea, have been sunk or killed almost to the man . . . [3]

MacArthur's favorable publicity caused many Republicans to look upon him as the candidate for president to oppose Roosevelt. In early 1943, the media began speculating on the Republican presidential nominee.

Wendell Willkie and Thomas E. Dewey were the front-runners, although MacArthur was prominently mentioned. In April 1943, Secretary Stimson contributed to a revival of political interest in MacArthur when he restated publicly a long-standing regulation that prohibited a regular army officer from becoming a candidate or accepting election to any political office not held by him when he began active military duty. Hamilton Fish, a New York Republican and vociferous critic of Roosevelt, charged that the statement was aimed at MacArthur. Other congressmen, including Senator Arthur Vandenberg, voiced the opinion that the move "was aimed at keeping MacArthur out of the next presidential campaign." [4]

On 10 April 1943, Vandenberg received a message from MacArthur, which was delivered by a staff officer who had just flown in from Brisbane. The letter expressed gratitude from MacArthur for Vandenberg's friendship and concluded with the statement, "I want you to know the absolute confidence I would feel in your experienced and wise mentorship." [5] In the months following, Vandenberg quietly assumed the unofficial leadership of a MacArthur for President movement. When Willoughby arrived in Washington in June 1943, he met with the senator and, after a long talk, agreed to act as liaison between MacArthur and Vandenberg.

After conferring with a number of influential friends in various parts of the country, Vandenberg formed what he called "our cabinet" to organize the MacArthur for President movement. This group included John Hamilton, a former chairman of the Republican National Committee who was to serve as campaign manager, and Gen. Robert Wood, the former head of the America First isolationists' movement. Wood agreed to act as the chief financial backer. Other group members were Frank Gannett, a conservative Republican publisher of some influential newspapers in the Northeast; Roy Howard, of the Scripps-Howard newspaper syndicate; Kyle Palmer, a reporter for the *Los Angeles Times*; Joseph Pew, Jr., a leading Republican in Pennsylvania; and Col. Robert R. McCormick of the *Chicago Tribune*.

Based on instructions from the Joint Chiefs, MacArthur on 7 May 1943 issued a directive to Blamey's New Guinea Force to seize the Japanese strongpoints of Lae, Salamaua, Finschhafen, and Madang in 1943. Describing the direction of attack, the instructions stated that the general lines of attack by Halsey's South Pacific Command and MacArthur's Southwest Pacific Command would proceed along two axes, one along the northwest New Guinea coast to seize Lae and secure airfields in the Markham River Valley, then to seize western New Britain airdromes, then along the coast of New Guinea to the seizure of Madang. In the east, Halsey's South Pacific Force would move through the Solomons to seize southern Bougainville. "All operations are preparatory to the eventual capture of Rabaul and the occupation of the Bismarck archipelago." [6]

MacArthur directed the Sixth Army to occupy and defend Kiriwana and Woodlark islands, replace Australian ground troops on Goodenough Island, and occupy western New Britain for subsequent operations against Rabaul. Krueger's Sixth Army was given the status of a task force under MacArthur's direct command. General Blamey recognized that he had become commander of Allied Land Forces in name only. MacArthur wanted an Australian force and a separate American army.

When Blamey met with Rear Adm. Daniel E. Barbey on 16 May, he explained his plan for the capture of Lae and the Markham Valley and its airfield in the first phase. Next, he would round the coast to Finschhafen and Madang.

The seizure of Lae necessitated a seaborne landing. Blamey's report demanded the prior seizure of a shore base within sixty miles of Lae, this being the maximum range of the small landing craft that could carry the troops by night to the assault. Nassau Bay was selected as the area most suited for Blamey's purpose.

Blamey's New Guinea Force at the end of May 1943 numbered 53,564 Australian soldiers and 37,200 Americans. In addition, there were about 9,000 men of the RAAF and 19,100 of the U.S. Army Air Force.[7] General Adachi's Eighteenth Japanese Army consisted of three divisions, namely the 20th, the 41st, and the 51st.[8] These divisions would normally consist of about 31,000 men. The Australians estimated that Adachi's troops deployed in Australian New Guinea numbered between 31,600 and 34,200 with a further 38,000 in Dutch New Guinea.[9] In Australian New Guinea, Adachi's troops occupied strongpoints along the north, primarily Lae, Madang, and Wewak.

The Fifth Air Force now claimed substantial control over all of Australian New Guinea. Its mission was to defend Allied bases against the enemy air force, carry troops and supplies when needed, and prevent enemy troops or supplies from reaching the Salamaua-Lae area by sea. General Adachi realized that he could no longer reinforce his garrisons by shipments from Rabaul during daylight.

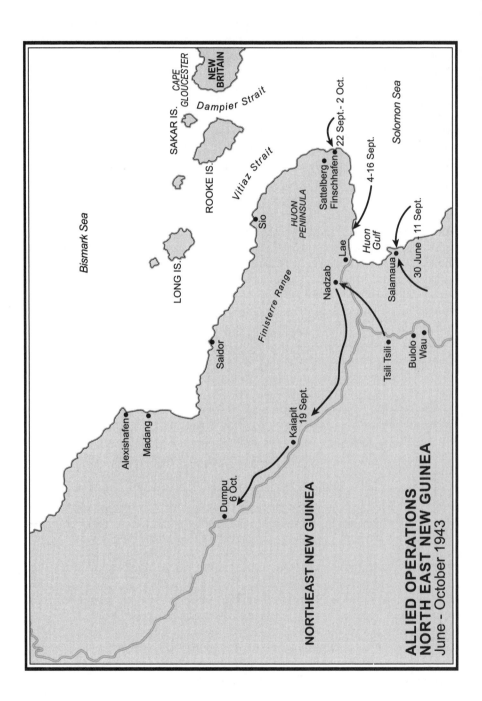

**ALLIED OPERATIONS
NORTH EAST NEW GUINEA**
June - October 1943

NORTHEAST NEW GUINEA

NEW BRITAIN

CAPE GLOUCESTER

SAKAR IS.

Dampier Strait

ROOKE IS.

Vitiaz Strait

Bismark Sea

LONG IS.

Solomon Sea

Sio

HUON PENINSULA

Sattelberg
Finschhafen
22 Sept. - 2 Oct.

4-16 Sept.

11 Sept.

Lae

Huon Gulf

Salamaua
30 June

Finisterre Range

Saidor

Nadzab

Tsili Tsili

Bulolo
Wau

Kaiapit
19 Sept.

Alexishafen
Madang

Dumpu
6 Oct.

On 29 and 30 June, elements of the U.S. 41st Infantry Division landed at Nassau Bay. According to the division historian, everything went wrong. Nevertheless, because enemy forces did not oppose this operation, the Americans joined Australians to consolidate positions during the month of July. The experienced Australian 7th and 9th Divisions launched an attack on Salamaua and Lae in mid-August. Fierce fighting continued through the month.

On 30 August MacArthur wrote to Blamey about "three items of major importance which are not clear to me and which should, I believe, be clarified." The first point was the silence of New Guinea Force's orders of 9 August and 25 August regarding the consolidation of the Huon Peninsula and the seizure of Finschhafen; second, the specific agency charged with the arrangement of over-water transportation for elements of the Allied Air Forces and Lae; and third, that only the commander in chief (MacArthur) was in a position to coordinate the activities of New Guinea Force, Allied Naval Forces, and Allied Air Forces. Therefore, it was not right to delegate to the commander of one Australian corps "the authority to arrange details of air support and naval support for the operation."

Next day, Blamey replied to point one: The resources and facilities available do not permit a simultaneous action against Lae, Markham Valley, and Finschhafen; therefore, the Lae and Markham Valley areas have been selected as the primary objective. On points two and three, Blamey said his orders had, in fact, provided for the transport of rear elements mentioned by MacArthur and that "it was not intended, nor could it be read, by an Australian commander, to mean that the arrangement of details in any way affected the 'coordination' of the work of the three Services on the level of the higher command." [10]

Australian historian David Dexter pointed out that "This misunderstanding underlined the weakness whereby since April 1942 an American general headquarters on which there was quite inadequate Australian representation reigned from afar over a field army that was, for present purposes, almost entirely Australian, and whose doctrines and methods differed from those of GHQ. It was evidence of the detachment of GHQ that, after sixteen months, its senior general staff officers had little knowledge of the doctrines and methods of its principal army in the field." [11]

In addition to being a man of great charm and intellect, MacArthur was foremost a showman. When the 503rd Parachute Regiment arrived from the United States, he staged a show for stateside consumption. He planned a jump on the morning of 5 September a few miles west of Lae where a company of Royal Australian Engineers, already on the ground, planned to develop runways capable of handling transport planes. With fighter planes as guides, aircraft carrying the parachutists took off from airfields in Moresby and Dobadura. A selected group of journalists and photographers occupied one B-17, flying above the transports; General MacArthur rode in another. Colonel Leif Sverdrup landed in a Piper Cub the next morning, 6 September, and by sundown fifty plane loads of troops—mainly Australian and American engineers—had been delivered. Three Americans were killed and thirty-three injured during the drop. There were no Japanese casualties, as none were in the area.

Blamey's forces continued the fight against the Japanese at Salamaua and Lae. Salamaua fell to the Allies on 13 September; Lae, three days later. On 8 September, MacArthur's communiqué claimed that, "elements of four Japanese divisions aggregating 20,000 at the beginning are now completely enveloped with their supply lines cut." [12] Captured enemy documents revealed that the Japanese soldiers in both locations combined numbered something less than 10,000. All were part of the 51st Division and the 238th Regiment.

As early as June 1943, the Joint Chiefs informed MacArthur that some Pentagon officers felt that Rabaul could be cut off and left to rot. MacArthur vehemently objected by claiming he needed an adequate forward naval base there to protect his right flank. He claimed the capture of Wewak prior to Rabaul would involve hazards rendering success doubtful. Wewak should be heavily bombed and neutralized, he said, but the base was too strongly fortified to be assaulted, particularly if the garrison was supported by air and naval strikes from Rabaul. MacArthur made this argument even though Rabaul had nearly ten times the number of troops than at Wewak, estimated at only 11,000.

In August 1943 at Quebec, the Quadrant Conference resolved the issue as well as others for the Pacific theater. Rabaul, with its garrison strength of 90,000 to 135,000 soldiers, sailors, and marines—always more than three times the number of enemy troops on all of Australian New Guinea—would be bypassed. Sir Alan Brooke again raised the question, "Might we not obtain the collapse of Japan without invasion." [13] The answer as reflected in the minutes of the meeting reads:

> It was also generally agreed that while blockade and air bombardment might produce the collapse of Japan without invasion, it was necessary to plan on the assumption that the country itself would have to be attacked by land forces. [14]

The British advocated that the American offensive against Japan be mounted on a single front: Adm. Chester Nimitz's in the Central Pacific. It was clearly the shortest ocean highway to Japan except through the Aleutians, where weather conditions prohibited a major drive. Admiral Ernest J. King, though sympathetic, did not agree with the British. The British claimed that King's staff had unilaterally developed the plans for war against Japan while ignoring British planners. From a strategic point of view, a single thrust across the Central Pacific made good military sense. However, it was untenable from a political viewpoint. In battles against the Japanese, Nimitz's command would have no difficulty in always meeting the enemy with overwhelming force, provided additional resources contemplated for the Southwest Pacific Command were placed under his control. But if a Central Pacific single thrust was chosen, MacArthur would play a minor role for the remainder of the war. Roosevelt recognized that MacArthur had a huge following in the United

States, his political influence much greater than the Baptist ministers in the South. Marshall opposed a single thrust move because he was in no mood to see the U.S. Army play a minor role.

In the end, the president sided with George Marshall, MacArthur's strong supporter at the conference. As a result, Part 35 of Quadrant's Final Directive ordered the seizure or neutralization of New Guinea as far west as Wewak. Rabaul was to be neutralized rather than captured. The Burma Road would be reopened. Lord Louis Mountbatten would assume the role as overall commander for Southeast Asia. Nimitz's command would start his drive through the Central Pacific.

The most far-reaching decision made at the Quebec Conference was not recorded. This was the so-called Quebec Agreement between Roosevelt and Churchill over the future of nuclear research and the development of the atomic bomb. Until early 1942, the British had been ahead in terms of original research. At Birmingham University, Professor Rudolf Peierls and Dr. Otto Frisch, both German-born physicists, had determined how an atomic bomb might be made. In early 1943, the United States reached agreement for the entire Canadian output of uranium and the Canadian heavy water plant upon which the British themselves had been counting. The British recognized that they could not spare the industrial resources to continue with their own nuclear development.

Previously Roosevelt and Churchill had agreed to work together to produce atomic weapons at the Argonaut Conference in Washington, D.C., in June 1942 and again at the Trident Conference in May 1943 where tensions had been removed over sharing information. The agreement reached said, in part:

> . . . in view of the heavy burden of production falling upon the United States as a result of a wise division of war effort the British Government recognize that any post-war advantages of an industrial or commercial character shall be dealt with as between the United States and Great Britain on terms to be specified by the President of the United States to the Prime Minister of Great Britain. The Prime Minister expressly disclaims any interest in these industrial and commercial aspects beyond what may be considered by the President of the United States to be fair and just and in harmony with the economic welfare of the world.[15]

MacArthur became most unhappy by the decisions reached at Quebec, especially the announcement that Lord Louis Mountbatten would lead a new Southeast Asia Command. On the evening of 21 September MacArthur complained that his plans "for winning the war in the Pacific had been scrapped . . . and that he had been relegated to a third-rate role in favor of the campaigns of Lord Louis Mountbatten and the island-hopping strategy of the Navy." [16] He gave vent to his feelings to a reporter of the *New York Times*. A report on the newspaper's front page on Wednesday, 22 September 1943, said: "the general went about as far as a commander on active service could in expressing his disapproval of the course of events." Having approved the island hopping in the 1935 Plan Orange, which advocated the Central Pacific drive, MacArthur now expressed his disapproval to the press and public. The article read:

> My strategic conception for the Pacific theatre contemplates massive strokes against only the main strategic objectives, utilizing surprise and air and ground striking power, supported and assisted by the fleet. This is the very opposite of what is termed island hopping, which is the gradual pushing back of the enemy by direct frontal pressure, with the consequent heavy casualties which will certainly be involved . . .
>
> Island hopping, with its extravagant losses and slow progress—some press reports indicating victory as late as 1949—is not my idea of how to end the war as soon as and as cheaply as possible.

MacArthur's statement against island hopping touched two raw nerves with the American public: the excessive loss of human life and a prolongation of the Pacific War.

The Washington *Times-Herald* and the New York *Herald Tribune* gave considerable attention to MacArthur's criticism of the decisions made at Quebec. In addition to his hostility at island hopping across the Central Pacific, he vehemently opposed the appointment of Lord Louis Mountbatten to head the newly formed Southeast Asia Command. MacArthur inferred that his role would be subordinated to those of Nimitz and Mountbatten.

On 30 September, the London *Daily Mirror* published a dispatch from its New York correspondents that said:

> A strong group of United States senators will open a campaign in Congress next week to have General MacArthur made supreme commander of the Asiatic war theatre. This group openly expresses disapproval of the appointment of Lord Louis Mountbatten to Southeastern Asia, believing that the entire campaign should be under MacArthur.

It reported that Senator Styles Bridges was leading the Senate campaign for MacArthur. Bridges later claimed that he had taken no part in such a move. The London *Daily Mirror* article pointed to the Ohio *State Journal*, which contrasted the "sincere attitude" of MacArthur with "the somewhat flamboyant air of Mountbatten," adding, "It would be a tragic thing if MacArthur were to be shorn of his authority while a London glamour boy is elevated." Continuing, the report said, "Some [American] papers are publishing letters from readers containing insulting references to Mountbatten." [17]

Churchill protested to Roosevelt about the American press's slurring remarks about Mountbatten. In the presence of an American guest, he pointed out on the globe the 6,600 miles' distance between Mountbatten's and MacArthur's headquarters. He then asked, "Do you think that's far enough apart?" [18]

A frustrated MacArthur was greatly relieved by the 26 October announcement that Vice Adm. Thomas Kinkaid would replace Vice Adm. Arthur S. Carpender as commander of the Seventh Fleet. On two prior occasions, MacArthur had requested King to replace Carpender. Yet, he had not been consulted in the selection of Kinkaid. To smooth the general's feathers, George Marshall wrote:

> Kinkaid has performed outstanding service against the Japs as naval commander in the North Pacific. His relations have been particularly efficient and happy with Army commanders, and he had the admiration of both services in that theater. I think you will find him energetic, loyal and filled with desire to get ahead with your operations. I think he is the best naval bet for your purpose.[19]

Kinkaid arrived in Brisbane on 23 November, two days before Thanksgiving. He was quartered in Lennons Hotel, where almost all American senior officers in MacArthur's command resided. Kinkaid wrote his wife, Helen, about his first meeting with his commander. He concluded, "I could not have asked for a more cordial reception." [20] However, he learned that quarreling among the U.S. Army, U.S. Navy, and Army Air Corps staff members in Brisbane had grown to epidemic proportions by the time he arrived. MacArthur claimed otherwise. He said, "General Headquarters has successfully developed an attitude that is without service bias." [21]

Kinkaid chafed at the U.S. Navy's lack of input when GHQ was working up an operation. He knew the source of friction could not be alleviated until MacArthur ordered changes in U.S. Army planning practices, which later he did. Kinkaid learned early that GHQ was dominated by the Bataan Gang, officers who had served with MacArthur in the Philippines, and were driven by the general's desire to avenge his defeat there.[22]

At this time, the Seventh Fleet possessed two air wings, a patrol aircraft, a submarine force divided between the east and west coast of Australia, a small cruiser force, four squadrons of destroyers, and ten motor torpedo boat squadrons. In addition, it contained a large number of ships and small craft appropriate for amphibious assault operations. With the arrival of his new fleet commander, MacArthur had hoped he would soon receive carriers, cruisers, and some battleships. Kinkaid quickly informed the general there would be no carriers except those loaned by the commander in chief, Pacific Fleet (CINCPAC) for specific SWPA operations. He further told MacArthur he did not believe these larger units should be given to the Seventh Fleet.

Kinkaid recognized that MacArthur's unhappy relationship with the U.S. Navy was caused by the Joint Chiefs of Staff's current strategy that called for an approach to the Philippines and China coast along two lines of advance, the primary route being through the Central Pacific.

By the fall of 1943, MacArthur's constant complaint—that of being inadequately supplied—no longer, if ever, had any merit. Much of his food and military supplies had always come from Australia and New Zealand. Australian troops had shouldered most of the burden in the Papua and New Guinea campaigns to this point. After Krueger's arrival, new American divisions began pouring into the Southwest Pacific Area so that by late summer 1944, fifteen American divisions would be at MacArthur's disposal. Already, by the fall of 1943, General Adachi's three decimated divisions were woefully outmanned by Australian and American troops.

After the capture of Lae, the Australians moved along the Huon Gulf in conjunction with an amphibious landing to attack Finschhafen. The Australians faced imminent danger in early October because they were unable to get reinforcements. On 4 October MacArthur announced that all enemy forces between Finschhafen and Madang had been outflanked and contained. Not being privy to this announcement, the Japanese 20th Division launched a series of counterattacks against the Australian 9th Division from 16 through 25 October. By holding the key positions on the Finschhafen perimeter, fourteen Japanese were lost for every Australian killed.[23]

The heavy casualties suffered by the failed breakthrough compelled Adachi to go on the defensive in the mountains between Sattelberg and Warco. Wootten's 9th Division began an offensive that seized Sattelberg after eight days of heavy fighting, then Warco on 8 December. The Japanese retreated toward Sio.

MacArthur determined to use Krueger's Sixth Army to invade the western end of New Britain, with the main landing to be at Cape Gloucester. Kenney tried in vain to persuade his chief against the Gloucester assault. He felt it would not be feasible to construct an air base there before the next major operation. At a conference in Brisbane in late November, the landing had to be postponed for two weeks for lack of ships. Vice Admiral Barbey, the commander of the amphibious force, remembered MacArthur's words as they filed out of the room: "There are some people in Washington who had rather see MacArthur lose a battle than America win a war." [24]

Major General William Rupertus, whose 1st Marine Division was to attack Cape Gloucester, persuaded MacArthur to change his original plan. A proposed paratroop drop by the 503rd Regiment southeast of the airfield in conjunction with a single regiment of the marine division to land on D-day did not make sense to U.S. Marine staff planners. The occasion of bad weather often experienced could prevent the timely arrival of the parachutists. The Guadalcanal marines had already learned some sad lessons about maneuvers in the jungle terrain. To his credit, MacArthur approved the plan proposed by the U.S. Marines.

The overall operation would be the first major undertaking by Krueger's Alamo Force. The 112th Cavalry Regiment and a field artillery battalion would go ashore at lightly defended Arawe. The 1st Marine Division reinforced by miscellaneous supporting units, including the U.S. Army's 2nd Engineer Special Brigade, would take Cape Gloucester. The 32nd Division would constitute the Alamo Force reserve. Unlike the initial Guadalcanal landing, for the rest of the war, all division-size operations in the Pacific were performed with sufficient

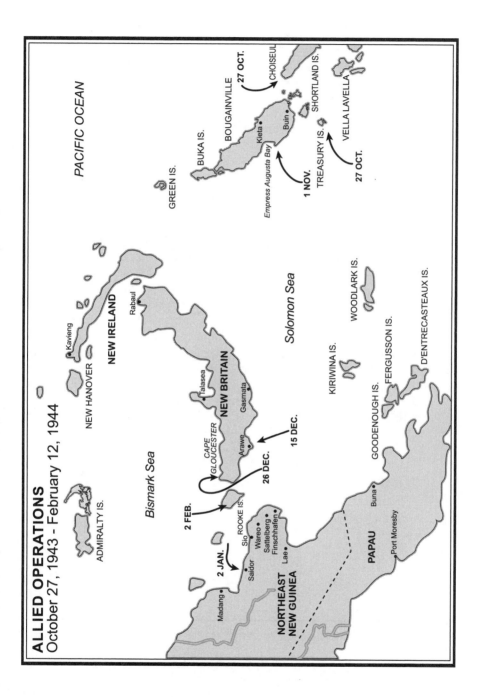

ALLIED OPERATIONS
October 27, 1943 - February 12, 1944

PACIFIC OCEAN

Bismarck Sea

Solomon Sea

ADMIRALTY IS.

Kavieng

NEW HANOVER

NEW IRELAND

Rabaul

Talasea

CAPE GLOUCESTER

NEW BRITAIN

Gasmata

Arawe

15 DEC.

26 DEC.

2 FEB.

ROOKE IS.

Sio

Wareo

Saidor

2 JAN.

Madang

Sattelberg

Finschhafen

Lae

NORTHEAST NEW GUINEA

PAPAU

Buna

Port Moresby

GOODENOUGH IS.

FERGUSSON IS.

D'ENTRECASTEAUX IS.

KIRIWINA IS.

WOODLARK IS.

GREEN IS.

BUKA IS.

BOUGAINVILLE

27 OCT.

CHOISEUL

Kieta

Buin

Empress Augusta Bay

1 NOV.

TREASURY IS.

SHORTLAND IS.

VELLA LAVELLA

27 OCT.

reserves. A few hours before the U.S. Marines embarked for Cape Gloucester on Christmas Day, MacArthur told Rupertus, "I know what the Marines think of me, but I also know that when they go into a fight they can be counted on to do an outstanding job. Good luck." [25]

Though planning for the Arawe and Cape Gloucester operations was well advanced before he arrived, Admiral Kinkaid made significant input. He explained the need for appropriate air cover to General MacArthur on his verandah at Port Moresby. Kinkaid reported that army runways can be repaired when receiving bomb hits, but ships often sink. MacArthur understood and promised that the landing force would receive more fighter coverage than ever seen before. General Kenney's Fifth Air Force fulfilled MacArthur's promise; however, his fighters were unable to prevent the loss of one destroyer, *Brownson*, three others damaged, plus two landing ship, tanks (LSTs) from enemy air attacks. [26]

The U.S. Marines landed against only slight resistance on beaches east and south of Cape Gloucester on 26 December. Fighting accelerated as they pushed westward toward the two Japanese airstrips, which were overrun by 30 December. For two more weeks, the Japanese 17th Division put up a weak defense. The Japanese soldiers were in poor physical condition because their supply line from Rabaul had been cut off by air strikes.

The U.S. Army troops met little opposition at Arawe. Neither Arawe nor Cape Gloucester would develop into a major air or naval base. Just as General Kenney had predicted, both assumed little significance in the staging of future operations. After two years, the Southwest Pacific Command held overwhelming strength against the enemy in every category—air, sea, and land. Better still, MacArthur had a top-level American army-navy-air force team in the persons of Generals Krueger and Eichelberger, Vice Admirals Kinkaid and Barbey, and General Kenney on whom he could depend for the rest of the war.

Chapter 14
China

*I*NVOLVING CHINA IN THE WAR AGAINST JAPAN had no part in Plan Orange. Yet for the better part of the Pacific War, the Joint Chiefs, especially Admiral King, considered an enclave on the China coast as a major goal for Allied forces. However, the Asian war differed greatly from the war in the Pacific. There were many more ground troops involved, yet the war there had little influence on final victory.

After the Japanese captured Singapore and Burma, the Allies inherited a tremendous logistical problem in maintaining a viable Chinese army. From the very start, the Joint Chiefs of Staff envisioned the erection of air bases on China's east coast. These would be used to bomb the Japanese home islands as well as cut off supplies from the south. In China itself, the poorly equipped, ill-fed, ineptly led Chinese troops were pitted against a Japanese army containing substantially more ground forces than all Allied commanders combined would meet in the Pacific War.

Generalissimo Chiang Kai-shek commanded the main Chinese force opposing the Japanese. He had the moral support of the American public plus Franklin D. Roosevelt, who gave him substantial military aid prior to Pearl Harbor. During the years that China fought the undeclared war against Japan, the Soviet Union also provided Chiang's Nationalist Chinese with military supplies, as Stalin considered the Japanese a mutual enemy. Not fully appreciated at the time was the fact that Chiang Kai-shek had to fight a war within a war for his survival. Previous political and military events in China created Chiang's dilemma:

In 1911, Dr. Sun Yat-sen led the revolution that established the Republic of China the following year. Sun Yat-sen's political entity, the Kuomintang Party, attracted two men of similar backgrounds but widely different personalities, Chiang Kai-shek and Mao ZeDong. After Sun's death in 1925, Chiang Kai-shek made himself commander in chief of the National Revolutionary Army. In 1927, he turned on the Shanghai Workers' organization, killing some 300

Communist and labor leaders. Six days later he organized his own national government in Nanking.

On 1 August of that year, at Nancheng, the Communist Party's central committee organized an insurrection of officers against the Kuomintang, giving birth to the People's Liberation Army. That winter Mao ZeDong was elected commander of the Red Army, which then consisted of a few thousand half-starved, miserably equipped men. "Without a people's army, the people have nothing," Mao insisted. "Political power grows out of the barrel of a gun!"

Lin Piao, a graduate of Whampoa Military Academy, China's finest military school, gave the Communists their first major victory over Chiang Kai-shek's Nationalist troops. In line with the military doctrine developed by Sun-tzu, he lured five Nationalist regiments into pursuing his Red Force into the mountains in Yungshin country. By erecting a roadblock at a narrow pass held by one-third of his force, then sending a small force to the enemy's rear to prevent escape, the major portion of Lin Piao's command swooped down from both sides of the entrapped Nationalists, cutting them to pieces.

To combat the Communists, Chiang waged what he called Bandit Extermination campaigns against them. When he launched his Fifth Bandit Extermination campaign in 1933, the Chinese Reds planned their celebrated Long March, which became one of their most cherished traditions. Breaking out of Chiang's encirclement in October 1934, they took a circuitous 6,000-mile route to avoid Nationalist armies. Of 90,000 who started, only 6,000 were left a year later when the Communists reached Yenan in Shensi Province. There Mao alternately fought against and negotiated with the government.

After the Japanese marched into Peking on 8 August 1936, Chiang Kai-shek and Chou En-lai concluded a United Front agreement, whereby Mao's Red Army became the Eighth Route Army of the National Revolutionary Army. Under the United Front policy, the Communists were allotted a quarter of the seats in the 200-member People's Political Council established by Chiang in April 1938 as the supreme policy-making body for the duration of the war. The mere nature of the parties involved made a long-term reconciliation impossible.

In the spring of 1938 the remnants of the Red Army south of the Yangtze were allowed to constitute the New Fourth Army under the Communist Yeh T'ing but on paper to take orders from the Nationalist General Chu-t'ung. The Eighth Route Army and the New Fourth Army were designed to fight the Japanese. Instead, they took advantage of their autonomy to eliminate Nationalist forces in their way and extend their political control over ever-expanding areas. "According to official Communist history, the Eighth Route Army grew from 45,000 in 1937 to 400,000 by 1940, while the New Fourth Army increased from 15,000 to 100,000 in the same period." [1] While the numbers are most probably exaggerated, the Communist armies showed substantial growth during this three-year period.[2] The Japanese took the Nationalists more than the

Communists as their number one enemy; accordingly, they concentrated 70 percent of their forces against the former.[3] Beginning in May 1939 through 1941, the Japanese bombed Chungking, the Nationalist capital. Lacking anti-aircraft guns and sufficient aircraft, the residents of Chungking built air raid shelters plus dugouts and stayed put.

In May 1939, the Japanese army tested the Soviet will to fight with an attack on the frontier of Soviet-protected Outer Mongolia. The Russians, under General Zhukov, hit back hard and on 20 August inflicted a stinging defeat on the Japanese. Three days later, Nazi Germany and the Soviet Union signed a non-aggression pact.

In fights against the Japanese during the same year, Chiang's forces lost, then regained, Changsha in south China with a final assault on 31 December. Thereafter, Chiang's troops did little fighting against the Japanese until the Americans entered the war. But by Chiang's retreat into the interior, one million Japanese soldiers were required to hold their military gains because they were always surrounded by a hostile civilian population.

On 12 July 1940, the British closed the Burma Road for a period of three months. This was China's only link with the outside world. The stated reason was to give Japan and China a further chance to reach a peaceful settlement.

The United Front between the Nationalists and Communists finally broke down in early 1941. Previously, the New Fourth Army was ordered to cross the Yellow River and take up new positions with the Communist Eighth Route Army. Instead, the Communist chief of staff, Hsiang Ying, began moving his forces south. On 4 January 1941, the Nationalists' 4th Division clashed with the New Fourth Army, killing Hsiang Ying. Its commander, Yeh T'ing, was wounded and taken prisoner, whereby on 17 January the National Military Council ordered the disbandment of the New Fourth Army. For weeks, Communist propaganda violently denounced the Nationalists, attributing the decision to disarm the New Fourth Army to a pro-Japanese clique.

On 6 March 1941, Chiang Kai-shek sent a long message to the People's Political Council charging the Communists with bad faith and adding:

> I need scarcely assert that our government is solely concerned with leading the nation against the Japanese invaders and extirpating the traitors, and is utterly without any notion of again taking up arms to "suppress the Communists." It desires never again to hear of that ill-omened term which now has a place only in Chinese history. Let them obey orders, give up their attacks on their comrades-in-arms and cease all their provocative acts; the government will then treat them with all possible consideration.[4]

Chiang Kai-shek fully recognized his most formidable long-term enemy when he said privately, "The Japanese are a disease of the skin. The Communists are a disease of the heart."[5]

Later, concrete evidence came to the Generalissimo when a copy of Mao ZeDong's secret directives to the Eighth Route Army came into Nationalist hands:

The Sino-Japanese War affords our party an excellent opportunity for expansion. Our fixed policy should be 70 percent expansion, 20 percent dealing with the Kuomintang, and 10 percent resisting Japan. There are three stages in carrying out this fixed policy:

The first is a compromising stage, in which self-sacrifice should be made to show our outward obedience to the Central Government and adherence to the Three People's Principles; but in reality this will serve as camouflage for the existence and development of our party.

The second is a contending stage, in which two or three years should be spent in laying the foundations of our party's political and military powers, and developing these until we can match and break the Kuomintang, and eliminate the influence of the latter north of the Yellow River.

The third is an offensive stage, in which our forces should penetrate deeply into Central China, sever the communications of the Central Government troops in various sectors, isolate and disperse them until we are ready for the counter-offensive, and wrest the leadership from the hands of the Kuomintang.[6]

For the rest of the war against Japan, the United Front remained irrelevant as well as impractical.

In April 1941, Chiang Kai-shek received another blow when he learned that the Soviets and Japan had signed a neutrality pact. With military aid from the Soviets eliminated, he now had to rely solely upon the United States for weapons to fight the Japanese. These had to be transported first to Rangoon in Burma, then by rail north to Lashio. From there, trucks carried the supplies to Kunming, China, over a narrow, twisting 681 miles of road that rose to 9,000 feet when traversing the Himalayas and through mile-deep gorges of the Mekong and Salween rivers. This means of supply was eliminated in April 1942 when the Japanese overran Burma, seized Lashio, and thus closed the Burma Road at its source. By the seizure of Lashio, the Japanese restricted outside support to a thin line of air supply over 500 miles across the Himalayan Mountains called the Hump between Assan, India, to the Yunnan Plateau in China. In the face of only a trickle of material, Chiang Kai-shek's political and military condition grew progressively worse.

Prior to Pearl Harbor, Brig. Gen. John Magruder had been placed in charge of an American military mission to China. He supervised the distribution of U.S. lend-lease military supplies as well as the reorganization and training of Chinese armies under American advisors. The Nationalist Chinese supposedly had three hundred divisions. Magruder's duties envisioned the equipment and training of thirty divisions to fight against the Japanese. Americans stationed in Chungking recognized that top-ranking Nationalists plus a few Americans were using lend-lease for their own private benefit. Colonel George Sliney, the mission's artillery expert, reported that China's demand for war material was not for "the purpose of pressing the war against Japan but to make the central government safe against insurrection. The general idea in the U.S. that China has fought Japan to a standstill and has had many glorious victories is a delusion." [7]

Before the Japanese captured Lashio, goods shipped under lend-lease piled up on the docks at Rangoon and Lashio to the point that Harry Hopkins, Roosevelt's personal advisor, sent Daniel Arnstein, a transport expert, to the area for an appraisal. He reported that the situation on the nine-foot-wide, single-lane Burma Road between Kunming and Lashio was appalling. At Kunming, truck drivers had to pass through eight customs desks, which often occupied the whole day, before obtaining permission to proceed. At a dozen more check-points along the way, provincial officials took their toll for permits to pass. On the China-Burma border, 250 trucks waited anywhere from twenty-four hours to two weeks for customs clearance. Only 6,000 tons per month were reaching the Nationalists, when the total should have been at least 30,000 tons.[8]

Maintaining the flow of supplies over the Burma Road was a primary function of Lt. Gen. Joseph "Vinegar Joe" Stilwell in his new assignment as commanding general, U.S. Army Forces in the China-Burma-India theater; chief of staff to the supreme commander, China theater; and supervisor of lend-lease.

From a purely military standpoint Stilwell's appointment made good sense, but his selection as chief of staff under Chiang Kai-shek proved to be a poor choice politically. When on 28 December 1938 Col. Joseph W. Stilwell, the American military attaché in China, met with the Generalissimo, he formed an unfavorable view of Chiang. He accused the latter as being "directly responsible for much of the confusion that normally exists in his command." [9]

Stilwell was already a major general when the United States entered the war against Japan. Highly regarded by Gen. George C. Marshall, Stilwell was promoted to lieutenant general when ordered to China in early 1942. He arrived at Chungking by March. With the concurrence of Chiang Kai-shek, he became commanding general of U.S. forces in the China-Burma-India theater and chief of staff to Chiang. Graduated from West Point in 1904, Stilwell's military career was closely associated with Asia, especially China. In his previous tours of duty in China, he had become fluent in the language. Admiral Leahy described him as "tactless, and with a tongue too sharp for his own good. He was an excellent fighter and knew what to do on the ground." [10]

When he reported to Chiang Kai-shek on 6 March, Stilwell believed that Burma could be saved by offensive action. In his first conference, Chiang promised to set up a joint staff for the Burma campaign the next day. While waiting for staff and divisions to be assigned to him, Stilwell wrote down his strategy for Burma and activity in China. The next day, 7 March, the Japanese entered Rangoon. Stilwell recognized that it was important to formulate plans the British would accept, as Burma was a British colony. In China itself, his

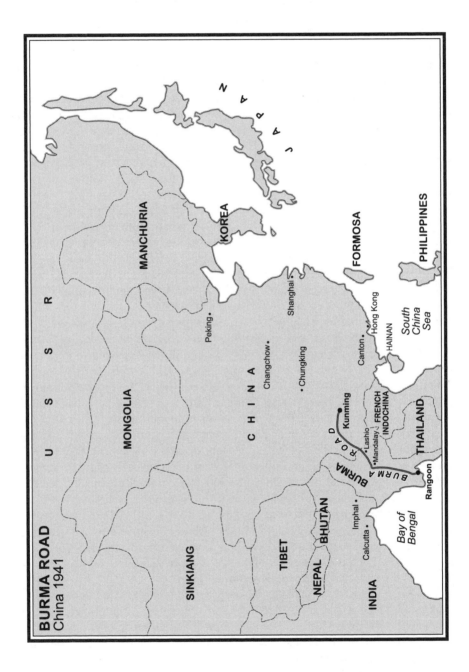

BURMA ROAD
China 1941

main endeavor would be to get the thirty trained divisions program under way, but which divisions had not yet been designated.

After waiting three days, Stilwell was invited to the home of the Generalissimo and Madame Chiang Kai-shek. In a two-hour discussion after dinner, Stilwell listened to Chiang's view of military tactics. Chiang said it required three Chinese to one Japanese division to hold a defense and five to one for an attack. He wanted no attack until it was known whether the Japanese were being reinforced.

On 11 March, Chiang verbally placed the Fifth and Sixth Armies under Stilwell's command. These were supposedly his best troops. However, Chiang attempted to run the campaign in Burma from his headquarters in Chungking. This resulted in chaos. The Chinese divisions retreated in defiance of Stilwell's orders. When Stilwell attempted to move northward, the Japanese blocked him. The lack of bridges strong enough to carry tanks blocked his attempt to march westward into India. Reduced to a portion of his staff and a few dozen others—some 114 people in all—he walked out of Burma, 150 miles through steep, jungle-covered terrain to Imphal, India. His march took two weeks. He arrived safely just before monsoon rains began.

From Imphal, Stilwell went at once to General Wavell's headquarters in New Delhi. Disregarding congratulations from Marshall and Roosevelt and British communiqués, which described the Burma debacle as a voluntary withdrawal, Stilwell gave his views at a large press conference on the evening of his arrival in New Delhi. Somehow, his statements passed the censors. He said bluntly, "In the first place, no military commander in history ever made a voluntary withdrawal, and in the second place, there is no such thing as a glorious retreat. All retreats are ignominious as hell. I claim we got a hell of a licking. We got run out of Burma and it's humiliating as hell . . ." [11]

His published remarks joined with his description of the walkout made him a famous man in Britain and the United States. Later, when asked by *Time* reporter Theodore H. White to give a quick overview of the situation in China, Stilwell replied, "The trouble in China is simple: We are allied to an ignorant, illiterate, superstitious, peasant son of a bitch." [12]

The loss of Burma completed the blockade of China. This defeat raised fears in the United States that China's will to resist could not survive her isolation. Allied strategy in Asia was still uncertain. Nevertheless, the Joint Chiefs—especially Admiral King—felt the need to keep China in the war as a future base for air operations against Japan's sea lanes plus the ultimate bombing of the home islands.

Stilwell had a plan by the time he reached New Delhi. It called for American divisions. On 25 May he wired the War Department: "My belief in [the] decisive strategic importance of China is so strong that I feel certain a serious mistake is being made in not sending American combat units into this theater." [13]

General George Marshall could not be persuaded. He recognized the extreme difficulty in maintaining a large contingent of American troops in Asia in light of other commitments around the globe. With Marshall's refusal, Stilwell determined to train a Chinese task force in India.

Having departed New Delhi, Stilwell met the Generalissimo and Madame Chiang Kai-shek on June 3. Both complained due to the lack of supplies.

On 25 May Chiang Kai-shek had warned the United States, "Chinese confidence in their Allies will be completely shaken" unless the Chinese saw visible evidence of help. Morale was "never lower," Madame wrote to the lend-lease administrator.[14] Chiang followed with a letter to Roosevelt asking him to send Harry Hopkins to China in lieu of coming himself because the situation was at a "crucial stage such as I have never experienced before." [15]

Stilwell put the blame on the Generalissimo. Because Stilwell did not hesitate to tell the Generalissimo and Madame Chiang Kai-shek the truth as he saw it, he never developed a close relationship with either. Stilwell saw Chiang Kai-shek as a peanut dictator and a "stubborn, ignorant, prejudiced, conceited despot who has never heard the truth except from me." [16]

Stilwell's relations with Maj. Gen. Claire Chennault were also less than satisfactory. This conflict stemmed from an honest difference about the best way to defeat Japan. "It's the man in the trenches that will win the war," Stilwell was supposed to have said. Chennault replied: "Goddammit, Stilwell, there *aren't* any men in the trenches." [17] Stilwell was convinced—and he so warned Chennault—that if his air boys ever seriously threatened the Japanese, the latter would simply take his airfields away from him, that he needed ground troops to protect the airfields.

Five years previously, Chennault had become the aviation advisor to the Chinese government. He had grown up in Louisiana. He joined the army in 1917, earned a reserve commission, and completed pilot training in 1919. After obtaining a regular commission in 1920, Chennault remained in the Army Air Force until his retirement as a captain in 1937 when he came to China. While an aviation advisor to Chiang Kai-shek, Chennault recruited a number of aviators, officially the American Volunteer Army, but more prominently known as the Flying Tigers. He rejoined the U.S. Army Air Force after the Japanese attack on Pearl Harbor. Chennault became a major general in February 1943 and took command of the new United States Fourteenth Air Force in China.

On Independence Day 1942, Chennault's American Volunteer Group passed into history. Some stayed in China as part of the Fourteenth Air Force; some returned to the United States. One—Greg Boyington—rejoined the U.S. Marine Corps and formed the Black Sheep Squadron, which served with distinction at Guadalcanal.

Stilwell and Chennault remained in China to fight the Japanese and each other over the meager supplies flown over the Hump. Each general had a different view of how to fight the war as well as a different opinion of Chiang Kai-shek.

Stilwell believed that first priority must be given to the reopening of the Burma Road and, if not, to an alternate route from India into China. Only then could he get the necessary supplies to fight the Japanese. He felt strongly that some American divisions should be sent to the China-Burma-India (CBI) theater in order to achieve this purpose. Marshall never agreed, as he recognized that keeping them adequately supplied would constitute a logistical nightmare.

In a letter dated 8 October 1942, "Chennault claimed that with only 105 modern fighters and 30 medium and 12 heavy bombers, maintained at that level by replacements, he could accomplish the downfall of Japan . . . probably within six months, within one year at the outside." [18] This was the message he gave to Roosevelt's personal representative, Wendell Willkie, for transmittal to the president. In his letter, Chennault said, "I have no doubts of my success, and if given real authority, I can cause the collapse of Japan." [19]

Chennault's easy solution for victory impressed Chiang Kai-shek, so much so that he wanted the Fourteenth Air Force to launch a major air offensive against the Japanese. He requested Roosevelt to confer with Chennault in Washington. Marshall insisted that Stilwell should visit the president together with Chennault. They both arrived in Washington a few days prior to the Trident Conference, which began on 12 May 1943.

Chennault's plan called for "a six-month program of combat to obtain air superiority over the Japanese, then against river and coastal shipping extending to the South China Sea. By the end of the year, the Fourteenth Air Force would bomb Japan itself. To supply this program, he wanted the entire over-the-Hump tonnage for May and June, 4,700 tons from July through September and more than 7,000 tons a month later." [20] Stilwell believed that Chennault's plan would cause the Japanese to wipe out the useful airfields in China even though Chiang Kai-shek "gave his personal assurance to Roosevelt that if the enemy moved against the air bases they could be halted by existing Chinese ground forces." [21]

Both Marshall and King sided with Stilwell's view, which meant that both the Americans and the British had to make a greater effort in the opening of a land route to China. Roosevelt agreed with Churchill that the necessary resources were not yet available. Near the end of the Trident Conference, the Combined Chiefs consented to increase the amount of military supplies over the Hump without making a final decision on the Burma campaign. As always, the British and the Americans divided strongly on the need to keep China in the war.

After the formal session, Roosevelt asked Stilwell and Chennault for their opinion of Chiang Kai-shek. "He's a vacillating tricky undependable old scoundrel who never keeps his word," Stilwell replied. Chennault countered, "Sir, I think the generalissimo is one of the two or three greatest military and political leaders in the world today. He has never broken a commitment or promise made to me." [22]

The debate over the importance of China continued through August 1943, when the Combined Chiefs met again in Quebec for the Quadrant Conference. Churchill did not believe as Roosevelt did that it was important to keep Chiang Kai-shek afloat, although he was anxious to regain the British lost colonies of Burma and especially Singapore. The Joint Chiefs agreed to form a special American unit to penetrate behind the Japanese lines in Burma. This was needed to interdict Japanese supply and communications in order to reopen the Burma Road. Finally, at the behest of Churchill, Vice Adm. Lord Louis Mountbatten was made supreme commander of the Southeast Asia Command with Stilwell as his deputy. Stilwell would continue in his other posts, including chief of staff to Chiang Kai-shek.

After Quadrant, Roosevelt issued a presidential call for volunteers for a dangerous and hazardous mission. Approximately 3,000 American soldiers volunteered to answer the call. The unit, officially designated as the 5307th Composite Unit, later became known as Merrill's Marauders after its leader, Brig. Gen. Frank Merrill. This command formed into six combat teams (400 per team), two teams to a battalion, with the rest placed into headquarters and air transport. After some training in the jungles of central India, the Marauders began the long march in February 1944 up the Ledo Road over the lower ranges of the Himalayan Mountains into Burma. In the days and weeks ahead, they stayed in constant contact with the enemy. Finally, the Marauders surprised the Japanese and seized the airfield at Myitkyina, which together with Chinese troops they were able to hold. By 1 June after being in constant action for three months, the Marauders suffered greatly from malaria, exhaustion, and malnutrition. No other American force except the 1st Marine Division at Guadalcanal had seen as much uninterrupted jungle service. However, no other American force had marched as far or hard to display such endurance. At the end of the campaign, even those still in action were evacuated to hospitals, as they suffered from tropical diseases and malnutrition.

Because of the decisions reached at Quadrant, the British greatly increased their efforts against the Japanese in Burma. In China itself, Chiang Kai-shek's armies continued to do very little fighting. This lack of aggressiveness failed to make a big difference because the Japanese troops were always surrounded by a hostile population in a country of more than 400 million Chinese.

In the months and year ahead, Stilwell dedicated himself to completion of the alternate land supply route from India into China known as the Ledo Road. Before the Japanese occupied Rangoon, the Chinese formally requested lend-lease material to construct a road from Ledo in Assam across the rugged territory of north Burma to tie in with the Burma Road on the Chinese side at Lungling. Even though this engineering and construction project proved far more difficult than the air route over the Hump, the War Plans Division recommended it as an "urgent military necessity."

Work on the road inched forward against extreme obstacles of terrain and climate. Mountains, canyons, and torrential streams marked the path as annual rainfall amounted to 150 inches, sometimes as much as 14 inches in 24 hours during the monsoon season. Army engineers, including a battalion of black troops, began to work together with Indian contract labor. Ultimately, 80,000 men including 50,000 Americans were used to finish the project. Keeping the Japanese from encroaching on this road during construction was equally difficult.

Chapter 15
Rabaul

*R*ABAUL IS THE ONE NAME that all veterans who served in the southwest Pacific during the first two years of the war will remember. It's a place that only the fighter and bomber pilots ever saw. Then why remember? Because Allied troops—air, ground, and navy—recognized it as the source of all trouble in the Solomons, Papua, eastern New Guinea, and surrounding waters. On the light side, some veterans wondered if the "Kilroy was Here" signs that showed up on the islands in the South Pacific, often in remote places, would be seen by the first waves invading Rabaul's shores.

General Douglas A. MacArthur advocated its seizure in early June 1942. The Joint Chiefs of Staff quickly determined that forces were not available for its capture, an opinion shared by MacArthur before the end of the month.

Located at the northeast corner of New Britain, Rabaul lay 800 miles southwest of Truk, headquarters of the Japanese Combined Fleet. The Allies had no air or sea bases that could interdict enemy ships carrying troops or supplies before arriving at Rabaul's harbor. The Japanese dislodged the small Australian garrison there in January 1942 and subsequently developed five airfields around its natural harbor, together with storage facilities for food and ammunition for their troops in the Solomons and New Guinea. Prior to the Japanese occupation, Rabaul was capital of the Australian mandated territory of New Guinea. In the Pacific War, the Joint Chiefs of Staff were focused on the campaigns in the Solomon Islands and MacArthur's battles in New Guinea.

MacArthur did not accept the "beat Hitler first" strategy, as he repeatedly complained to the press and the Joint Chiefs for more support in the southwest Pacific. Admiral Ernest J. King also made the Pacific War his primary interest, but he emphasized the Central Pacific command of Adm. Chester W. Nimitz as the highway leading to Japan's defeat. However, as yet there had been no move on behalf of the Joint Chiefs to implement the prewar Plan Orange.

At the first meeting of the Combined Chiefs at Casablanca on 14 January 1943, the British invited King to enlighten them on the Pacific War. He made it clear that the Americans intended to take a different direction during the ensuing year from the fighting solely in the Solomon Islands and New Guinea.

After summarizing the previous year's operations, King argued for increasing the pressure against Japan, emphasizing the importance of seizing the Marianas because of their central position astride Japanese sea lanes of communication. King said he took no pride of authorship in the strategy that he was advocating. It had been developed at the Naval War College and it was understood and accepted by nearly all naval officers.[1] To show their unanimity, Gen. George C. Marshall and Gen. Hap Arnold reinforced King's arguments, including a plan to aid China by opening the Burma Road.

King criticized the small dimensions of the Allied effort against Japan. He stated that in December 1942 he had made an estimate of the percentage of the total war effort (men, ships, planes, munitions) of all the Allies, including China, then used in the Pacific. His conclusion was that only 15 percent of the total Allied resources went to the Pacific theater. The remaining 85 percent was being used in Europe, Africa, the Battle of the Atlantic, and in the build-up of forces in Britain.

A close examination of the facts paints a different picture. At that time, the greater part of the United States Navy was in the Pacific; nine infantry divisions and two marine divisions were also there, whereas there were only eight American infantry divisions in the United Kingdom and North Africa. There were more American air groups in the Pacific than elsewhere—thirty-four against twenty-five. "American army strength alone in the Central, South, and Southwest Pacific theaters totaled 374,000 men, which was, despite the Germany-first strategy, considerably greater than that in the Mediterranean (298,000) or in the United Kingdom (107,000).[2] King's statistics indicated his determination to spare no efforts to have larger forces allotted to the Pacific.

Although Admiral King and General Marshall agreed with their British counterparts that Germany must be defeated first, both urged that the successes in the Pacific must be followed up promptly and that Japan must not be allowed to build up her strength for another offensive.

Marshall informed the British that the American Chiefs of Staff thought the Japanese were establishing a strong defensive line from the Solomons to Timor. King stated that the fighting in the Solomons and eastern New Guinea was designed to secure the approaches to Australia.[3] He agreed with MacArthur that Rabaul was the key to the situation. After the capture of Rabaul, which, at Casablanca, was taken for granted, King urged that the Philippines be attacked across the Central Pacific, using stepping-stones in the Marshalls, Carolines, and Marianas. The Combined Chiefs received a memorandum from General Marshall, Admiral King, and General Arnold that the Allies in 1943 would "work towards positions from which land-based air can attack Japan." At this stage in the war the Joint Chiefs believed in the prewar Plan Orange to the extent that their memorandum continued, "assault [by ground troops] on Japan is remote and may well not be found necessary."[4]

Near the end of the conference, under the heading "Operations in the Pacific and Far East," there were three major statements:

1) Operations in these theaters shall continue with the forces allocated, with the object of maintaining pressure on Japan, retaining the initiative and attaining a position of readiness for the full scale offensive against Japan by the United Nations as soon as Germany is defeated.
2) These operations must be kept within such limits as will not, in the opinion of the Combined Chiefs of Staff, jeopardize the capacity of the United Nations to take advantage of any favorable opportunity that may present itself for the decisive defeat of Germany in 1943.
3) Subject to the above reservation, plans and preparations shall be made for:
   a. The recapture of Burma (Anakim) beginning in 1943.
   b. Operations, after the capture of Rabaul, against the Marshalls and Carolines if time and resources allow without prejudice to Anakim.[5]

For the first year of the war, events dictated the plans and decisions of the Joint Chiefs. At this conference it was clear the Joint Chiefs intended to resort to the prewar Plan Orange.

The most newsworthy event of the conference dealt with President Franklin D. Roosevelt's press release. It stated:

I think we have all had it in our hearts and heads before, but I don't think that it has ever been put down on paper by the Prime Minister and myself, and that is the determination that peace can come to the world only by the total elimination of German and Japanese power . . . The elimination of German, Japanese and Italian war power means the unconditional surrender of Germany, Italy, and Japan.[6]

Although Roosevelt's words met with the overwhelming approval of the public, they caused deep divisions inside Japan before she finally decided to surrender.

MacArthur strongly opposed the concept that the main advance against Japan as advocated in the latest Plan Orange and now by the Joint Chiefs was the quickest way to defeat Japan. He advocated the occupation of Rabaul plus a series of moves along the New Guinea coast, then to the Philippines. At Casablanca the Joint Chiefs believed that the Allies needed a base on the China coast from which to bomb Japan. This was not part of the prewar Plan Orange strategy.

On 28 February 1943, MacArthur's staff completed an outline plan for the achievement of the second and third tasks set forth in the Joint Chiefs' directive of July 1942. No fixed dates were established for the five operations advocated. The first of these would be the capture of Lae by an airborne force landing in the Markham Valley cooperating with an amphibious force moving along the coast in small craft. Salamaua would be bypassed, but important bases in the

Huon Peninsula-Vitiaz Strait area such as Finschhafen would be captured, and a combined airborne and amphibious attack would be launched against Madang. The second operation, after the capture of the Huon Peninsula-Vitiaz Strait area, would be the capture of New Georgia in the Solomons by Adm. William F. Halsey's South Pacific Command. The Southwest Pacific and South Pacific Commands would then launch amphibious assaults on New Britain and Bougainville. The fourth and fifth operations would be the capture of Kavieng and Rabaul, respectively. Kavieng, with its airfield north of Rabaul, would be the final key in neutralizing Rabaul's air arm.[7]

To carry out his part of this plan, MacArthur said he needed to be reinforced by five infantry divisions and 1,800 combat and transport aircraft.[8] With this extra strength, his command and the South Pacific Command, which needed no reinforcement, would be able to drive the Japanese back to Truk and Wewak during 1943. Rabaul itself might even be captured.

On the day the Casablanca Conference ended, Admiral Nimitz met Adm. William F. Halsey at Noumea to plan future operations before the seizure of Rabaul. Shortly after Nimitz returned to Hawaii, he received a disquieting message from Halsey.

In February 1943, while the Japanese were evacuating Guadalcanal, they staged diversionary raids by sea and air. To meet the apparent crisis, Halsey asked MacArthur for the loan of a few heavy bombers. The general refused, saying, "My own operations envision the maximum use of my air forces." He concluded by adding, "Before considering the dislocation of my plans and the diversion of my air force to your operations, it is necessary that I have some knowledge of your intentions . . ." In a letter to Nimitz, Halsey said of MacArthur, "I refuse to get into controversy with him or any other self-advertising Son of a Bitch." [9]

Nevertheless, because he needed to synchronize his invasion of New Georgia with plans of the Southwest Pacific Command, Halsey concluded that he should confer with MacArthur. He wrote to the general proposing a meeting and received a cordial invitation to come to Brisbane on 15 April. When Halsey arrived at Brisbane in midafternoon on the 15th, General MacArthur with some of his staff met him at the wharf. Halsey's party was comfortably billeted at Brisbane's fine Lennons Hotel. When MacArthur turned on the charm, Halsey's bias against the general evaporated. Halsey later wrote:

> Five minutes after I reported, I felt as if we were lifelong friends. I have seldom seen a man who makes a quicker, stronger, more favorable impression. He was then about sixty-three years old, but he could have passed as fifty. His hair was jet black; his eyes were clear; his carriage was erect. If he had been wearing civilian clothes, I still would have known at once that he was a soldier.[10]

Afterward, the two remained lasting friends. By a combination of distinguished looks, erect bearing, and articulate speech, MacArthur captivated most others who came within his presence.

On 26 April, Halsey's and MacArthur's staffs worked out a plan consisting of thirteen amphibious landings within six months code-named Cartwheel. In the first phase, to begin in June, Woodlark and Kiriwina were to be occupied. In the second phase, the seizure of Salamaua, Lae, and Finschhafen was to be accomplished by the time New Georgia was secured. (The seizure of Salamaua was a reversal of MacArthur's 28 February 1943 plan.) The third phase involved landings at Cape Gloucester in New Britain while South Pacific forces attacked Kieta in Bougainville.

The Japanese were far from idle during this planning stage by the Americans. The troops in New Guinea and the Solomons consisted of the Eighth Area Army, commanded by Lt. Gen. Hitoshi Imamura, who was under the direct control of Imperial General Headquarters. Under Imamura were Lt. Gen. Haruyoshi Hyakutake's Seventeenth Army in the Solomons and Lt. Gen. Hatazo Adachi's Eighteenth Army (20th, 41st, and 51st Divisions) in New Guinea.

From Rabaul, Imamura set about reinforcing his troops in New Guinea while Yamamoto developed a bold plan of massive air attacks to destroy Allied air power and shipping in the Solomons and New Guinea. Hundreds of planes were transferred from Truk to Rabaul as Yamamoto himself flew to Rabaul on 3 April to head the operation. Considerable damage was done by the Japanese, but the American airmen and anti-aircraft crews took a heavy toll on the attacking formations.

Halsey's South Pacific cryptanalysts learned that on 18 April Yamamoto intended to inspect naval air bases in south Bougainville. The exact flight plan was revealed. Halsey sought Admiral Nimitz's advice as to whether an attempt should be made to shoot down Yamamoto's plane. The inquiry went all the way to the White House, where President Roosevelt made the final decision to go after Japan's most brilliant naval officer. P-38s from Guadalcanal intercepted the admiral's plane. Yamamoto died in the flaming crash of his bomber in the jungle of Bougainville. He was given a hero's burial in Tokyo. Already his prediction of what would happen after a year of war with the United States had come to fruition.

Throughout 1943, Japan and the United States engaged in a war of attrition in the Solomons, the type of war Yamamoto knew Japan could not win in the long term. The battle for New Guinea was primarily an Australian show with increasing help from the Americans.

The Australian historian Dudley McCarthy noted that April 1943 marked "the end of the first year of the formal existence of the South-West Pacific Area, which had begun with the Japanese at the peak of their success and confidence and with corresponding despondency in Australia—a despondency shared in full measure by General MacArthur after his arrival there, the memory of a great defeat dogging him. Then came the forward move by the Allies to fight the war in New Guinea, not because MacArthur at once inspired this on his arrival, (as he was later to claim) but because the Coral Sea and Midway battles, and the development of airfields and air power, made possible the achievement of conditions which were fundamental to such a move." [11]

The change in circumstances did not go unnoticed by the Combined Chiefs. They gathered in May in Washington, D.C., for the Trident Conference. There, the idea of a Central Pacific offensive was approved. The Papuan and Guadalcanal campaigns had taken far longer than anticipated, and the seizure of the all-important Rabaul was not yet in the foreseeable future. The British disagreed with the Joint Chiefs' memorandum that stated: "Simultaneously, in cooperation with our allies," it read, "to maintain and extend unremitting pressure against Japan in the Pacific and from China." [12] That kind of pressure, said British Chief of Staff Field Marshal Alan Brooke, could well cause a vacuum that would suck forces away from Europe and jeopardize the war against Germany. The disagreement between Admiral King and Field Marshal Brooke over Pacific War strategy would continue until the end of the war. Yet, the Joint Chiefs determined to maintain the initiative in the Pacific in spite of British misgivings.

On 12 May 1943, the U.S. Army's 7th Infantry Division made an amphibious landing on fog-covered Attu in the Aleutians. After some bitter fighting, the island was declared secure by 31 May. In the last days of battle, the Japanese made a banzai attack that penetrated to the hospital tents, where some American wounded were killed before the last enemy could be wiped out.

Because of bad weather and the remoteness of Kiska from any American military outpost except Attu, the Japanese decided to secretly abandon the island. American cryptanalysts learned of this decision, which enabled the U.S. Navy to sink three I-class Japanese submarines assigned to the evacuation.[13] Major General Holland Smith, USMC, the amphibious training officer for the American and Canadian troops engaged, was convinced the Japanese had evacuated Kiska. In spite of Smith's misgivings and the cryptanalysts' pre-knowledge, a large American-Canadian force landed on unoccupied Kiska on 16 August apparently still expecting enemy opposition. For the remainder of the war, Kiska had little military value to either country. General Smith wrote later:

> In the Aleutians, we had all the means at our disposal to determine definitely whether the Japanese had evacuated Kiska but we failed to use them. This negligence on the part of the high command was inexcusable.[14]

On 15 June, the Joint Chiefs notified MacArthur that landings in the Marshalls were tentatively set to begin in mid-November. The 1st and 2nd Marine Divisions together with two bomber groups from either the South or southwest Pacific would have to be employed in the Marshalls. MacArthur responded strongly, stating, "Air supremacy is essential to success. With my present strength, this (success) is problematical. The withdrawal of two groups of bombers would, in my opinion, collapse the offensive effort in the Southwest Pacific Area."

He advised the Joint Chiefs, "In my judgment the offensive against Rabaul should be considered the main effort, and it should not be nullified or weakened by withdrawals to implement a secondary attack" in the Central Pacific.[15] MacArthur then told Marshall:

From a broad strategic viewpoint I am convinced that the best course of offensive action in the Pacific is a movement from Australia through New Guinea to Mindanao. This movement can be supported by land-based aircraft, which is utterly essential and will immediately cut the enemy lines from Japan to his conquered territory to the southward. By contrast a movement through the mandated islands will be a series of amphibious attacks with the units and ground troops supported by land-based aviation. Midway stands as an example of the hazards of such operations. Moveover no vital strategic objective is reached until the series of amphibious frontal attacks succeed in reaching Mindanao. The factors upon which the old Orange Plan was based have been greatly altered by the hostile conquest of Malaya and the Netherlands East Indies and by the availability of Australia as a base.[16]

Self-interest can cloud the thinking of an otherwise brilliant mind. In 1935, as U.S. Army Chief of Staff, MacArthur had approved Plan Orange, which called for a thrust across the Central Pacific. Just as Eisenhower had previously predicted, MacArthur demanded more support than militarily necessary when placed in command of the southwest Pacific theater. Overlooked in MacArthur's letter to Marshall, the geography of the Pacific had not changed. Japan was still an island kingdom and if surrounded by ships with nearby air bases she could not conduct offensive war from the home islands. Its military power was useless without a means of delivery. Marshall recognized this fundamental principle at the very beginning of hostilities when he importuned Roosevelt to build more ships of all types in order to move his troops to the battlefront. Although Marshall did not endorse the proposition that the southwest Pacific route was necessarily the best, he did agree that the diversion of forces from the Southwest Pacific Area should not be made. Accordingly, the Joint Chiefs declined to send the 1st Marine Division and two bomber groups to Nimitz.

The move north to Rabaul called for the capture of the air base at Munda on the northwest coast of New Georgia. This operation began the night of 29 and 30 June 1943. Army troops under Halsey's command easily seized beachheads to the south at Rendova from a small enemy garrison. Further advances were both slow and costly. Major General Oscar W. Griswold, commander of the army's XIV Corps, took charge of operations in mid-July. Intended to be a one-division operation against a garrison of approximately 10,000, the conquest of New Georgia ultimately involved three army divisions plus elements of another, together with several marine battalions. The campaign precipitated large-scale naval and air battles that caused heavy casualties to both sides. Munda was not secured until 6 August.

Although Halsey's command directed the New Georgia campaign and the capture of the airfield at Munda, this island was located in MacArthur's area.

Accordingly, public relations were handled through Southwest Pacific Command headquarters, which spotlighted MacArthur in practically all news releases. This prompted Marshall on 14 July 1943 to ask MacArthur, "Is there objection to releasing the fact that troops of the 37th and 43rd Divisions are engaged in the New Georgia operations and the names of division commanders?" [17] American newspapers published very few stories on the defeat of the Japanese at Munda.

On 21 July, Marshall radioed MacArthur that after Cartwheel he should seize Wewak in northeastern New Guinea and Manus in the Admiralty Islands and that Halsey's forces should capture Kavieng in New Ireland. By these maneuvers Rabaul would be encircled and isolated and no longer a threat to Allied forces. MacArthur responded that Rabaul had to be taken in order to provide him with an adequate forward naval base together with security on his right flank as his forces advanced up the coastline of New Guinea.

Through the year the Allies maintained air superiority in the lower Solomons and New Guinea, making it virtually impossible for the Japanese to take men and supplies from Rabaul to the front during daylight hours. Operating from Henderson Field, marine Maj. Gregory "Pappy" Boyington and his Black Sheep scored numerous kills against enemy aircraft on a daily basis. Boyington himself was credited with downing twenty-eight enemy aircraft before he himself was shot down and captured by the Japanese. So confident that he could not be killed, he told members of his squadron, "If you ever see me go down . . . I promise I'll meet you in a San Diego bar six months after the war." [18] *Life* magazine ran photographs of the Boyington party (held in San Francisco) in its 1 October 1945 issue.

In addition to land-based planes on Guadalcanal, PT boats played a major role in preventing supplies from reaching the Japanese at forward areas. Headquartered at Tulagi, the PTs intercepted numerous barges carrying enemy troops and supplies during the hours of darkness. Byron "Whizzer" White, later a Supreme Court justice, acted as the intelligence officer for the direction of the PTs against the best targets. The PTs operated most often in enemy waters. PT 109, commanded by John F. Kennedy, was among the many sunk in the process of interdicting Japanese movements to the front.

The slow progress made by a vastly superior force in numbers against the Japanese in the New Georgia campaign must have affected the Joint Chiefs' thinking about Rabaul. After Munda, it was obvious that the capture of Rabaul with its garrison strength of more than 100,000 enemy soldiers would entail tremendous Allied casualties, a fact recognized in both Washington and Brisbane. In August, the Combined Chiefs at Quadrant agreed that Rabaul would be bypassed.

Chapter 16
Strategy Change

THE 1935 PLAN ORANGE called for island hopping across the Central Pacific to Truk, Japan's strong navy base in the western Pacific. Islands not needed for U.S. bases would be bypassed and left to wither on the vine. Truk itself would be used as the U.S. Navy's main base in place and stead of the Japanese.[1]

The historian Edward S. Miller observed that "far more Japanese defenders were isolated on bypassed islands than were destroyed in invasion battles. It was one of the most farsighted campaign doctrines handed down from the authors of Plan Orange to the wartime architects of victory." [2]

Beginning in the summer of 1943 and throughout the remainder of the Pacific War, the art of bypassing became the rule rather than the exception until MacArthur's forces reached the Philippines, a strategy change from the previous year and a half. In mid-August, Halsey's forces captured lightly defended Vella Lavella, bypassing the heavily defended Kolombangara. In anticipation of the 3rd Marine Division's landing at Bougainville on 1 November, a combination of airplanes from Guadalcanal, Kenney's Fifth Air Force, and Halsey's Third Fleet pounded Rabaul in September and October. Ten enemy cruisers were put out of action together with two-thirds of Adm. Meinichi Koga's naval air strength. Koga had succeeded Yamamoto as commander of the Combined Fleet. Later events showed that once the Allies occupied an airstrip on Bougainville capable of handling a large number of fighter planes, Japan's most formidable base in the southwest Pacific would no longer be an offensive threat.

At war, the side that gains control of the sky also gains control of the sea underneath, although the nearby land may be under the domination of the enemy. To reduce Rabaul to impotency, the Allies needed airstrips within close range so that U.S. fighter planes could operate around the clock against this Japanese stronghold.

By September 1943, MacArthur had accepted the Joint Chiefs' decision to neutralize rather than capture Rabaul. Halsey's fighter aircraft had to be established within close range of the fortress itself. MacArthur and Halsey exchanged a number of ideas as to where to acquire the needed airstrips. On 17 September, MacArthur stressed the importance of landing on the mainland of Bougainville but left the decision to Halsey as to where.

Bougainville, the largest of the Solomon Islands, is approximately 125 miles long and 30 to 40 miles wide. Two active volcanoes, 10,000-foot Mount Balbi and 8,000-foot Mount Bagana, send continual clouds of steam and smoke into the skies. Mount Bagana overlooks Empress Augusta Bay, the area selected by Halsey to land troops.

In 1943, the native population consisted of more than 40,000 Melanesians, who were slightly darker in color than those in the southern Solomons. Before the war, about a hundred Australian missionaries, planters, traders, and government officials lived on the island. Many of these stayed on as coast watchers. During the early part of 1943, some natives aided the Japanese in rooting out these brave Australians who gave valuable information to the Allies of Japanese planes and ships moving south.

United States Intelligence estimated enemy strength on Bougainville at about 37,500 soldiers, belonging to the Seventeenth Army under General Hyakutake, and about 20,000 sailors.[3] More than 25,000 of Hyakutake's men were thought to be in the Buin-Shortland area, with an additional 5,000 on the east coast plus 5,000 more at Buka and Bonis. Only slightly more than 1,000 Japanese occupied the Empress Augusta Bay area. Before making his final decision, Halsey sent submarines to the east and west coast to gather soil samples. He needed ground for the building of two airstrips. The east coast patrol delivered an unfavorable report. To the west, the submarine *Guardfish* landed a marine patrol north of Cape Torokina. When tested, the soil samples showed this area suitable for airfield construction.

By invading Empress Augusta Bay, Halsey's forces would bypass the main enemy strength in both north and south Bougainville. There was no intent to capture the entire island. To achieve military objectives, the Allies called for an enclave in width and depth large enough to establish two airfields within its perimeter. Thick jungles surrounding the enclave would deny the Japanese easy access.

Halsey's airstrips would be within close fighter range of Rabaul as well as all bases on Bougainville. Prior to invasion, he used all his air strength including his carrier planes, those at Guadalcanal and Munda as well as the Fifth Air Force, to eliminate all Japanese planes on the island itself in advance of the intended main landing on 1 November 1943.

A coastal plain of about seven square miles lay between the sea and the mountains at Cape Torokina. So forbidding were the jungle-covered mountains that surrounded the proposed landing area that Halsey's planners correctly estimated it would take three to four months for the Japanese to bring enough artillery and heavy equipment to launch an effective counterattack. However, heavy surf in Empress Augusta Bay made landing operations difficult.

On 20 October, Admiral Koga ordered carrier planes from Truk dispatched to Rabaul. By November, 173 carrier planes—82 fighters, 45 dive-bombers,

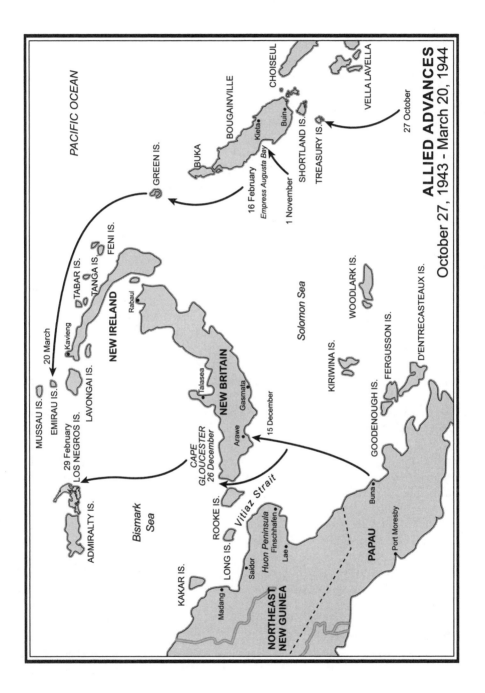

PACIFIC OCEAN

CHOISEUL

VELLA LAVELLA

27 October

BOUGAINVILLE

BUKA

Kieta

Buin

SHORTLAND IS.

TREASURY IS.

16 February

Empress Augusta Bay

1 November

GREEN IS.

TABAR IS.

TANGA IS.

FENI IS.

Rabaul

Kavieng

NEW IRELAND

20 March

MUSSAU IS.

EMIRAU IS.

LAVONGAI IS.

29 February
LOS NEGROS IS.

ADMIRALTY IS.

Bismark
Sea

Talasea

Gasmata

NEW BRITAIN

15 December

CAPE
GLOUCESTER
26 December

Arawe

Solomon Sea

WOODLARK IS.

KIRIWINA IS.

FERGUSSON IS.

GOODENOUGH IS.

D'ENTRECASTEAUX IS.

Buna

Port Moresby

PAPAU

ROOKE IS.

Vitiaz Strait

Huon Peninsula

Finschhafen

Lae

Saidor

LONG IS.

KAKAR IS.

Madang

NORTHEAST
NEW GUINEA

ALLIED ADVANCES
October 27, 1943 - March 20, 1944

40 torpedo bombers, and 6 patrol planes—reached Rabaul to team with Kusaka's 200 already there. Some of the fiercest sky battles in the Solomons took place in late October and the month of November after Allied troops landed.

Ground forces assigned to the attack included the 3rd Marine Division, the U.S. Army 37th Division and 8th Brigade Group, the 3rd New Zealand Division, the 3rd Marine Defense Battalion, the 198th Coastal Artillery Regiment (anti-aircraft), the 2nd Provisional Marine Raider Battalion, the 1st Marine Parachute Battalion plus naval construction and communications units. Prior to the landing day, the 2nd Marine Parachute Battalion made a twelve-day raid on Choiseul intended to mislead the enemy into believing that the main Allied objective lay on Bougainville's east coast.

The 3rd Marine Division less the 21st Regiment made the assault attack on D-day at Empress Augusta Bay. The 37th Division arrived a few days thereafter. The Japanese fully expected Halsey to attack Bougainville. In September, Imperial Headquarters stressed the importance of this island as the outpost for Rabaul. The Japanese planned to use air and surface strength to smash any Allied invasion attempt. If troops did succeed in getting to shore, the Japanese planned to destroy their beachhead. The nature of the terrain on the west coast of Bougainville convinced Hyakutake that the Allies would not attempt to land there.

The first American troops reached the beach at 7:26 A.M. In a matter of minutes, all of the assault waves came ashore. Only at Puruata Island and Cape Torokina did the marines meet strong opposition. On Cape Torokina, the enemy had built about eighteen log and sandbag pillboxes, each with two machine guns mutually supporting, camouflaged and arranged in depth. By 11:00 A.M., the marines eliminated the Japanese at a cost of 78 men killed and 104 wounded. Elsewhere, those landed pushed slowly inland through dense jungle and a knee-deep swamp that ran two miles inland and backed most of the beach north and east of Cape Torokina. Because of the dense overhead jungle, the swamp's existence had not been detected by Allied intelligence. Constant enemy air attacks plus the swampy terrain caused numerous halts in unloading supplies and equipment. Halsey said it was "worse than any we had previously encountered." [4]

For the first eleven days of November, the battle for the beachhead was fought in the air and on the sea. General Kenney's Fifth Air Force made Rabaul its primary target. By 11 November, 121 planes of Koga's carrier air force had been destroyed plus seventy more planes from the Japanese Eleventh Air Fleet. On 12 November, Koga withdrew his carrier planes back to Truk. The further withdrawal of his surface ships ended Rabaul's offensive threat; however, the enemy maintained sufficient aircraft to make air raids day and night against marine and army troops.

The 1st Battalion of the 21st Marine Regiment arrived on 6 November. Elements of the 37th Division began arriving on 8 November and continued through the third week of the month. The 2nd Battalion, 21st Marine Regiment, arrived on 11 November and the 3rd Battalion, 21st Marine Regiment, boarded four APDs (old converted destroyers) at Guadalcanal on 15 November. Japanese planes spotted the movements on the night of the 16th. Progress was slow, as the APDs zigzagged to their destination. One enemy plane placed a torpedo in the APD *McKean*. She sank within ten minutes along with a loss of ninety-eight sailors and marines. The next morning, destroyers fished approximately one hundred survivors out of the water. By late December, Allied ground-based fighter planes from Bougainville flew daily missions against Kavieng and Rabaul.

In mid-January, the 3rd Marine Division returned to Guadalcanal. No longer did planes from Rabaul bomb Henderson Field on moonlight nights. The troops tented in a large coconut grove some miles east of Henderson Field. At night, the marines watched movies or regimental boxing matches. The Seabees had constructed roads connecting bivouac areas to other features of the island including a fine medical facility staffed by army and navy doctors plus female nurses. The latter had to reside in heavily fenced-in quarters for protection.

Often at night men gathered around the communications jeep to listen to the Radio Tokyo broadcast "Zero Hour." After playing American band music, it featured an English-speaking female that servicemen named Tokyo Rose. Periodically, she made comments such as, "You orphans of the Pacific . . . Why should you be suffering such hardships while your wives and sweethearts are running around with 4Fs in the states?" Her comments caused more laughter than any adverse effect upon morale. However, most military personnel were intrigued by her knowledge of happenings in the Pacific. She often referred to battles and events prior to information received through normal channels. After the war, it was learned that the real Tokyo Rose was Iva Toguri, a Japanese-American graduate of the University of California at Los Angeles who just happened to be in Japan when war started. In 1949, she was tried for treason in San Francisco and sentenced to ten years' imprisonment plus a $100,000 fine.

Mail call plus overseas editions of *Time*, *Newsweek*, and *Life* were especially popular with the troops.

To further his drive to the Philippines, MacArthur planned for the invasion of Hansa Bay on 1 February 1944. On 1 March, Halsey's South Pacific Force would take Kavieng, while MacArthur would move into the Admiralties. Seeadler Harbor in the Admiralties would become a principal navy base while Kavieng would be developed into a major air base with six airfields. The day after Christmas, Halsey departed Noumea for a visit with Nimitz at Pearl Harbor. After his arrival, Nimitz advised that he and King had decided to have him alternate command of the big Pacific Fleet with Spruance. Halsey would command the Third Fleet, Spruance the Fifth Fleet. The ships commanded by both would be the same. The designation "Third Fleet" or "Fifth Fleet" depended on which admiral was in command.

In early January 1944, Halsey and Nimitz conferred with King on the West Coast. Here, and later in Washington, Halsey made known his view of bypassing Kavieng in favor of Emirau Island. While unable to carry his point, the Joint Chiefs agreed to provide the necessary support for the Admiralties and Kavieng landings. Halsey returned to the South Pacific in late January 1944.

The capture of Madang completed Cartwheel except for the isolation of Rabaul. Plans now called for the seizure of Hansa Bay, about midway between Madang and Wewak, beginning in February 1944, and the invasions in March of Manus in the Admiralties by MacArthur's forces, and of Kavieng in New Ireland by Halsey's forces. Besides being ideally situated in severing Rabaul's line of communications, the Admiralties—consisting mainly of Manus and Los Negros islands—had one of the finest potential fleet anchorages in the Pacific, at Seeadler Harbor. The U.S. Navy determined to establish a major fleet base there to support future operations.

In December 1943, Halsey and MacArthur did not see eye to eye on the necessity for taking Kavieng. MacArthur argued that its capture was essential to provide air bases to cover later advances, but Halsey contended that Kavieng, known to be strongly fortified, could be bypassed in favor of seizing lightly held Emirau, to the north. Having been unsuccessful with Nimitz and King to bypass Kavieng, Halsey designated the 3rd Marine Division to lead the assault.

Already, however, Japan had moved its ships and planes from Rabaul to Truk. The Joint Chiefs reviewed their strategy after a fast carrier task force under Admiral Spruance on 16 and 17 February destroyed most of the aircraft stationed there together with about 200,000 tons of enemy shipping. As a result, the Japanese fleet abandoned Truk in favor of the Palau Islands.

Meanwhile, in order to have better fighter bases within range of Kavieng, Halsey sent elements of a New Zealand division into the Green Islands on 15 February. The New Zealanders successfully completed the operation within five days. By early March, a fighter strip became operational on one of the Green Islands, which lay only 220 miles southeast of Kavieng and 117 miles east of Rabaul.

By March of 1944, Japanese troops at Rabaul and Bougainville were stranded. With air and naval strength gone, they were incapable of affecting the course of the war. However, Generals Imamura and Hyakutake refused to accept defeat. They planned the capture of Empress Augusta Bay. Unfortunately, Hyakutake's intelligence estimate placed Allied strength at Empress Augusta Bay at about 30,000, of whom 10,000 were aircraft ground crews.[5] His figure for Maj. Gen. Oscar W. Griswold's XIV Corps was too low by half. The main ground combat elements were the Americal and 37th Divisions, which numbered about 27,000 men. The 3rd Marine Defense Battalion plus other attached units placed Griswold in charge of 62,000 men altogether.[6]

Against the American XIV Corps, Hyakutake planned to attack with a total Japanese strength reported as 15,000 to 19,000 men.[7] During the early part of 1944, Japanese engineers built roads, trails, and bridges so that the Seventeenth Army could move from north and south Bougainville to assembly areas in the hills around the American perimeter.[8] But Griswold's men were not asleep. All units strengthened positions on the main line of resistance, which consisted of rifle pits and earth, log, and sandbag pillboxes behind double apron or concertina barbed wire. Minefields and grenade booby traps were established along obvious approach routes.

Hyakutake organized his infantry into three forces, each named for its commander: General Iwasa, Colonel Magata, and Colonel Muda. The Japanese plan of maneuver involved two thrusts from the north coupled with an attack from the northeast, all on a prearranged schedule starting on 11 March. All units were to drive southward on a broad front to capture the Torokina fighter strip by 17 March.

Hyakutake's plan was fatally flawed from the very beginning. He lacked strength in both manpower and artillery and had no air support whatsoever. Furthermore, the desired element of surprise did not exist. Beginning on 7 March, Allied infantry patrols reported many enemy contacts prior to the initial assault. Although the Japanese made penetrations in the American perimeter, they were always beaten back in the bloodiest fighting on Bougainville.

On 27 March, Hyakutake decided to withdraw, having sustained more than 8,000 casualties.[9] In spite of the serious losses by the Japanese Seventeenth Army, it still engaged in several sharp fights with the XIV Corps in early April. Thus ended the last Japanese offensive effort in the Solomon Islands.

The Joint Chiefs rescheduled the Admiralty Islands and Kavieng invasions to 1 April. During January and early February, the Fifth Air Force systematically bombed Japanese air bases at both places. By mid-February, airmen reported no enemy planes at either base; moreover, neither anti-aircraft fire nor troop activity was observed.

On 29 February, elements of the U.S. 1st Cavalry Division, labeled a reconnaissance in force by MacArthur, landed at Los Negros in the Admiralties and captured the Momote Air Field within two hours. MacArthur received numerous accolades by military chiefs at the time and by historians later for what appeared to be a risky gamble that succeeded. The army's historian states that MacArthur's decision regarding Los Negros had the very great virtue of hastening victory while reducing the number of dead and wounded.[10] Australian historians tell a different story, which is set forth in Chapter 19 of this book.

On 5 March 1944, MacArthur advised the Joint Chiefs that the initial success of the Admiralty reconnaissance in force operation presented an excellent opportunity to accelerate his westward move along the north coast of New Guinea. He suggested that Kavieng be seized, Hansa Bay be bypassed, and that he next advance all the way to Hollandia in Netherlands New Guinea, provided Admiral Nimitz furnish him aircraft carriers. This move would bypass Adachi's main strength at Madang and Wewak.

Finally the Joint Chiefs, having been influenced by Halsey's arguments, supported by Nimitz, ordered the cancellation of Kavieng. Instead, the Joint Chiefs agreed with MacArthur's advance on Hollandia and Halsey's seizure of Emirau Island.

Halsey selected the U.S. 4th Marine Regiment, created out of the recently disbanded Raider battalions, for the Emirau landing. On 23 March, while four old battleships pounded Kavieng with tons of 14- and 5-inch shells, the 4th Marines went peacefully ashore at Emirau. As there were no Japanese, air bombardments and naval gunfire were unnecessary. Halsey wrote that this operation established "a record of six days between 'Stand by to shove off.' And 'Well done!' "[11]

Within a month 18,000 men and 44,000 tons of supplies had been ferried to Emirau. The first airstrip was opened in May. Allied planes and torpedo boats patrolled the waters leading to New Ireland and Rabaul. With Allied control of all sea lanes and straits as well as the air, the more than 150,000 Japanese at Kavieng, Rabaul, and Bougainville for all practical purposes were now out of the war.

An examination made after Japan's surrender showed the wisdom of Admiral Halsey's and the Joints Chiefs' decision to bypass Kavieng and Rabaul. There were 12,400 Japanese repatriated from New Ireland, which houses Kavieng's airfields. A total of 95,396 Japanese army, navy, and civilian workers still occupied Rabaul on surrender day.[12] The Australians who took charge of the repatriation noted that the Japanese troops "were found to be well fed and in fairly good health." [13]

The official Australian history reported that Rabaul's port and airfield were in ruins, with the town overgrown in jungle. "The Japanese had honeycombed the hills around Rabaul with a system of tunnels totaling more than 150 miles in length." [14] Around the town, they had gardens aggregating thousands of acres. In the harbor, "31 sunken ships could be seen from the air." [15] The Japanese troops hid themselves from aerial view as they lived "and kept their vehicles, stores, and even workshops underground. Some tunnels were concreted and had stairways, telephones, electric light, and built-in furniture. Men's quarters were lined with tiers of bunks. Hundreds of tons of rice were in underground stores. The underground radio station was about 40 feet below the surface and 60 feet long." [16] Clearly, had the Allies determined to attack Rabaul head-on, the result would have been the worst bloodbath of the Pacific War.

Pearl Harbor as viewed by a Japanese aircrew on 7 December 1941. Battleship Row stretches across the photo; Ford Island is at lower right. *U.S. Navy photo*

USS *Lexington*'s Capt. Frederick Sherman orders "Abandon ship" at 5:01 in the afternoon of 8 May 1943 during the Battle of the Coral Sea. The destroyer at right (just visible through the smoke) is taking on the wounded. Other crewmembers slide down ropes to the water to be picked up by small boats. Not a man was lost in abandoning the ship. *U.S. Navy photo*

A Japanese cruiser (lower right) and smaller ships flee Rabaul harbor during a devastating raid by carrier-based U.S. Navy planes on 5 November 1943. The crushing blow nullified for a time the Japanese attempt to strengthen the Rabaul garrison with reinforcements from Truk. *U.S. Navy photo*

Sprawled bodies on the beach of Tarawa testifies to the ferocity of the struggle for this stretch of sand. *U.S. Navy photo*

The 4th Marine Division attacks Roi Island, Kwajalein Atoll, Marshall Islands. Japanese installations on nearby Namur go skyhigh as demolition squads go into action. *U.S. Navy photo*

Heavily loaded LSTs (Landing Ship, Tank) hit the beach of Tanahmerah Bay in the Hollandia area of Dutch New Guinea on 22 Aprill 1944. Three airfields were seized within five days. *U.S. Navy photo*

Left to right: Gen. Douglas MacArthur, President Franklin Roosevelt, and Adm. Chester W. Nimitz aboard the heavy cruiser USS *Baltimore* in Pearl Harbor on 26 July 1944. *U.S. Navy photo*

President Roosevelt is greeted by a long line of enlisted men in whites as he inspects the Submarine Base at Pearl Harbor during his July 1944 visit. *U.S. Navy photo*

President Roosevelt surveys military facilities during a brief tour of the island of Oahu, July 1944. *U.S. Navy photo*

Left to right: Adm. William Leahy, Lt. Gen. Robert Richardson, President Roosevelt, and Col. William Saffarans watch soldiers drill in tropical combat at the U.S. Army's Jungle Training Unit in Hawaii. *U.S. Navy photo*

Left to right: Gen. Douglas MacArthur, President Roosevelt, Adm. Chester W. Nimitz, and Adm. William Leahy discuss Pacific strategy in Oahu, Hawaii, July 1944. *U.S. Navy photo*

MacArthur, Roosevelt, Nimitz, and Leahy. Later meetings were less ceremonial. During these meetings it was decided that bypassing Luzon in the Philippines was not feasible. *U.S. Navy photo*

Marines entrench themselves and inch forward against determined Japanese resistance on Peleliu Island. *U.S. Navy photo*

Heavy columns of smoke rise over the Philippines as U.S. Navy carrier-based planes and naval guns hammer the shores of Leyte prior to the landing of troops, 20 October 1944. *U.S. Navy photo*

The top brass in the Pacific (left to right): Adm. Chester W. Nimitz, Adm. Ernest King, and Adm. Raymond Spruance aboard the USS *Indianapolis*, 1944. *U.S. Navy photo*

A task force of Adm. William Halsey's Third Fleet enters the South China Sea for the first time on 11 January 1945 and batters Japanese ships. Smoking, burning ships dot the sea. Forty-one ships were sunk. *U.S. Navy photo*

A coordinated amphibious assault moves against Iwo Jima, 19 February 1945. *U.S. Navy photo*

Gen. Mitsuru Ushijima, commander of
the Japanese 32nd Army on Okinawa.
U.S. Navy photo

The IJN *Yamato* explodes in a giant ball of fire and smoke after concentrated air attacks
from U.S. carrier-based Helldivers and Hellcats on 7 April 1945. *U.S. Navy photo*

Lt. Gen. Simon Buckner, Commanding General of the Tenth Army (left), and U.S. Marine Major General Roy Geiger, Commanding General of III Amphibious Corps (right), discuss the situation during a meeting on Okinawa. *U.S. Navy photo*

The ground the 184th Infantry Regiment fought over to gain the "Rocky Crag" on Okinawa, 22 April 1945. *U.S. Navy photo*

Vice Admiral Marc Mitscher (left) and Adm. Chester W. Nimitz aboard USS *Indianapolis*, 1945. *U.S. Navy photo*

Left to right: Adm. Raymond Spruance, Adm. Chester W. Nimitz, and Lt. Gen. Simon Buckner at an airfield before a tour of inspection of Tenth Army Headquarters and XXIV Corps Headquarters on Okinawa, 22 April 1945. *U.S. Navy photo*

Heavy rains have slowed mechanized warfare on Okinawa, but these infantrymen of the Tenth Army's 77th Division plod ahead despite the sticky terrain. *U.S. Navy photo*

Japanese POW stands at the graves of Lt. Gen. Isamu Cho and Gen. Mitsuru Ushijima on Hill 98, Okinawa, June 1945. *U.S. Navy photo*

Ruins of Shuri Castle walls after the town was captured by Tenth Army forces. *U.S. Navy photo*

A flame-throwing tank neutralizes a position as a 96th Division infantryman covers it against a potential rush by desperate enemy soldiers, 21 June 1945. *U.S. Navy photo*

Chapter 17
The Central
Pacific Drive

*I*MPLEMENTATION OF PLAN ORANGE began with the battle for Tarawa on 20 November 1943. Beforehand, in August 1943, Roosevelt and Churchill called for another conference at Quebec under the code name Quadrant. Decisions had to be made about operations following the invasion of Sicily in July, the opening of the Burma Road in China, and the long-range strategy for the defeat of Japan in the Pacific.

Before Quadrant, Admiral King had wanted action in the Central Pacific. He first considered taking the Marshalls, although Nimitz and Spruance had doubts. In July, Spruance reported back to Nimitz that Japanese fortifications in the Marshall Islands were too strong for the limited American forces then available to attack at this time. He recommended that American forces should first seize the Gilbert Islands, which the fleet strategists suspected were not so heavily defended. From airfields in the Gilberts, land-based air could reconnoiter plus soften up the Marshalls prior to an invasion.

Japan lay 5,000 miles from Hawaii, and the path the U.S. Navy would have to take was blocked by hundreds of Japanese-held islands in the Central Pacific, many studded with air bases. Fleet Admiral Meinichi Koga, commander in chief of the Japanese Imperial Combined Fleet, having succeeded the late Isoroku Yamamoto in May 1943, told his staff, "There was only one Yamamoto and no one is able to replace him. His loss is an insupportable blow to us." [1] Indeed, Koga, like Yamamoto, recognized early that whichever nation had the superior fleet at the end would win the war.

In meetings at Truk, Vice Adm. Ryusonuke Kusaka, commander of Japanese South and southwest Pacific, complained about the advances being made in New Guinea and the Solomons. "(Admiral William) Halsey, in particular," Kusaka told Koga, "is making dangerous progress." [2]

During the first week of September 1943, Koga issued the "New Operational Policy." It was centered on the Yogaki plan, or "waylaying attack," a strategy to wait for the enemy fleet to enter Japanese waters and then fight a decisive naval engagement. Koga had numerous air bases in the potential battle areas, including facilities in the Marshalls, Gilberts, Solomons, Carolines, and New Britain. His land-based air forces combined with his carrier fleet could destroy the Americans when they came forward. The Japanese fleet occupied three large naval anchorages in the South and Central Pacific: one at Truk in the Caroline Islands, one at Kwajalein in the Marshall Islands, and the heavily fortified Rabaul on the northeast coast of New Britain.

In September, Koga had available in his main striking force three carriers with nearly 200 combat aircraft, the super battleships *Yamato* and *Musashi*, two smaller battleships, and a destroyer squadron from the 1st Fleet. On island bases at the Marshalls, Gilberts, and Carolines, he had another 150 land-based planes. Also available was a third fleet that had a combined strength of three carriers with 150 aircraft, two battleships, eleven heavy cruisers, three light cruisers, and scores of destroyers. Vice Admiral Masashi Kobayashi's 4th Fleet contributed two light cruisers, four destroyers, and six submarines. In addition, Rear Adm. Takeo Takagi's 6th Fleet included twenty-four submarines.

Koga's strategy for battle in the Gilberts was drawn up on 8 September 1943. Rear Admiral Keiji Shibasaki, who had previously been named commander of the Gilberts and Nauru, commanded 8,000 naval infantry and support troops. Of these, 5,000 were based on Tarawa atoll with the rest dug in on Makin, Ocean, and Nauru islands. Koga intended to make the Gilberts even stronger with the addition of 2,500 Imperial Marines. He had available the 22nd Air Flotilla at Truk, which would attack the American carrier forces from bases throughout the Marshalls.

Yet, advances by the Americans in the Solomons greatly hindered Koga's strategy. In September and October of 1943 the combination of airplanes from Guadalcanal, Maj. Gen. George C. Kenney's U.S. Fifth Air Force, and "Bull" Halsey's Third Fleet had pounded Rabaul in anticipation of the 3rd Marine Division's landing on 1 November at Bougainville, the largest of the Solomons.

In the first two weeks of November, all but one of the eleven cruisers that Admiral Kurita's 2nd Fleet had deployed in September had been put out of action. Equally important, Admiral Koga's naval air strength at Rabaul had been ravaged: 121 planes, or roughly two-thirds of the entire force, had been lost in air battles. Of the 192 highly trained carrier flight crews dispatched from Truk to Rabaul, 86 had been lost. Koga, with great disappointment, recalled the survivors to Truk on 12 November. By mid-November Koga's losses in planes and cruisers had been such that only nine submarines and a reduced number of aircraft could be sent to the Gilberts to combat Vice Admiral Spruance's fleet.

The first major U.S. offensive aimed against Japan as envisioned in Plan Orange called for the use of the U.S. Army's 27th Division to capture Makin Island, occupied by between 650 and 800 men, of whom 280 were combat troops. The 2nd Marine Division would take Tarawa, while Nauru and Ocean islands would be bypassed. The lightly defended Abemama Island required only a small marine landing force. Vice Admiral Spruance would be in overall command. Rear Admiral Richmond Kelly Turner would command the amphibious forces assigned to Tarawa and Makin. Rear Admiral Harry W. Hill, commander of the Southern Attack Force, would actually direct the Tarawa invasion. Major General Holland Smith, USMC, would command the assault units under the designated V Amphibious Corps. Major General Ralph C. Smith commanded the U.S. Army's 27th Infantry Division. Major General Julian C. Smith was in command of the 2nd Marine Division. The operation was code-named Galvanic, but both before and after the battle the news media referred mostly to Tarawa. Major General Holland Smith approved the 2nd Marine Division's blueprint for Tarawa on 14 September.

The 2nd Marine Division had a motley collection of one hundred landing vehicles, tracked (LVTs), in New Zealand, but to ensure success the marines estimated they needed a minimum of one hundred more. They suggested that the lack of intelligence concerning tidal conditions in the Gilberts alone was reason enough to employ more tracked landing craft. Any possibility that the tides might be low on D-day could mean disaster for the assault troops, who would have to wade ashore under fire.

"How soon can we have the vehicles, Kelly?" asked "Howlin' Mad" Smith of Admiral Turner. In Turner's opinion, there would be favorable tidal conditions. The marines would have to get along with what they had. Smith raised his voice. "By God, Kelly, I want amtracs and I'll have them!" "On Oahu, I obtained irrefutable proof of the amtrac's efficiency," Smith wrote later. ". . . If the reef proved impassable for boats—and it did—the only way to get the men ashore was in amtracs."

Turner tried to mollify Smith. "There's no need to blow up, General," he said. "You won't need amtracs." Facing Turner, Smith said, "Admiral, don't tell me what I need. You handle your ships, and I'll take care of my men. I'm telling you straight out, Admiral, either produce a hundred amtracs or the deal's off." Turner remained adamant in his opposition.

"Kelly, it's like this. I've got to have those amtracs. We'll take a helluva licking without them. No amtracs, no operation. You know me, Kelly. I mean it." Turner threw up his arms in exasperation and sighed wearily. "Yes, General, I know you. I'll rustle up a hundred amtracs for you and find room for them on the ships. Now let's get back to business—there's been enough bullshit." [3]

By the middle of November, on the eve of battle, Tarawa could not have been much stronger, although American submarines in the Marshalls and around Truk had sunk supply ships and slowed to a trickle the flow of steel, cement, and other supplies to Tarawa. The last Japanese port call had been a small coastal freighter from Jaluit in late September.

Rear Admiral Keiji Shibasaki commanded the 3rd Special Base Defense Force on Betio islet, the most heavily fortified garrison in the Tarawa atoll. Shibasaki had directed the construction of bombproof shelters, perhaps the most extensive encountered anywhere except at Iwo Jima. Coconut logs strengthened

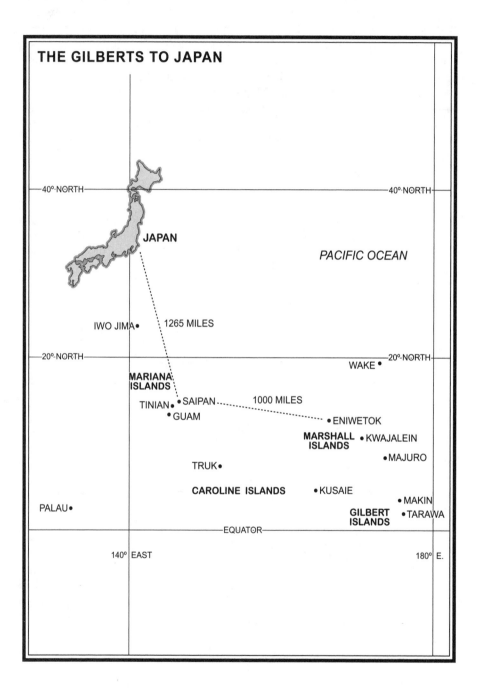

THE GILBERTS TO JAPAN

40°·NORTH — 40°·NORTH

JAPAN

PACIFIC OCEAN

IWO JIMA• 1265 MILES

20°·NORTH — 20°·NORTH

WAKE •

MARIANA
ISLANDS

TINIAN• •SAIPAN 1000 MILES
•GUAM •ENIWETOK

MARSHALL •KWAJALEIN
ISLANDS
•MAJURO

TRUK•

CAROLINE ISLANDS •KUSAIE

PALAU• •MAKIN

GILBERT •TARAWA
ISLANDS

EQUATOR

140° EAST 180° E.

by angle irons and roofs, six feet and thicker, were so well constructed of sand, logs, and corrugated iron that only direct hits by large-caliber or delayed-action high-explosive shells could penetrate them.

The Allied plan called for the army's 27th Division and the 2nd Marine Division to simultaneously attack Makin and Betio in early morning 20 November and quickly reduce the enemy. Betio was the main prize because of its airfield, but it was by far the most heavily defended. The marines would attack across a coral reef on the lagoon side of Betio on beaches designated Red 1, Red 2, and Red 3, all in close proximity to the airfield. A seawall lined the beach areas next to the lagoon. On the second day, a fourth landing would be made from the western tip of the island on an area designated Green Beach.

Shortly before the assault, Col. David M. Shoup, USMC, who commanded the assault troops at Tarawa, explained the situation to *Time-Life* correspondent Robert Sherrod:

What worries me more than anything is that our boats may not be able to get over that coral shelf that sticks out about 500 yards. We may have to wade in. The first waves, of course, will get in all right on the "alligators" (LVTs), but if the Higgins boats draw too much water to get in fairly close, we'll either have to wade in with machine guns shooting at us, or the amtracs will have to run a shuttle service between the beach and the end of the shelf. We have got to calculate high tide pretty good for the Higgins boats to make it.[4]

On landing day, Shoup realized his worries. Low tide prevented the Higgins boats from getting over the coral shelf. Unaccountably, the low tide lasted for the better part of two days.[5]

At 4:00 A.M. on 20 November, the marines boarded the amtracs in anticipation of the landing. Four hours of heavy bombardment preceded their arrival on the beach at eight o'clock. Just as the LVTs crossed the line of departure, the naval bombardment lifted to allow the last air assault to come in. The planes roared over the beaches, strafing and bombing. The LVTs still had 3,500 yards to go. Landing hour was postponed to 9:00 A.M.

When the LVTs approached the reef, matters changed quickly—for the worse. Many LVTs came to a complete stop. Marines had to leap over the sides into the water and begin wading, their weapons held high. Other LVTs managed to go on, though incredibly slowly. It did not take long to realize that the worst possible scenario had become a reality: numerous marines would die as they struggled to get ashore. Higgins boats had no chance of crossing the reef because of the low tide. Shibasaki's garrison survived the unprecedented naval and air gunfire in large numbers. Attacking marines were shocked to find that the naval bombardment had eliminated so few defenders. The Japanese destroyed the incoming amtracs with such regularity, it is difficult to see how any marines survived to reach the protection of the seawall. Enemy machine gun and rifle fire mowed down large numbers of those wading to shore with rifles held high.

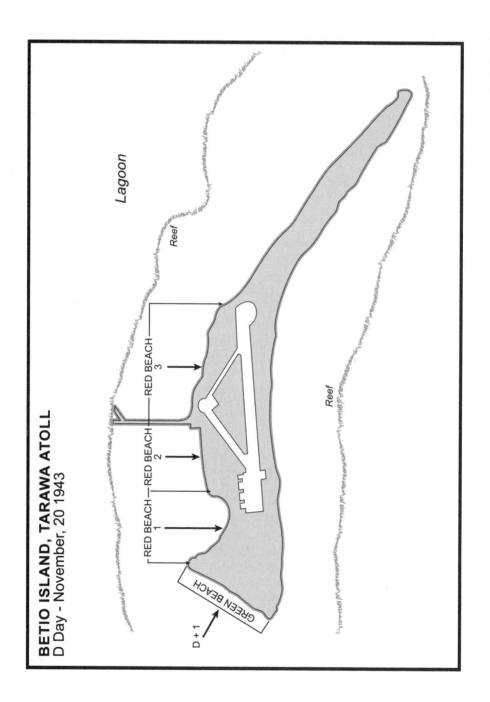

BETIO ISLAND, TARAWA ATOLL
D Day - November, 20 1943

Lagoon

Reef

Reef

RED BEACH 3

RED BEACH 2

RED BEACH 1

GREEN BEACH

D + 1

When Colonel Shoup hit the beach near noon, a large shell landed nearby, killing two riflemen. The concussion dropped Shoup to his knees. "Keep away!" he shouted to his staff as he led them inland. About fifteen yards from the water's edge he found a bunker in which five Japanese had been killed. The structure was forty feet long, eight feet wide, and ten feet high. Here, Shoup established his headquarters and proceeded to direct his troops. The carnage among assault troops had been disastrous. Instead of 3,000 marines landed by noon as planned, fewer than 1,200 had reached shore. Luckily for the marines, Shibasaki was killed the afternoon of this first day of fighting.

Historian Joseph H. Alexander explains:

> We now know from recent translations of Japanese accounts of the battle that Shibasaki died that first afternoon . . . He gave up his concrete blockhouse to be used as a hospital for his hundreds of casualties, assembled his staff in the open, and began to move to a secondary command post several hundred yards away. In one of the ironic flukes of battle, a Marine with perhaps the only working field radio on the island spotted the cluster of officers in the open and quickly called in naval gunfire. The two destroyers in the lagoon, *Ringgold* and *Dashiell*, cut loose with salvos of 5"/38 rounds fused as air bursts. Steel shards rained over the exposed Japanese, killing Shibasaki and his entire staff. By these few salvos, the Navy fire support task group made up for all its shortcomings of the day.[6]

By the end of the day, the marines held only a narrow strip along the seawall. Some had advanced to shell holes on the landing strip plus a toehold at the northern tip of Green Beach. With more than 1,300 casualties, success lay very much in doubt. With Shibasaki's death the Japanese failed to make the counterattack, which otherwise might have wiped the marines off the island.

On the second day, the U.S. Marines advanced across the airfield to the southern beach, and those landing in rowboats at Green Beach made solid progress. Only after marines had secured Green Beach and the laggard tide finally came in did the situation ashore begin to improve. General Julian Smith for the first time was able to act with confidence. He deployed his fully equipped three battalions of the 6th Marine Regiment. Until then it had been touch and go, although this second day of fighting claimed almost as many casualties as day one.

Correspondent Richard Johnston also sensed that the worst had passed. He scribbled in his notes: "It has been my privilege to see the Marines from privates to colonels, every man a hero, go up against Japanese fire with complete disregard for their lives. Men had died around me, many lie dead up ahead and more are going to die. The situation at one time was critical, but the valor of the Marines (has) won the battle." [7]

However, the battle was far from over.

By the end of the second day, the Japanese were divided into two groups, the redoubt between the airfield and the seawall (called The Pocket by the marines) and the main body still holding on savagely south and east of the airfield. With material getting ashore, the picture brightened immensely. Colonel Shoup observed, "Well, I think we're winning but the bastards have got a lot of bullets left. I think we'll clean up tomorrow." [8] As night came, the colonel grabbed his first real sleep in sixty hours.

Elsewhere within the American lines, few men slept easily for fear of counterattack. As the Japanese were driven in upon themselves in narrow fronts, the danger of a banzai attack had become more acute. But again on this second night, no Japanese counterattack occurred.

Shoup was right. On the third day, the Japanese defense began falling apart. The 6th Marine Regiment went into action for the first time since landing the previous evening, and with maximum fury. The 1st Battalion made an early morning rush. They faced the narrow hundred-yard-wide corridor of heavily fortified ground between the airfield and the ocean. The strip was studded with pillboxes and bunkers, hiding an untold number of Japanese riflemen. The marines moved swiftly, knocking out numerous Japanese pillboxes as they advanced while taking only minimal casualties.

On the fourth day, marines surrounded the last bastion of Japanese resistance on Betio, the notorious redoubt they had dubbed The Pocket. The Japanese had suffered heavy losses, were losing ground, and had lost elsewhere on Betio. At a midmorning conference, Gen. Julian Smith decided to mount an all-out attack led by the remnants of the 2nd Marines. Surrounded though they were, the Japanese would not surrender. The 1st Battalion, 8th Marines, and 3rd Battalion, 2nd Marines, moved against Japanese fortifications from all sides, including a hastily organized frontal amphibious assault from the lagoon. Supported by tanks, flamethrowers, LVTs, demolitions, and half-tracks mounting 75mm howitzers, they swarmed into and over individual pillboxes and bunkers. This furious action, in which two dozen marines were killed or wounded, was completed by the afternoon. No Japanese offered themselves as prisoners, and none were taken. Finally, at 1:30 P.M. Smith notified: "Betio has fallen."

At the end of the day after four full days of practically nonstop combat, the cost to the marines and attached naval and coast guard personnel was an astonishing 3,129 casualties. For this, the 2nd Division had bought only the most important of all the incredibly small islands that make up Tarawa atoll. The 2nd Battalion, 6th Marines, was even now still working its way up the rest of the tiny chain in pursuit of a fleeing enemy force that numbered close to 200. On day five, the marines eliminated the last of the enemy on Tarawa atoll. On the island of Abemama, only three marines were killed or wounded. The U.S. Army suffered 305 casualties taking Makin.

Time, *Newsweek*, and *Life* all carried the news and pictures of the Tarawa invasion, including editorial comment. *Time* commented on the change in attitude by the navy toward U.S. newsmen covering the Pacific Fleet. It spoke with approval of the directive issued by Chester W. Nimitz ordering fleet, force, and unit commanders to extend the fullest cooperation to correspondents

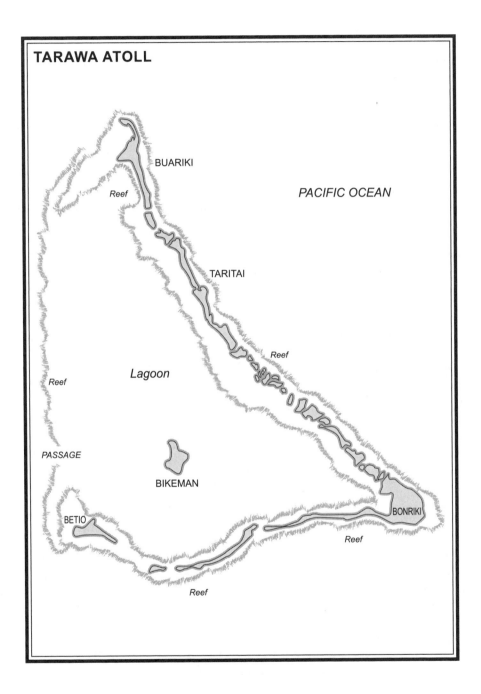

TARAWA ATOLL

PACIFIC OCEAN

BUARIKI

Reef

TARITAI

Reef

Lagoon

Reef

PASSAGE

BIKEMAN

BONRIKI

BETIO

Reef

Reef

everywhere. Twenty-five writers, five photographers, two artists, and a newsreel man flew over, cruised near, or landed with combat troops on the Gilbert Islands. The news reports to the States were generally positive in spite of the heavy casualties sustained. By reading the news coverage, it becomes obvious that the reporters were not privy to the strategy adopted by the Joint Chiefs of Staff. Many clearly had doubts about whether a drive across the Central Pacific was the best way to achieve victory.

In its 6 December 1943 issue, *Time* labeled the operation "The Admirals' Show." It said the U.S. Navy at last had opened its chosen theater: the Central Pacific. It observed that in the southwest Pacific, "General Douglas MacArthur glowered, let a spokesman grumble his dissent, and edged restively toward Rabaul." [9] Tarawa's heavy casualties gave support to MacArthur's opposition to island hopping as expressed in his 22 September 1943 interview in the *New York Times. Time* magazine observed that in the navy's drive through the mid-Pacific, "(the admirals) may then abandon island hopping for something much more direct and decisive . . . then General Douglas MacArthur has a strong case for his plaints—and for his road to the Philippines and east China (which in the end the admirals' plans need not rule out). For better or worse the Admirals' Show will bear watching." [10]

Both *Time* and *Newsweek* had maps that showed MacArthur's and Nimitz's drives toward the Philippines, with the ultimate objective being the east coast of China where airfields would be established for the bombing of Japan. Although the prewar Plan Orange did not envision the China coast as necessary for the ultimate blockade of Japan, the Joint Chiefs and news media seemed to consider it essential. The capture of Tarawa marked the beginning of the campaign that in time would change the mind of the Joint Chiefs on the need to reach the China coast.

Aside from Tarawa, *Time* and *Newsweek* contained articles about the home front that pointed out why the defeat of Japan was inevitable. In *Time*, navy Secretary Frank Knox announced that in the past eleven months the U.S. Navy had built 419 combat ships, doubling its strength. In *Newsweek*, columnist Raymond Moley observed that in two years the United States had increased its normal production 250 percent with a labor force increase of less than 30 percent. [11] Obviously Rosie the Riveter was more than upholding her share.

Admiral Spruance concluded, "The highlight of the campaign, and the part that will be longest remembered in American history, was the magnificent courage and tenacity of the 2nd Marine Division in carrying on their assault on Betio Island for a period of four days after suffering staggering losses. Nothing in the record of the Marine Corps can exceed the heroism displayed at Tarawa by the officers and men of the 2nd Marine Division and by the naval units that accompanied them in their landings." [12] Later Spruance declared that Tarawa taught him to use "violent overwhelming force swiftly applied." [13]

Nimitz told Admiral King that things would only get worse. [14]

Prior to Tarawa, Spruance's Task Force 58 had been assigned the mission to take Kwajalein, Wotje, and Maloelap in the Marshalls simultaneously with a target date of 1 January 1944. As a result of his experience at Tarawa, Holland Smith contended that enough troop support was not available for the three simultaneous assaults. Spruance concurred and accordingly recommended to Nimitz that Wotje and Maloelap be taken first for use as bases to support a later attack on Kwajalein. Nimitz rejected this recommendation. Instead, he directed that Wotje and Maloelap be bypassed in favor of the assault on Kwajalein alone.[15]

After it became clear that Nimitz's mind could not be changed, Spruance asked to include Majuro as an additional objective. One of the undefended atolls of the Marshalls, Majuro had a protected harbor with a lagoon twenty-one miles long and six to eight miles wide. This atoll also had room for airfields within supporting distance of Kwajalein.

The Joint Chiefs, especially King, wanted an early commencement of the operation, originally set for 1 January 1944 as D-day. Both Nimitz and Spruance contended that this timetable (1 January 1944) could not be met, as there was not enough planning time available to meet such an early date. It was finally decided that troops would land on Kwajalein on 31 January 1944. This atoll comprised about thirty-two islands surrounding one of the largest lagoons in the world, 655 square miles. The key islands of Kwajalein Atoll were Roi and Namur islands at the northern tip and Kwajalein Island at the southern tip. Roi had a fine airfield. Kwajalein had a 5,000-foot runway, which had nearly been completed by the Japanese.

The heavy casualties at Tarawa gave MacArthur the ammunition he needed to block the U.S. Navy's island-hopping campaign across the Central Pacific. He began a campaign to make the navy's role merely supportive of his own offensive.[16] He sent General Sutherland to Washington to urge the Joint Chiefs that after taking the Marshalls to switch Nimitz's Central Pacific Force southward to support MacArthur's advance to Mindanao.[17] After the Joint Chiefs rejected MacArthur's plan, he decided to go over their heads.[18] In mid-January, when Brig. Gen. Fredrick H. Osborn of the War Department staff visited the southwest Pacific, MacArthur gave Osborn a statement of his views and asked him to bring them to the attention of Secretary Stimson and, through him, to the president.[19] He claimed his own forces would be in Mindanao by the end of the year, provided he was given control of the ships, men, and equipment now in the Pacific. He said:

I need only that; what is now in the Pacific is sufficient if properly directed. . . . I do not want command of the Navy, but must control their strategy, be able to call on what little of the Navy is needed for a trek to the Philippines. The Navy's turn will come after that. These frontal attacks by the Navy, as at Tarawa, are tragic and unnecessary massacres of American lives. . . . The Navy fails to understand the strategy of the Pacific, fails to recognize that the first phase is an Army phase to establish land-based air protection so the Navy can move in. . . . Mr. Roosevelt is Navy minded. Mr. Stimson must speak to him, must persuade him.

Give me central direction of the war in the Pacific, and I will be in the Philippines in ten months. . . . Don't let the Navy's pride of position and ignorance continue this great tragedy to our country.[20]

Osborn showed MacArthur's message to General Marshall, who decided it should go no further, so there it stayed.

The Marshalls were part of the numerous islands, formally belonging to Germany, which were mandated to Japan after World War I. As the Japanese began to develop military bases on this newly acquired territory, foreigners were allowed to visit only on carefully conducted tours. By 1938 all foreign ships were officially barred from the islands. Strategically, the Japanese conceived a sound defense system. They developed military bases stretching across the Pacific Ocean from Singapore to Wake and from Formosa to the Solomons. Each island supplemented the defense of its neighbors. Because no island could be garrisoned heavily enough to repel a determined invasion, the Japanese counted on their fleet and air force to do the heavy work in driving off amphibious attempts.

At war's beginning, the enemy had the ability to concentrate overwhelming power on almost any point they chose. By the end of 1943 this situation had been reversed.

Throughout December 1943 and January 1944, land-based planes operated from new fields in the Gilberts, mainly Tarawa, photographing the Marshalls. In addition, bombers from the Gilberts flew almost daily missions against Mili, Wotje and Maloelap, Roi-Namur and Jaluit, which destroyed most of the enemy air power as well as shipping in the east Marshalls.

The operation, assigned the code name Flintlock, involved somewhat larger forces than did the Gilberts, but the task organizations were similar. With Vice Admiral Spruance in overall charge, Rear Admiral Turner was again the Joint Expeditionary Force commander, composed now of the Southern Attack Force under Turner, the Northern Attack Force under Rear Adm. R. L. Conolly, and the Majuro Attack Force commanded by Rear Adm. H. W. Hill. Major General Holland Smith was again Spruance's choice to command the expeditionary troops, which included the army's 7th Infantry Division under Maj. Gen. C. H. Corlett as the Southern Landing Force, and the 4th Marine Division, commanded by Maj. Gen. Harry Schmidt as the Northern Landing Force. Rear Admiral Marc A. Mitscher commanded the Fast Carrier Force. The land-based air came under Rear Adm. J. H. Hoover, who controlled about 1,200 planes of the U.S. Army, Navy, and the Marine Corps in the Gilberts.

The 4th Marine Division embarked from San Diego. The 7th Infantry Division had seen combat in the Aleutians, but a somewhat different kind of combat than that for which it now trained and rehearsed in the Hawaiian Islands.

On 29 January, fast U.S. carrier force planes struck Maloelap and Wotje, destroying every plane in the Kwajalein Atoll. Nightly ship bombardments prevented the Japanese from flying in reinforcements from Eniwetok. The U.S. Navy achieved such air superiority in the Marshalls that no Japanese aircraft interfered or damaged a ship on D-day.

The Japanese had left the Majuro atoll nearly three months earlier, leaving behind a number of buildings, barracks, seaplane hangers, and equipment. At 9:50 A.M. on D-day, Majuro was secured. United States ships anchored inside the lagoon as work of marking the channels and anchorage area proceeded expeditiously. Large-scale anchorage charts were available for use by fleet forces by 2 February. On that day, the battleship *Washington* limped in to repair a huge hole in her side, the result of a collision with another battleship.

Units of the mobile service squadrons were ordered into the lagoon at Majuro. Soon repair ships, provisions ships, ammunition ships, and floating dry docks could service the fleet there. Most damaged ships no longer needed to return to Pearl Harbor for servicing. Only individual ships requiring major repairs returned to Hawaii.

The Northern and Southern Attack Forces reached their objectives at dawn on 30 January and began their systematic bombardment of Roi-Namur and Kwajalein. Throughout 30 and 31 January and early on 1 February, their gunfire was coordinated with carrier air attacks using both high-capacity and armor-piercing shells as required. The scale of the pre-invasion bombardment was of unprecedented magnitude. For two and a half days, battleships, cruisers, and destroyers poured fire into the main objective islands, keeping up harassing fire during the nights. Even Holland Smith praised its superabundance at Kwajalein and Roi-Namur.

The main landings on Roi and Namur were made on the morning of D-day plus 1. Already stunned by the intense bombardment, the Japanese offered little resistance to the landings but fought desperately as the marines crossed the islands. The momentum of the marines could not be stopped. Roi was secured at 5:35 P.M. on D-day plus 1, and Seabees with equipment to repair the airfield were landed on the same day. Namur, more heavily defended than Roi, was secured by the marines at 2:18 P.M. on D-day plus 2. The 7th Army Division met determined resistance at Kwajalein; however, by D-day plus 5 this island was in American hands.

By 7 February all of the islands of the atoll had been secured. Many were unoccupied. Ebeye, location of the enemy seaplane base just north of Kwajalein and garrisoned by 400 Japanese, resisted strongly but was secured by noon on 4 February.

Compared to the Gilberts operation, American casualties were surprisingly light. More than 41,000 troops were committed, about twice the number in the Gilberts, but only 372 Americans were killed and 1,582 wounded, compared with about 1,000 troops killed and 3,100 wounded in the Gilberts. There were no naval casualties, since enemy submarines did not appear and the Japanese air was effectively prevented from interfering. Altogether, the Japanese lost approximately 9,000 men. The 14 February issue of *Newsweek* said in the battle of Kwajalein Atoll "the U.S. Navy won the most brilliant victory of the Pacific War."

The U.S. news media, in general, now saw that the drive across the Central

Pacific made good military sense in spite of MacArthur's objections. The defeat of Japan took on an added sense of urgency when the army and navy released a story to the Associated Press on 28 January that described the atrocities perpetrated by the Japanese on the hapless prisoners of Bataan and Corregidor.

It told of deliberate starvation, torture, and death. In one camp, Camp O'Donnell, about 2,200 American prisoners died in April and May 1942. In the camp at Cabanatuan about 3,000 Americans had died up to the end of October 1942. Three escapees, namely navy Cmdr. Melvin H. McCoy, Lt. Col. S. M. Mellnick, and Lt. Col. William E. Dyess, gave sworn statements as to what they experienced and observed in these prison camps. They told of deliberate starvation, the shooting in cold blood of the thirsty who sought water, of watching sick men writhe when denied medicine, and the horsewhipping of those who helped their fallen comrades. The three American prisoners of war (POWs) were transferred to a penal camp near Davao, Mindanao. They, together with four marines, namely Maj. Michiel Dobervitch, Maj. Austin C. Shoffner, Maj. Jack Hawkins, and Cpl. Reid Carlo Chamberlain, at nightfall overpowered a Japanese guard. They struck out over miles and miles in the mangrove swamp, finally connecting with a Philippine guerrilla group. The Filipinos made contact with an American submarine, which took the escapees to Brisbane, Australia.[21]

Military service to one's country in time of war brings out the best in the great majority of American servicemen. Yet, it brings out the very worst in a small minority. The escapees had to be very secretive in their planning, as they were aware that a number of American POWs collaborated with the Japanese and informed on their fellow prisoners.[22]

Because the Kwajalein operation proceeded more expeditiously and with far fewer casualties than expected, the tentatively scheduled capture of Eniwetok for 1 May was accelerated to 17 February.

D-day at Eniwetok would coincide with large-scale carrier strikes on Truk, which was only 660 miles away. The expeditionary group was composed of the 22nd Marine Regiment reinforced by two battalions of the 27th Infantry Division with Brig. Gen. T. A. Watson, USMC, in overall command of troops. The general plan called for:

1) Sweeping a channel into and across the lagoon
2) Occupying and siting artillery on small islands adjacent to Engebi, location of the airfield and believed to be the only defended island
3) Assault and occupation of Engebi
4) Landings on Parry and Eniwetok Islands
5) Mopping up the rest of the small islands[23]

Captured documents on Engebi showed Parry and Eniwetok to be defended also. Actually, there were 1,347 enemy troops on Parry and 808 on Eniwetok as against 1,276 on Engebi. Artillery was emplaced on Rujiyori Island, just south of Engebi, the afternoon of 17 February. The landing on Engebi was made on the

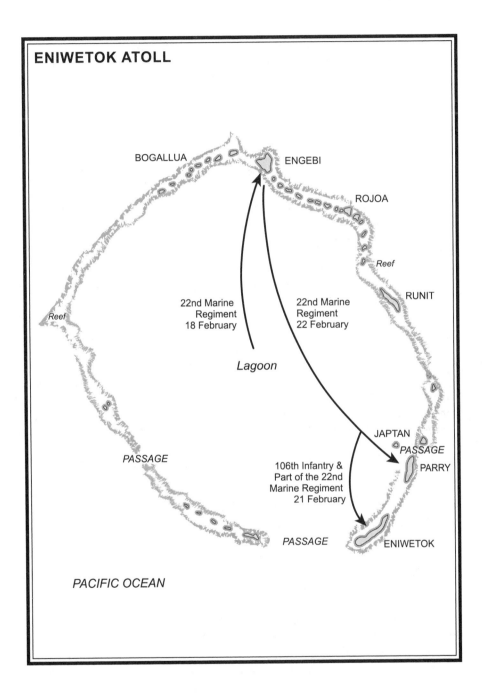

ENIWETOK ATOLL

BOGALLUA

ENGEBI

ROJOA

Reef

RUNIT

Reef

22nd Marine
Regiment
18 February

22nd Marine
Regiment
22 February

Lagoon

JAPTAN

PASSAGE

PARRY

PASSAGE

106th Infantry &
Part of the 22nd
Marine Regiment
21 February

PASSAGE

ENIWETOK

PACIFIC OCEAN

morning of the 18th and the island was secured that day.

Because the Americans had only a three-to-one numerical advantage over the defenders, as compared to a six-to-one ratio at Kwajalein, the three occupied islands had to be taken one at a time.[24] It took the marines one day each to secure Engebi and Parry islands, but the army became so bogged down on Eniwetok that a marine landing team had to be rushed in to take over the brunt of the fighting. Unlike the 7th Infantry Division, the 27th Infantry Division was beginning to get a reputation for being poorly trained and poorly led.

By 22 February the entire atoll was declared secured. The lagoon at Eniwetok was capable of holding more than 2,000 ships. Located 2,500 miles west of Pearl Harbor and 1,000 miles east of the Marianas, Eniwetok became an important forward supply base for the remainder of the war. Earl Ellis had told of it in "Advance Based Operations in Micronesia."

After making an inspection tour of the Marshalls, Admiral Nimitz said, "Never before in the Pacific war had an American victory of such magnitude been won at so cheap a cost." [25]

Tokyo seemed dismayed by this American victory at such a bargain price. Ichiro Kiyose, the permanent director of Japan's Imperial Rule Assistance Association, said in an address to the nation, "The Marshall Islands are the front-porch entrance to Tokyo, with only the Bonin Islands before it. The enemy is probably finally thinking of some such thing as bombing Tokyo in dead earnest . . . It would absolutely not do for the people to devote ourselves to panic." [26]

A decision whether the Central Pacific Force should turn northward through the Marianas and Bonins toward Japan depended on two main considerations. One was that an operation against Truk seemed likely to precipitate a decisive fleet action and, by 1944 onward, the U.S. Pacific Fleet was so strong that it welcomed such an action. It was decided that strong carrier attacks should be undertaken to test the strength of Truk; the final decision whether to capture it or not would depend on the result.

The other consideration was how to employ the big B-29 bombers (Superfortresses) now being produced in large numbers. At first the Joint Chiefs planned to use the B-29s to bomb Japan from airfields in China, but General Arnold was not confident that the Chinese could hold the necessary airfields. On the other hand, Saipan and Tinian in the Marianas were closer to Tokyo than the airfields in China. Admiral King always favored the plan to advance by way of the Marianas.

Prior to the Eniwetok landing, Admirals Nimitz and Spruance hoped to strike a major blow against the Japanese Combined Fleet at Truk. On 4 February a Marine Corps B-24 from Bougainville reported numerous targets afloat at the Truk anchorage. Afterward, traffic analysis indicated that the Combined Fleet was abandoning Truk in favor of the Palau Islands, westernmost of the Carolines.

Because Admiral Spruance determined to keep radio silence during 16, 17, and 18 February, most of the information gathered at Central Pacific Headquarters came from the Japanese. By nightfall of the 16th, Truk reported one of its cruisers afire, five destroyers damaged, and three freighters sunk. Reports by the Japanese showed the three-day raid as sinking fifteen naval vessels including two light cruisers and four destroyers plus nineteen cargo vessels and five tankers. In addition, 200 enemy aircraft were destroyed. In anticipation of the Truk attack, submarines were ordered to the scene to pick up downed American flyers.

Not being satisfied with the tremendous success he had achieved in the Marshalls and at Truk, Spruance continued west to Adm. Mineichi Koga's new base, the Palau Islands, westernmost of the Carolines.

In his approach to Palau, Spruance gave his force the mission of destroying enemy ships, aircraft, and installations and mining the three deep-draft entrance channels into the lagoon. Palau, a stronghold of the Japanese inner defense zone, was almost 1,200 miles west of Truk. No such operation could have succeeded a few months earlier.

The initial strike was made at dawn on 30 March. Forewarned by his reconnaissance sighting, the day before the strike, Admiral Koga ordered his principal combat ships and a number of merchant ships to retire out of harm's way. En route to Davao, Koga's plane crashed. The admiral's body was never recovered.

In two days of strikes at Palau, 150 enemy aircraft were destroyed along with 104,000 tons of shipping. Channels were successfully mined, the first time carrier planes had undertaken such a task. Total U.S. losses were twenty-five planes, although twenty-six of the forty-four downed air crewmen were recovered by air and submarine rescue operations. The objective of immobilizing Palau for the duration of the Hollandia operation had been accomplished. No interference or enemy reinforcements could come through this stronghold. The usefulness of another enemy base had been ended for a period of weeks. Spruance's task force returned to its new base at Majuro in the Marshalls.

On 13 April, Spruance's Task Force 58 left Majuro to aid MacArthur's troops in the Hollandia operation. From 21 to 24 April his planes struck airfields against light opposition in support of the landings in Humboldt Bay. On 29 April, he was notified of the death of Secretary of the Navy Frank Knox, who had had a heart attack the previous day. Knox was immediately succeeded by his undersecretary, James Vincent Forrestal, born 15 February 1892 in Beacon, New York. Forrestal had served as a naval aviator in World War I and had experienced a very successful financial career in New York City prior to coming to Washington.

On Spruance's return trip to Majuro, his task force dealt another blow at Truk on 29 to 30 April, destroying ninety-three Japanese planes in the air and on the ground while losing twenty-six of its own planes in combat. Of the forty-six U.S. air personnel shot down, twenty-eight were rescued. The task force re-entered Majuro and Kwajalein on 4 May to prepare for the Marianas operation.

Admiral King's book, *Fleet Admiral King*, says of the Marshalls operation, "King was well pleased, not only with Spruance's excellent planning but with the almost perfect timing of his forces in the execution of these plans. He considered the operation a noteworthy example of the results that may be expected when good staff work is implemented by efficient fleet operations under superior leadership." [27]

In recognition of his increased responsibilities, Spruance was given his fourth star and promoted to the grade of full admiral. After the Kwajalein operation, Spruance's Central Pacific Force became the U.S. Fifth Fleet.

Chapter 18
Submarine Warfare

*T*HE SUBMARINE SERVICE PLAYED A SIGNIFICANT ROLE in MacArthur's return to the Philippines, but a far greater role in the ultimate defeat of Japan. No branch of the U.S. armed services did as much to prevent men and materials from moving on or off the Japanese home islands. The dearth of news about its activities caused newsmen to label it the silent service. During and after the war, the American public failed to appreciate its importance in causing the Japanese surrender. Yet, the American submarines' performance for the first year and a half of war duty was less than satisfactory.

On 7 December 1941, fifty-five submarines were assigned to the Pacific in two uncoordinated commands, twenty-eight at Cavite in the Philippines and the other twenty-seven at Pearl Harbor. A dozen of these were obsolete S-class relics of the 1920s. They lacked adequate range, firepower, and under-water endurance. Eleven more were unavailable due to undergoing overhauls in stateside ports or patrolling coastal waters. One boat, the *Sealion*, became the first U.S. submarine casualty during the initial Japanese air raid at Cavite. Pre-World War II submarine doctrine did not help performance.

The United States had been an enthusiastic signatory to the 1930 London Naval Arms Limitation Treaty, which declared that submarines "may not sink or render incapable of navigation a merchant vessel without having first placed passengers, crew and ships papers in a place of safety." A submarine that observed this amendment stood an excellent chance of being sunk by an armed merchantman. Submarine captains were warned that if they attacked enemy merchant ships without prior warning, they would be subject to a war crime trial. The Japanese attack on Pearl Harbor eliminated these restrictions. Within six hours after the first planes struck, the Navy Department in Washington ordered: EXECUTE UNRESTRICTED SUBMARINE WARFARE AGAINST JAPAN.

ULTRA gave the United States priceless information on the movements of all Japanese shipping. In the beginning, shore commanders failed to realize that battleships and carriers were faster than submarines and difficult to sink even if successfully intercepted. The slow cargo ships were extremely vulnerable, but initially had a lower priority as targets. Senior naval officers stressed caution because of the perceived risk of aerial detection. Many submarine captains pursued the caution theme with excessive zeal through most of 1942. The result was inevitable. By the end of the first year of combat, "forty skippers had been relieved of command, mostly . . . for unproductive patrols." [1]

In the beginning, every sort of problem plagued the American submarine service, including old and crude equipment. Worst of all, its new equipment had not been properly tested. Yet, for all its shortcomings the U.S. submarine service had one great strength at the start: its junior officers and enlisted men. Every man and officer was a volunteer. They had been pronounced fit by a battery of physicians, psychologists, and senior submariners. Regardless of rank, the submariner received 50 percent more than standard pay as hazardous duty pay. Obviously, he considered himself a member of an elite force, although he learned early that he needed all of his well-honed skills to survive the war's hectic patrols.

In December 1941, the submarines in the Philippines should have wreaked havoc with Japanese landings. Instead, they were practically useless as attack weapons. Submarines sank three merchant ships, one very small. After the Japanese wrecked the Cavite Naval Station at Luzon, the submarine command of the Asiatic Fleet immediately began a series of base changes that took them farther and farther from Japan. They first stopped at Surabaya in the Dutch East Indies, then to Tjilatjap on the south coast of Java, and finally to Fremantle on the southwest coast of Australia.

Fremantle is the port for nearby Perth, the largest city in Western Australia. Its close proximity to the Netherlands East Indies made it an ideal base for attacking the Japanese merchant fleet. The navy dispatched Catalinas to patrol the sea approaches to the submarine base. It also built a recreation center in Perth so that the crews could enjoy their leave time upon return from hazardous duty. In time, the submarines from Fremantle practically owned the South China Sea.

Initially, the submarine fleet at Pearl Harbor did not perform very well. While ULTRA pinpointed numerous enemy targets, patrol after patrol came back empty handed. Most boats were equipped with the top-secret Mark 14 torpedo, which the U.S. Navy had developed over a period of fifteen years. The U.S. Navy's top commanders had the utmost confidence in this explosive device, a confidence utterly misplaced.

The Mark 14 and its exploder, the Mark 6, proved to be the U.S. submarine force's most serious and persistent problem of the entire war. Time and again, submarine commanders came back empty handed due to faulty torpedoes. Inevitably, top-rank naval officers blamed the skipper rather than the torpedo. When complaints reached the navy Bureau of Ordnance (BuOrd), it firmly denied that there was anything wrong with the Mark 14 or its exploder. Prior to the war, each torpedo cost $10,000. Frugal officers at BuOrd regarded it too extravagant to blow them up in test programs. Instead, BuOrd tested the Mark 14 with water-filled warheads so that each torpedo could be retrieved from the sea and used for subsequent tests. In tests performed with dummy warheads, the Mark 14 ran straight and true. No test was made with a live warhead.

The turning point in submariners' fortunes took place when Capt. Andrews Lockwood became commanding officer of the submarine station at Fremantle in April 1942. The next month, Lockwood became a rear admiral. During his career, Lockwood, at age fifty-two, had commanded no fewer than seven submarines. He empathized with his skippers' complaints.

Lockwood immediately focused his attention on the Mark 14 problem. He erected a deep-sea fishing net 500 feet long from the surface to the bottom in waters near Albany, Australia. Mark 14s with dummy warheads, yet weighted to match live warheads, were fired at the net from a range of 850 yards. One fish, set to run ten feet deep, punched a hole at twenty-five feet below the surface. Another torpedo set for a ten-foot depth went through the net at eighteen feet. A third, set to run on the surface, sliced the net at eleven feet under the water. Lockwood determined that he had tracked down the torpedo's flaw and so reported to BuOrd. BuOrd responded that no reliable conclusions could be drawn from these inadequate tests.

Lockwood repeated his experiments, which produced the same results. He again notified BuOrd and urged the experts to make their own tests. This time, a copy of his request came to the attention of Admiral King. A one-time submarine skipper himself, King demanded BuOrd make the test. Finally, in August 1942, the U.S. Navy Bureau of Ordnance admitted that the Mark 14 ran ten feet deeper than set. Commanders at both Fremantle and Pearl Harbor were instructed to subtract eleven feet from whatever depth they chose to attack.

At the end of 1942, American Pacific-based submarines had made approximately 350 war patrols. They had been assigned numerous missions other than their intended use: the sinking of enemy vessels. They had delivered supplies and evacuated personnel from Corregidor. In spite of the many difficulties experienced, including the lack of a unified strategy for submarines, postwar Japanese records reported 180 ships sunk for 725,000 tons for the year 1942.[2]

On 20 January 1943, Rear Adm. Robert H. English, commander, Submarines Pacific Fleet, was killed in a flight to the West Coast when the Pan-Am plane in which he was a passenger ran into a mountain 115 miles north of San Francisco during a bad rain and wind storm. Admiral King directed the Bureau of Personnel to name Lockwood to replace English. Lockwood took command at Pearl Harbor in late February. Here was another clear example of the right man being in the right place at the right time in the naval command structure.

Before leaving Australia, the achievements of Dudley Walker Morton came to Lockwood's attention. Known throughout the service as "Mush" Morton, he became skipper of the *Wahoo* in early January 1943. Described by one of his crew members as "built like a bear and as playful as a cub," he told his crew upon assuming command, "We will take every reasonable precaution, but our mission is to sink enemy shipping . . ."[3]

He was first ordered to reconnoiter Wewak, a Japanese supply base on the north coast of New Guinea. Morton kept *Wahoo* on the surface as it moved boldly ahead nine miles inside the harbor. He sent his crew to battle stations in preparation to attack a stationary Japanese destroyer. As *Wahoo* prepared to shoot, the Japanese destroyer got under way. Morton then shifted his plan by firing three torpedoes at the moving target. All missed. The destroyer headed straight for *Wahoo*, as Morton prepared for a down-the-throat shot. Another torpedo missed as the Japanese destroyer closed to 1,200 yards. At a range of 800 yards, Morton fired a sixth torpedo, which hit the destroyer, causing a massive explosion before sinking.

That night, *Wahoo* headed for Palau. The next day, he found a four-ship convoy: two freighters, a huge transport, and a tanker. Hits were scored on both freighters and the transport. One freighter sank. The other limped away, while the transport—with thousands of Japanese soldiers aboard—stood dead in the water. Morton fired another torpedo, which failed to explode, then a last torpedo, which blew the transport "higher than a kite, as the soldiers aboard her commenced jumping off the side like ants off a hot plate." [4] Needless to say, Morton had gained the respect of Lockwood.

On 21 May, Morton stormed into Lockwood's office. He had just returned from a patrol that had sunk three Japanese ships but, according to Morton, should have sunk three more had it not been for the Mark 14 torpedo. Morton pointed out the torpedo's failure to detonate on impact as well as its tendency to explode prematurely. After considerable investigation, part of the problem turned out to be a matter of physics and the super sensitivity of the Mark 6 exploder. Every steel-bottomed ship was encased in a magnetic field that radiated in all directions. What was not understood was that the magnetic field encasing the ship varied in shape depending on circumstances. Acting on these discoveries, Admiral Nimitz, in June 1943, ordered the Pearl Harbor submarines to deactivate the magnetic feature of the Mark 6. Admiral Kinkaid, commanding the U.S. Seventh Fleet, made the same order for the submarines stationed in Australia.

Yet, there still remained the problem that too many torpedoes failed to explode on contact. The solution was found by experiments conducted by Admiral Lockwood at Kahoolawe Island in the Hawaiians. He reported to Admiral King that after extensive testing his men had discovered that the contact exploders were too flimsy. The sailors themselves could modify the exploders to make them reliable. Lockwood requested permission from King to make the change immediately without approval from BuOrd, which could take months. King complied. By the fall of 1943, nearly two years after the attack on Pearl Harbor, U.S. submarines in the Pacific went to sea with torpedoes that worked.

The number of enemy ship sinkings climbed dramatically in 1943. According to postwar records, 335 Japanese ships representing 1.5 million tons were sent to the ocean's floor. Imports of bulk commodities to the home islands showed a sharp drop for the year, from 19.4 million tons in 1942 to 16.4 million tons in 1943. Among the ships lost was the Japanese steamer *Konron Maru*, with a loss of 544 lives, plus three other ships, for a total of about 13,000 tons. All were sunk by *Wahoo* off the west coast of Honshu in October.

Morton changed the procedure for torpedo attacks. Previously the submarine captain made all periscope observations. "Believing that this placed too much pressure on the captain, [he] assigned periscope observations and the ordering of torpedo firing to his executive officer," Lt. Dick O'Kane.[5]

O'Kane was assigned to captain the submarine *Tang* prior to October 1943.

Japanese records report that on 11 October 1943, the date *Wahoo* was due to exit, a Japanese aircraft attacked a submarine by dropping three depth charges. After Lockwood examined these records, he concluded that *Wahoo* and all hands—including "Mush" Morton—had plunged to the bottom. *Wahoo* was among the fifty-two American submarines that failed to return from a patrol during World War II. But by January 1944, American submarines posed the greatest menace to Japanese chances of winning the war. What Adm. Karl Donitz had tried, almost succeeded, and failed in the battle of the Atlantic, U.S. submarines would achieve in the Pacific.

No longer could Japanese ships sail with safety in any part of the Pacific. Although the Japanese submarines were equipped with good torpedoes from the start and were well manned, after the year 1942, they were far less a threat than the submarines of the Americans, but for different reasons.

After the war, Mochitsura Hashimoto, one of the few surviving enemy submarine captains, explained, "The Japanese policy was to use submarines primarily for attacking enemy naval forces. Merchant ships were legitimate targets only when there were no warships to be considered." [6] Submarine commanders were given a schedule for torpedo expenditure: enemy battleships and aircraft carriers rated all torpedoes; cruisers ranked three torpedoes; but only a single torpedo should be used for a destroyer or merchant vessel. The disciplined Japanese stuck to this policy long after it had demonstratively failed.

The Japanese naval academy at Etajima modeled itself after Great Britain's Dartmouth. Ensigns served to the rank of lieutenant junior grade before they could apply for submarine service, then came two years aboard submarines. Crewmen and officers received an extra 30 percent in pay, plus service on a submarine counted double when figuring retirement benefits. As in the United States, the Japanese submariner had to meet rigid physical requirements.

Unlike the U.S. Navy's cost-conscious Bureau of Ordnance, each Japanese submarine had practiced firing a live Model 95 torpedo against the steep shores of Oshima, a desolate island south of Tokyo Bay. The Model 95 could travel at forty-nine knots for a distance of nearly eleven miles, leaving no telltale wake. It packed an explosive charge of 1,000 pounds, almost twice that of American torpedoes, and, best of all, it detonated on impact with none of the troubles the Americans had experienced.

From their other equipment, Japanese submariners received mixed performances; most notably, Japan had a deficiency in radar that proved disastrous. As Hashimoto expressed it, "The submarine crews in the forward areas were longing for radar as farmers look for rain in a long drought." [7] Above all, the Japanese had no information system comparable to ULTRA to pinpoint the whereabouts of American ships.

At the outbreak of the war, Japan's force of sixty submarines was a shade larger than the American strength of fifty-five. Of these sixty submarines, fourteen were obsolete or second-line boats usable only in coastal waters. The backbone of the Japanese undersea force lay in the versatile I-class or first-line fleet boats. These displaced from 1,600 to 2,200 tons and carried up to twenty torpedoes. They had a maximum range of 1,600 miles with a top speed of more than twenty knots on the surface and seven to nine knots underwater. The twenty-five submarines and five midgets figured in the surprise attack on Pearl Harbor. The midget was a two-man, two-torpedo vessel, 78.5 feet long and driven by a 600 horsepower electric motor. They were carried aboard regular fleet submarines.

Although the performance of the Japanese submarines during the first year of the war was a disappointment to Imperial Headquarters, by contrast with the Americans, the Japanese submarine effort in 1942 against U.S. surface forces was very rewarding. Its submarines sank the damaged carrier *Yorktown* at Midway, and the carrier *Wasp* plus the light cruiser *Juneau* in the Solomons. Twice they torpedoed *Saratoga*, putting her out of action for most of the year. They also badly damaged the new battleship *North Carolina* plus a destroyer, *O'Brien*, which sank after leaving the port of New Caledonia. Yet, thanks to ULTRA, American ships and planes sank twenty-three Japanese submarines during the year.

Because of a decision made at the highest command, Japanese submarine results went steadily downhill after 16 November 1942. On this day, Vice Adm. Teruhisa Komatsu announced that submarines henceforth would carry provisions to Guadalcanal. This decision eliminated the submarine as an attack weapon as well as an efficient means of supply. When junior submariners asked, "How can submarines carry out their foremost mission—attack— when we are forced into this stupid work?" The troops on Guadalcanal are starving, replied the admiral. "We must help them," he insisted, "no matter what sacrifices must be made." [8]

By directing their main effort to supply missions, Japanese submarines no longer posed a major threat for the remainder of the Pacific War. In 1943, Japanese submarines sank only three worthwhile U.S. Navy vessels: the jeep carrier *Liscombe Bay*, the submarine *Corvina*, and the destroyer *Henley*. In so doing, the enemy lost twenty-two submarines during the year. Later, Lt. Cmdr. Zenji Orita complained to Vice Adm. Takeo Takagi that "using submarines for transport is throwing away the reason for their construction." [9]

In spite of this opposition, by mid-1944, transportation operations to isolated islands had become the chief purpose of Japanese submarines. The *Sen-Tei* Type D1 was especially built for this purpose. This type of submarine could carry some 350 troops and approximately 700 tons of military supplies. [10] By early 1945, American planes and submarines had sunk six of this new series. This caused the Japanese to abandon submarine transport operations. Altogether, the Japanese suffered losses of 127 of about 160 large submarines in service by war's end. [11]

MacArthur also used his submarines for supply, albeit more judiciously than the Japanese. He used American submarines stationed at Brisbane extensively, though not exclusively, for supply and intelligence missions to the Philippines. Lieutenant Commander Charles "Chick" Parsons, an officer in the Naval Reserve, was placed in charge of a most worthwhile operation known as "SpyRon," short for spy squadron. He had previously managed a stevedore company in the Philippines when taken prisoner by the Japanese upon the fall of Manila. He left the Philippines on the repatriation ship *Gripsholm* by virtue of the fact that he had been filling in for the absent consul of Panama. Now back in the Philippines, he had the duty to organize, coordinate, and supply the guerrillas, and this he did. "Forty-one SpyRon missions to the Philippines delivered more than 330 agents and 1,325 tons of supplies. More than 470 passengers made the return trip to Australia. Nineteen submarines took part, with *Narwhal*, *Nautilus*, and *Stingray* undertaking the lion's share of the missions." [12] By the time the Americans landed at Leyte, there were approximately 180,000 guerrilla troops operating throughout the Philippines. Numerous Japanese ships of all kinds were sent to the ocean's floor by other American submarines.

Dick O'Kane became America's most successful submarine skipper during World War II. In *Tang* in just over four patrols, he was credited with sending twenty-four enemy ships to the bottom, which made him the leading skipper of the submarine war in terms of ships sunk. He also held the record for saving downed airmen, having rescued twenty-two at the fleet's air battle over Truk. Mush Morton was credited with sinking nineteen ships. Many other skippers received credit for double-digit sinkings. In the early hours of 23 October, O'Kane found a ten-ship convoy near the China coast—five freighters and five escorts. Postwar records credit him with sinking three small freighters that night. On the evenings of 24 and 25 October, O'Kane found another convoy. He fired ten torpedoes, sinking two heavily laden freighters and damaging another. With only two torpedoes left, he attempted to polish off the cripple. The first ran true but the second torpedo began a circular turn, turning back to hit the *Tang*.

O'Kane and others on the bridge were hurled into the water. In all, eight men, including O'Kane, survived. A Japanese patrol boat picked them up and administered a severe beating to all. O'Kane said later, "When we realized that our clubbing and kickings were being administered by the burned, mutilated survivors of our own handiwork, we found we could take it with less prejudice." He and the seven served out the remainder of the war in a POW camp. [13]

At the behest of Admiral Nimitz, Lockwood developed an effective rescue operation for downed U.S. Navy and U.S. Army pilots. Beginning in 1943 through the remainder of the war, Pacific Fleet headquarters dispatched submarines to areas where U.S. planes were engaged in combat with the Japanese. A future president, George H. W. Bush, would be one of the numerous beneficiaries of this program.

On 2 September 1944, Bush piloted a torpedo plane aboard the aircraft carrier USS *San Jacinto*. His target was an enemy radio station on ChiChi Jima, located about 600 miles southwest of Japan in the Bonin Islands. Shells from Japanese anti-aircraft batteries hit his plane during his dive to drop his payload. Bush delivered four 500-pound bombs on the radio station, causing considerable damage. He then maneuvered his plane over the ocean in hopes of getting back to San Jacinto. With the plane on fire, Bush and one air crewman managed to leap out from about 1,500 feet. One crewman went down with the plane while the other fell helplessly to his death because his parachute failed to open properly. Once in the water, Bush unleashed his inflatable yellow lifeboat, crawled in, and paddled out to sea. A Japanese boat sent out to capture him was stopped by a fellow air pilot who strafed the boat. The U.S. submarine *Finback*, patrolling twenty to thirty miles from the island, picked up Bush a few hours later.

By the year 1944, Lockwood and Nimitz had developed a strategy for submarines to complement the many needs of the U.S. Pacific Fleet. With 140 boats operating out of Pearl Harbor and Australia, U.S. submarines—more than all other military services combined—would curtail the flow of needed supplies, especially fuel oil, to Japan.

The ensuing year became the most productive by far for U.S. submarines. Japanese records after the war showed that Japan lost 603 ships for more than 2.7 million tons to the U.S. silent service in 1944.

While the American public received stories about the victories in the Central and southwest Pacific, untold triumphs of equal importance were taking place around the Philippines. A group of three submarines, patrolling the same as the German wolf pack, sank three Japanese merchant ships bound for Manila in mid-July 1944. On 26 and 27 July, they sank a tanker-freighter and a transport off the northwest coast of Luzon. On the night of 31 July and 1 August, an American submarine group sank two Japanese tankers and two transports with more than 5,000 Japanese troops of the 26th Division aboard. A Japanese convoy southwest of Manila lost four more transports on 23 August. Five more merchantmen went down over the next two weeks. The historian Clay Blair points to the unqualified success of wolf packs operating in Luzon strait prior to the Leyte invasion. Lockwood sent eight packs composed of twenty-five submarines to the area. In short order, they sank fifty-six ships for 250,000 tons.[14] Lockwood's boats continued to slaughter Japanese shipping in Philippine waters through the remainder of the year.

Boats from Fremantle patrolled the South China Sea while those from Pearl Harbor concentrated in the East China Sea, the Yellow Sea, and around the Japanese home islands. Unfortunately, on 7 September 1944, the U.S. submarine *Paddle* sank the *Shiniyo Maru* with hundreds of Allied POWs aboard. After the *Maru* was hit, Japanese guards opened fire on the POWs with machine guns. A number of POWs managed to escape by jumping over the side; "81 reached shore on Mindanao and made contact with friendly guerrillas." [15] Beginning with the work of the *Paddle*, plus other sinkings, U.S. submarines accidentally killed or drowned well over 4,000 Allied POWs in a period of six weeks.[16]

At the beginning of 1944, the Japanese had 4.1 million tons of merchant shipping, excluding tankers. At the end of the year, this figure had declined to about 2 million tons.[17] The flow of oil from the Netherlands East Indies to Japan had been reduced to a monthly total of only 200,000 tanker tons.

With the move of the main submarine base from Pearl Harbor to Guam in the latter part of 1944, the submarines' efficiency greatly improved, although against a dwindling number of ships. By March of 1945, oil tankers from the south could no longer reach the Japanese home islands. For the remainder of the year, U.S. submarines confined Japanese shipping to the home islands, the waters of the Sea of Japan, and the Yellow Sea.

In the course of the Pacific War, American submarines would sink 201 Japanese warships for a total of 540,192 tons, which included one battleship, four large carriers, four small carriers, three heavy cruisers, eight light cruisers, forty-three destroyers, and twenty-three large submarines. Of greater importance to the war's outcome, U.S. submarines would sink 4,779,902 tons of Japanese merchant ships. Altogether, they would sink 55 percent of all Japanese ships lost in the war.[18] The U.S. surface navy, carrier planes, marines, and army air force combined to send the remaining 45 percent to the ocean's floor.

The lack of appreciation by the American public for the role played by the submarine service was a part of the latter's strategy. As Adm. Charles Lockwood recalled that

> great pressure was being put on the Navy Department to publish play-by-play accounts of the war. We of the submarines wanted no part of this.
>
> To keep the enemy guessing about what became of his ships which never reached port would, I felt, not only wear down his nerves but would deny him information on which to base changes in his routines, or improve his antisubmarine measures. We wanted him to think that his existing methods were highly effective and that every time he dropped a depth charge, another American submarine went to Davy Jones's locker.[19]

Chapter 19

The Netherlands New Guinea

*F*ORTHEFIRSTTWOYEARSOFTHEWAR,Australiashoulderedthemajorburdenof its own defense as well as the recapture of lost territories in Papua and Australian New Guinea. When the Japanese removed their ships and airplanes from Rabaul in January 1944, the war in the southwest Pacific took on an entirely different flavor from the two previous years. MacArthur's command, including the general himself, became much more aggressive. In liberating the Philippines, his main objective in the Pacific War, MacArthur used sound strategy and tactics for the remainder of the war. The phrase "I shall return" had caught the imagination of the American public, which clearly applauded MacArthur's performance during the months ahead.

Halsey's command had almost complete control of the sea and air in the Solomons, although there were approximately 150,000 Japanese isolated at Bougainville, Rabaul, and Kavieng. By late February 1944, MacArthur's troops could reflect on slow-to-moderate movement against a determined enemy. The Allies had advanced about 300 miles, or less than one-third of the way along the northern New Guinea coast. In contrast, Admiral Nimitz's command had jumped 2,000 miles from Hawaii, first to the Gilbert Islands in November 1943, then to the Marshalls in February 1944. The Southwest Pacific Command now had overwhelming strength in comparison to the Japanese on ground, sea, and air, and soon it would be aided by the most important intelligence find for Allied infantry troops in the Pacific War.

Lieutenant General Hatazo Adachi had the unenviable task of defending the lengthy coastline in eastern New Guinea with his three divisions decimated by disease and malnutrition. Any attempt to receive supplies from Rabaul in 1944 during daylight hours would be a repeat of the Battle of the Bismarck Sea as Kenney's Fifth Air Force was now stronger than ever.

Imperial General Headquarters, having recognized Adachi's plight, sent the 50,000-man Second Army under Lt. Gen. Fusataro Teshima with approximately 300 aircraft of the 6th and 7th Air Divisions to Wakde, Sarmi, Biak, and Manokwari bases in Dutch New Guinea. This force had been stationed east of Java. The two Japanese armies that defended New Guinea were widely separated. Between Teshima's 36th Division in the Wakde-Sarmi vicinity and Adachi's 51st Division in Wewak lay a 300-mile stretch of coastline. Supplies to both Teshima and Adashi's armies now had to come from the Netherlands East Indies, where the Japanese still controlled both air and sea. Nevertheless, Kenney's Fifth Air Force could prevent reinforcements to the enemy in all of east New Guinea and much of Dutch New Guinea.

To gain control of the sea between New Guinea and Mindanao in the Philippines, the U.S. Navy was particularly anxious to occupy the Admiralty Islands. The Admiralties comprise two main islands, Manus and Los Negros, and a large coral atoll. Situated just south of the equator and north of New Guinea, the atoll creates in Seeadler Harbor one of the finest landlocked anchorages in the Pacific. Approximately fifteen miles long and four and a half miles wide, the lagoon is large enough to contain all ships of the U.S. Fleet.

The Joint Chiefs of Staff believed the U.S. Pacific Fleet needed Seeadler Harbor as a base for ship repair. They planned for the Seabees to develop the largest naval base west of Pearl Harbor complete with two giant floating docks. The Joint Chiefs first intended to occupy the Admiralty Islands in March 1944 with overwhelming strength by use of Halsey's Third Fleet. The planned invasion was rescheduled to 1 April. A chance discovery by the Australians accelerated the Admiralties attack by one month.

After the capture of Finschhafen in 1943, the Australians moved west to occupy the main Japanese administration area at Sio. The Japanese left behind a metal box in a water-filled pit that was found by the Australian 9th Division engineers. The box contained Japanese codebooks from which the covers had been removed, the covers being retained as evidence that their contents had been destroyed.[1] However, the codebooks at Sio were intact plus the currently used cipher keys. This discovery proved to be the most important intelligence coup for ground troops in the Pacific War.

The codebooks were used "to encrypt such sensitive material as daily ration states, reports of casualties, transfers, arrival of reinforcements and the evacuation of casualties." [2] The Allies could use this intelligence to know the Japanese order of battle. So sensitive was this captured material that it could be delivered to Washington only by "safe hand" courier.

By mid-February 1944, before anyone outside his headquarters knew of the existence of the Sio codes, MacArthur possessed a tabulated list of the Japanese army units present in the Admiralties. It revealed there were 4,000 Japanese in the islands with only 2,200 combat troops available. This knowledge gave him the opportunity to attack without any outside help from Halsey's fleet.

MacArthur was particularly angered when told that Seeadler Harbor was to be developed as a major base for Nimitz's Pacific Fleet as well as the Seventh Fleet, whereby Marshall had suggested that he delegate the development of the Manus-Los Negros facilities to Halsey. In a message to King with copy to

MacArthur, Nimitz recommended that for this project Halsey remain under CINCPAC command. Thus resulted in an explosive confrontation between the U.S. Army and U.S. Navy.

In a two-and-a-half page letter to Marshall dated 27 February 1944, MacArthur stated, in part:

> I am in complete disagreement with the recommendation of Admiral Nimitz regarding the Bismarck Archipelago. He thus has proposed to project his own command into the southwest Pacific by the artificiality of advancing South Pacific Forces into the area . . .
>
> It is quite evident that the ultimate issue in question is the control of the campaign in the Pacific, and immediately, that for the initial major objective, the Philippine Islands, which have always been in my area. This has been entrusted to me from the very beginning and has been reiterated in directives from the Joint Chiefs of Staff and the Secretary of War. While I do not for a moment believe this will be changed, my professional integrity, indeed my personal honor would be so involved that, if otherwise, I request that I be given early opportunity personally to present the case to the Secretary of War and to the President before finally determining my own personal action in the matter.[3]

Manus Island is mountainous and by far the largest in the Admiralties group. Los Negros is a long, narrow, low-lying island that lies east of Manus and is separated from it only by a narrow passage at its western end, easily crossed. The Japanese garrison was completely cut off from support by its navy and air force. There was simply too much coastline to guard for so few troops.

On 24 February, MacArthur directed Admiral Barbey to prepare for a landing on Los Negros, D-day to be no later than 29 February. His order referred to the operation as a "Reconnaissance in Force." This term describes a fighting patrol, an armed probe of the enemy's defenses to test its strength, but MacArthur already knew the size of the enemy forces. The attack force would number just over 1,000 men including 882 frontline troops from the 1st Cavalry Division. Under MacArthur's plan, this force would be on its own for about forty-eight hours before reinforcements could arrive.

MacArthur and Admiral Kinkaid traveled aboard the cruiser *Phoenix*, accompanied by the *Boise*. The troops landed at Hyane Bay adjacent to the Momote Air Strip on Los Negros' southeastern shore. A small "party of Japanese manned heavy machine guns and a 20-mm cannon on the headland, well dug in and camouflaged." After the troops came ashore torrential rains fell for more than four hours, and "by the time the rain eased to a drizzle, infantrymen had made their way around the headland and killed the gun crews." [4]

At 2:00 P.M., MacArthur came ashore for an inspection. One of five Japanese who had stayed behind to contest the issue was found in the area where MacArthur landed. He had been killed hours before the general came ashore. His body was photographed with MacArthur looking on. The picture, along with the story of the bold stroke to capture the Admiralties, was sent to newspapers in the States. At 5:30 P.M. on D-day, *Phoenix* sailed for Oro Bay with the *Boise* and eleven other destroyers that had accompanied the landing force. Next morning, MacArthur flew back to Brisbane.

Brigadier General William C. Chase and some troops from the 1st Calvary Division were there to stay. On the night of D-day Chase's small force was almost overrun by a battalion-strength attack. The two destroyers left behind provided defensive fire and star shells to help the infantry locate its attackers. The cavalrymen took heavy casualties yet managed to hang on, but it was the naval gunnery that saved the day. General Chase said of the destroyers, "They didn't just support us, they saved our necks." [5]

On the night of D-day plus 2, the Japanese launched a powerful and sustained attack. By the time reinforcements arrived the morning of 3 March bringing artillery and tanks, the worst of it was over. Organized enemy resistance did not cease until mid-March, and it was 3 April before unrestricted work on a naval base could commence.

By going in light and without artillery or air support, casualties were excessively high for the original landing force. In the first three days, more than 60 percent were killed or wounded. Total casualties for this operation amounted to 337 killed plus 1,189 wounded. The loss should have been insignificant had the operation been carried out using overwhelming force as originally scheduled for the 1 April landing. Indeed, little if any time was gained in the development of the naval base.

MacArthur's objection to Nimitz's proposal was so great that he indicated that he would close Seeadler Harbor to all but the Seventh Fleet and other ships under his command. "Recognizing the foolish nature of the issue, Admiral Kincaid got MacArthur to invite Halsey to Brisbane to thrash out the problem." [6]

E. B. Potter spells out what transpired in his book, *Bull Halsey*, paraphrased as follows: MacArthur was waiting for Halsey and his entourage upon their arrival the afternoon of 3 March. At the first session, MacArthur launched into a tirade lasting for about a quarter of an hour. He voiced his decision to restrict the use of Manus-Los Negros facilities to his Seventh Fleet until the question of jurisdiction was settled. Then he pointed his pipe stem at Halsey and demanded, "Am I not right, Bill?"

With one voice, Admirals Halsey and Kinkaid together with Captains Carney and Johnson who were present replied, "No sir." [7]

MacArthur said, "Well, if so many fine gentlemen disagree with me, we'd better examine the proposition once more. Bill, what's your opinion?"

"General," replied Halsey, "I disagree with you entirely. Not only that, but I'm going one step further and tell you that by limiting use of the Manus naval base to the Seventh Fleet you'll be hampering the war effort." [8]

At length, MacArthur said, "Well, okay. You can have it your way." [9] But by the next morning, the U.S. Navy officers were told that the general had changed his mind. The course was run a second and then a third time. On the last

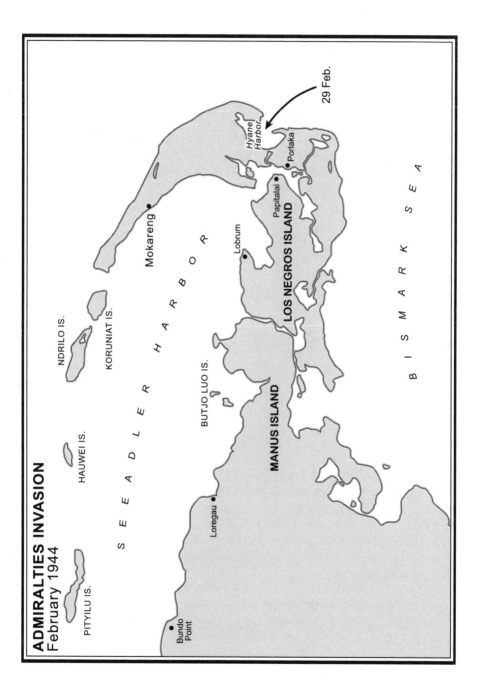

ADMIRALTIES INVASION
February 1944

PITYILU IS.

HAUWEI IS.

NDRILO IS.

KORUNIAT IS.

S E E A D L E R   H A R B O R

Mokareng

Lobrum

Papitalai

Hyane
Harbor

Porlaka

29 Feb.

LOS NEGROS ISLAND

BUTJO LUO IS.

MANUS ISLAND

Loregau

Bundo
Point

B I S M A R K   S E A

occasion, MacArthur emphasized Nimitz's insult to his personal honor at which Halsey said, "General, you're putting your personal honor before the welfare of the United States." [10]

Shocked, MacArthur said, "My God, Bull. You can't really mean that? We can't have anything like that." Turning to Sutherland, he said, "Dick, there will be nothing like that." [11]

Halsey returned to Noumea thinking that the problems concerning the naval base at Seeadler Harbor had been settled, but this was not to be. On 11 March, Leahy, King, and Nimitz brought the matter to the president. Roosevelt replied that the command problem was something the Joint Chiefs should handle. They did, leaving MacArthur in overall command. However, Marshall wrote, "You should control base facilities in your area unless you yourself see fit to turn over control of them." But he added that, "there should be a clear understanding that the Pacific Fleet will have unrestricted use of them." [12] Within a short time, the Seventh and Fifth Fleets operated from the Admiralties, the best fleet base west of Pearl Harbor until Ulithi was captured.

The historian Gerald E. Wheeler observed: "It is hard not to conclude that General MacArthur's concern about control of the Seeadler Harbor Naval Base was simply another instance of vanity and ego overriding sound military judgment, or even common sense." [13]

With the recent accomplishments enjoyed by Nimitz and MacArthur's commands, optimism reigned supreme with the military commanders in Washington. Seizure of the Admiralties influenced the Joint Chiefs to reassess specific strategy. On 2 March, they directed MacArthur and Nimitz to submit their respective plans for an advance to the Luzon-Formosa-China coast triangle.

MacArthur proposed to Marshall and the Joint Chiefs that two southwest Pacific divisions supported by the U.S. Fleet attack Hollandia on 15 April, a step in MacArthur's ultimate goal of returning to the Philippines. His justification for the change in plan was based primarily in what had been learned from the Sio codes. MacArthur told Marshall, ". . . the enemy has concentrated the mass of his ground forces forward in the Madang-Wewak area, leaving relatively weak forces in the Hollandia Bay area. He is attempting to concentrate land-based air forces in the area of western New Guinea and is developing additional fields in order to consolidate this area into a bulwark of air defense." [14] Only deciphered army communications could have given such accurate intelligence about enemy deployments and intentions.

On 8 March, Sutherland, who was visiting Washington, briefed the Joint Chiefs on the revised plan to strike Hollandia. Four days later, in a closed session on 12 March, the Joint Chiefs approved a directive for MacArthur and Nimitz that was to govern their operations until February 1945:

- MacArthur would complete the isolation of Rabaul.
- MacArthur would proceed westward along the northern coast of New Guinea, followed by the seizure of Mindanao on 15 November 1944.

- Nimitz would bypass Truk, seize the southern Marianas on 15 June and isolate the Carolines, then seize the Palaus on 15 September in order to provide a base from which the Pacific Fleet could support MacArthur's attack against Mindanao.
- Nimitz would seize Formosa on 15 February 1945, or, if first necessary to support an attack on Formosa, MacArthur would seize Luzon on 15 February.[15]

It is obvious from this directive that the Joint Chiefs still envisioned an enclave on the east China coast, yet they placed a greater emphasis on the Central Pacific drive.

After the neutralization of Rabaul, MacArthur changed his military strategy as expressed in his statement to the *New York Times* of 22 September 1943. In the defense of New Guinea, General Adachi's troops had occupied enclaves on the northern coasts of Papua and New Guinea, with many miles of land space between each enclave. Apparently, MacArthur considered each enclave, or Japanese strongpoint, as a strategic objective, in that during 1942 and 1943 Australian and American troops were ordered to attack each strongpoint. In 1944, during the drive across northern New Guinea, bypassing became the password. This change in strategy proved very successful in accelerating MacArthur's move to the Philippines.

In his *Reminiscences* MacArthur later commented, "It was the practical application of this system of warfare . . . to bypass Japanese strong points and neutralize them by cutting their lines of supply . . . to . . . 'hit 'em where they ain't'—that from this time forward guided my movements and operations."[16]

From the Sio codes, MacArthur learned that Wewak and Hansa Bay were heavily defended, whereas some 12,000 men, only about one-fifth of whom were combat troops, occupied the Japanese base at Hollandia. On 15 March, MacArthur proposed to the Joint Chiefs that the scheduled landing at Hansa Bay be canceled. At the same time, he submitted complete plans for the ships and troops allotted for that venture to land at Hollandia instead.

Hollandia and Aitape, west of Wewak, would be attacked simultaneously during the third week of April. Hollandia's harbor provided the best-sheltered anchorage between Wewak and Geelvink Bay. Hollandia's airstrips could support ground-based aircraft sufficient to dominate the airspace all the way to the Vogelkop at the western end of New Guinea. The Hollandia landing represented a giant leap forward as its nearest Pacific base lay nearly 600 miles down coast at Saidor.

During this operation, MacArthur had 217 ships of all types available to the 7th Amphibious Force to transport and put ashore a total of 79,800 army and air force personnel. On D-day (22 April), 35,800 combat soldiers went ashore at Hollandia at the adjacent Tanah Mera Bay and at Aitape, 120 miles to the east. Overwhelming force overran the enemy at Hollandia in two days at a cost of 159 lives. Only two Americans fell at Aitape, and Tanah Mera Bay was undefended.

Eight days after the Hollandia landing, MacArthur took himself out of the race for the Republican nomination for president. For months, MacArthur would neither affirm nor deny that he was interested in seeking the Republican nomination for president. He did express the opinion to Frank Kluckhohn, a *New York Times* correspondent, that an experienced soldier in the White House would bring an earlier victory in the war.[17] By the beginning of 1944, the MacArthur for President movement was gaining momentum.

On 26 January 1944, MacArthur visited Eichelberger's I Corps about 300 miles north of Brisbane, near Rockhampton. Eichelberger's troops were engaged in "a very realistic scene" of mock jungle warfare in the hilly countryside. MacArthur arrived in a Packard, followed by a battery of photographers who took numerous pictures of him after he had transferred to a Jeep. A number of these pictures were sent to newspapers in the United States under such captions as "General MacArthur at the Front with General Eichelberger in New Guinea." Eichelberger later became amused when he saw one of the photographs in an American newspaper. "The dead giveaway," he noticed, "was the unmistakable nose of a Packard motorcar in one corner of the picture." [18] Obviously, there could be no Packards in New Guinea in 1944. MacArthur knew that it is the perception of the public that really counts in politics.

On 12 February 1944, Vandenberg wrote an article published by *Colliers* magazine, "Why I Am For MacArthur." He reasoned that MacArthur's military genius was such that the country should

promote him to commander in chief and thus give him total sway over the military decisions which we think he is so incomparably qualified to make. . . . MacArthur is the embodiment of loyalty to our American destiny at any cost. . . . More than any other Presidential possibility, he would be elected as a great unifying American who would win his country's unified support by deserving it. . . . Although MacArthur has been a soldier all his life, I never knew a man in whom spiritual values are more predominant. . . . If nominated, he will be elected. If elected, he will bring a great mind, a great heart, a great capacity and a great devotion to the proud leadership of a great nation." [19]

His campaign seemed to be gaining momentum until 14 April 1944. On that day, Representative Albert L. Miller of Nebraska, a conservative Republican, startled the nation by releasing to the press his correspondence with MacArthur during the previous half year. This consisted of two letters to the general and two in return. Miller said in a letter on 18 September 1943 that "You owe it to civilization and to the children yet unborn" to run and defeat Roosevelt for "unless this New Deal can be stopped our American way of life is forever doomed." MacArthur replied on 2 October, "I thank you so sincerely for your fine letter . . . I do not anticipate in any way your flattering predictions, but I do unreservedly agree with the complete wisdom and statesmanship of your comments." [20]

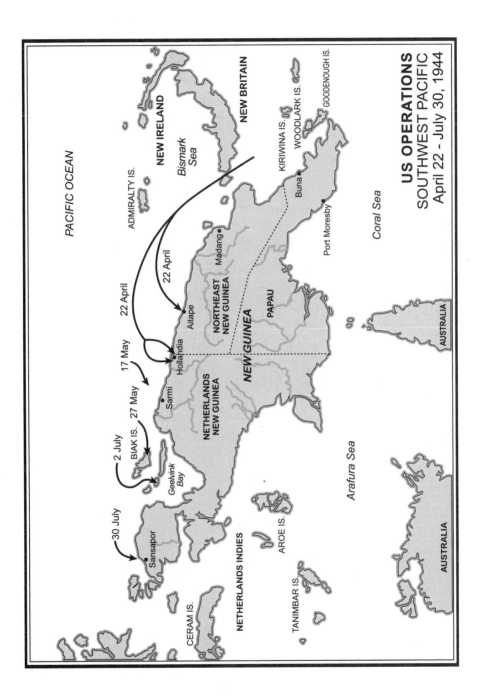

PACIFIC OCEAN

NEW IRELAND

NEW BRITAIN

Bismark
Sea

ADMIRALTY IS.

KIRIWINA IS.

WOODLARK IS.

GOODENOUGH IS.

Buna

Port Moresby

Coral Sea

22 April

22 April

17 May

27 May

2 July

BIAK IS.

30 July

Sansapor

Geelvink
Bay

Sarmi

Hollandia

Aitape

Madang

NORTHEAST
NEW GUINEA

NETHERLANDS
NEW GUINEA

NEW GUINEA

PAPAU

NETHERLANDS INDIES

CERAM IS.

AROE IS.

TANIMBAR IS.

Arafura Sea

AUSTRALIA

AUSTRALIA

US OPERATIONS
SOUTHWEST PACIFIC
April 22 - July 30, 1944

Again Miller denounced the Roosevelt administration in a letter on 27 January 1944 to MacArthur in which he said, "If this system of left-wingers and New Dealism is continued another four years, I am certain that this Monarchy which is being established in America will destroy the rights of the common people." To which the general answered, "Your description of conditions in the United States is a sobering one indeed and is calculated to arouse the thoughtful consideration of every true patriot . . . Like Abraham Lincoln, I am a firm believer in the people, and, if given the truth, they can be depended upon to meet any national crisis." He continued, "Out here we are doing what we can with what we have. I will be glad, however, when more substantial forces are placed at my disposition." [21]

Although most columnists agreed that MacArthur's letters showed that he was a receptive candidate for the Republican presidential nomination, most agreed the publication of his answers had spoiled his chances. Vandenberg called Miller's action a tragic mistake that made the general's position untenable. MacArthur recognized that derailment of his campaign was partially of his own making.

It was soon learned that soil conditions at Hollandia precluded the speedy development of any bomber base there that could support the advance to the Vogelkop as well as the heavy bombardment of the Palaus. It was thus decided that the Wakde-Sarmi area be taken to provide the necessary airfields. When it was learned that Sarmi was heavily defended, its seizure was canceled and only Wakde Island, known to have an excellent airstrip, was taken. MacArthur also decided that an assault on the island of Biak in Geelvink Bay, the location of excellent sites for bomber bases, would be undertaken on 27 May with the attack covered by Wakde-based aircraft.

The capture of Wakde on 18 to 21 May involved difficult fighting against a small enemy force. Wakde was developed into a key air base supporting two heavy bomber groups, two fighter groups, and two reconnaissance squadrons, which proved to be very important in the forthcoming invasion of Biak, Noemfoor, and Morotai. Later, bombers flew support missions for Nimitz's assault of the Palaus.

Biak became a hard nut to crack. Following an intensive aerial and naval bombardment on 27 May, American troops landed nine miles east of the airfield area. They encountered little opposition until 29 May when they were stopped by well-positioned enemy fire, which forced a retreat. The Japanese under Col. Naoyuki Kuzume had based defensive plans on the assumption that the airfields were the principal objectives of the invaders. He therefore concentrated his troops in the cave-pocked hills so that his forces could prevent the Americans from using the airfields. On 28 May, MacArthur's communiqué from Brisbane stated that the impending capture of Biak "marks the practical end of the New Guinea campaign." [22] On 1 June, he reported that enemy resistance was collapsing, and a short time later his communiqué announced that mopping up was proceeding on Biak. Neither American nor Japanese forces on the island agreed with these reports, as heavy fighting continued throughout the month of

June. This prevented the Fifth Air Force from attacking Japanese bases in the Carolines, which MacArthur had promised Nimitz for the invasion of Saipan on 15 June. Although American fighters could use the easternmost airfield on 22 June, other strips did not become operational until early August. Krueger declared the end of the Biak operation on 20 August. His command had lost approximately 400 men killed, 2,000 wounded, and 7,400 non-combat casualties against approximately 4,700 Japanese killed plus 220 captured.

Although the delay at Biak prevented air missions against the Carolines before and during the Saipan operations, the assault against the Marianas was a tremendous benefit to the Allied forces in Geelvink Bay. When Admiral Toyoda learned of the Biak invasion, he ordered his surface units and naval aircraft into action. In one surprise attack, the Japanese destroyed on the ground approximately sixty Allied planes that had been flying missions in support of Biak. Toyoda abruptly diverted the Japanese Fleet in the Netherlands East Indies from Biak to the Philippine Sea west of the Marianas. Accordingly, the attack on Saipan lured the Japanese fleet away from the Southwest Pacific Area forces in Geelvink Bay.

A naval history co-authored by Nimitz states, "The two Allied forces advancing across the Pacific operated as a team, each relieving the other of a portion of its burden . . . Had there not been a Central Pacific drive to attract and hold Japanese forces elsewhere, the southwest Pacific forces would have met far greater resistance in the New Guinea area." [23]

MacArthur never admitted to any benefits accruing from the Saipan invasion and to the end viewed it as an unwise decision.

On 2 July while the battle was still raging on Biak, a task force of about 8,000 American troops landed on lightly defended Noemfoor. Construction of airfields began in mid-July, although mopping-up activities were not completed until the end of August. Again, the bypassed Japanese at Wewak were not content to stay out of action. As early as late April 1944, Adachi announced to his soldiers at Wewak, "I am determined to destroy the enemy in Aitape by attacking him ruthlessly with the concentration of our entire force in that area." [24]

The 32nd Division occupied the beachhead at Aitape. In May, American patrols clashed with Adachi's forward units about thirty-two miles east of the Americans' main base. As a result of intelligence data supplied by Willoughby that Adachi would attack with a strong force of approximately 20,000 to 30,000 men between 5 and 10 July, the 43rd Division and elements of two other divisions were sent to reinforce the 32nd Division. On 27 June, Maj. Gen. Charles P. Hall was placed in overall charge of the command at Aitape. Hall placed an initial defensive line along the west side of the Driniumoor River twenty-two miles east of Aitape, a second line four miles to the rear, and a third line in the Aitape vicinity.

Adachi's main force of the 20th and 41st Divisions and parts of two other divisions attacked the Americans at the Driniumoor line on the night of 10 to 11 July. The Japanese units threw back the Americans, crossed the river, then broke through the covering force. Hall ordered a withdrawal to the second defensive line but was criticized by Krueger, who felt the retreat was unnecessary and demanded a counterattack.

In compliance, Hall's units regained the offensive and, within a few days, restored their line on the Driniumoor. Fighting continued through July and most of August until Krueger announced on 25 August the official termination of the Aitape-Driniumoor operation. Hall's force lost 450 men killed and more than 2,500 wounded while the Japanese Eighteenth Army deaths amounted to almost 10,000.

In anticipation of an invasion of the Philippines, MacArthur established an Army Service Command (ASCOM) to provide immediate logistical support as well as base and airfield construction. In the early stages of a task force assault, Maj. Gen. Hugh J. Casey was placed in charge with Brig. Gen. L. "Jack" Sverdrup, his chief engineer. Casey's unit was placed under the direct control of General Krueger.

Chapter 20
The Marianas

O N 12 MARCH 1944, THE JOINT CHIEFS OF STAFF directed the occupation of the Mariana Islands, specifically Saipan, Tinian, and Guam, the largest of the group and the only ones militarily required. They directed a target date of 15 June.

As Gen. Holland Smith later wrote, "Saipan was Japan's administrative Pearl Harbor, without massive permanent naval and military installations. It was the naval and military heart and brain of Japanese defense strategy. In itself it was a fortified island of considerable strength." [1] He pointed out that Saipan harbored Japan's Central Pacific Fleet headquarters under Vice Adm. Chuichi Nagumo, who had commanded the striking force at Pearl Harbor and Midway, the Thirty-first Army headquarters comprising all Central Pacific army troops under Lt. Gen. Hideyoshi Obata, the Northern Marianas Defense Force under Lt. Gen. Yoshijo Saito, and the Japanese 5th Naval Base Force under Rear Admiral Tsujimura.

Although the Marianas, including Saipan, proved to be the most valuable real estate captured by the Americans in the Pacific War, the decision to occupy them was a battle in itself. When Adm. Ernest J. King met with Admirals Nimitz and Halsey in San Francisco on 3 and 4 January 1944, he advised that the Mariana Islands were the key to the Pacific. Lieutenant General Walter Kruger reached the same conclusion as far back as 1936. [2] The meeting was arranged to discuss the implications of the Cairo-Teheran Conference.

Roosevelt and Churchill for the first time brought Generalissimo Chiang Kai-shek of China into their planning at the Cairo Conference, which began 22 November 1943. The communiqué from Cairo said, "The three great Allies are fighting this war to restrain and punish the aggression of Japan," reaffirming that Britain would continue fighting Japan after Germany was defeated. The communiqué continued that the Allies "in harmony with those of the United Nations at war with Japan will continue to persevere in the serious and prolonged operations necessary to procure the unconditional surrender of Japan." [3]

The three powers agreed that Japan would be stripped of all conquests she had made since 1894. Manchuria and Formosa would be returned to China in due course. Korea would regain her independence. It was intimated that the Soviet Union would obtain the Kurile Island chain and the southern half of Sakhalin, while the United States would acquire the Japanese mandated islands in the Central Pacific.

After the Cairo meeting, Roosevelt and Churchill met with Stalin at Teheran on 18 November through 1 December 1943. The Big Three drafted long-range military operations against Germany. Without prompting, Stalin indicated that the Soviet Union would join the Allies in the war with Japan after Germany had been defeated. At a party in celebration of Churchill's sixty-ninth birthday, the staffs of all three countries were invited to the British embassy. There, Stalin made three memorable toasts: one, "to my fighting friend Roosevelt" and another, "to my fighting friend Churchill." Then he asked the assemblage to stand and raise glasses for his last toast: "Without American production the United Nations could never have won the war." [4] Like Yamamoto, Stalin recognized the importance of the American home front.

With respect to Japan, King stressed that all operations were to be aimed at getting to China in order to exploit Chinese manpower and establish bases for the final assault against the Japanese mainland. King explained that in American hands the Marianas could block Japanese lines of communication to the Carolines, and that their central position made them an ideal base for the advance westward to the China coast. Forrest Sherman, Nimitz's war plans officer, noted that by seizure of the Marianas Truk might well be bypassed.

On 27 and 28 January representatives of Nimitz, Halsey, and MacArthur met in Pearl Harbor to coordinate their immediate operations. "Lieutenant General Richard Sutherland, MacArthur's chief of staff, argued that pooling all Pacific resources in the Southwest Pacific Area was the quickest way to seize the Philippines and move on to China." [5] MacArthur's strong objection to seizing the Marianas seemed to have obtained the agreement of Nimitz and Sherman. Sutherland wired MacArthur that he had won Nimitz's support.[6]

After reading the minutes of the Pearl Harbor conference, King became enraged at Nimitz. He wrote:

> I have read your conference notes with much interest and I must add with indignant dismay. Apparently, neither those who advocated the concentration of effort in the Southwest Pacific, nor those who admitted the possibility of such a procedure, gave thought nor undertook to state when and if the Japanese occupation and use of the Marianas and Carolines was to be terminated. I assume that even the Southwest Pacific advocates will admit that sometime or other this thorn in the side of our communications to the western Pacific must be removed. In other words, at some time or other we must take our time and forces to carry out this job . . .

A number of conferees, particularly Towers, stated, and his statements were allowed to go unrefuted, that the object of taking the Marianas was to provide for B-29 bombing attack against the Japanese Empire. Of course, that was never the object. That was merely one of the results that would ensue from this operation, which was to be taken to dry up the Carolines, facilitating the capture or neutralization of the Carolines, and to speed up the clearing of the line of communications to the northern Philippine area . . .

The idea of rolling up the Japanese along the New Guinea coast, throughout Halmahera and Mindanao, and up through the Philippines to Luzon, as our major strategic concept, to the exclusion of clearing our Central Pacific line of communications to the Philippines, is to me absurd. Further, it is not in accordance with the decisions of the Joint Chiefs of Staff.[7]

King wrote to Gen. George C. Marshall that apparently General MacArthur had not accepted the Combined Chiefs of Staff decisions at Cairo that there would be a dual drive across the Pacific and that the Central Pacific took priority in scheduling and resources. Now was not the time to change those decisions. King ended by recommending that Marshall tell MacArthur to obey orders.[8]

On 12 March when the Joint Chiefs went into closed session to consider the directives to Nimitz and MacArthur, they clearly envisioned moving to China's east coast following the fall of Formosa. However, Gen. Hap Arnold considered the Marianas as an ideal base for his new B-29 bombers.[9]

A study showed the Marianas operation would provide the following benefits: 1) interruption of the Japanese air pipeline to the south, 2) development of our own advanced naval base for submarine and surface operations, 3) establishment of a B-29 base from which to bomb Japan proper, 4) occupation of a position from which there would be a choice among several possible objectives for the next operations, keeping the enemy uncertain of our intentions. Too, it was hoped that this penetration of the Japanese inner defense zone, little more than 1,250 miles from Tokyo, might force them to bring their fleet out for decisive engagement.[10]

Admiral Raymond A. Spruance commanded all forces for the Marianas operation. The naval forces assigned to his command consisted of 535 combat ships and auxiliaries for three and a half marine divisions and one reinforced army division, a total of more than 127,500 troops. The target islands were 1,000 miles west of Eniwetok, the nearest anchorage; 3,500 miles from Pearl Harbor; and approximately 1,250 miles from Tokyo.

The bombardment groups totaling eight battleships, eleven cruisers, and twenty-six destroyers arrived off Saipan and Tinian at dawn on 14 June. When U.S. Marines of the 2nd and 4th Divisions landed at 8:44 A.M. on 15 June, the Japanese mortar, artillery, and machine gun fire was so effective that the first day's objective was not reached until Day 3. The Japanese considered these islands of such importance that they must oppose with all possible resistance.

On 12 June, Adm. Soemu Toyoda ordered Vice Adm. Matome Ugaki to proceed with his super battleships *Yamato* and *Musashi* with cruisers and destroyers to rendezvous with Vice Adm. Jisaburo Ozawa in the Philippine Sea. Ozawa, commanding the main body of the mobile fleet, began threading through the Philippine islands toward the rendezvous on 13 June. The submarine *Redfin* reported Ozawa's movement of four battleships, six carriers, and six destroyers heading north through Sibutu passage. Admiral Spruance, believing the Marianas area as Ozawa's destination, calculated it would take until 17 June to reach there.

Since the beginning of the war, the naval general staff in Tokyo was obsessed with the belief that Japan had to defeat the American fleet in a decisive engagement. By May 1944 Admiral Toyoda, the new commander in chief of the Combined Fleet, believed the time for a showdown was close at hand.

American submarines tracked and reported the movements of the Japanese to the advent of battle. The Japanese fleet consisted of nine aircraft carriers with 439 planes, five battleships, thirteen cruisers, and eighteen destroyers, a formidable force indeed. But by now the American home front showed its superiority, as Spruance had at his disposal fifteen aircraft carriers with 819 planes, seven battleships, twenty-one cruisers, and sixty-nine destroyers. This was a very large force, able to assembled in spite of the fact that even more combatant ships had been involved in the recent D-Day landings at Normandy on 6 June.

Spruance advised his two fleet commanders, Vice Adm. Marc A. Mitscher and Vice Adm. Willis A. Lee:

> In my opinion the main attack will come from the west but might be diverted to come from the southwest. Diversionary attacks could come from either flank or from the empire. *Task Force 58 must cover Saipan and the forces engaged there* and this can be done best by proceeding west in daylight and towards Saipan at night. Consider it unwise to seek a night engagement in view of our superiority but earliest possible strike on enemy carriers is necessary. [11]

On the morning of 19 June, Ozawa launched planes from his carriers aimed at destroying the U.S. Fleet. The planes came in four separate raids, all of which were intercepted by U.S. planes before any major damage was done. So many enemy planes were shot down at minimal loss to the Americans that airmen labeled it the Marianas Turkey Shoot.

Spruance had directed Mitscher to keep Guam and Rota neutralized; nevertheless, there was so much enemy activity on the Guam fields that reinforcements were needed. About fifty Guam-based planes were destroyed, mostly in attempted takeoffs, while many others were shot down in an attempt to land there.

Submarines took an aggressive part in the day's actions. The *Albacore* torpedoed the *Taiho*, the newest and largest Japanese carrier, and Ozawa's flagship. At first it appeared she had not been badly damaged, but in late afternoon the *Taiho* sank following a violent internal explosion that resulted from the torpedo damage. The U.S. submarine *Cavalla* sent three torpedoes into the carrier *Shokaku*. She sank within three hours, taking most of her planes with her.

As reports came in to Spruance at the end of the day, it was clear he had won an overwhelming victory in the air; however, he did not then know that two enemy carriers had been sunk. Japanese aircraft losses approached 400, compared to a U.S. loss of only thirty planes and twenty-seven airmen.

Spruance now knew that the bulk of the Japanese air force had been spent and amphibious forces at Saipan were no longer threatened from seaward. He decided to pursue the enemy to the westward and sent the following message to Mitscher:

Desire to attack enemy tomorrow if we know his position with sufficient accuracy. If our patrol planes give us the required information tonight no carrier searches should be necessary. If not, we must continue searches tomorrow to ensure adequate protection for Saipan. Point Option should be advanced to the westward as much as air operations permit. Damaged ships tomorrow proceed Saipan anchorage.[12]

Patrol planes were directed to conduct searches up to 700 miles the next morning. After many hours of flying time, the enemy fleet could not be found. Ozawa had set a northwest course intending to refuel the next day, then return to battle. When he learned that only 100 of his 430 carrier planes were operable, he changed his mind.

At 3:40 P.M. an *Enterprise* pilot reported the enemy 220 miles to the northwest. Mitscher advised Spruance that he would launch an all-out deck strike, which would require a night recovery. At 4:30 P.M., 216 planes were in the air and had just started for the target when a corrected report placed the enemy 275 miles away. This was extreme range. It was almost certain that many planes would exhaust their fuel supply before coming in for the night landing.

The U.S. planes ripped up the flight decks in the carriers *Chiyoda* and *Zuikaku* and damaged a battleship and cruiser. Two enemy oilers plus the carrier *Hiyo* were sunk. At 8:00 P.M. the planes began their return. As they approached, Mitscher ordered lights to be turned on to facilitate recovery. Normally the dimmest match light is forbidden aboard ships in the war zone, but in this case the safety and recovery of pilots came first. A group of destroyers was left behind to search the area in daylight. Although one hundred U.S. planes were lost, rescue operations saved all but sixteen pilots and thirty-three crewmen.

On Saipan, the Japanese grudgingly gave ground after fanatic, stubborn fighting. The marines captured Aslito airfield in the south on 18 June. Seabees placed the field in use for army P-47 planes by the 22nd.

On 22 June, the front of the northbound 2nd and 4th Marine Divisions widened to such a degree that Holland Smith ordered the army's 27th Division, less one battalion, to take over the line in the center, between the two U.S. Marine divisions. The 27th Division was late taking its position and was late in making advances so that the inner flanks of the marine divisions became exposed. A giant U was formed with the 27th at the base 1,500 yards behind the advancing formations, thus presenting the Japanese an unrivaled opportunity to exploit it.

Holland Smith became highly displeased. He decided that Gen. Ralph C. Smith, the commanding general of the 27th Division, lacked aggressive spirit and must be replaced. As commanding general of the landing force, he had authority to make such replacements as he deemed necessary. Aware of possible inter-service repercussions if he, a U.S. Marine, replaced a U.S. Army officer, he took his problem to Admirals Turner and Spruance on 24 June. Admiral Spruance had no hesitation in backing up Holland Smith. He "authorized and directed" the relief and replacement of the commanding general of the division "in order that the offensive on Saipan may proceed in accordance with the plans and orders of the Commander, Northern Troops and Landing Force." [13]

This episode created the loudest explosion in the Pacific's army-navy rivalry. Prior to Saipan, five army generals had been relieved in the Pacific, but by army generals. For a marine general to remove an army general was unpardonable. Although Spruance had approved Holland Smith's actions, he escaped criticism altogether. Smith's relief of an army general infuriated both Admiral Nimitz and Gen. George Marshall to the point they never forgave him.

Saipan's southern extremity, Nafutan Point, was secured on 27 June after the Japanese trapped there expended themselves in a desperate attempt to break through. To the north, Mount Tapotchau, the highest point on the island, was taken on 27 June. Thereafter, the marines' northward advance was steady if not rapid.

On the night of 6 to 7 July, Admiral Nagumo and General Saito ordered a banzai attack in which three to four thousand Japanese made a fanatical charge that penetrated the lines near Tanapag before being wiped out. Following this futile attack, both General Saito and Admiral Nagumo committed suicide; thus the commander of the striking force at Pearl Harbor and Midway brought his career to an end. Following the deaths of Saito and Nagumo, hundreds of the native population committed mass suicide by throwing themselves off the cliffs onto the rocks below near the northern tip of the island. Mothers would throw their children, then themselves, from the cliffs, in spite of the fact that the marines had set up loudspeakers nearby that broadcast reassurances in Japanese that the civilians would not be ill-treated.

On 9 July, two days after the banzai attack, organized resistance on Saipan ceased. The U.S. Marines reached Marpi Point, northernmost tip of Saipan, twenty-four days after the landing. Thereafter, only isolated groups of hiding Japanese remained. The stubborn enemy had made the island's capture costly. Of the 64,500 troops landed, 3,400 had died and 13,000 others were wounded. Twenty-four thousand Japanese were killed.

In reference to the heavy casualties, the New York *Journal-American*, a Hearst publication, commented on 18 July:

The important and significant thing the American people DO know is that equally difficult and hazardous military operations conducted in the

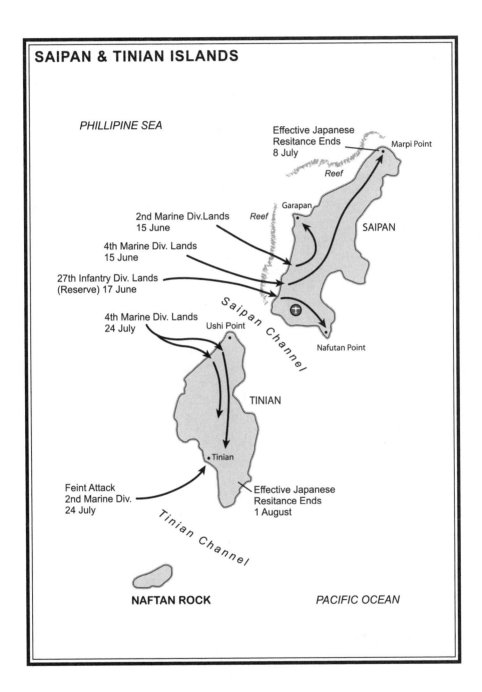

SAIPAN & TINIAN ISLANDS

PHILLIPINE SEA

Effective Japanese
Resitance Ends
8 July

Marpi Point

Reef

Garapan

2nd Marine Div.Lands
15 June

Reef

SAIPAN

4th Marine Div. Lands
15 June

27th Infantry Div. Lands
(Reserve) 17 June

Saipan Channel

4th Marine Div. Lands
24 July

Ushi Point

Nafutan Point

TINIAN

• Tinian

Feint Attack
2nd Marine Div.
24 July

Effective Japanese
Resitance Ends
1 August

Tinian Channel

NAFTAN ROCK

PACIFIC OCEAN

Pacific War under the competent command of Gen. Douglas MacArthur have been successfully completed with little loss of life in most cases and with an obvious MINIMUM loss of life in all cases.[14]

Actually, up to this point in the Pacific War, Allied troops had not encountered Japanese defenses as powerful as those on Saipan, nor would they capture territory of equal military value. While the news media and the American public did not generally recognize the true value of Saipan's defeat, Imperial Japan saw its significance. Upon announcing the fall of Saipan to the Japanese public, Hideki Tojo and his entire cabinet resigned. For the first time, knowledgeable Japanese began thinking of the worst for their country in the days ahead. Indeed the time was close at hand because the Seabees were heavily engaged in the construction of airdromes for long-range bombardment of the home islands. Vice Admiral Shigryoshi Miwa, a trusted advisor to the emperor, confided to Hirohito that, "Hell is upon us." [15]

A Japanese officer, Major Yoshida, who surrendered to the Americans in the last days of battle, pointed out the main reason the Japanese should be despondent. He told U.S. intelligence officers:

> The Japanese can never hope to defeat a nation that produces soldiers like your Marines. In the Japanese army, we revere the spirit of Yamato Damashii, which means the Spirit of Old Japan, and our soldiers will die for it. We have learned that the American Marine also reveres the spirit of his country and is just as willing to die as the Japanese soldier. Moreover, the Marine is a better soldier than the Japanese. His individuality is stronger, his training and fighting technique better. He has arms, ammunition, and engineering equipment far superior to ours. Had I not believed this, I would not have surrendered.[16]

Having secured Saipan, Spruance decided next to invade Guam. D-day for the Guam landing, originally set for 18 June, was delayed until 21 July. The Philippine Sea Battle and the character of the Saipan fighting showed the need for three divisions instead of the originally planned two.

Guam was the largest landmass yet to be assaulted in the Central Pacific, which gave the defenders room for withdrawal to the hills. The air and surface bombardment, which began on 11 June, made the landings easier by reducing coast defenses. From 14 July on, Rear Adm. R. L. Conolly, Southern Attack Force commander, supervised the systematic bombardment, which was both thorough and prolonged.

Early in the morning of 21 July, the III Amphibious Corps under Maj. Gen. Roy S. Geiger, USMC, landed in amtracs, preceded by a rolling naval bombardment. The 3rd Marine Division came ashore north of Orote Peninsula with the 1st Provisional Marine Brigade to the south, followed by the 77th Army Division. These beaches were chosen because Apra Harbor and Orote Peninsula, with its airfield, lay between them.

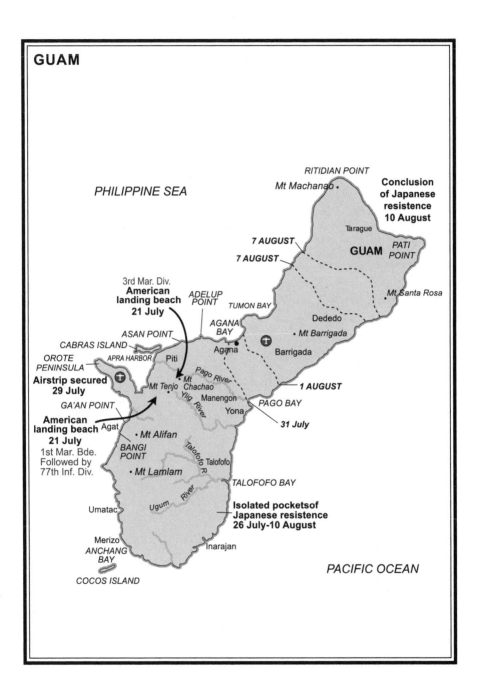

GUAM

RITIDIAN POINT

PHILIPPINE SEA

Mt Machanao •

Conclusion of Japanese resistence 10 August

Tarague

7 AUGUST

7 AUGUST

GUAM

PATI POINT

3rd Mar. Div.
American landing beach 21 July

ADELUP POINT

TUMON BAY

Mt Santa Rosa

AGANA BAY

Dededo

ASAN POINT

• Mt Barrigada

CABRAS ISLAND

Agana

Barrigada

OROTE PENINSULA

APRA HARBOR

Piti

Pago River

Airstrip secured 29 July

• Mt Chachao

Mt Tenjo

1 AUGUST

GA'AN POINT

Ylig River

Manengon

PAGO BAY

Yona

American landing beach 21 July

Agat

31 July

1st Mar. Bde.
Followed by
77th Inf. Div.

• Mt Alifan

BANGI POINT

Talofofo R.

Talofofo

• Mt Lamlam

TALOFOFO BAY

Umatac

Ugum River

Isolated pocketsof Japanese resistence 26 July-10 August

Merizo

Inarajan

ANCHANG BAY

PACIFIC OCEAN

COCOS ISLAND

The enemy had concentrated its strength near the landing area. Japanese air was no longer a factor, in that all enemy aircraft based on Guam had been eliminated and the Orote airfield rendered unusable.

The first seven days of fighting proved to be the worst for the Americans, but the two landing forces closed the gap between them on 28 July. The U.S. Marine brigade then pushed its way to the tip of Orote Peninsula by the next afternoon. Orote airfield and Apra Harbor were quickly put to use. On 30 July American planes landed on the airstrip. The backbone of Japanese resistance had been broken before General Obata withdrew to the northern part of the island for a last-ditch stand. The U.S. Marines and the 77th Division followed north through dense jungle, wiping out pockets of resistance on the way. General Geiger announced the end of organized resistance on 10 August 1944.

Although 11,000 Japanese had been killed, about 9,000 remained in small, scattered bands hidden in the jungle and hills. Some isolated groups had not been found until after the war ended. The U.S. suffered 1,400 killed and missing and about 7,100 wounded. The Tinian operation would prove much less costly.

The invasion of Tinian followed the initial assault on Guam by only three days. The best landing beaches by far lay near Tinian Town, which the Japanese considered most likely for an assault. They concentrated their defenses there with dug-in positions, underwater obstacles, and beach mines. Next best came the Yellow beaches on the northeast shore, but a navy-marine reconnaissance team revealed heavy surf and many offshore mines plus numerous underwater obstacles. The only other possible landing place involved two short beaches on the northwest side, designated White One and Two. These were only 65 and 135 yards long, far short of the 2,000 yards normally required to land a division. Yet, "three important considerations favored their use, namely 1) a landing there could be supported by artillery on the south shore of Saipan, 2) there was an excellent airfield nearby on the north end of Tinian, which, after capture, could be used by supply planes and 3) the Japanese had concluded these tiny beaches were too poor to use." [17]

A demonstration of transports and landing craft off Tinian Town deceived the Japanese as to the landing place. It pinned down the bulk of Japanese defenders there while the 4th Marine Division shuttled across the three miles of water between Saipan and the White beaches for a practically unopposed landing. The 2nd Marine Division followed the next day. Two pontoon piers established at White Two enabled a steady stream of pre-loaded trucks to be ferried in LSTs from nearby Saipan. Ammunition and supplies could be carried to inland dumps without rehandling on the beach. For the first time, new incendiary bombs filled with napalm, a highly flammable petroleum jelly, were used, with excellent results.

Vigorous resistance became disorganized by 27 July. The island was declared secured on 1 August. Some 9,000 had been wiped out at the cost of 389 marines killed and 1,816 wounded.

For the rest of the war, these islands proved more valuable than even Admiral King had envisioned. King saw them as key to the advance across the Pacific; in reality, they were key to the destruction of Japan's manufacturing capability. The Seabees built huge runways on all three for use by the B-29 Superfortresses. Apra Harbor was cleared for the westernmost large submarine base. Later, as B-29s leveled Japanese cities, the greatly reduced round-trip mileage for submarines accelerated the demise of the Japanese Merchant Marine.

The original Plan Orange envisioned that Japan must sue for peace when its troops, supplies, and people could not move on or off the home islands. Each day saw the enemy's movements become more restricted.

Admiral Nimitz transferred his headquarters from Pearl Harbor to Guam to be closer to the action. Truk and the rest of the Carolines could now be bypassed, and China was no longer needed for an air attack on Japan. At last, most U.S. news media saw the value of the U.S. Navy's island-hopping campaign across the Pacific, which some had questioned after the Tarawa campaign. In a period of less than ten months, American forces had advanced 3,500 miles across the Pacific from Oahu to within striking distance of Tokyo, only 1,250 miles away.

Although most comment in the American press was highly favorable about the Marianas campaign, a number of military historians would later question Admiral Spruance's decision-making at the Philippine Sea Battle. Spruance received criticism by many for not proceeding westward to meet Ozawa. In hindsight, he missed his chance to destroy the Japanese fleet; however, at that time the amphibious landing on Saipan was at a critical stage, with troops ashore and only partial supplies unloaded. Needless to say, his primary mission was to take Saipan, Tinian, and Guam. Admiral King repeated many times that in his view Spruance's decision had been entirely correct.

High-ranking Japanese officers agreed with Admiral King on the importance of the Marianas for Allied victory. After the war, Prince Higashikuni, commander in chief of Home Defense Headquarters, testified:

The war was lost when the Marianas were taken away from Japan and when we heard the B-29's were coming out. . . . We had nothing in Japan that we could use against such a weapon. From the point of view of the Home Defense Command, we felt that the war was lost and said so. If the B-29's could come over Japan, there was nothing that could be done.[18]

Chapter 21
The Philippines vs. Formosa Debate

*I*N THE EARLY PART OF 1944, Admiral King objected to the idea of "battering our way through the Philippines." He suggested the Philippines be bypassed altogether and that the Allied forces move directly against Formosa. He reasoned that the U.S. Navy could "put a cork in the bottle" of Japanese sea communications by choking off all shipping between Japan and its southern possessions.[1] MacArthur violently protested this strategy.

King reasoned that with Formosa in Allied hands and a submarine blockade imposed on the homeland, the flow of oil to Japan would be shut off completely. After war's end, the U.S. Strategic Bombing Survey found that Japan was "always hampered by a lack of oil." [2] With a total blockade, Japan would use up her remaining oil reserves, thereby immobilizing its ships, aircraft, and production lines in its manufacturing facilities.

MacArthur sent a three-page communication to the War Department dated 18 June 1944, which in part said:

> The Formosan campaign differs radically from operations that have been executed thus far in the Pacific. It is my most earnest conviction that the proposal to bypass the Philippines and launch an attack across the Pacific directly against Formosa is unsound. . . .
>
> Purely military considerations demand the reoccupation of the Philippines in order to cut the enemy's communications to the South and to secure a base for our further advance. . . .
>
> Even if this were not the case and unless military factors demanded another line of action, it would in my opinion be necessary to reoccupy the Philippines. Philippines is an American Territory where our unsupported forces were destroyed by the enemy. Practically all of the 17,000,000 Filipinos remain loyal to the United States and are undergoing the

greatest privation of suffering because we have not been able to support or succor them.

We have a great national obligation to discharge. Moreover if the United States should deliberately bypass the Philippines, leaving our prisoners, nationals, and loyal Filipinos in enemy hands without an effort to retrieve them at earliest moment we would incur the gravest psychological reaction. We would admit the truth of Japanese propaganda to the effect that we had abandoned the Filipinos and would not shed American blood to redeem them; we would probably suffer such loss of prestige among all the peoples of the Far East that it would adversely affect the United States for many years. I feel also that a decision to eliminate the campaign for the relief of the Philippines, even under appreciable military considerations, would cause extremely adverse reactions among the citizens of the United States. The American people I am sure would acknowledge this obligation. . . . [3]

By message dated 24 June 1944, General Marshall acknowledged the concerns of MacArthur's 18 June memorandum. It is clear that Marshall was seriously considering an early attack against Formosa. In part, he said:

It is also apparent from the information that the Japanese are seriously limited in their capacity to resupply or rearrange their troops due to limited shipping. . . .

Whether or not such operations should be carried out before a heavy blow is struck at the Japanese fleet is also of course a serious consideration. There is little doubt in my mind, however, that after a crushing blow is delivered against the Japanese fleet then we should go as close to Japan as quickly as possible in order to shorten the war, which means the reconquest of the Philippines.

With regard to the last (the reconquest of the Philippines) we must be careful not to allow our personal feeling and Philippines political considerations to override our great objective, which is the early conclusion of the war with Japan. In my view, "by-passing" is in no way synonymous with "abandonment." On the contrary, by the defeat of Japan at the earliest practicable moment the liberation of the Philippines will be effected in the most expeditious and complete manner possible. . . .

As to you [sic] expressed desire to be accorded the opportunity of personally proceeding to Washington to present fully your views, I see no difficulty about that and if the issue arises will speak to the President who I am quite certain would be agreeable to your being ordered home fo [sic] the purpose.[4]

At the time Marshall sent this message, he was aware that the U.S. Fleet had scored a decisive victory over the Japanese navy in the Battle of the Philippine Sea. Yet, he knew that the Japanese still had a substantial fleet left.

A good look at the map shows that Formosa had far more strategic value to the Allies than did the Philippines and probably could have been captured with fewer resources. It was much closer to Japan than the Philippines. When captured its air force could control the sea channels between Formosa and China as well as the waters to the south between Formosa and Luzon. Moreover, from airdromes on Formosa, U.S. planes could reach most military targets on the Japanese home islands whereas airfields on Luzon were too far away.

In the coming debate, MacArthur showed that he had few if any peers in the use of rhetoric—the art of persuasion. Nimitz supported King; yet, from his base in the Marianas he harbored doubts about whether his command alone had the strength to invade Formosa. Admiral Spruance objected because he felt that Okinawa was strategically more valuable than Formosa in carrying out the Plan Orange strategy for a total blockade of Japan. He so advised King, but he believed that Luzon should be seized first for needed fleet anchorage in Manila Bay. Spruance had not considered Ulithi atoll as a safe harbor when he, King, and Nimitz met at Saipan on 17 July 1944.

Few if any outside the U.S. Navy recognized that the Pacific Fleet would no longer need Manila Bay for fleet anchorage once Ulithi had been occupied and developed. By the fall of 1944, American submarines and the U.S. Pacific Fleet practically owned the South China Sea so that Luzon had little if any military value in the continuing war against Japan. Furthermore, the Japanese occupied the land area on the west side of the South China Sea. Airplanes alone from the Philippines could not interdict the north or south flow of Japanese shipping when it took a route near the China coast where it had friendly air cover. Yet, at no time did MacArthur downgrade the strategic importance of the Philippine islands landmass.

In the official history of General MacArthur's operations, compiled by his staff in Tokyo but not published until 1966, Chapter Seven, titled "The Philippines: Strategic Objective," states:

> The Philippine islands constituted the main objective of General MacArthur's planning from the time of his departure from Corregidor in March 1942 until his dramatic return to Leyte two and one half years later. . . .
>
> As the Allies advanced westward along New Guinea and across the Central Pacific, a wide divergence of opinion developed among international planners and military strategists on the methods of defeating Japan, but General MacArthur never changed his basic plan of a steady advance along the New Guinea-Philippine axis, from Port Moresby to Manila.[5]

In mid-July, MacArthur received a summons from Marshall to meet President Roosevelt at Pearl Harbor. It was one of the few instances where Admiral King and MacArthur agreed. Roosevelt had been nominated for a fourth term and was up for re-election in November. Both senior officers considered the meeting as a political ploy to enhance the president's re-election chances in the fall. At one point the Southwest Pacific commander exclaimed, "The humiliation of forcing me to leave my command to fly to Honolulu for a political picture-taking junket!" [6] King later said, "He had to show the voters that he was Commander in Chief." [7] Admiral Leahy, who accompanied Roosevelt on this trip and who harbored a good opinion of King and MacArthur, disagreed with both as to the president's motives. He would later say "to my knowledge he never made a single military decision with any thought of his own personal political fortunes." [8]

In spite of MacArthur's protest, he recognized that the coming meeting in Hawaii was extremely important. According to his flight pilot, Weldon E. "Dusty" Rhoades, he was very apprehensive about the outcome of his meeting with Roosevelt. Admiral Nimitz recognized that MacArthur had an emotional attachment to the Philippines. He had visited the general in March of that year and "found MacArthur highly intelligent with a magnetic personality but also with an unfortunate tendency to strike poses and to pontificate." [9]

In commenting on the MacArthur visit, Nimitz observed:

> His cordiality and courtesy to me and my party throughout my visit was complete and genuine, and left nothing that could be desired. Everything was lovely and harmonious until the last day of our conference when I called attention to the last part of the J.C.S. directive which required him and me to prepare alternate plans for moving faster and along shorter routes towards the Luzon-Formosa-China triangle if deteriorating Japanese strength permitted. Then he blew up and made an oration of some length on the impossibility of bypassing the Philippines, his sacred obligations there—redemption of the 17 million people—blood on his soul—deserted by American people—etc., etc.—and then a criticism of "those gentlemen in Washington, who, far from the scene, and having never heard the whistle of pellets, etc., endeavor to set the strategy of the Pacific War"—etc. When I could break in I replied that, while I believed I understood his point of view, I could not go along with him, and then—believe it or not—I launched forth in a defense of "those gentlemen in Washington" and told him that the J.C.S. were people like himself and myself who, with more information, were trying to do their best for the country, and to my mind, were succeeding admirably.[10]

MacArthur and Nimitz both met the president at Honolulu on 26 July. After dinner that evening the three, together with Leahy, discussed future moves in the Pacific. There is no written record of this conference. Although no final decision had been reached, the Joint Chiefs apparently favored the occupation of Formosa over a move into the Philippines. At the beginning of the meeting, the president seemed predisposed to the Formosa Invasion.

Various historical sources suggest Nimitz urged the invasion of Formosa, which appeared to be the Joint Chiefs of Staff's position. Certainly, Formosa was so located that the blockage of the flow of oil to Japan could easily be

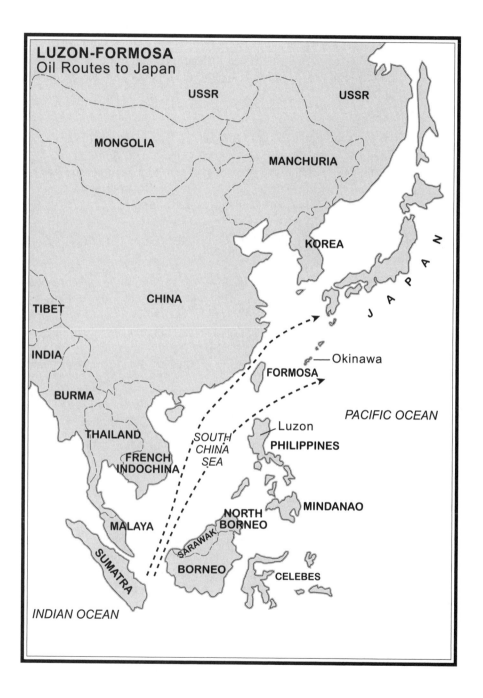

LUZON-FORMOSA
Oil Routes to Japan

USSR

USSR

MONGOLIA

MANCHURIA

KOREA

JAPAN

CHINA

TIBET

INDIA

Okinawa

FORMOSA

BURMA

PACIFIC OCEAN

THAILAND

SOUTH
CHINA
SEA

Luzon

PHILIPPINES

FRENCH
INDOCHINA

MINDANAO

NORTH
BORNEO

MALAYA

SARAWAK

SUMATRA

BORNEO

CELEBES

INDIAN OCEAN

accomplished. Furthermore, from its air bases, American planes could bomb the Japanese home islands, whereby those on Luzon were a bit too far away. Nimitz apparently stated that Formosa would provide a solid base of operations for the invasion of Japan.[11]

MacArthur is believed to have argued his case on both military and moral grounds, along the line expressed in his 18 June 1944 communication to the War Department.

The discussions ended at midnight. Leahy later wrote:

> After much loose talk in Washington, where the mention of the name MacArthur seemed to generate more heat than light, it was both pleasant and very informative to have these two men who had been pictured as antagonists calmly present their differing views to the Commander-in-Chief. For Roosevelt it was an excellent lesson in geography, one of his favorite subjects. The President was at his best as he tactfully steered the discussion from one point to another and narrowed down the area of disagreement between MacArthur and Nimitz.[12]

In the end, Roosevelt appeared to have adopted MacArthur's view. The two met privately the next morning. Some historians believe they reached a secret agreement whereby MacArthur would return to the Philippines but would take no part in supporting Roosevelt's opponent in the fall. On his return flight to Australia, MacArthur's pilot, Weldon E. "Dusty" Rhoades, asked the general if he had obtained what he wanted. Looking around so as not to be overheard, he said:

> "Yes, everything. We are going on."
> I asked, "To the Philippines?"
> He answered, "Yes. It will not be announced for a few days yet, but we are on our way."[13]

Rhoades observed that on the trip back MacArthur's good mood was like a child with a new toy.[14]

For security reasons, no mention of the president's visit was made in American newspapers until 11 August 1944, when the president was safely back in Washington, D.C. The *Honolulu Advertiser* in bold headlines reported the president's visit. The lead article on the front page of the paper stated he (meaning the president) declared, "1) General MacArthur will at the proper time return to the Philippines. 2) The only end for Japan is unconditional surrender."[15] A separate article on the front page said, "The President was tired. The lines on his face said so." A large picture of the president on the front page showed the president looking quite somber.

Additionally, a front-page article evidenced the tremendous popularity of MacArthur at the time. It said:

Gen. Douglas MacArthur was almost as much an object of public excitement as President Roosevelt during the Pacific war conference.

During drives on the streets of Honolulu and in the towns of the island, and on inspection tours of Army, Naval and Air installations, people lining the sidewalks craned their necks to catch a glimpse of the tall, handsome warrior.

Both Roosevelt and MacArthur drew loud applause at various stops.[16]

On the same date, 11 August, the *New York Times* headlined the meeting of the president, MacArthur, and Nimitz in Hawaii with a picture on the front page. Although the newspaper article was not as explicit as the *Honolulu Advertiser*, it was clear that a return to the Philippines was in the offering. The subtitle of the *New York Times* story said, "Roosevelt and Leaders Map Plans for Return to Philippines."

The record does not reflect that Roosevelt influenced the Joint Chiefs in making its decision. However, "Marshall, King, and Arnold were quite aware after Roosevelt and Leahy's return from Pearl Harbor that the President and his chief of staff favored the seizure of Luzon and gave considerable weight to MacArthur's moral and political arguments regarding the Philippines." [17]

Previously on 10 July, MacArthur had published his Musketeer Plan, which scheduled the invasion of Leyte and the Philippines on 20 December 1944. By late summer, it became obvious that this invasion could be accelerated to an earlier date.

Unlike Admiral King, General Marshall was always conscious of good public relations, especially for the U.S. Army. Accordingly, Marshall continued to be protective of MacArthur. For two and a half months after the Saipan invasion the American press devoted most of its coverage of the Pacific War to the Saipan, Guam, and Tinian campaigns, catering mostly to the U.S. Marines and U.S. Navy. On 8 September 1944, Marshall wrote MacArthur enclosing an article from *Time* magazine of 21 August regarding the fighting in New Guinea. *Time* had written the article at Marshall's request. Marshall stated:

I am writing you this note because I could not get an article of the character desired due to the fact, according to the *Time* people, that I gave them no name or units on which to hang the Aitape affair . . . The result was a very ineffective article whereas I think one redounding greatly to the credit of you and your command and which would have brought the American public to a far better understanding of what was being done, might have resulted.

All of which leads me to this suggestion, that your public relations people give us more names, otherwise you can expect much less of desirable credits for your command than would otherwise be the case. [18]

As late as the fall of 1944, nearly all communiqués from Southwest Pacific headquarters still featured MacArthur. Earlier in the year *Harper's Magazine* petitioned the Army Bureau of Public Relations for permission to publish a narrative entitled "MacArthur and His Command," which had been written by Walter Lucas, a correspondent of the *London Daily Express* who until recently had been accredited to the southwest Pacific area. Marshall was advised of the request in a memorandum for the chief of staff dated 16 February 1944. The memorandum explained:

> The article is highly critical of General MacArthur on grounds of vanity, aloofness, conceit, selfishness, histrionics, etc. It criticizes him for living in comfortable quarters at Port Moresby while his troops live in the jungle. It states that he has lost the confidence of the Australians. It states that his censors passed an article that implied that he would accept the Vice Presidency under either Willkie or Dewey provided the Presidential nominee would announce that he planned 'to let MacArthur handle the job of winning the war'. It quotes General Willoughby, G-2 of SWPA, as comparing General MacArthur in a published interview to Napoleon, Wellington, and Lee.
>
> On the other hand, it credits him with being a man of high intellect, great military ability, and thorough military knowledge. But the scales are so heavily weighted towards the sarcastic that one forgets any good before he has finished reading the article.[19]

Harper's request was killed by Marshall "on the grounds that the article will tend to undermine the confidence of General MacArthur's troops in him." [20] Clearly, heavy censorship prevented the American public from getting a balanced picture of the major players as well as strategy in the Pacific War. The many successes of the U.S. Fleet in its implementation of Plan Orange seemed to cause the Joint Chiefs to plan more army involvement rather than adhere strictly to this prescient prewar strategy.

At a meeting on 14 July of the Combined Chiefs, General Marshall explained, "as a result of recent operations in the Pacific it was now clear to the United States Chiefs of Staff that, in order to finish the war with the Japanese quickly, it will be necessary to invade the industrial heart of Japan." [21] In agreement with Marshall, the Combined Chiefs redefined the ultimate aim to force the unconditional surrender of Japan as:

1) Lowering Japanese ability and will to resist by establishing sea and air blockades, conducting intensive air bombardment, and destroying Japanese air and naval strength.
2) Invading and seizing objectives in the industrial heart of Japan.[22]

Invading Japan had not been contemplated in any of the prewar versions of Plan Orange as necessary to defeat the Japanese and was still not envisioned by the Joint Chiefs at the Casablanca Conference in January 1943. Inside the Joint Chiefs, there was still disagreement as to whether such action was necessary.

It seems that navy members had not changed their minds from their previous view. Commenting on this subject when this matter came up again before the Combined Chiefs in September, Admiral Leahy said in his memoirs:

A large part of the Japanese Navy was already on the bottom of the sea. The same was true of Japanese merchant shipping. There was every indication that our Navy would soon have the rest of Tokyo's warships sunk or out of action. The combined Navy surface and air force action even by this time had forced Japan into a position that made her early surrender inevitable. None of us then knew the potentialities of the atomic bomb, but it was my opinion, and I urged it strongly on the Joint Chiefs, that no major land invasion of the Japanese mainland was necessary to win the war. The JCS did order the preparation of plans for an invasion, but *the invasion itself was never authorized.* [emphasis his][23]

Nevertheless, the Combined Chiefs together with Churchill and Roosevelt formally approved the invasion at the September 1944 Octagon Conference.

A major source of disagreement at this conference was caused by Admiral King's opposition to the British Royal Navy being used in the Pacific War. King argued that the British had not developed the mobile logistical support perfected by the U.S. Pacific Fleet. King contended that, "the additional combat power of the Royal Navy would not compensate for the added logistical burden it would impose on American resources." Apparently, King looked upon the Pacific War as the U.S. Navy's war, and he did not want to share the honor for the ultimate triumph over Japan with any other nation or outside force.[24]

After a heated exchange between Churchill and King, Roosevelt agreed to use the British fleet in the Pacific. It would not be used extensively until the Okinawa campaign.

The final decision to invade the Philippines was reached at the Octagon Conference as a result of a report from Halsey to Nimitz on 13 September. Halsey said his planes had destroyed all but a handful of the Japanese air force in the Mindanao-Visayan region. His pilots found "the enemy's non-aggressive attitude unbelievable and fantastic"; the central Philippines lay "wide open" for assault.[25] One pilot who was downed and rescued by Filipinos on Leyte claimed there were no Japanese troops on the island. Halsey recommended cancellation of operations against the Palaus, the Talauds, Mindanao, and Yap. He urged an immediate invasion of Leyte.

Since the Palaus attack force was already at sea, Nimitz did not recommend its recall, but did endorse Halsey's other proposals. Marshall immediately decided to send a message to MacArthur asking for his opinion. Since MacArthur was aboard the *Nashville*, which was observing radio silence as it steamed toward the Morotai invasion, Sutherland gathered Kenney, Chamberlin, and other senior GHQ officers to discuss the decision. Kenney said, "Quite naturally everyone was reluctant to make so important a decision in General MacArthur's name without his knowledge of what was going on, but it had to be done." [26]

Sutherland replied in MacArthur's name that the immediate operations could be dropped in favor of a direct assault on Leyte. However, he disputed Halsey's claim that the island had no enemy forces.

Marshall received Sutherland's message while seated at a formal dinner given by Canadian Prime Minister Mackenzie King the evening of 15 September 1944. After excusing themselves from the dinner to confer, King, Leahy, Arnold, and Marshall reached an agreement. The Joint Chiefs ordered Nimitz and MacArthur to cancel the Talauds, Mindanao, and Yap operations in order to attack Leyte on 20 October. The die was now cast for entry into the Philippines.

When told of the decision of the Joint Chiefs, MacArthur joyfully made plans for the Leyte Gulf invasion. From the time he left Corregidor, he always viewed his mission as one to liberate the Philippines, although the Joint Chiefs had a different objective in mind. Shortly after he arrived in Australia, MacArthur began using his submarine force to arm Philippines guerrilla groups throughout the archipelago. Although this use curtailed the submarines' ability to sink enemy ships, it proved invaluable in aid to Allied troops throughout the Philippines campaign. This guerrilla force numbered approximately 180,000 by invasion day.

MacArthur once told General Kenney that he would return to the Philippines even if he were "down to one canoe paddled by Douglas MacArthur and supported by one Taylor Cub." [27] His obsession to return was matched by his emotional concern for the Filipino people. He took the unusual step of making all crew members of the Fifth Air Force read, understand, and sign a document prepared and signed by himself and General Kenney, which stated:

> It must be understood by all that the liberation of the Philippines is one of the purposes of the Philippines campaign. Liberation of the Philippines will not be understood by the Filipinos if their possessions, their homes, their civilization and their lives are indiscriminately destroyed to accomplish it. Throughout the Far East our moral standing and humility dictate that destruction of property and lives in the Philippines be held to a minimum in our military campaigns compatible with the insurance of success. Evidence is accumulating that the Japanese in some localities are leaving Filipinos in residence, evacuating cities, either compelling Filipinos to stay or failing to warn them. In order to insure our success, our objectives in areas we are to occupy is the total destruction of hostile effort. Aerial bombing offers by far the greatest destruction effect. Port facilities we plan to use we must preserve to the greatest possible effect. Our attack objectives are primarily shipping and airfields in the latter areas, not barracks, villages, or metropolitan areas.[28]

For more than a year prior to the Leyte invasion, MacArthur's headquarters had deluged the Philippines with materials proclaiming the general's forthcoming return. Both the Japanese and Filipinos made plans for the occasion.

The news media in the United States had made famous his words "I shall return," a promotional effort that advanced his cause with the general public. With 1944 being a presidential election year, Roosevelt himself needed little convincing. Not being privy to the background for the Joint Chiefs' agonizing decision in selecting Luzon over Formosa, the American public overwhelmingly supported a Philippines homecoming.

To the chagrin of Blamey, MacArthur determined that the Philippines operation would be an All-American affair. However, he needed the U.S. divisions that defended against the Japanese in the Solomons and New Guinea, especially those at Bougainville. These American divisions were assigned to MacArthur's command and replaced by Blamey's Australian troops, which took charge of all further operations in the Solomon Islands and New Guinea.

Throughout the Pacific War, Imperial General Headquarters envisioned the defeat of the U.S. Fleet by the one decisive naval battle. Recognizing that a vast armada of American vessels would be engaged in the Philippines invasion, the Japanese correctly assessed that this would be their last opportunity to destroy the U.S. Fleet short of the defense of their home islands. Accordingly, they made plans to commit their entire remaining fleet to such an attack. In contrast to the Battle of Midway, the U.S. Fleet would be vastly superior to its enemy.

Yet, this brings into question: Had the Joint Chiefs fully anticipated the success of the submarine fleet, would there have been any need to occupy either Luzon or Formosa? By August 1944, occupation of the Marianas had already eliminated any value the Allies could achieve by a move to the China coast.

Chapter 22
Ulithi

*B*Y SEPTEMBER 1944, THE JOINT CHIEFS could see light at the end of the tunnel in the Pacific War. The Marianas provided the base for bombing Japan and, almost as important, a forward submarine base at Guam. United States submarines could now reach both Tokyo and the straits between Luzon and Formosa in three days. Soon the U.S. Navy would have its most important base in the western Pacific, one that could service and house its entire fleet for the remainder of the war. Daily, the news media reported successes by the Allies on all fronts. In spite of the many setbacks suffered in the early months of the war, most Americans believed in ultimate victory; now, they knew it.

With 1944 a presidential election year, in the fall the public divided its attention between the war and presidential politics. The Democrats had nominated Franklin D. Roosevelt for a fourth term. He surprised the press and the public by selecting a little-known Missouri senator, Harry S. Truman, as his running mate for vice president. Governor Thomas E. Dewey of New York became the presidential nominee for the Republican Party. The Democrats had controlled the House, the Senate, and the Executive Branch for twelve years, which frustrated Republican lawmakers. Some Republicans claimed that Roosevelt and other higher-ups in his administration had known in advance of the Japanese air attack on Pearl Harbor and had failed to pass on this information to Kimmel and Short. This conspiracy theory seemed to be a good campaign issue.

In furtherance thereof, in September, Republican Congressman Forest A. Harness of Indiana said on the House floor that "the government had learned very confidentially that instructions were sent out from the Japanese government to all Japanese emissaries in this hemisphere to destroy the codes." [1] Harness' statement was correct, but he did not tell all. The Joint Chiefs of Staff and the Secretaries of Army and Navy did know that all Japanese codebooks had been ordered destroyed. This information had been sent to the Pacific Commands, including Kimmel and Short, on 3 December 1941, four days before the Pearl Harbor attack. Yet, at this time, neither the Joint

Chiefs nor anyone in the Executive Branch of government could comment for fear the Japanese would learn that the U.S. military was reading their secret messages. Such information, if known by the enemy, had deadly implications for Americans serving in the Pacific War.

General Marshall readily saw the danger. He took it upon himself to contact Governor Dewey by writing him a two-and-a-half page letter explaining the true situation, a copy of which was sent to Admiral King for his approval. In his memo to Admiral King, Marshall noted that "the whole thing is loaded with dynamite." [2]

On 25 September 1944, Marshall had Col. Carter Clarke hand-deliver the message to Governor Dewey in Tulsa, Oklahoma.[3] In it, he said, "I should have preferred to talk to you in person but I could not devise a method that would not be subject to press and radio reactions as to why the Chief of Staff of the Army would be seeking an interview with you at this particular moment." [4]

After addressing Dewey as "My Dear Governor," the first two paragraphs of Marshall's letter read as follows:

> I am writing you without the knowledge of any other person except Admiral King (who concurs) because we are approaching a grave dilemma in the political reactions of Congress regarding Pearl Harbor.
>
> What I have to tell you below is of such a highly secret nature that I feel compelled to ask you either to accept it on the basis of *your not communicating* its contents *to any other person* and returning this letter or not reading any further and returning the letter to the bearer. [emphasis his][5]

Recognizing that he may well be walking into a political trap, Dewey returned Marshall's message before reading beyond the second paragraph. Accordingly, Clarke returned to Washington. Marshall recognized that he needed to rely upon Dewey's integrity to get his message across. Two days later, Clarke again met Dewey back in Albany with the first two paragraphs of the 25 September 1944 letter deleted. "He said he was willing that Dewey read the entire letter provided he communicated to others only facts that he then had or that he received from someone other than Marshall." [6] Dewey replied that he owed it to his party to seek the counsel of a major political advisor. Marshall agreed to permit him to discuss the information in the letter with Elliott Bell, a close friend and political strategist.

Marshall's letter denied that code breaking prior to Pearl Harbor disclosed the Japanese intentions. He continued in part:

> Now the point to the present dilemma is that we have gone ahead with this business of deciphering their codes until we possess other codes, German as well as Japanese, but our main basis of information regarding Hitler's intentions in Europe is obtained

from Baron Oshima's messages from Berlin reporting his interviews with Hitler and other officials to the Japanese government. These are still in the codes involved in the Pearl Harbor events.

To explain further the critical nature of this set-up, which would be wiped out almost in an instant if the least suspicion were aroused regarding it, the battle of the Coral Sea was based on deciphered messages and therefore our few ships were in the right place at the right time. Further, we were able to concentrate our limited forces to meet their naval advance on Midway when otherwise we almost certainly would have been some 3,000 miles out of place. We had full information of the strength of their forces in that advance and also of the smaller force directed against the Aleutians which finally landed troops on Attu and Kiska.

Operations in the Pacific are largely guided by information we obtain of Japanese deployments. We know their strength in various garrisons, the rations and other stores continuing available to them and, what is of vast importance, we check their fleet movements and movements of their convoys. The heavy losses reported from time to time which they sustain by reason of our submarine action largely result from the fact that we know the sailing dates and routes of their convoys and can notify our submarines to lie in wait at the proper points . . .

The conduct of General Eisenhower's campaign and of all operations in the Pacific are closely related in conception and timing to the information we secretly obtain through these intercepted codes. They contribute greatly to the victory and tremendously to the saving in American lives, both in the conduct of the current operations and in looking towards an early termination of the war.

I am presenting this matter to you in the hope that you will see your way clear to avoid the tragic results with which we are now threatened in the present political campaign.[7]

After careful consideration, Dewey's patriotism trumped politics. His decision greatly relieved the Joint Chiefs, as they could continue concentrating on how best to defeat the Japanese.

The Republicans did have a valid campaign issue, one not fully exploited. The president's failing health was a concern to all of Roosevelt's close associates and was mentioned by Dewey and other Republicans during the campaign. The true status of Roosevelt's health did not come through to the public because the president campaigned principally by radio plus weekly announcements to the Washington press corps. Even though 65 to 70 percent of the news media was owned by those antagonistic to Roosevelt, his Washington press corps was highly favorable and rarely wrote anything negative about the president personally.

Being unaware of the decisions of the Joint Chiefs, Dewey campaigned primarily on the slow progress being made in the Pacific, especially Roosevelt's failure for purely political reasons to support MacArthur.

Politics was not confined to the fall's presidential election. In addition to making the decision to invade Leyte at the September 1944 Octagon Conference, the Combined Chiefs of Staff pursued new and old disputes for strategy and planning. China was an area of serious disappointment. The Japanese now occupied most of the airfields in south China, although in 1943 Chiang Kai-shek had assured Roosevelt that his armies could defend these bases.

The rift between Stilwell and Chiang Kai-shek reached a complete impasse. When the latter gave orders to Stilwell to use the Burma divisions to attack toward Bhamo, in effect this meant terminating the action in northern Burma just short of reopening the Ledo Road to China. "The crazy little bastard," Stilwell wrote. "The little matter of the Ledo Road is forgotten . . . It does not even enter that hickory nut he uses for a head . . . Usual cockeyed reasons and idiotic tactical and strategic conceptions. He is impossible." [8]

Stilwell immediately reported to Marshall the Generalissimo's intention saying, "(He) will not listen to reason . . . I am now convinced that he regards the South China catastrophe as of little moment, believing that the Japs will not bother him further in that area, and that he imagines that he can get behind the Salween front and there wait in safety for the U.S. to finish the war." [9]

Stilwell's telegram reached Marshall in the midst of the Quebec Conference. The strategic aim at Quebec was to keep China in the war and not much more. Marshall was determined that no U.S. divisions would be deployed to the China-Burma-India theater. All future operations in Burma would be left to the British so that the United States would not be involved in the reconquest of colonial territory. Particularly galling to Stilwell was Chiang Kai-shek's ambivalence toward breaking his own blockade from the south.

On 16 September, Marshall presented the gist of Stilwell's telegram to the conference in the presence of Roosevelt and Churchill. Marshall's staff at Quebec composed a 600-word telegram to Chiang Kai-shek with Marshall's recommendation that the president sign. The message repeated all the arguments that Stilwell had made to Chiang Kai-shek while at once placing Stilwell in unrestricted command of all Chinese forces. It concluded, "It appears plainly evident to all of us here that all your and our efforts to save China are to be lost by further delays." [10]

Stilwell delivered the message to the Generalissimo in person, which unquestionably shocked the latter. However justified the message, Roosevelt had plainly overreached. Chiang Kai-shek refused to give in. If the Americans succeeded in imposing Stilwell on him, they might do likewise in the matter of the Communists. He demanded Stilwell's removal. In so doing, he received the support of Patrick Hurley and Donald Nelson, who had been sent to China by the president as special envoys. Over the objections of Marshall, Roosevelt in mid-October gave orders to remove Stilwell from China without delay. Lieutenant General Albert C. Wedemeyer succeeded him as chief of staff to the Generalissimo and commander of American forces in China.

This marked the beginning of the end also for Chiang Kai-shek. Had he adopted Stilwell's program for the reform of the army, he may have been able to resist the Japanese offensive of 1944 and, possibly, to overcome the Communists in the clash that was sure to come. American support continued to Nationalist China, although John Patton Davis, Jr., a Foreign Service officer located there, said in one of his reports, "We must not indefinitely underwrite a politically bankrupt regime." [11]

Major General Frank Merrill attended the Octagon Conference. Upon his return to China, "he reported that statements of Admiral Nimitz and others about the needs for bases on the China coast were purely a cover for real operations." He said "that all plans for operations against the Japanese assumed no action by China beyond containing some enemy forces on the mainland. There was no intention to get mixed up on the Continent with large U.S. forces." [12]

With bases on the China coast eliminated from further consideration, the Joint Chiefs could now devote full time on how best to blockade the home islands. Liberation of the Philippines to satisfy MacArthur, supported by public opinion in the United States, remained the only diversion from clear, steadfast military strategy. Yet, the dual drive across the Pacific could arguably be justified up to this point even at its heavier cost from a logistics viewpoint.

Prior to the Octagon Conference, Nimitz and MacArthur made arrangements to invade Yap, the Palaus, the Talauds, Mindanao, and Morotai. Upon receiving Halsey's opinion that the central Philippines lay wide open for assault, invasion of the Talauds, Mindanao, and Yap were canceled in favor of an immediate invasion of Leyte.

Nimitz had planned to use the U.S. Army's battle-tested 7th and 77th Infantry Divisions plus the 96th Infantry Division in reserve for the Yap assault. He offered these divisions to MacArthur for use in Leyte. Halsey's fleet now had seventeen aircraft carriers. With the invasions of Morotai and the Palaus under way, Halsey's fleet gave simultaneous cover to each, as they lay only 500 miles apart.

In preparation for the initial Philippine invasion, the U.S. XI Corps, comprising the 31st Infantry Division and the 126th Regimental Combat Team of the 32nd Infantry Division, went ashore on the island of Morotai on 15 September 1944. Morotai is 300 miles south of Mindanao, the Philippine archipelago's second largest island. The XXI Corps quickly secured a defensive perimeter behind which airfields were constructed to provide air support for the future advance. The Japanese gave little resistance to this penetration of their last defense before the Philippines.

As on Bougainville, no effort was made to occupy all of the island; instead, the beachhead was expanded into a twelve-square-mile perimeter within which several new airfields were constructed. Two hours after American troops hit the undefended beaches, MacArthur came ashore and is said to have remarked, "We shall shortly have an air and light naval base here within 300 miles of the Philippines." Gazing to the northwest he is reported to have said, "They are waiting for me there. It has been a long time." [13]

Concurrently with the Morotai landing, Nimitz moved against the Palau Islands. There, he intended to gain the air bases and anchorage necessary to support the Leyte landings and to protect MacArthur's right flank. The Palau Islands formed a string of volcanic islets within a coral reef seventy-five miles long and twenty miles wide. They had provided the Japanese with anchorages and bases after the destruction of Truk. Through code breaking, Nimitz learned that the Japanese occupied three major islands: Peleliu, Angaur, and Babelthuap, the largest and most heavily defended with 25,000 Japanese troops. Accordingly, Nimitz determined to bypass Babelthuap, thus occupying only the small islands of Peleliu and Angaur.

Nimitz designated the U.S. Army's 81st Division to invade the lightly defended island of Angaur, immediately to the south of Peleliu. The 81st Division landed on 17 September and by the morning of the 20th it had killed 850 Japanese and reported the island secure. It was 21 October, however, before the last pockets of Japanese resistance were cleared. By that time 1,300 Japanese had been killed and 45 captured. The Americans lost 264 men killed. Casualties, including 244 cases of "battle fatigue," totaled 2,559 (nearly twice the strength of the enemy garrison).

At the southern end of the Palau Islands, immediately north of Angaur, lay Peleliu, an islet about six miles long and two miles wide at its broadest. In the south lay an excellent airfield, which had been in use before the war. The 1st Marine Division came ashore on 15 September and quickly occupied the landing strip. Commanding the airfield and running north for about two miles was a low wooded ridge the Japanese called Mornji Plateau, which the marines would later call Bloody Nose Ridge.

Imperial General Headquarters had adopted a strategy against beach-front defense and banzi charges in favor of a battle of attrition.[14] The Japanese placed Col. Nunio Nakagawa in charge of Peleliu's defense. Before the U.S. Marines landed, Nakagawa had fortified 500 caves, most of which were connected by interior tunnels. Some of the caverns were five- and six-stories deep and contained barracks and kitchens. The 1st Marine Division secured the southern part of the island with its important Japanese airfield by 17 September. Thereafter, the Japanese continued fanatic resistance from rough, dominating ground in the center of the island. Casualties were so high that the marines had to be reinforced by the U.S. Army's 81st Division from Anguar. Not until 25 November did all organized resistance cease.

The battle for Peleliu had been waged to protect MacArthur's right flank before his move into the Philippines. It was a pyrrhic victory at best. The Palaus operation cost the U.S. Army and Marine Corps approximately 2,850 men killed and 9,000 wounded. The Japanese lost about 13,600 men killed and 400 captured. It turned out to be one of the bloodiest battles in the Pacific. The seizure of Peleliu and Angaur did little, if anything, to aid the American invasion at Leyte, but the overall operation was a classic case of serendipity. On 22 September 1944, a regimental combat team from the 81st Division took a giant step on the road toward

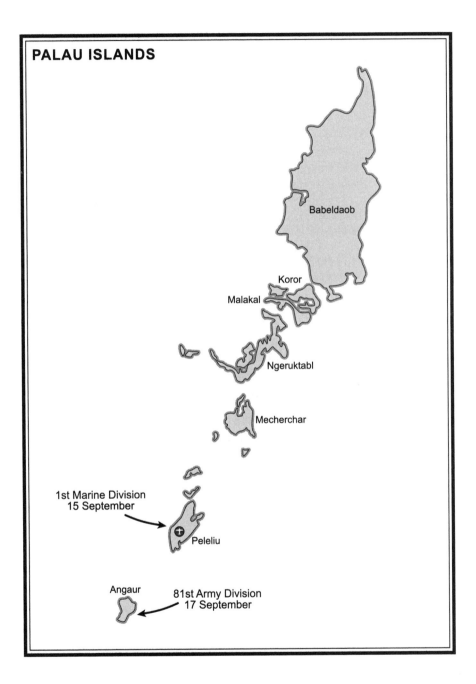

PALAU ISLANDS

Babeldaob

Koror

Malakal

Ngeruktabl

Mecherchar

1st Marine Division
15 September

Peleliu

Angaur

81st Army Division
17 September

the Japanese homeland at no cost whatsoever: The soldiers went ashore at Ulithi atoll. Through his constant study of maps, Nimitz discovered this atoll and readily saw its value. He called it the U.S. Navy's secret weapon, and his censors made sure that no reporter made mention of it. But the Japanese knew Ulithi was there, as it was only ninety miles distant from its Yap base, which the Americans had bypassed.

The Japanese had previously evacuated Ulithi atoll, which was now inhabited by about 400 natives. Ulithi is 360 miles southwest of Guam, 850 miles east of the Philippines, 1,500 miles south of Tokyo, and 1,200 miles from Okinawa. It is a typical volcanic atoll with coral, white sand, and palm trees. The reef runs roughly 20 miles north and south by 10 miles across enclosing a vast anchorage with an average depth of eighty to one hundred feet—the best suitable anchorage within 800 miles and certainly one of the finest natural harbors in the world. Three dozen little islands rise slightly above the sea, the largest only half a square mile in area.

Located northwest of Truk, once envisioned as the U.S. Navy's western fleet base, Ulithi is 250 miles closer to Tokyo than Manila Bay. Historians Samuel Morison and D. Clayton James acknowledged its vast military value. The latter said, "Ulithi was soon developed into the most important fleet anchorage and staging base in Nimitz's theater west of Hawaii." [15] Yet the American public knew nothing about this valuable military asset during the war although it rivaled the Marianas, Iwo Jima, and Okinawa in strategic value for the ultimate defeat of Japan. Interestingly enough little has been written about Ulithi in the aftermath of World War II.

Within a month of its occupation, a whole floating base operated at Ulithi. Six thousand ship fitters, artificers, welders, carpenters, and electricians arrived aboard repair ships, destroyer tenders, and floating dry docks. The USS *Ajax* had an air-conditioned optical shop, a supply of base metals from which she could make any alloy to form any part needed. Many refrigerator and merchant ships combined to form revolving supply teams. It has been estimated that over half of the ships were not self-propelled but were towed in. They then served as warehouses for a whole system of transports, which unloaded stores for distribution. This kind of chain went all the way back to the United States.

After leaving Pearl Harbor, the slow, military-laden Liberty ships could lay anchor at one of three lagoons in the Marshalls—Majuro, Kwajalein, and Eniwetok—the last being the farthest west. At each location, the ships would be immune from enemy attack by both submarine and surface ships. Under escort, they could proceed to Ulithi, the Allies' foremost forward base for supply and naval ship repair for the remainder of the war.

The natives on the four largest islands were moved to the smaller Fassarai, and every inch of these four was quickly put to use by Seabees. Asor became headquarters for the port director, radio station, evaporator (rain is the only fresh water supply), tents, small boat pier, and a cemetery. Sorlen was set up as a shop for the maintenance and repair of the smaller ships. Mog-Mog became

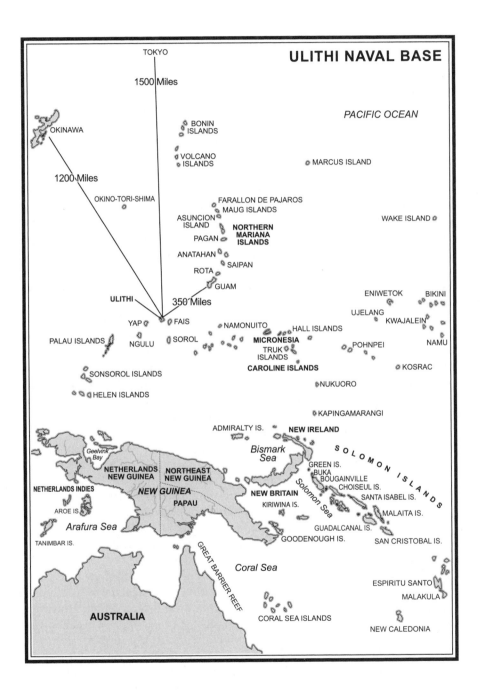

the recreation center. The largest island, Falalop, was just wide enough for a 3,500-foot airstrip for the handling of airplanes that flew in from Guam on a daily basis carrying sacks of mail and airfreight. Because of Ulithi's very small landmass, the U.S. Navy spent little in development in comparison with other bases in the Pacific, particularly Leyte, Samar, and Guam. The port facilities at the latter proved the costliest of any fleet base in the Pacific during World War II,[16] yet Ulithi accommodated more ships.

After the capture of the Marianas, every day saw an increase in U.S. military strength in the Pacific and a dramatic decrease in Japan's ability to stop the Americans. Imperial General Headquarters took drastic measures in hopes of slowing the American advance. Two new secret suicide weapons came into being. In August 1944, at a base on Otsujima in Japan's inland sea, more than 200 Japanese volunteers began training to pilot the kaiten. This was a fifty-foot-long torpedo with a small pilot's chamber, a periscope, and a 3,000-pound warhead. Although the kaiten's success spelled suicide for the pilot, there was never a dearth of volunteers for the kaiten or its airborne equivalent, the kamikaze, which was established two months later.

The kaitens were first used against the American ships at Ulithi. Early on the morning of 20 November, four kaitens slid off the deck of the *I-47*. One managed to get inside Ulithi's harbor to sink a U.S. Fleet oiler. The other three kaitens wrecked or were sunk by U.S. defenders. So far as is known, kaitens claimed only one other victim during the war. The Japanese kamikazes proved far more successful. One managed to reach Yap, then damaged the USS *Randolph*'s flight deck while the carrier was at anchor in Ulithi's lagoon on 11 March 1945. These two incidents caused only minimal damage when measured against the fact that literally thousands of sea vessels of all types anchored in safety at Ulithi during the last nine months of the war.

In addition to ship repair, military supply, and safe anchorage, Ulithi housed the tankers that were used to quench the U.S. Pacific Fleet's enormous thirst for fuel oil. An estimated monthly consumption of over 6 million barrels had to be met by commercial tankers bringing oil from the West Coast to Ulithi. There, a floating storage of more than 100,000 barrels was always maintained. A shuttle service of forty tankers operated between Ulithi and the U.S. Fleet in the western Pacific. In addition, 900,000 barrels of reserve fuel was divided among Saipan, Guam, and Kwajalein, plus a 5 million barrel reserve at Pearl Harbor.[17]

Before war's beginning, the Joint Chiefs adopted the Rainbow Five Plan. Because of the disadvantages involved in fighting a two-ocean war with equal vigor, this plan rightfully directed that Germany be defeated first. However, by the fall of 1944, Allied military strength in the Pacific had reached the point that ultimate victory appeared viable without any support from the European theater after Germany's defeat. The year saw Japan's military still determined to win, though losing. Courageous Japanese soldiers alone could not compensate for the Americans' overwhelming material strength, the fighting spirit of its young men, and a strategy designed to strangle Japan's ability to wage war. Yet, at no time would MacArthur adopt the basic winning strategy of the prewar Plan Orange. He was not alone among U.S. Army generals in his belief that winning the war required occupation of the enemy ground, a doctrine applicable to most wars in history.

In reference to the Palau Islands operation, most historians agree that the capture of Peleliu was not worth the cost. Nevertheless, American planes stationed there did prevent the large enemy garrisons on Babelthuap and Yap from moving to Ulithi.

Chapter 23

Leyte Gulf

*T*HE NAVAL BATTLE OF LEYTE GULF was the largest ever fought in terms of ships and men. Yet, all the fighting occurred outside of Leyte Gulf itself. Before war's beginning, Admiral Yamamoto correctly recognized that whichever country's battle fleet remained supreme at the end would win the war of the Pacific.

The great naval battle came about as a result of the American's first advance into the Philippines at the odd-shaped island of Leyte. This island is about 115 miles long, with a width ranging from 15 to 45 miles. In 1944, it had a population of approximately 915,000, of which 31,000 inhabited Tacloban, its capital and largest city. General Headquarters (GHQ) at Hollandia moved at full speed in the preparation of plans for the Leyte landing. Although present at his advance headquarters for only four days, MacArthur stayed in constant touch from Brisbane.

MacArthur hoped to develop a large air and logistical base in the Leyte Valley to support future operations. The Seventh Fleet could take advantage of the spacious anchorage in Leyte Gulf, off the east coast. The Japanese had built six airfields, which, when captured, could support offensive actions against the islands to the north or south.

On Leyte, MacArthur could count on the support of Col. Ruperto K. Kangleon's guerrilla force, together with thousands of Filipinos who would assist his service units. Kinkaid's Seventh Fleet constituted the central Philippines attack force, which would be responsible for the invasion, from staging through the amphibious landings. Krueger's Sixth Army headquarters would assume control of ground operations upon arrival. Eichelberger's Eighth Army was to be held in reserve.

In preparation for the Leyte invasion, both MacArthur and Nimitz committed all available U.S. air power in the Pacific to weaken the Japanese, especially enemy air power in and adjacent to the Philippines. China-based B-29s and medium bombers of the Fourteenth Air Force operated against Formosa. Kenney's planes struck at Japanese airfields in Mindanao.

On 6 October, Halsey's Third Fleet sailed from Ulithi to patrol the northern flank, a great arc extending from the central Philippines through Formosa and the Ryukyus to southern Japan. Halsey's Third Fleet contained four task forces, one each commanded by Vice Adm. John S. McCain, Rear Adm. Gerald F. Bogan, Rear Adm. Forrest P. Sherman, and Rear Adm. Ralph E. Davison. The four combined task forces contained ninety-six combat ships, including eight fleet carriers, seven light carriers, six battleships, six heavy cruisers, eight light cruisers, and sixty-one destroyers,[1] substantially more offensive power than held by the entire U.S. Pacific Fleet prior to Pearl Harbor Day, and far more powerful than the remaining Japanese combined fleet.

To deceive the Japanese, a cruiser-destroyer group attacked Marcus Island on 9 October. On the 10th, Halsey's carrier planes flew 1,396 sorties on and around Okinawa. A submarine tender, a dozen torpedo boats, two midget submarines, and four freighters were sunk. The Third Fleet destroyed almost a hundred Japanese planes at the cost of twenty-one of its own.[2]

On 12 October, Halsey launched his planes from a position about ninety miles east of Formosa. The Americans destroyed about two hundred enemy aircraft, but at the heavy cost of forty-eight of their own.[3] On the next day, his task force flew 974 sorties, which concentrated on airfields, hangars, and other installations at Formosa.[4] At dusk, a Japanese plane struck the heavy cruiser *Canberra* with an aerial torpedo. She immediately became dead in the water. Being 1,300 miles from Ulithi and within range of a number of enemy airfields, the severely damaged *Canberra*'s fate had to be addressed: Should she be abandoned and sunk or should an attempt be made to save her? Halsey decided that *Canberra* should be towed to Ulithi by a heavy cruiser guarded by destroyers.[5]

On 14 October, the Twentieth Bomber Command sent 109 B-29s from China to bomb the airfields around Takao, Formosa. By the end of the three-day Formosa air battle, U.S. aircraft had destroyed nearly 600 enemy planes, sunk three dozen freighters and small craft, and inflicted substantial damage on hangars, barracks, ammunition dumps, and industrial plants.[6] Nevertheless, in late afternoon, a Japanese plane slammed a torpedo into the light cruiser *Houston*, completely flooding her engineering spaces. Halsey dispatched another heavy cruiser to tow her to Ulithi.

After Japanese planes seriously damaged the two American cruisers off Formosa, reports to Tokyo grossly exaggerated the losses. The Japanese official communiqué reported that "the intrepid Japanese aviators in a series of successful attacks had virtually annihilated the U.S. Fleet."[7] Imperial General Headquarters, by accepting these estimates, concluded that the Allies could not mount an invasion of the Philippines before December.

On 16 October, Japanese planes attacked the towed cruisers, which could make less than four knots on their 1,300-mile journey. One enemy aircraft succeeded in putting another torpedo into *Houston*, yet it did not sink. Both damaged cruisers reached Ulithi's safe lagoon on 27 October.

On 17 to 18 October, while the invasion convoys began closing in for the final approach, the 6th Ranger Battalion seized Dinagat, Sulaun, and Homonhon islands at the entrance of Leyte Gulf. Only Sulaun had a few enemy occupants, who were quickly eliminated.

After the Rangers installed navigation lights on the islands, minesweepers and underwater demolition teams scoured the entrance to the gulf. They encountered only a few mines along the approach to the gulf entrance.

On 16 October, MacArthur left Hollandia aboard the cruiser *Nashville*. He became elated as he traveled north amid the huge Seventh Fleet armada containing 738 ships, which later would be joined by the 96 combat ships of the Third Fleet. In size, the Leyte landing rivaled the Allied invasion of Normandy four months earlier.[8] This force provided cover for the transports containing Lt. Gen. Walter Krueger's Sixth Army.

"To supply the huge invasion force during the landing, the War Department estimated 1.5 million tons of general equipment, 235 tons of combat vehicles, 200,000 tons of ammunition and 200,000 tons of medical supplies were required. Thereafter, 332,000 tons of equipment would be required every thirty days."[9] Logistical supply necessitated use of nine staging bases widely scattered over the southwest and Central Pacific: Oro Bay, Finschhafen, Manaus, Hollandia, Biak, Noemfoor, Morotai, Guam, and Oahu.[10]

On the morning of 20 October, shells rained down on the beachhead at sunrise as MacArthur's vessel steamed up the gulf and anchored two miles away. At 10:00 A.M., four divisions of the Sixth Army landed simultaneously. The XXIV Corps, consisting of the U.S. Army's 7th and 96th Infantry Divisions, quickly secured the beachhead near Dulag against light opposition. The 7th Division, commanded by Maj. Gen. Archibald V. Arnold, landed at beaches in front and on either side of Dulag. Although the town was quickly overrun, the Dulag airfield was not taken by nightfall.

MacArthur notified President Sergio Osmeña and his party on a nearby transport to be ready for pickup at 1:00 P.M. for the ride to shore. He was disturbed, yet later elated, after he saw the worldwide publicity received by the photograph of him walking ashore in knee-deep water.

As rain began to fall on the beach, men of the Sixth Army Signal Corps brought up a weapons carrier with a radio transmitter for the scheduled broadcast by MacArthur and Osmeña to the Philippine nation. The portable transmitter was linked to a master transmitter aboard *Nashville*, which broadcast on several wavelengths known to guerrilla forces and Filipinos who had radios.[11]

At 2:00 P.M., MacArthur delivered a two-minute, emotion-packed address:

People of the Philippines, I have returned! By the grace of Almighty God, our forces stand again on Philippine soil . . . Rally to me! Let the indomitable spirit of Bataan and Corregidor lead on. As the lines of battle roll forward to bring you within the zone of operations, rise and strike! . . . For your homes and hearths, strike! In the name of your sacred dead, strike! . . . Let no heart be faint. Let every arm be steeled. The guidance of divine God points the way. Follow in His name to the Holy Grail of righteous victory![12]

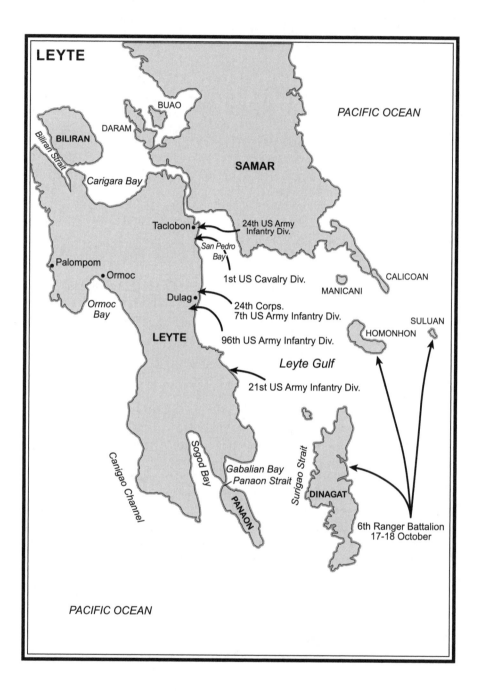

One bystander observed that the general was " 'genuinely moved,' as he spoke. His hands shook and his voice took on the timbre of deep emotion." [13]

The Philippines president followed with a ten-minute speech. Osmeña said that "Roosevelt had asked him to be the bearer of a message of congratulations to the people of the Philippines on regaining freedom." [14]

Earlier in the day, the 1st Cavalry Division, commanded by Brig. Gen. Verne D. Mudge, seized the Tacloban airfield against spotty Japanese resistance, then crossed Highway 1, the main road on the east coast. When darkness arrived, it occupied ground within a mile of the city of Tacloban. The 24th Infantry Division, to the south on the X Corps' front, encountered the heaviest Japanese opposition of the day. However, by nightfall, it had captured Hill 522, which dominated Highway 2, the key route into Leyte Valley.

Meanwhile, the 21st Infantry Regiment landed seventy miles to the south. It encountered no Japanese troops as it occupied points on both sides of Panaon Straits. Forty-nine Americans were killed on all fronts this first day. However, 60,000 men and 100,000 tons of supplies had been unloaded by nightfall.[15] The 1st Cavalry Division seized Tacloban near dusk on 21 October. The XX and XXIV Corps steadily enlarged their beachheads from 21 October through 25 October.

On 23 October, with fighting only two miles outside the city, MacArthur and Osmeña and many senior officers assembled at Tacloban for a ceremony to officially re-establish the commonwealth government in the Philippines. The ceremony was broadcast throughout the archipelago. After short speeches by MacArthur and Osmeña, Sutherland read a proclamation from Roosevelt making official the restoration of civil government. A bugler sounded colors as the flags of the United States and the Philippines were hoisted simultaneously at opposite ends of the provincial capitol building. MacArthur then presented the army's Distinguished Service Cross to Col. Ruperto K. Kangleon, the guerrilla leader designated to serve as acting governor of Leyte.

MacArthur visited the Walter Price residence, a spacious house that would serve as his quarters and GHQ offices. This elegant two-story stucco house was located three blocks from the provincial capitol, which served as the Philippine capitol until Osmeña could return to Manila. Prior to MacArthur's arrival, the Japanese had used the Price house as an officers club, having killed its owner, Walter Price.

After the Battle of the Philippine Sea, the Japanese naval staff began designing a plan for the next battle, named Sho-Go, or victory operation. Four Sho-Go plans were developed depending on strike location. The plan for the attack on Leyte Gulf called for three naval forces to converge on the landing area. The Northern Force, under Vice Adm. Jisaburo Ozawa, would advance on Leyte from the north in an attempt to lure away the American Third Fleet. The main striking force, called the Center Force by the Americans and commanded by Vice Adm. Takeo Kurita, would come through the San Bernardino Strait to the east of Samar, then converge on the ships in Leyte Gulf. This force was composed of twenty-five warships, including the *Yamato* and the *Musashi*, the largest battleships afloat. The remaining ships, designated as the Southern Force by the Americans, were under the control of Vice Adm. Shoji Nishimura, who had at his command two older battleships, the *Fuso* and the *Yamashiro*; one heavy cruiser; and four destroyers. Vice Admiral Kiyohide Shima's 2nd Striking Force, consisting of two heavy cruisers, one light cruiser, and seven destroyers, would join Nishimura.[16]

On 18 October at 1:00 A.M., Kurita's Center Force left its base at Lingga Roads near Singapore. On 20 October, it anchored in Brunei harbor in Borneo, where all ships were refueled. On 22 October at 8:00 A.M., Kurita's fleet left Brunei heading for the Philippines.

Two American submarines, the *Darter* and the *Dace*, were on patrol west of Palawan Island and were about to depart for Australia because they were running low on food and fuel. For security reasons, they had not been warned of the Philippines assault. They were alerted by a broadcast from Tokyo Rose, who said the Americans "had landed in Leyte and they would all die." [17] As a result, they decided to stay in the area. The two stalked the Japanese fleet en route, sinking the heavy cruiser *Maya* together with *Atago*, Vice Admiral Kurita's flagship. The vice admiral had to jump in the water and swim for his life. A total of 350 officers and men were lost on *Atago*.[18] Two other heavy cruisers were badly damaged: *Takao*, which made its way back to Brunei Bay, and *Aoba*, which was towed to Manila Bay. Afterward, the *Darter* ran aground on a reef, her crew being saved by the *Dace*.[19]

To counter the Japanese, Nimitz directed all Pacific Fleet units to cover and support forces of the southwest Pacific in the seizure of Leyte. The Third Fleet was directed "to destroy enemy naval and air forces in or threatening the Philippine area." It would occupy waters to the north of Leyte Gulf. Halsey's instructions included one unnumbered sentence that caused considerable controversy later. It read, "In case opportunity for destruction of major portion of the enemy fleet offer or can be created, such destruction becomes the primary task." [20] This sentence differed from Spruance's operation directive in June that ordered him only to capture, occupy, and defend Saipan, Tinian, and Guam. Spruance received criticism for not being more aggressive in pursuing the Japanese fleet to his west.

On 24 October, air attacks by Halsey's carriers, though damaging to the Japanese fleet, were not the knockout blows reported by the pilots. Kinkaid informed Halsey by dispatch that the Seventh Fleet could handle the enemy's southern force, but expected the Third Fleet to take care of Kurita's striking force. By 4:00 P.M. on the 24th, Halsey apparently believed he had already defeated Kurita's fleet. His carrier groups had launched 259 sorties against the Japanese. When his reconnaissance planes spotted Ozawa's carriers, Halsey abandoned patrol off San Bernardino Strait. The Third Fleet proceeded north at full speed. In so doing, Halsey failed to inform Kinkaid that the vital strait above Samar was being left unguarded.

To the south of Leyte Gulf, Kinkaid placed a large force at the north end of Surigao Strait under the tactical command of Rear Adm. Jesse B. Oldendorf.

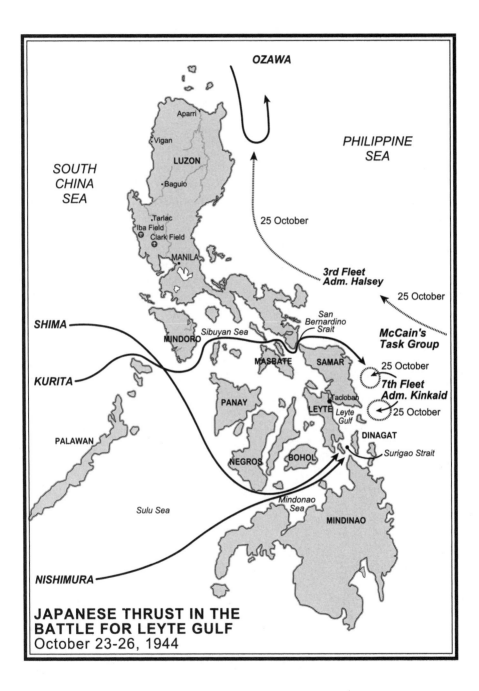

**JAPANESE THRUST IN THE
BATTLE FOR LEYTE GULF**
October 23-26, 1944

Oldendorf's destroyers sank a battleship and three destroyers of Nishimura's fleet as they came through the strait on the night of 24 to 25 October. By the end of the battle, Oldendorf's ships sank Nishimura's entire fleet, with the exception of one destroyer.

Shima arrived into Surigao Strait later that night. At 5:32 A.M. on the morning of 25 October, Shima radioed Kurita that Nishimura's force had been destroyed.[21] After a brief encounter with American firepower, and upon recognizing Nishimura's fate, like Shakespeare's Falstaff, Shima decided that "discretion is the better part of valor." Turning southward, he fled the scene. Carrier planes constantly harried his ships the next day.

Despite Halsey's belief that Kurita's strong central force had been badly mauled and was turning west in the Sibuyan Sea, Kurita continued forward through San Bernardino Strait. He had thus far lost three heavy cruisers to American submarines and his super battleship *Musashi* to Halsey's carrier aircraft on 24 October. *Musashi* exhibited incredible strength before sinking. She was attacked by hundreds of American aircraft to little effect. The Americans scored some twenty torpedo hits and seventeen bomb drops to eventually bring her down. Her sister ship, *Yamato*, sustained severe damage yet stayed with the fleet. A one-thousand- pound bomb penetrated through five decks of the *Yamato*. When it exploded, it blew two holes below the water line near the starboard bow. As one compartment filled with water, the great ship shuddered and began to heel slightly. Flooding a compartment on the port side allowed the *Yamato* to right itself and plow on.[22]

Having come through San Bernardino Strait, Kurita faced three escort carrier groups with radio call signs Taffie 1, under command of Rear Adm. Thomas Sprague; Taffie 2, commanded by Rear Adm. Felix Stump; and Taffie 3, commanded by Clifton "Ziggy" Sprague (no relation to Thomas Sprague). Each Taffie contained six carrier escorts, three destroyers, plus three destroyer escorts for protection. The eighteen escort carriers carried 304 fighter planes plus 109 torpedo planes. The Taffie planes were armed with one-hundred-pound anti-personnel bombs, not the five-hundred- to two-thousand-pound bombs carried by planes of the Essex class fast carriers. Clifton Sprague's Taffie 3 occupied space off the east coast of Samar directly in the path of Kurita's move south. Taffie 2 occupied space approximately thirty miles south, followed by Taffie 1 thirty miles due south of Taffie 2.

The destroyers and destroyer escorts had the duty to protect the carriers. In this battle, the destroyers, led by the *Johnston*, went far beyond the call of duty. The captain of the *Johnston* was Cmdr. Ernest Edwin Evans, a mixed-blood Cherokee Native American from Oklahoma who somehow managed to enter the U.S. Naval Academy and graduate in the class of 1931. According to his biographical entry in The Lucky Bag, "his philosophy was 'life is what one makes it.' "[23] Nicknamed "The Chief" by his classmates, a name often bestowed on the numerous Native American volunteers in the U.S. Marine Corps, his yearbook described him as "never gripes, always ambitious."[24]

After making a smokescreen to obscure the escort carriers, the *Johnston* charged the oncoming Japanese fleet. Evans waited until his ship got within eight hundred yards of the leading Japanese ship before firing his torpedoes. A torpedo ripped into the *Kumano*, flagship of one of Kurita's cruiser divisions. "The cruiser's bow was blown off." [25] Thereafter, Japanese shells came from every direction until the *Johnston* was hit and later sunk. A wounded Evans vanished with his sinking ship. He was posthumously awarded the Medal of Honor. The destroyer escort *Samuel B. Roberts* also went down in this phase of battle while planes from all three Taffies swarmed Kurita's ships.

Admiral Kincaid frantically called on Halsey as he feared the loss of his escort carrier fleet to Kurita's fleet. Admiral Nimitz followed the progress of the battle from Hawaii by wireless telegraph. He was concerned by Halsey's dispatch of 8:24 P.M. the night before, "am proceding north with three groups." [26] Kincaid's desperate pleas the morning of 25 October caused Nimitz to be even more perturbed. He sent a message to Halsey: "Where is Task Force Thirty-Four? Repeat, where is Task Force Thirty-Four? The world wonders." Halsey felt insulted by Nimitz's inquiry. Shortly thereafter, he gave the order to change course from due north to due south. He did not expect his fleet to arrive at Leyte Gulf until 8 A.M. the next morning, too late to engage Kurita's fleet.

Clifton Sprague's force put up a gallant and heroic fight against a superior force, yet before being annihilated Kurita retired northward backward through the San Bernardino Strait. Kurita later explained that an intercepted message led him to conclude that Halsey's fleet was bearing down on him. In reality, Halsey, after sinking all of Ozawa's carriers, did turn south, but not in time to have prevented Kurita from moving into Leyte Gulf, had he so desired. Had he done so, the Japanese could have caused untold havoc with shipping and beachhead positions. After the war, the U.S. Strategic Bombing Survey reported that Kurita testified that lack of expected land-based air support and air reconnaissance, fear of further losses from air attack, and worry as to his fuel reserves induced him to withdraw.

With Kurita's departure, the battle ended. During the next few days, ships from the Seventh Fleet scoured the seas off the coast of Samar looking for lost sailors and downed pilots. With the sinking of the *Johnston* alone, an estimated 270 officers and men had to cling to life rafts and bits of wreckage to prevent drowning. For more than two days and nights, they swam in shark-infested waters before being saved. By then only 141 from the *Johnston* managed to survive. Yet the Japanese sustained many times the number of personnel losses as did the Americans. In ships sunk, the American fleet lost six combat ships while the Japanese lost three battleships, four carriers, ten cruisers, and nine destroyers.

Afterward, most historians and admirals censured Halsey for his decision to leave the Leyte beachhead in pursuit of Ozawa, as they claim his departure could have caused a disaster, which indeed it might have, to the supply ships still unloading in Leyte Gulf. However, by 25 October all troops and the bulk of supplies had already been unloaded, most supply ships having departed. To speculate further, had Kurita brought his fleet inside Leyte Gulf, would he have been able to escape back through the San Bernardino Strait before being annihilated by Kincaid's fleet and land-based planes, which had already disposed of the southern Japanese naval thrust?

Admiral King was not among Halsey's critics; neither was MacArthur. The latter later commented that

the near disaster can be placed squarely at the door of Washington. In the naval action, two key American commanders were independent of each other, one under me, and the other under Admiral Nimitz 5,000 miles away, both operating in the same waters and in the same battle.[27]

MacArthur himself exacerbated the divided command problem by insisting on maintaining the independence of his command. In so doing, he "forbade any uninterrupted channel of communication from the Seventh Fleet to the Third." [28] Unity of command in the Pacific meant he would be the commander. Fortunately for the Allies, the Joint Chiefs controlled the direction of the war in the Pacific.

In the evening of 25 October, Halsey sent a dispatch addressed to Nimitz, MacArthur, Kinkaid, and King to clarify his position, "So that there be no misunderstanding concerning recent operations of the Third Fleet." He argued that once he located Ozawa's carrier forces, "to statically guard San Bernardino Strait until enemy surface and carrier attacks could be coordinated would have been childish." [29] In spite of the controversy surrounding Halsey's actions, this naval battle assured the ultimate defeat for Japan.

Chapter 24
The March to Luzon

WHEN THE JOINT CHIEFS AT THE OCTAGON CONFERENCE directed MacArthur to invade the Philippines at Leyte, they obviously had Luzon in mind as the main objective. Occupying territory to the south was not envisioned.

In response to Dr. Van Mook's plea for Allied forces to move into the Netherlands East Indies, Admiral Leahy explained:

> Our main object was to bring about the defeat of Japan at the earliest possible moment and to this end our strategy was directed to the fullest exploitation of our superiority in naval and air power.
>
> In this general conception, our idea was to close in on Japan, cut the sea and air communications, and strike at the heart of Japan as rapidly as possible.[1]

In answer to the inquiry of Sir Alan Brooke, General Marshall and Admiral King added:

> With regard to operations in the Philippines it was not visualized that major United States forces would be used in mopping-up operations nor that the island of Mindanao and others to the south would be assaulted by United States forces. Rather, it was hoped that with U.S. troops holding certain key positions, the rearmed Philippine army and guerrillas would be able to carry out the necessary mopping-up operations.[2]

MacArthur had a different plan in mind. He never intended to abide by the Joint Chiefs' wishes pertaining to the Philippines. In 1941, he had rejected the Plan Orange strategy for the defense of Luzon, only to adopt it when he saw that he had no other choice. Now, he continued to ignore the Plan Orange strategy, which clearly was the quickest and best way to achieve victory against Japan.

As early as September 1944, MacArthur determined to send the Eighth Army into the central and southern Philippines after the Sixth Army was well established on Luzon. Even as the Combined Chiefs met, MacArthur busied himself and staff with his Oboe Plan for using Australian troops for the invasion of the Netherlands East Indies.

The string of Allied successes caused the Joint Chiefs on 3 October 1944 to authorize the invasion of Iwo Jima on 20 January 1945 and Okinawa on 1 March 1945. On 4 October the Joint Chiefs authorized the occupation of Luzon. In view of Halsey's assessment about Leyte, the Joint Chiefs contemplated the march to the Philippine's largest island to be quick and easy. The Japanese had a different opinion.

Upon learning of the Leyte landing, the Japanese Fourth Air Army was heavily reinforced by planes from the home islands and Formosa. It now had up to 2,500 planes available. On 24 October, the Japanese undertook a massive air offensive against the Leyte beachheads, which caused major damage to Fifth Air Force planes and facilities. Somehow, the Japanese Fourth Air Army had failed to coordinate its attack so as to give Kurita the air cover he needed in his approach to Leyte Gulf.

General Tomoyuki Yamashita, the conqueror of Singapore, who had arrived in Manila on 9 October, assumed command of the Japanese Fourteenth Area Army, consisting of about 224,000 troops, with 23,000 in the Japanese garrison at Leyte, substantially more than Halsey's report.[3] Imperial General Headquarters instructed Yamashita to abandon plans for annihilation at the beachhead and to prepare instead for resistance in depth in the interior, out of range of American naval bombardments. Accordingly, the Japanese established their main defense line in the middle of Leyte Valley, with its principal supply base at Jaro in the central mountains. The Japanese Fourth Air Army boosted a large force in early September, most planes located at Luzon bases.

General Hisaichi Terauchi, commander of Japanese forces in the southern Philippines, persisted in demanding that Yamashita send large ground reinforcements to assist Lt. Gen. Sosaku Suzuki, the commander of troops on Leyte. Although Imperial General Headquarters wanted most of the Fourteenth Area Army to be held on Luzon, between 23 October and 11 December, Yamashita dispatched nine convoys. American aircraft sank nearly 80 percent of the ships involved, yet the Japanese succeeded in getting an additional 45,000 to 50,000 troops and about 10,000 tons of supplies and equipment to Leyte.[4]

On 25 October, the Japanese introduced its kamikaze corps to the American navy. Kamikazes hit three escort carriers off Samar. Several more attempted crashes on ships in Leyte Gulf but were shot down. The crashing tactics of this group of suicidal aviators became the United States Navy's greatest fear for the remainder of the war. Censorship prevented any mention in the American press of the kamikazes until the Okinawa campaign.

On 26 October, MacArthur moved ashore to formally open his new headquarters at the Price residence in Tacloban. With the naval battle for Leyte Gulf now history, the campaign for Leyte Island had just begun.

Kamikazes made damaging hits on the carriers *Franklin* and *Belleau Wood*. Between them, 148 men were killed, another 70 injured, and forty-five planes were lost. Both carriers retired to Ulithi under escort.

Kinkaid requested that Halsey provide combat air patrol over Leyte Gulf on 26 October. In reply, Halsey dispatched a message to MacArthur that evening:

After 17 days of battle, my fast carriers are unable to provide extended support for Leyte, but two groups are available on October 27. The pilots are exhausted and the carriers are low in provisions, bombs, and torpedoes. When will land-based air take over at Leyte?[5]

In his autobiography, Halsey made note of the fact that pilot fatigue had tilted upward the normal level of accidents. He said, "For instance, a flight surgeon on the *Wasp* reported that only 30 of his 131 pilots were fit for further fighting." [6] Nevertheless, on the next day, two groups provided fighter cover over the gulf and set sweeps over the central Philippines. On 28 October, two of Halsey's groups gave close support to U.S. ground forces while the remaining two groups journeyed to Ulithi for rest and replenishment.

After the first two squadrons of P-38s landed at Tacloban airfield, MacArthur announced that his air force could assume control of air operations, which allowed Halsey to withdraw his remaining carriers to Ulithi. During the first week ashore, Krueger's Sixth Army advanced quickly inland. By the beginning of the second week, progress on the ground slowed for two reasons: heavy Japanese opposition and heavy rain. On 28 October, a typhoon raged across the island followed by two more in the next ten days. Altogether, thirty-five inches of rain fell during the Americans' first forty days on Leyte. With the airfields waterlogged and matted runway construction moving slowly, only 150 fighters of Kenney's air force had reached Leyte when MacArthur called on Nimitz for a return of carrier aircraft. Halsey's Third Fleet at Ulithi had planned on using Mitscher's carrier groups to strike Japan proper in mid-November. Nimitz agreed to resume carrier operations in support of MacArthur's ground forces until 25 November. "A bitterly disappointed Halsey accepted the decision with good grace." [7]

On 30 October, MacArthur's communiqué gave a grossly exaggerated picture of progress thus far in the Philippines. The synopsis appearing on the front page of the *New York Times* read, "Two-thirds of Leyte Island, an area of 1,800 square miles, was firmly in American hands, and only a few isolated garrisons remained to be cleaned up on Samar. The speedy liberation of the Philippines had already set free 1,500,000 Filipinos." [8]

MacArthur's statement came just eight days before the presidential election. On Tuesday, 7 November, the American public re-elected Roosevelt for a fourth term as president on the theme "You don't trade horses in the middle of a stream." Because Thomas E. Dewey, his opponent, was a relatively short man, many Democrats added, "You don't trade a horse for a Shetland pony." Unlike the political atmosphere in 1942, America and its Allies were winning on all fronts, and in the minds of the public, MacArthur's return to the Philippines and this early success in Leyte was a huge boost for Roosevelt's re-election. Going into the Philippines alone assured the president's victory, as it undercut Dewey's claim that Roosevelt for political reasons failed to support MacArthur. Whatever agreement the president and MacArthur reached at Honolulu in July was now history.

In fact, on 30 October most of the major fighting for Leyte clearly laid ahead, so much so that by mid-November, it became obvious to MacArthur that the 20 December invasion of Luzon would have to be delayed. The Japanese continued to land reinforcements on the west coast of Leyte at the town of Ormoc, while planes from Luzon repeatedly harassed American troops and supplies at night.

Halsey advised MacArthur that he most needed U.S. Marine night fighters that had been trained in the Solomons. Nimitz agreed to their use, and the fighters began arriving at Tacloban on 3 December. For the next five weeks, the eighty-seven U.S. Marine aircraft proved invaluable in defending the Leyte Gulf area against Japanese night raiders. From landing day through Christmas, army-navy-marine planes plus anti-aircraft guns accounted for an estimated 1,480 enemy aircraft destroyed in operations.[9]

The U.S. Army's Maj. Richard I. Bong received the Medal of Honor at the Tacloban airfield on 12 December after downing his thirty-eighth plane. Like many medal winners in the Pacific War, the twenty-four-year-old Bong came from a small midwestern village. He was raised in a farmhouse two miles outside of Poplar, Wisconsin, a town of 461 people according to the 1940 census. Bong was a first-generation American, his father having arrived from Sweden at the age of five. Before going back to the States on leave, Bong scored his fortieth kill, making him the number one American ace for World War II. In explaining his success, he claimed, "I am strictly a one-airplane man and the P-38 is it." On leave in February, the major married twenty-one-year-old Marjorie Vattendahl of Superior, whom he met while on leave in 1943. Bong died in a plane crash in California eight days before the war's end.

In terms of developing potential air bases for the invasion of Luzon, Leyte was a keen disappointment. Monsoon rains and washed-out roads also slowed Krueger's force in its push across the island. The slowness of the Leyte conquest caused MacArthur to postpone the Mindoro invasion, originally scheduled for 5 December, to 15 December. This enabled Krueger to make an amphibious assault against Ormoc, which closed the avenue of enemy reinforcements as well as split Japanese forces.

The U.S. Army's 77th Division captured Ormoc on 10 December. This seizure marked a turning point in the Leyte campaign. MacArthur joyfully announced in a communiqué the next day that the Ormoc operation had "split the enemy's force in two, isolating those in the valley to the north from those along the coast to the south. Both segments are now caught between our columns, which are pressing in from all fronts." [10] In spite of MacArthur's communiqué, the courageous but vastly outnumbered Japanese would take a long time in dying.

Back in Washington, the unity of command issue was again revisited as the Joint Chiefs discussed plans for the invasion of Japan. The March 1942 directive to MacArthur and Nimitz placed MacArthur's area slightly north of the Philippines. Operations against the Japanese home islands were in Nimitz's command area. Recognizing that an invasion of the Japanese home islands would incur a large army force but that the navy would object to him being the unified commander, MacArthur wrote Marshall on 17 December 1944:

I do not recommend a single unified command for the Pacific. I am of the firm opinion that the Naval forces should serve under Naval Command and that the Army should serve under Army Command. Neither service willingly fights on a major scale under the command of the other . . . The Navy, with almost complete naval command in the Pacific, has attained a degree of flexibility in the employment of resources with consequent efficiency that has far surpassed the Army. It is essential that the Navy be given complete command of all its units and that the Army be accorded similar treatment. Only in this way will there be attained that complete flexibility and efficient employment of forces that is essential to victory.[11]

On the day after Christmas, MacArthur's communiqué proclaimed that, "The Leyte-Samar campaign could now be regarded as closed except for minor mopping up . . . General Yamashita has sustained the greatest defeat in the military annals of the Japanese Army." [12] Eichelberger's Eighth Army assumed control of operations by relieving Krueger's Sixth Army. The mopping-up phase delegated to the Eighth Army lasted until May 1945. Upon leaving, Krueger estimated that only about 5,000 Japanese remained on Leyte and Samar. Eichelberger disagreed. He said that between Christmas Day and the end of the campaign, "We killed more than 27,000 Japs." [13]

The unexpected length of the Leyte conquest forced delay in launching the invasion of Luzon but, more importantly, a delay in Central Pacific operations. Because airfield construction proved unsatisfactory, Leyte never became an important base for air operations in the Philippines.

The amphibious landing on Mindoro proceeded as planned near San Jose on 15 December. Without Japanese opposition, the Americans established a beachhead sixteen miles long and seven miles deep by nightfall. The invasion force, consisting of the 19th Regimental Combat Team of the 24th Division and the 503rd Parachute Regimental Combat Team, departed Leyte on 12 December.

On the afternoon of 13 December kamikazes crashed into the *Nashville*, killing 133 persons and injuring 190 more. Two hours later, a kamikaze dove into a destroyer, causing forty more casualties. Both ships had to return to Leyte en route to Ulithi for repairs. On the day of the landing, kamikazes broke through the air cover and crashed into three landing ships, two destroyers, and an escort carrier. For the next three weeks, kamikazes made repeated attacks on supply convoys. Nevertheless, by Christmas Day, Fifth Air Force planes operated from two airfields near San Jose as a third strip neared completion.

This air base construction proved invaluable, as the Third Fleet had to withdraw to Ulithi on 19 December after being struck by a typhoon in the Philippine Sea. Three destroyers capsized and seven other ships were heavily damaged. The typhoon destroyed 186 carrier planes and took the lives of nearly 800 men. Prior to running into heavy weather, Halsey's Third Fleet moved eastward in the Philippine Sea. On the morning of 17 December, Halsey received a weather warning from a seaplane tender at Ulithi that reported a storm center less than 200 miles southeast of his position. Not being fully advised of the severity of the storm, Halsey took a course that placed his ships directly into the path of an oncoming typhoon.[14] In his autobiography, Halsey described the storm's peak:

No one who has not been through a typhoon can conceive its fury. The 70-foot seas smash you from all sides. The rain and the scud are blinding; they drive you flat-out, until you can't tell the ocean from the air. At broad noon I couldn't see the bow of my ship, 350 feet from the bridge . . . [15]

Nimitz appointed a court of inquiry to determine why the carrier force had been caught by the typhoon. The court placed most of the blame on Admiral Halsey. Nimitz's endorsement of the court's record moderated the verdict by saying, "Halsey's mistakes were errors of judgment committed under stress of war operations and stemming from a commendable desire to meet military requirements."[16] After the word "judgment," King added, "resulting from insufficient information" so that he practically nullified the court's verdict. Halsey never made any mention of the court's verdict or endorsements in his autobiography. Having failed to support MacArthur at Mindoro, Halsey made plans for the Luzon landing.

On 1 January 1945, control of operations on Mindoro passed from the Sixth to the Eighth Army. Only sixteen American ground troops had been lost. About 170 Japanese died in action, while the remainder fled into the mountainous interior. By the time of the Luzon invasion, the Fifth Air Force had a powerful support force of three fighter groups, two medium bomber groups, and seven other miscellaneous squadrons on Mindoro. The official army history said:

It seems safe to assume that without the Mindoro airfields, MacArthur would not have been able to move to Luzon when he did. Certainly, without those fields his forces would have found the invasion of Luzon, and post assault operations as well, considerably more hazardous and difficult. [17]

The command structure for the Luzon landing was not unlike that of the Leyte invasion. MacArthur chose Krueger to head the ground forces, with Kinkaid retaining control of the operation until Krueger established his headquarters ashore. The Fifth Air Force, the main air assault force, was supported by the Thirteenth Air Force and carrier planes of Halsey's Third Fleet. B-29s of the Twentieth Air Command conducted strategic bombing attacks against targets in the Ryukyus and Japan.

The best intelligence estimates at GHQ placed Yamashita in control of about 152,000 troops of all types on Luzon. Krueger's command totaled 203,000, including 131,000 combat troops. With the addition of later reinforcements plus organized guerrilla groups, the troops engaged against the Japanese on Luzon exceeded 280,000.[18]

During the first eight days of January, hundreds of carrier- and land-based planes struck at enemy airfields and shipping in the Luzon-Formosa area. Kamikaze planes had wrought serious damage on naval vessels off Leyte and Samar and even more severe against U.S. ships in the Mindoro operation. The U.S. Navy feared that the full fury of the kamikazes would be unleashed against the Luzon attack force. However, the overwhelming air cover from the Third Fleet and ground-based planes of the Fifth Air Force on Mindoro greatly minimized the damaging effect of the kamikazes on troop and supply ships for the Luzon landing.

On 8 January 1945, Halsey's Third Fleet moved into the South China Sea. He attacked shipping and airplane facilities from Formosa to Hong Kong all along the coast as far south as Camranh Bay. He continued south while Kincaid's Seventh Fleet protected the landing in Luzon. On 12 January Halsey claimed forty-one ships sunk, totaling 127,000 tons. After the war, Japanese records showed the number to be forty-four ships, totaling 132,700 tons. Twelve of the sunk marus were oil tankers. Halsey called this "one of the heaviest blows to Japanese shipping of any day of the war," further stating that "Japanese supply routes from Singapore, Malaya, Burma, and the Dutch East Indies were severed, at least temporarily."[19]

Chapter 25
Philippine Liberation

*I*N THE INITIAL INVASION OF LUZON, MacArthur entered the same area as the Japanese 48th Division had utilized in December 1941. At sunrise on 9 January, nearly 1,000 American ships occupied Lingayen Gulf. The dreaded kamikazes arrived but in smaller numbers than in previous days. They crashed into one battleship, two cruisers, and one destroyer escort, all of which were badly damaged but not sunk. At 10:00 A.M., the assault waves went ashore. Lieutenant General Oscar W. Griswold's XIV Corps, with the 37th Division on the left and the 40th on the right, went ashore between the towns of Lingayen and Dagupan. To the north, Maj. Gen. Innis P. Swift's I Corps' 6th and 43rd Divisions landed on each side of San Fabian. Neither ran into any opposition at the beachhead, although the 6th Division encountered Japanese mortar and artillery fire after pushing three miles inland. At nightfall, the Americans occupied the enemy airfield outside Lingayen.

At 2:00 P.M., four hours after the first assault waves went ashore, MacArthur and members of his staff landed south of San Fabian. The Seabees ashore had taken a bulldozer and pushed out sand, forming a little pier where the boat could land. When MacArthur saw the pier, he refused to land there. Instead, he jumped out into the water and waded ashore. While his Leyte wading scene, though unintentional, had brought worldwide attention, MacArthur could not resist another big splash of publicity. *Life* magazine showed him wading through the surf in three separate photos.

The next day, on 10 January, MacArthur again went ashore, making an inspection trip to all four divisional sectors. Unlike the Leyte operation, he routinely visited his division commanders throughout the Luzon campaign. "During his ten weeks at Tacloban, MacArthur ventured outside the city only four times, three times to visit Krueger at his headquarters and once to the nearby Tacloban airfield." [1] On the second day on Luzon, his communiqué announced, "The decisive battle for the liberation of the Philippines and the control of the South West Pacific is at hand. General MacArthur is in personal command at the front and landed with his assault troops." [2] He stayed aboard the *Boise* on

11 and 12 January. On the afternoon of the 13th, he moved his advance GHQ to buildings at Dagupan. The beachhead had been expanded to nearly thirty miles in length and an average of fifteen miles in depth.

Fortunately, the kamikazes had spent themselves. Since the Lingayen invasion force had left Leyte Gulf, Japanese direct assaults, mostly kamikazes, had sunk four ships and damaged forty-three others, causing casualties of more than 2,100 men, including 738 killed. By nightfall of the 13th, the Lingayen airfield, though small, was in the hands of the Fifth Air Force. Best estimates claimed that fewer than a dozen Japanese aircraft were left in service on Luzon. Until the later Iwo Jima and Okinawa campaigns, U.S. ships could feel secure that the terrifying kamikaze threat was over.

With American submarines and Halsey's fleet in complete control of the waters to the north and west, Yamashita knew that reinforcements for his troops were nonexistent. "Although he commanded 275,000 troops instead of 152,000 (as Willoughby estimated), his Japanese Fourteenth Area Army was dangerously short of munitions, supplies, and transportation." [3] With the Americans in control of the sky, Yamashita determined to offer a static defense to delay the Allied advance to the Japanese homeland. He divided his forces into three regional defense zones, each centered in easily defended mountainous areas.

Major General Rikichi Tsukada's Kembu Group, numbering about 30,000 troops, defended the Clark Field area, which also included the Bataan Peninsula. Lieutenant General Shizuo Yokoyama's Shimbu Group, consisting of about 80,000 men, occupied the mountains to the east of Manila. Yamashita ordered him first to complete the evacuation of supplies from the capital city, then to control the dams that supplied its water. Rear Admiral Sanji Iwaburchi's defense force in Manila, numbering approximately 17,000 and included in the Shimbu Group, had orders to withdraw into the mountains and join Yokoyama's group, yet it failed to do so. Yamashita's 152,000-troop Shobu Group guarded the west coast above San Fabian along Lingayen Gulf. Yamashita's Fourteenth Area Army combined headquarters with the Shobu Group at Baguio.

On 22 January, the Third Fleet departed the South China Sea for rest at Ulithi, having destroyed some 300,000 tons of enemy shipping during the month. In his flagship, the *New Jersey*, Halsey arrived in Ulithi atoll on the afternoon of 25 January. He wrote: "The outer defenses of the Japanese empire no longer include Burma and the Netherlands East Indies. Those countries are now isolated outposts, and their products are no longer available to the Japanese war machine except with staggering and prohibitive losses en route." [4]

In response to pressure from MacArthur, Krueger on 18 January ordered Griswold's corps to seize Clark Field without delay. After advancing below Tarlac, Griswold's corps encountered heavy fighting from the Kembu Group. The U.S. Army's 40th Division secured the complex of airfields known as Clark Field on 28 January; yet, it would take three more weeks to dislodge the Kembu Group's forces only two miles in the hills to the west.

In the meantime, the U.S. Army's 6th Infantry Division drove past Guimba to the outskirts of Cabanatuan. A ranger unit with aid from Filipino guerrillas conducted a daring raid on a prison camp beyond Cabanatuan. The rescue of 400 Bataan veterans made front-page news in the States. In its 10 February issue, *Life* magazine ran an in-depth story with pictures of the Cabanatuan rescue together with that of the 3,500 Allies liberated at St. Thomas. In the eyes of the American public, the liberation of these prisoners alone more than justified the U.S. campaign for Luzon.

Throughout the month, American troops continued to pour into Luzon. On 27 January the 32nd and 1st Cavalry Divisions landed at Lingayen Gulf, while on 29 January, Maj. Gen. Charles P. Hall's XI Corps, consisting of the U.S. Army's 38th Infantry Division and the 34th Regimental Combat Team, landed unopposed northwest of Bataan. Again on 31 January the 11th Airborne Division arrived unopposed at Nasugbu, approximately forty-five miles southwest of Manila.

In mid-January, Nimitz and MacArthur disputed over the latter's refusal to release naval units borrowed from the Pacific Fleet. By radiogram, Nimitz reminded MacArthur that according to their agreement at Tacloban the vessels would be returned to Ulithi by 19 January for maintenance and replenishment in preparation for the Iwo Jima assault.[5] MacArthur insisted on retaining six battleships and twenty-six destroyers of the Pacific Fleet. Nimitz came out second best in the argument. Only two battleships in bad shape from kamikaze attacks plus four destroyers left for Ulithi on 22 January. MacArthur insisted he needed a strong surface force in Philippines waters during the crucial period between the loss of the Third Fleet's air cover and the movement of Kenney's aircraft to Clark Field. The remaining ships were not released in time for service in the Iwo Jima assault.

At midnight on 26 January, Adm. Raymond A. Spruance assumed tactical command of the fleet, which under him was numbered the Fifth Fleet. Samuel Eliot Morison noted, "he had a wonderful reputation to live up to, and that he did." [6] Spruance commented that the Philippines operations necessitated last-minute changes, which reduced the total number of ships that had been previously allocated to Iwo Jima. General Howland Smith felt that MacArthur's belated release of the ships significantly weakened the naval gunfire support for the marine landing, causing more American casualties. Although MacArthur's refusal may have necessitated some delay, it is doubtful that it contributed to any significant increase in casualties at Iwo Jima.

On 28 February after a visit with MacArthur at his headquarters, Forrestal wrote in his diary, "The units General MacArthur needs to accomplish his objectives are obviously a thing of vital interest to him, but the determination of when ships need overhaul or may be necessary for other operations is obviously the interest of Admiral Nimitz." [7] MacArthur's biographer, D. Clayton James, wrote, "To the SWPA commander in January 1945, however, the occupation of Manila, whether for strategic, tactical, logistical, or personal reasons, had become an obsession, blocking consideration of the Central Pacific theater's needs." [8]

Major General R. S. Beightle's 37th Infantry Division, Maj. Gen. V. D. Mudge's 1st Cavalry Division, and Maj. Gen. J. M. Swings' 11th Airborne Division began the race to Manila on 1 February. When MacArthur visited the 1st Cavalry's assembly area near Guimba on 30 January, he gave Mudge the order to pass on to his men: "Go to Manila. Go around the Nips, bounce off the Nips, but go to Manila. Free the internees at Santo Tomas. Take Malacanan Palace and the Legislative Building." [9]

Arriving in the Grace Park suburb of north Manila on 3 February, 1st Cavalry vehicles crossed the city limits about 6:00 P.M., becoming the first American troops to re-enter the Philippine capital. The 37th Division entered north Manila on the morning of 4 February and quickly moved to Old Bilibid Prison to free about 500 civilian internees and 800 U.S. Army prisoners of war. The Japanese guards fled as the 37th Division troops arrived.

Far to the south, units of Swings' 11th Airborne Division traveled north on Highway 17 at high speed toward Manila, only to be stopped four miles short by intense artillery, mortar, and machine gun fire. The 11th Airborne had the distinction of becoming the first division to engage a part of the main Japanese defense force of Manila.

Spanish colonists had founded the city of Manila in 1571. By 1945, Manila proper had a population in excess of 800,000. With its surrounding suburbs, greater Manila included more than a million inhabitants. Located south of the Pasig River was Intramuros, a centuries-old Spanish walled city. The twenty-foot-high walls stretched for two and a half miles. In places they reached twenty-five feet in height and had a thickness of up to forty feet at the bottom. Effectively utilizing the Intramuros District together with the city's strongly reinforced concrete buildings of prewar construction, the Japanese brought in heavy-caliber guns from damaged and sunken ships in the harbor. From 1935 to 1941, MacArthur resided in a penthouse atop the Manila Hotel, off the southwest corner of Intramuros.

By 7 February the 37th Division had secured the western half as the 1st Cavalry cleared the eastern half of north Manila by the 10th. MacArthur's 6 February communiqué announced: "Our forces are rapidly clearing the enemy from Manila. Our converging columns . . . entered the city and surrounded the Jap defenders. Their complete destruction is imminent." [10] On 10 February MacArthur sent word to his Sixth and Eighth Army commanders that he planned a grand victory parade of his units through the main streets of Manila although the battle for the city's center had barely begun.

Having refused his commanders the use of air strikes, MacArthur authorized artillery within the city. By 22 February the Japanese had been driven into the northwest corner of south Manila, which included the Intramuros, the south port area, and the commonwealth government buildings. The reduction of the many strongpoints leading to Intramuros produced heavy casualties among the American units and devastation of the city from Pasay to the Pasig River. The helpless Filipinos caught within the defense perimeter suffered greatly from American artillery as well as ill treatment by the doomed Japanese soldiers.

On 16 February, Griswold asked for dive-bombing and napalm strikes against this last Japanese stronghold. The Sixth Army commander approved, pending a reply from the SWPA chief. MacArthur responded immediately:

The use of air (attacks) on a part of a city occupied by a friendly and allied population is unthinkable. The inaccuracy of this type of bombardment would result beyond question in the death of thousands of innocent civilians. It is not believed moreover that this would appreciably lower our own casualty rate although it would unquestionably hasten the conclusion of the operations. For these reasons I do not approve the use of air bombardment on the Intramuros District.[11]

Accordingly, Griswold employed every available artillery piece against the enemy inside the Intramuros walls from 17 to 23 February. The shelling finally breached the thick walls in several places in the northeast corner of the walled city. Although MacArthur's heart was in the right place, in reality the use of artillery within a crowded city will cause as much or more collateral damage, that is, damage to the civilian population, as will pinpointed air strikes.

On 17 February, MacArthur presided over a ceremony held at Malacanan Palace marking the re-establishment of the commonwealth government in Manila. According to witnesses, he spoke slowly, sometimes pausing as if unable to control his emotions. Near the end of MacArthur's prepared speech, he said: "Your capital city, cruelly punished though it be, has regained its rightful place—Citadel of Democracy in the East. Your indomitable . . ." At this point his voice trembled and broke. MacArthur paused for a moment, then concluded, "In humble and devout manifestation of gratitude to Almighty God for bringing this decisive victory to our arms, I ask that all present rise and join me in reciting the Lord's Prayer." [12]

On 23 February the first American assault troops entered Intramuros. Both within and outside the walled city, vicious hand-to-hand combat ensued. On 3 March Griswold reported to Krueger that organized resistance had ceased. Manila, once known as the pearl of the Orient, lay devastated. A victory parade in the streets seemed inappropriate.

Meanwhile, on the continent of Asia, on 25 January 1945, the Allies completed the Ledo Road plus an oil pipeline that tied into the old Burma Road. Twenty-four days after a truck convoy left Assam, it entered Kunming to the cheers of thousands of Chinese who waved banners in Chinese characters, which proclaimed, "Welcome First Convoy Over Stilwell Road." Chiang Kai-shek proclaimed, "We have broken the siege of China. Let me name this road after General Joseph Stilwell in memory of his distinctive contribution and of the signal part which the Allied and Chinese forces under his direction played in the Burma campaign and in the building of the road." [13] United States headquarters for the India-Burma theater confirmed the name in an official order. In a broadcast over an "Army Hour" radio program, Stilwell paid tribute to "all the men—infantry, engineers, medics, air crews, truck crews and laborers—'who fought for it and built it.'" [14]

Operations in Burma during 1945 were largely a British display. The ultimate objective of the British was the recapture of Singapore more than the reconquest of Burma or help for China. The British attacked from India across the Irrawaddy River to Mandalay, which was captured in March after tremendous difficulties because of the terrain, the malaria-carrying mosquito, and crack Japanese troops. The battle that ensued involved some of the heaviest fighting of the war against Japanese ground troops. After the fall of Mandalay, the drive to the south was relatively fast. The capture of Rangoon on 3 May 1945, for practical purposes, completed the reconquest of Burma.

The Allies had no difficulty in moving military supplies over the Stilwell Road into Nationalist China for the remainder the year. Chiang Kai-shek stockpiled these weapons for use against his mortal enemy: Mao ZeDong. During 1945, neither the Chinese Communists nor Nationalists did any significant fighting against the Japanese before the latter's surrender.

By January 1945, it was evident to the Joint Chiefs that Japan would have to surrender within the following year to year and a half. The prewar Plan Orange had always been the dominant strategy for winning the war, although there had been deviations in thinking along the way, namely establishing a base on the China coast and the thrust from Australia through New Guinea to the Philippines. But as 1945 arrived, two more deviations from this prewar strategy appeared, namely an invasion of the Japanese homeland and bringing the Soviets into the war.

During the early months of the year, the Joint Chiefs concerned themselves with Soviet participation against Japan. In anticipation of the Yalta summit in February, Marshall and Stimson sought MacArthur's views on handling the Soviets and assuring their cooperation in Japan's defeat. MacArthur's statements to others are inconsistent with his *Reminiscences*. He wrote:

> Toward the end of 1944 and in early 1945 the question of Russian intervention in the Pacific was seriously considered in such international discussions as Yalta. The political, economic, and military effect of such intervention seemed to have become a vital factor in those secret understandings. I was never invited to any of these meetings, and my views and comments were never solicited. From my viewpoint, any intervention by Russia during 1945 was not required. The substance of Japan had already been gutted, the best of its army and navy had been defeated, and the Japanese homeland was now at the mercy of air raids and invasion.[15]

To correct this last sentence, the best of the Japanese army had not been defeated; the great majority of the Japanese soldiers were deployed in China, East Asia, Netherlands East Indies, and bypassed islands in the Pacific. In contrast to his statements in *Reminiscences*, MacArthur told a visiting member of the general staff that he considered it inevitable that the Soviets would take all of Manchuria, Korea, and possibly parts of north China. "The United States should press Russia to pay her way by invading Manchuria at the earliest moment." [16] After the Yalta Conference, MacArthur told Marshall's deputy, Maj. Gen. George A. Lincoln, that the War Department must make "every effort to get Russia into the Japanese war before we go into Japan." [17]

In expressing MacArthur's view, biographer Michael Schaller wrote, "Although Stalin would demand compensation in the form of Manchurian rail and port privileges, MacArthur felt it would be impractical to refuse, given the Soviet strength and America's desire that they should share the cost in blood in defeating Japan." [18] After a talk with MacArthur on 28 February, Secretary of the Navy Forrestal wrote in his diary:

> He said he felt that our strength should be reserved for use in the Japanese mainland, on the plain of Tokyo, and that this could not be done without the assurance that the Japanese would be heavily engaged by the Russians in Manchuria. He expressed doubt that the use of anything less than sixty divisions by the Russians would be sufficient.[19]

Later, in March, MacArthur told Robert Sherwood of the Office of War Information that the administration should condemn Soviet actions in Europe and make no deal to assure Russia's assistance in the Pacific War. MacArthur predicted the Japanese would surrender when he subdued Luzon but, if not, American forces would need Soviet help.[20] MacArthur's many conflicting statements concerning the Soviets' entry into the war against Japan give some credence to historian Stephen Ambrose's observations. He said, "MacArthur— this sounds terrible, but it's true—MacArthur lied his way out of every difficulty he ever got into." [21]

At a meeting of the Combined Chiefs of Staff at Yalta, it was apparent to all that the defeat of Germany and Japan was assured. With victory in sight, the British, the Dutch, and the Joint Chiefs of Staff each had a different goal in mind: The British, to regain its lost colonies, especially Burma and Singapore; the Dutch, to regain control of the Netherlands East Indies; and the Joint Chiefs, to bring on Japan's defeat as soon and with as little cost as possible.

The U.S. Navy had achieved a significant victory in the Battle of Leyte Gulf. The Joint Chiefs no longer envisioned the seizure of Formosa or an enclave on the China coast, although some Washington planners, including Admiral King, still toyed with this idea. In Ulithi, the Pacific Fleet had the best staging base for the jump to Iwo Jima, Okinawa, and the Japanese home islands. The completion of huge airdromes at Saipan, Tinian, and Guam enabled the U.S. Twentieth Air Force to strike at the heart of Japan. American submarines had swept the South China Sea almost clean of enemy targets. Admiral Lockwood wrote in a top-secret report after the war that

> in early 1945 it was learned from a Japanese prisoner of war that it was a common saying in Singapore that you could walk from that port

to Japan on American periscopes. This feeling among the Japanese was undoubtedly created, not by the great number of submarines on patrol, but rather by the fact, thanks to Communication Intelligence, the submarines were always at the same place as Japanese ships.[22]

Prior to moving his headquarters to Manila on 5 March, MacArthur transferred the equivalent of three of Krueger's divisions to Eichelberger's Eighth Army. Eichelberger was charged with retaking the rest of the central and southern Philippines beginning with an assault on 28 February on Palawan, the westernmost large island of the Philippine archipelago. This was the beginning of MacArthur's Victor Series, which included Palawan, Zamboangaon, Mindanao, Panay-Northern Negros, Cebu-Southern Negros-Bohol, and Central Mindanao—in that order. Airfield sites on Palawan were 250 miles southwest of Mindoro airfields and 400 miles south-southwest of Clark Field. The intended airfield for Palawan would be 150 miles farther west than either.

MacArthur reasoned that Palawan's seizure would assure a more effective blockade of the South China Sea as well as provide adequate air support for the invasion of Borneo. To use an old cliché, this strategy was a classic case of "locking the barn door after the horse has departed." Halsey's Third Fleet and U.S. submarines had already effectively cut off shipping from the Netherlands East Indies to Japan, and the invasion of Okinawa on 1 April would bypass any tactical value Palawan Island could provide even if an adequate airstrip could be developed there.

Kinkaid's Seventh Fleet, supported by Kenney's Fifth Air Force, carried out more than twenty major and minor amphibious operations, starting with Corregidor and Mariveles Point landing on 15 February, ending with the capture of Balut Island off the southernmost tip of Mindanao on 20 July 1945.[23] Obviously, they had no time to interdict Japanese shipping in the South China Sea. Kenney would claim his Fifth Air Force had been instrumental in stopping the flow of Japanese sea traffic without identifying the sinking of a single enemy ship.[24] The official Army Air Force's history of World War II agrees that the contribution of the Fifth Air Force did not "loom so large as it did in the eyes of its commanders at the time. It is now clear that submarines of the U.S. Navy already had gone far toward choking off the sustenance received by Japan from her southern conquests by the time the Fifth Air Force was in position to render major assistance, and the underwater blockade of Japan was to continue with increasing effectiveness." [25]

Arrangements were made in the early part of 1945 to move the submarines headquartered at Brisbane and Fremantle to Subic Bay. Seabees were ordered to finish the base before the heavy rains came in mid-May. Due to the dearth of Japanese targets, submariners were not happy upon returning from patrols, where they experienced many happy hours on liberty in Brisbane and Perth.

On 6 March MacArthur's wife, Jean, and son arrived from Brisbane. He had made previous arrangements for the use of the fine Bachrach House in north Manila, which he continued to occupy until his arrival in Japan.

On 18 March, MacArthur approved the first of six phases of his Oboe (East Indies) Plan, which called for the invasion of Tarakan Island off the east coast of Dutch Borneo. Afterward, the Oboe operations called for landings at Balikpapan, Bandjermasin, Surabaya, or Batavia, followed by the seizure of the rest of the Netherlands East Indies and British Borneo. Although unenthusiastic, the Joint Chiefs approved the invasion of Tarakan on 29 April, Brunei Bay on 23 May, and Balikpapan on 15 June. Because of shipping difficulties, the target dates were delayed to 1 May, 10 June, and 1 July, respectively.

The British considered the Brunei Bay operation to be useless. General Blamey also had misgivings; however, Curtin favored the use of Australian forces in seizing Borneo. The Joint Chiefs approved MacArthur's plan to go into Borneo knowing full well that the island's petroleum resources were not needed for the invasion of Japan. In fact, the oil fields and refineries could not be rehabilitated for many months after the Pacific War ended.

In April, the Joint Chiefs reluctantly approved three of MacArthur's six proposed assaults on Borneo in addition to the seizure of the central and southern Philippines. By the time MacArthur received the Joint Chiefs' directive, his Eighth Army had already invaded Palawan, Zamboanga, Tawi Tawi, Basilan, Panay, Guimaras, Negros, and Cebu. Only the Jolo, Bohol, and eastern Mindanao invasions remained. Morison's history of U.S. naval operations in the war states:

> It is still somewhat of a mystery how and whence . . . MacArthur derived his authority to use United States Forces to liberate one Philippine island after another. He had no specific directive for anything subsequent to Luzon. He seems to have felt that, as Allied theater commander in the southwest Pacific, he had a right to employ the forces at his command as he thought best for the common cause; certainly he went ahead with his plans. And as Seventh Fleet and Eighth Army were not urgently required at Iwo Jima . . . or Okinawa . . . the J.C.S simply permitted MacArthur to do as he pleased, up to a point.[26]

MacArthur's actions in liberating all Philippine islands south of Luzon clearly challenged the authority of the Joint Chiefs, yet they took no action against him. His biographer, D. Clayton James, said:

> The unauthorized initiation of his Victor Plan was surely MacArthur's most audacious challenge to the Joint Chiefs during the war, but neither he nor they seem to have regarded his action as an affront to them. It is little wonder that the same commander less than six years later would act with insolence toward his superiors in Washington.[27]

During the months of March, April, and May, soldiers of Krueger's Sixth Army helped rehabilitate life in devastated Manila as well as maintain pressure on Yamashita's Fourteenth Area Army, located in the mountains of north Luzon. In April, Krueger's troops captured Ipo Dam, which provided one-third of Manila's water supply. Eichelberger's Eighth Army continued to eliminate organized Japanese resistance south of Luzon with the exception of Mindanao.

On 5 July MacArthur's communiqué proclaimed the termination of operations in the Philippines. In part, he said:

The entire Philippine islands are now liberated and the Philippines Campaign can be regarded as virtually closed. Some minor isolated action of a guerrilla nature in the practically uninhabited mountain ranges may occasionally persist, but this great landmass of 115,600 square miles with a population of 17,000,000 is now freed of the invader. . . .

Naval and air forces shared equally with the ground troops in accomplishing the success of the campaign. Naval battles reduced the Japanese Navy to practical impotence and the air losses, running into many thousands, have seriously crippled his air potential. Working in complete unison the three services inflicted the greatest disaster ever sustained by Japanese arms. . . .[28]

In sharp contract to General MacArthur's view, a historian for the Twentieth Air Force wrote:

In MacArthur's case, he may have considered his return to the Philippines a "sacred duty" but this unnecessary operation caused the deaths and injuries of thousands of Americans and Filipinos. With the U.S. Navy in command of the seas, the Philippines should have been bypassed. The Philippine islands weren't needed even if an invasion had been necessary.[29]

In reality, organized resistance had not collapsed on Luzon and Mindanao. Fighting continued until Japan surrendered 15 August. On this date almost 115,000 Japanese, including some non-combatant civilians, were still at large. On the surrender date, the equivalent of three and two-thirds U.S. Army divisions were engaged in combat against Yamashita's units in the mountains of north Luzon. Some 21,000 Filipino guerrillas were also engaged, while another 22,000 were being used in patrolling and mopping-up activities. To the south, another 75,000 Filipino guerrillas were occupied in engagements against the Japanese.

Although Marshall and King had reported to the Combined Chiefs that U.S. troops would be used only to hold key positions in the Philippines—namely Luzon—9,060 American casualties were sustained in operations to recapture the central and southern islands. Excluding the campaign for the seizure of Leyte and Samar, the Sixth and Eighth Armies suffered almost 47,000 battle casualties, with 10,380 killed and 36,550 wounded. The U.S. Army casualty figure for the liberation of the Philippines totaled 60,628 killed, wounded, and missing.[30]

The Sixth Army alone sustained more than 93,400 non-battle casualties, which included 86,950 men hospitalized, 6,200 injured by accidents, and 260 troops dead from sickness or injury. The official U.S. Army history stated, "It is doubtful that any other campaign of the war had a higher non-battle casualty rate among American forces." [31] In addition, approximately 100,000 Filipino civilians were killed in the capture of Manila.

Despite the cost, Admiral Halsey would declare the Philippines campaign as "a model of generalship throughout" [32] and it kept MacArthur on the front pages of United States newspapers for the better part of ten months. Except for the naval battle at Leyte Gulf, the Philippines campaign was not a definitive factor in achieving victory in the Pacific. For as the official Australian history correctly observed:

Indeed, as soon as the Japanese ceased to dominate the sea and the sky above it, the loss of their new island empire was just as inevitable as the loss of the British, American and Dutch island empires off southeast Asia had been in the opening months of the war. And thenceforward the decisive struggle was the one between Nimitz's naval forces with their attendant infantry and the Japanese opposing them; the operations in the South-West Pacific and Burma became subordinate ones.[33]

Chapter 26
Iwo Jima

*T*HE MOST DEPRESSING MILITARY DECISION a commander must make is to knowingly spend numerous young lives for a vital strategic objective. So it was at Iwo Jima. On 19 February 1945, the largest number of U.S. Marines ever assembled for combat—three full divisions, the 4th and the 5th with the 3rd in reserve—began landing on a tiny island of only eight square miles.

Why this force for such a small island? Iwo Jima provided an essential element for control of airspace over Japan by the U.S. Twentieth Air Force. However, the island was strategically important to the Japanese as well. They effectively used it for early warnings to advise Tokyo of impending B-29 raids and as a base for fighter interceptors and bombers to attack American planes at Saipan, Tinian, and Guam.

General H. H. "Hap" Arnold readily saw Iwo Jima's military value as early as 14 July 1944. He recommended its taking to the Joint Chiefs. At that time, the U.S. Marines had not yet finished with Saipan and still had Guam and Tinian ahead. Arnold drew a line from the Marianas to Japan that ran straight through Iwo Jima. The B-29s badly needed it for fighter escort and emergency landings. In a visit by Maj. Gen. Curtis E. LeMay to the *Indianapolis*, Admiral Spruance's flagship, LeMay said Iwo Jima "would be of tremendous value—as a staging field, as an emergency landing field for B-29s in distress, as a base for air-sea rescue, and as a base for fighter escorts. Without Iwo Jima," he said, "I couldn't bomb Japan effectively." [1]

In 1941, Boeing Aircraft Company began work on the design and production of the B-29 Superfort. When finished, this plane was twice the size of any other; weighing sixty-nine tons, it had a range of 3,500 miles with a four-ton bomb load compared to the B-17's 2,400 miles and two-ton bomb load. Its four special Wright engines gave it a speed of 350 miles per hour, 50 miles per hour more than the latest B-17. Upon completion of the Marianas campaign, the U.S. Army Air Force had 500 such planes with crews ready to go.

Iwo Jima was the only island between the Marianas and Japan where an airfield could be built to handle the B-29s. While the fighting was still going on in the Marianas, Seabees began leveling space to build the largest airdromes in the Pacific.

Unfortunately for the U.S. Marines, Japanese Imperial Headquarters recognized the strategic importance of Iwo Jima as well. In late May 1944, Premier Gen. Hideki Tojo called Lt. Gen. Tadamichi Kuribayashi to his office. After telling him that he would be in charge of the defense of Iwo Jima, Tojo said, "Only you among all the generals are qualified and capable of holding this post. The entire Army and the nation will depend upon you for the defense of that key island." [2] Kuribayashi replied that he was honored to be chosen; however, when he left home on 10 June he did not take his sword, said nothing to his wife and children, but wrote to his brother, "I may not return alive from this assignment, but let me assure you that I shall fight to the best of my ability so that no disgrace will be brought upon our family. I will fight as a son of Kuribayashi, the Samurai, and will behave in such a manner as to deserve the name of Kuribayashi. May ancestors guide me." [3]

The general was fifty-three years old and tall for a Japanese, nearly 5 feet 9 inches. In the service for thirty years, Kuribayashi had served all over the world. In 1928 he went to Washington as deputy military attaché. In 1931 he was sent to Ottawa as military attaché. Again he had the opportunity to see America and there acquired the same impression as Yamamoto. To his wife, Yoshii, he wrote, "The United States is the last country in the world that Japan should fight. Its industrial potentiality is huge and fabulous and the people are energetic and versatile. One must never underestimate the American's fighting ability." [4]

Early on, Kuribayashi ordered all civilians sent back to Japan. By the end of July, only servicemen and Korean laborers remained. He then embarked on a program of tunnel and cave development. Many natural caves already existed on the island, as the soft volcanic stone made it easy for tunneling. Cave specialists came from Japan knowledgeable in ventilation and how to neutralize blast shocks near the openings. Digging wells and erecting storage tanks solved the island's serious water problem. Kuribayashi determined not to resist the landing but to wage war from his powerfully equipped underground fortifications.

American B-24s began hitting Iwo Jima in August 1944. By September, the United States conducted twenty or more raids each month. The Japanese first retaliated with nine twin-engine bombers against Saipan. They lost three without any favorable results. Five days later, ten more enemy bombers attacked Saipan without scoring any significant damage.

In late September 1944, Adm. Chester W. Nimitz flew to San Francisco to meet with Fleet Adm. Ernest J. King. He, King, and Spruance gathered around a table with Forrest Sherman. Captain Sherman read from a paper that recommended instead of the Formosa-China axis, the next targets for the Pacific Fleet would be the Iwo Jima-Okinawa axis. King listened in silence, studied for a while, and then rejected the suggestion. The Joint Chiefs of Staff had already decided on Formosa-China. Formosa was still considered the next step after Luzon. Nimitz and Sherman set out to change King's mind. Eventually, King turned to Spruance. "Haven't you anything to say?" he asked. "I understand Okinawa's your baby."

"I have nothing to add to Chester," Spruance replied. After further thought, King capitulated. The admirals had their answer by the next night.[5] On 3 October 1944 the Joint Chiefs directed Nimitz to proceed with planning for the capture of Iwo Jima and Okinawa. Yet, having made this decision, was there any military reason to invade Luzon? Some believed that a direct jump to Okinawa was a bit too long before eliminating most of the air power located in Formosa and the Philippines. However, by the time MacArthur's troops landed at Lingayen Gulf, Japan had only a few planes left in the Philippines.

On 24 November, 111 Superfortresses made the first strike on Tokyo. They were met by about 125 Japanese fighters. Flying at an altitude of 30,000 feet in bad weather, the results were less than spectacular. One B-29 fell, the first lost in combat. Another ditched on the way back to the Marianas.

Now it became the Japanese's turn. On 27 November, two twin-engine bombers attacked early in the morning as the B-29s were being loaded for a Tokyo strike. One B-29 was smashed and eleven others were damaged. A second raid later in the day knocked out three more B-29s. The worst was still to come. In a high- and low-level attack on 7 December, the Japanese smashed three B-29s and damaged twenty-three more.

The United States struck back. A combination of 28 P-38 fighters, 62 B-29s, 102 B-24s, plus 6 destroyers and the heavy cruisers *Chester*, *Pensacola*, and *Salt Lake City* knocked out the airstrips on Iwo Jima, only to have them back in business the next day. In spite of the heavy bombardment, the enemy's position improved daily. Reconnaissance photos showed the island's defenses steadily going underground.

In planning the Iwo Jima landing, a serious difference arose between the U.S. Navy and the Marine Corps. As early as 24 October, the marines requested ten days of bombardment by a cruiser division and three battleships directly before going ashore. Vice Admiral Richmond Kelly Turner refused the request. On 8 November the U.S. Navy rejected the plea of Maj. Gen. Harry Schmidt, USMC, for nine days' bombardment. Turner insisted that the U.S. Navy's original plan of three days' bombardment would stand. Holland Smith then got into the argument, to no avail. The U.S. Navy had planned an air carrier attack on the Japanese homeland by Task Force 58, its first big offensive showpiece. This would be carried out simultaneously with the Iwo Jima invasion.

Spruance later rejected a fourth day, to which Holland Smith said in his memoirs: "To my way of thinking—and I am sure I was right—the operation was planned for the capture of Iwo Jima, but Spruance permitted the attack on Japan to overshadow the real objective."[6] Opinions of Iwo Jima survivors divide as to the effect of a longer prelanding bombardment. Some say it would have helped, others claimed not, as the already heavy bombardment only rearranged the sand. The reporter, Robert Sherrod, who was there, said, "On Iwo the Japs dug themselves in so deeply that all the explosives in the world could hardly have reached them."[7]

The U.S. armada assembled at Ulithi consisted of 116 warships including 16 aircraft carriers mounting 1,200 planes. Around them were 8 new battleships, 15 cruisers, and 77 destroyers. These ships carried a total of 100,000 sailors, marines, and airmen under the command of Vice Adm. Marc A. Mitscher.

Smith became bitter when he learned that Spruance had withdrawn the two new battleships *Washington* and *North Carolina* from the bombardment force. These had the 16-inch cannon, which could do the most damage to underground emplacements.

During the first day's bombardment, Turner held a press conference in the wardroom of the *Eldorado*. Secretary Forrestal had initiated a policy of good relations with the press and was present for the occasion. More than seventy correspondents representing news media from all over the world crowded into the room. Turner, Holland Smith, and Forrestal all spoke. Prior to this meeting, Smith, after studying the aerial photographs, pronounced Iwo Jima as "the toughest place we have had to take" and somberly predicted 20,000 American casualties.[8] It is said that Smith could barely control his emotions at the thought of sending so many young marines to face death, knowing that such a large percentage would not return.

After three days of intense bombing, on 19 February at 6:40 A.M. the U.S. Navy began its heaviest prelanding barrage in the Pacific War. There were seven battleships, four heavy cruisers, three light cruisers, and numerous destroyers and smaller vessels. When navy gunfire stopped at 8 A.M., 120 carrier planes began working up the landing beaches, dropping napalm on the first run. Iwo Jima was part of the Japanese homeland, and no foreigner had ever set foot on the island. Shortly there would be a change.

Marines in the assault waves left the line of departure at 8:30 A.M. Soon they would hit the beaches. The Japanese had installed 750 blockhouses and pillboxes around the island virtually impervious to artillery rounds. They had positioned their gun sights from holes in the ground, which could not be seen by approaching marines. A sophisticated tunnel system crisscrossed the island. Sixteen miles of tunnels connected 1,500 manmade caverns. From the very start, the marines fought an unseen enemy. Kuribayashi had positioned his invisible gun sights to achieve maximum slaughter after the marines' arrival on the beaches.

Kuribayashi watched from his underground defense until the first few waves had come ashore. He then ordered his artillery, mortars, and machine guns to fire. Wounded marines began returning to the ships. By noon, the dead and dying sprawled everywhere about the ship decks.

During the first few hours, advancing marines threw grenades into Japanese pillboxes, blowing up some along the way and bypassing others. By 10:30 A.M. they had reached the western shore of the island. Among those pushing west was Gunnery Sgt. John Basilone, the first enlisted U.S. Marine in World War II to receive the Medal of Honor for his daring exploits at Guadalcanal. Having been honored in his hometown of Raritan, New Jersey, he chose to return to the fighting front. Leading his machine gun platoon past the southern end of the airfield, he became the victim of a mortar shell that killed him and four others. On his left arm was a favorite tattoo of many marines previously stationed at Quantico, Virginia: a dagger through a heart with the inscription underneath, "Death Before Dishonor."

As the day progressed, it became apparent that this battle was not like any other thus far in the Pacific, or in World War II for that matter. Japanese defenses were almost impervious to the U.S. Navy's powerful guns, marine artillery, mortar fire, or even close air support. Individual marines had to dig out, burn out, blow up, or cover up the Japanese defenders position by position. At the end of the day nearly 600 men ashore and afloat were dead and 2,000 more maimed, some only barely alive. The 133rd Seabees Battalion came ashore with the 4th Division this first day, when little construction work could begin. It suffered the heaviest casualties of any Seabees battalion in the war.

Around 5:00 P.M. Robert Sherrod boarded a landing craft to go ashore. He met Keith Wheeler of the *Chicago Times* returning from the beach. "I wouldn't go in there if I were you," Wheeler advised. "There's more hell in there than I've seen in the rest of the war put together." [9]

The next morning, Sherrod, who thought he'd seen the worst of the Pacific War, wrote that Iwo revealed nothing less than "a nightmare in hell. About the beach in the morning lay the dead . . . They died with the greatest possible violence. Nowhere in the Pacific have I seen such badly mangled bodies. Many were cut squarely in half. Legs and arms lay fifty feet away from any body." [10]

In spite of the heavy casualties, the U.S. Marines captured more ground this first day ashore than on any day of the battle. Troops stood on both beaches around Mount Suribachi. They had reached Air Field No. 1 and were stretched halfway up the island along the eastern beach, where in most places they had penetrated a half mile inland. The 28th Regiment, Col. Harry "the Horse" Liversedge's outfit, occupied the narrow neck of the island isolating Suribachi just a few hundred yards to the south. His marines began their advance south while others pushed north toward the airfields.

On the second day, soon after daybreak, Liversedge's 2nd and 3rd Battalions began assaulting the invisible enemy on Suribachi. Bombardments had little effect on the underground enemy. The ground assault—made up of flame-throwers, grenades, hand-held guns, and demolitions—advanced less than seventy-five yards through the morning. From a hole on the side of Suribachi an enemy gun would appear, discharge a round, then close again before a marine could fix on the hole. All through the day, Kuribayashi's guns refused to let up. By nightfall, the 5th Division had lost 1,500 men killed or wounded, and the 4th Division about 2,000.

During these two days of unbroken turmoil, Navajo code talkers played an important role in bringing some order out of chaos. Working around the clock, they sent and received more than 800 messages, all without error. Regimental and battalion commanders gave orders by walkie-talkie and telephone without being translated by the enemy. [11] Although skilled code breakers, the Japanese were never able to decrypt the Navajo language. Lieutenant General Seizo

Arisue, chief of intelligence, said that while the Japanese were able to decipher the codes of the U.S. Army and U.S. Air Corps, they never cracked the code used by the U.S. Marines.[12]

The 21st Regiment of the 3rd Marine Division, which had been held in reserve, was called into action. Its boats circled for six hours before they were ordered back to their transports. During the third day, the marines made solid progress, though not spectacular. The 21st Regiment, 3,000 fresh men, began landing in the morning and by nightfall had assembled near Air Field No. 1. This day, the U.S. Navy also experienced heavy casualties.

Near dusk, about fifty kamikazes from Hatori, outside of Tokyo, began attacking the assembled fleet. The *Saratoga* was badly damaged; 123 men of her crew were killed and 192 wounded, and she was knocked out of service for four months. The *Bismarck Sea* had worse luck; 218 men of her crew were lost in the cold dark waters as she rolled over and sank. Ashore, marine casualties at the end of the third day stood at 2,517 men of the 4th Division and 2,057 men of the 5th Division.

The fourth day dawned with a cold hard rain. Liversedge's 28th Regiment again moved against Suribachi. Too close now for artillery or air support, the men picked their way through the rubble by blasting and burning as they went. One company alone smashed twenty-five pillboxes. By Friday, 23 February, Suribachi's caves were almost reduced of enemy. Marines had blasted the pillboxes by closing the tunnels or leaving them smoking. Some men of the 28th Regiment managed to reach the top, where they found a piece of pipe. By lashing the American flag to it, the Stars and Stripes rose above the mountain. On the beach below, tired, unshaven men celebrated. Nearby, ship whistles, horns, and bells rang out. Secretary Forrestal told Holland Smith, ". . . the raising of that flag on Suribachi means a Marine Corps for the next 500 years." [13] Events during the next hour would thrill the nation even more.

Because Joe Rosenthal had poor eyesight, no branch of the service would take him. Thus he became a combat photographer for the Associated Press and had made war photographs in the Pacific since March 1944. He landed with the U.S. Marines on D-day and daily made trips back and forth to his ship to transmit his pictures. He was present shortly after a patrol of the 28th Regiment raised the American flag on Mount Suribachi. As he arrived at the top of the mountain, a marine told him that the first flag was being replaced with a larger one. From about twenty-five feet away, Rosenthal clicked his camera at the raising of the second flag. He didn't know it at the time, but he had just taken the most famous photograph of World War II.

It was one of seventeen photographs sent off to Guam by plane. He captioned the negative, "Atop 550-foot Suribachi Yama, the volcano at the southwest tip of Iwo Jima, Marines of the 2nd Battalion, 28th Regiment, 5th Division hoist the Stars and Stripes, signaling the capture of this key position." [14] As author-historian Richard F. Newcomb describes it, "Only one face could be seen and that could not be identified. It was a bad news photograph but a masterpiece of composition. It had movement and drama, and it told a story that needed no caption. The moment it began to come up in the developing tank at Guam it was recognized for what it is, a military work of art." [15]

The *New York Times* showed the flag raising on the front page of its Sunday, 25 February, paper under the caption "OLD GLORY GOES UP OVER IWO." The accompanying news article stated the marines were benefiting from the capture of Mount Suribachi but also pinpointed the problem that would be faced hundreds of times before the island could be secured. It said:

> In a single area of 400 by 600 yards on the east coast, the marines had to neutralize about 100 caves, thirty to forty feet deep, indicating clearly why the seventy-four-day aerial bombardment of the island and the three-day ship shelling prior to our landing failed to decimate the garrison or its supplies.

The number of casualties was not given, although the headlines stated that "Marines Smash Through Maze of Defenses in Bloody Iwo Battle." The news article also noted that Tokyo radio claimed a total of 17,000 American casualties up to Friday night. The Japanese radio claimed continued fighting on Mount Suribachi "without distinction to day or night, as our matchless drawn swords continue to penetrate into the enemy midst."

John Bradley, one of the six men shown in the photo, wrote his parents at the time: "You know all about our battle out here. I was with the victorious (Easy Company) who reached the top of Mt. Suribachi first. I had a little to do with raising the American flag and it was the happiest moment of my life." [16] When President Roosevelt first saw the photograph, he was so moved that he ordered the six men be brought back to the States. By the time they could be identified, three had already been killed and another badly wounded.

As a force in readiness, the Marine Corps prides itself on the training of its enlisted men and junior officers. In the summer, fall, and winter of 1944, numerous officers who had fought in the battles of Guadalcanal, Bougainville, Tarawa, New Britain, the Marshalls, and the Marianas were rotated back to the United States and placed in charge of training at Camp Lejeune in North Carolina and at Camp Pendleton, California. After graduation from Parris Island boot camp or officers' school, young marines and second lieutenants on the East Coast received six weeks to three months of training at Tent Camp, Camp Lejeune. They were then sent overseas as a replacement in one of the six marine divisions. Similar training was given on the West Coast. The Marine Corps was still segregated so that blacks in the eastern part of the country were trained at Montford Point.

Officer instructors who were engaged in the Tarawa campaign told of the importance of flamethrowers and hand grenades in eliminating the dug-in Japanese. Accordingly, at Camp Lejeune, Col. William N. McKelvy, Jr., a Guadalcanal veteran who was in charge of all training at tent camp, insisted that no marine should leave without first having used a flamethrower and thrown a live hand grenade. Instructors who taught a large number of troops that made up the 4th and 5th Divisions had never experienced a defense with interlocking caves and pillboxes as seen on Iwo. Yet, from the very first day of fighting there, hand grenades and flamethrowers became the main weapons of choice for the individual marine to annihilate the enemy.

The recruits trained at Camp Lejeune were mainly eighteen- and nineteen-year-olds, a significant number coming from white middle-class and upper-middle-class families. Harry Hopkins, Roosevelt's chief advisor, and Senator Leverett Saltonstall of Massachusetts had sons who, after having enlisted in the Marine Corps, were killed in action in the Pacific. The second lieutenants were mostly twenty-one- and twenty-two-year-olds. General George Marshall observed that:

> Men of 18, 19, and 20 make our finest soldiers. The excellent Marine divisions are made up largely of men of these age groups. They have stamina and recuperative power far beyond that of older men and this physical superiority often determines the issue in heavy and prolonged fighting.[17]

About five hundred Montford Point trainees courageously served as ammunition carriers on Iwo Jimo.[18] Later, Lt. Gen. Alexander Vandergrift, commandant, U.S. Marine Corps, said, "Negro Marines are no longer on trial. They are Marines, period." [19]

At the end of five days of fighting, marines had captured all of Air Field No. 1 and were positioned to move on Air Field No. 2. The task ahead was assigned to the 2nd and 3rd Battalions of the 21st Marines. Lieutenant Colonel Wendell H. Duplantis, commanding the 3rd Battalion, determined to capture the No. 2 airfield by the end of the sixth day. Captain Rodney L. Heinze was badly wounded when he reached the runway. Two grenades ripped open the inside of his thighs as he dived for cover. They were thrown from a hole with a metal cover. When the lid opened again, the Japanese soldier was killed by a Browning automatic rifle (BAR) man. Captain Clayton Rockmore, who commanded L Company, was killed shortly thereafter by a bullet to his throat. Within minutes, three lieutenants were badly wounded. Of the company commanders of the 3rd Battalion, 21st Marines, who came ashore at Iwo Jima, Heinze was the only one to survive. First Lieutenant Raoul Archambault took charge of both companies. He had won a Silver Star at Bougainville and a Bronze Star at Guam. By nightfall, his men had advanced 800 yards to secure most of the second airfield.

By the end of the first week, all of Air Field No. 1 and most of Air Field No. 2 were in friendly hands. Nevertheless, the bitterest and bloodiest part of the campaign lay ahead. The cost to the U.S. Marines was 1,605 men killed, 5,496 wounded, and 657 cases of combat fatigue for a total of 7,758 casualties.

Forrestal was correct in his view that the U.S. Navy needed good public relations, but Iwo Jima did not paint the picture to the American public that he would have liked. Too many American boys were being slaughtered on a small island whose tremendous strategic value was unknown to the average citizen. One mother wrote Forrestal, "Please, for God's sake, stop sending our finest youth to be murdered on places like Iwo Jima. Why can't objectives be accomplished some other way?" Forrestal replied, "There is no short or easy way." [20]

After the first week of fighting, the marines had captured only two-fifths of the island for which they had paid a heavy price. On the plus side was the completion of a strip 1,500 feet long and 150 feet wide, which had been made ready by the Seabees for light planes. Each day this airfield would be improved.

During the next week the 9th Regiment, 3rd Marine Division, succeeded in getting a flamethrowing tank in position to incinerate many enemy in tunnels and those running from them. On Wednesday, the tenth day ashore, elements of the 3rd Division made good gains in the center of the island, although slightly less than half the island lay in marine hands. In the push north the bulldozer became an important weapon. Numerous Japanese were entombed forever in their caves and tunnels.

Shortly after dawn on Saturday, 3 March, the first plane arrived from the Marianas, a navy C-47 hospital plane. Planes brought in mortar ammunition the rest of the day. Then, on Sunday afternoon, the first crippled B-29, the *Nine Bakecable*, attempted an emergency landing.

Transport planes coming in from the Marianas were warned off as the field was cleared. After three tries, the *Nine Bakecable* plane skidded down the runway with the engine sending up a giant dust cloud. Hundreds cheered as the plane came to a halt at the end of the runway. In thirty minutes on the ground, the plane's problem was fixed. She again became airborne fifty feet from the end of the runway.

The advance by the marines continued to be a "kill and be killed" battle. Taking prisoners was out of the question. The heavy casualties being sustained caused some newspapers to advocate the use of gas; in fact, in early 1944 the Joint Chiefs began investigating such use. The subject was discussed between Stanley P. Lovell of the Office of Strategic Services and Admiral Nimitz in June 1944. The plan was apparently approved at all levels except that of Franklin D. Roosevelt, commander in chief, who rejected it.[21]

In spite of the daily heavy casualties, on 10 March, D-day plus 20, some units of the 3rd Marine Division reached the sea at the top of the island, leaving two large pockets still in the hands of the enemy. During the next six days these pockets were reduced so that Admiral Nimitz declared the battle officially over. He gave the official casualties sustained through 16 March as 4,189 killed, 441 missing, 15,305 wounded. But there was still mopping up to do.

Secretary of War Henry L. Stimson wrote to Secretary Forrestal, "My personal congratulations and the congratulations of the entire army. The price has been heavy but the military value of Iwo Jima is inestimable. Its conquest has brought closer the day of our final victory in the Pacific." [22]

Yet, Stimson's opinion was not shared by some of the pro-MacArthur American press. On 27 February the *San Francisco Examiner*'s front-page editorial deplored the heavy casualties being sustained at Iwo as at Tarawa and

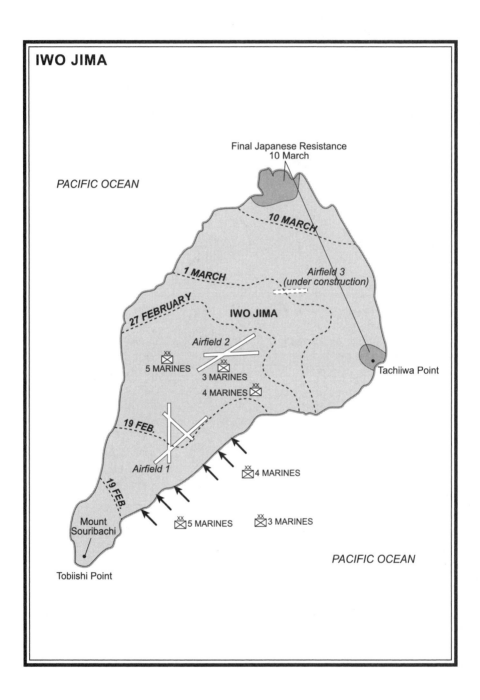

IWO JIMA

PACIFIC OCEAN

Final Japanese Resistance
10 March

10 MARCH

1 MARCH

Airfield 3
(under construction)

27 FEBRUARY

IWO JIMA

Airfield 2

5 MARINES

3 MARINES

4 MARINES

Tachiiwa Point

19 FEB.

Airfield 1

4 MARINES

19 FEB.

Mount
Souribachi

5 MARINES

3 MARINES

Tobiishi Point

PACIFIC OCEAN

Saipan, a common theme in Hearst and McCormick newspapers. It stated no such thing happened in General MacArthur's campaigns:

GENERAL MacARTHUR is our best strategist:
He is our most SUCCESSFUL strategist.
He wins all his objectives.
He outwits and outmaneuvers and outguesses and outthinks the Japanese.
HE SAVES THE LIVES OF HIS OWN MEN, not only for the future and vital operations that must be fought before Japan is defeated, but for their own safe return to their families and loved ones in the American homeland after the peace is won.[23]

The editorial exhibited the writer's ignorance of the military strategy designed to win the war in the Pacific. As an educated Californian, the editor instinctively knew that an acre of land in San Francisco at the corner of California and Mason streets had an economic value many times that of 1,000 acres in the arid portion of the San Joaquin Valley without water rights or access to reclamation water. Not knowing what was then necessary to defeat Japan, the editor could not see that for the remainder of the war Iwo Jima's military value far exceeded that of all the Philippine islands combined. Yet, marine casualties were extremely heavy among both officers and men. The average battalion landed with 36 officers and 885 enlisted men and was reduced to approximately 16 officers and 300 men at the end of the campaign.[24]

On 26 March 1945, D-day plus 35, Kuribayashi committed suicide. His body was never found. The few Japanese survivors staged one last banzai charge. Iwo was now completely secure in American hands. The bloodletting was over. All but a handful of the 21,000 Japanese died. Most were entombed in their underground defensive positions.

At the end of the thirty-six-day battle, Nimitz said:

The battle of Iwo Island has been won. The United States Marines by their individual and collective courage have conquered a base which is as necessary to us in our continuing forward movement toward final victory as it was vital to the enemy in staving off ultimate defeat.

By their victory, the 3rd, 4th, and 5th Marine Divisions and other units of the Fifth Amphibious Corps have made an accounting to their country which only history will be able to value fully. Among the Americans who served on Iwo Island uncommon valor was a common virtue.[25]

In speaking of valor, Nimitz referred to the American troops, but his statement was equally applicable for Japanese defenders as well. A message in a cave, where four Japanese were found dead, read: "To the Americans: We have fortified this island for over a year, but we cannot win this war alone, with just the *Yamato* (warrior) spirit. We cannot match your superiority. There is no other road for us to follow but to die." [26]

Chapter 27
Okinawa

ADMIRAL RAYMOND A. SPRUANCE'S NAVAL WAR COLLEGE background came to light when Adms. Ernest J. King and Chester W. Nimitz paid him a visit at Saipan on 17 July 1944. King decided to discuss future strategy with Spruance aboard the latter's flagship, the *Indianapolis*.

Spruance and Vice Adm. R. Kelly Turner did not favor Formosa at the exclusion of the Philippines. Both believed that Luzon should be seized first for a fleet anchorage in Manila Bay. They reasoned that the Marianas could not provide adequate base facilities to support an assault against Formosa. At this meeting, Spruance was not cognizant of the many advantages posed by the later occupation of Ulithi atoll, which was slightly nearer to Tokyo than Manila Bay and could accommodate more ships.

King then asked Spruance what he would recommend after the Marianas.

"Okinawa," Spruance replied.

"Can you take it?" King asked.

Yes, said Spruance, if he could find a way to transfer heavy ammunition at sea.[1] Spruance reasoned that he could not send his ships 1,400 miles to Okinawa with the nearest American anchorage at Saipan.

Spruance recommended Iwo Jima be seized first as an air base to support fleet operations against Okinawa. Okinawa itself would serve as an air base to interdict Japanese shipping in the East China Sea and would forever sever Japanese lines to the south, thus completing the Japanese blockade. Spruance maintained the war could be won without invading the Japanese mainland. King respected Spruance's opinion but did not change his mind about Formosa at this time.

Nimitz, King, Spruance, and Capt. Forrest Sherman reached the decision to invade Okinawa at a conference in San Francisco. The Joint Chiefs of Staff approved their decision on 3 October 1944 and directed Nimitz to proceed with the Iwo Jima and Okinawa operations.

At his staff study of 25 October 1944, Nimitz visualized the Okinawa operation in three phases:

Phase 1: Occupation of southern Okinawa and adjacent small islands beginning on "L" day (Landing Day) and development of base facilities.

Phase 2: Seizure of the remainder of Okinawa and Ie Shima and the development of additional base facilities, of a tentative target date of L plus 30.

Phase 3: Seizure and development of additional positions in the Nansei Shoto: Okino Daito Jima, tentatively L plus 60; Kume Shima, tentatively L plus 70; Miyako Retto, tentatively L plus 90; Kikai Jima, tentatively L plus 120.[2]

Spruance, the overall commander in charge, issued his operation plan on 3 January 1945 with the assault set for 1 April. Vice Admiral Marc A. Mitscher once more commanded the Fast Carrier Force, Task Force 58, now grown to eleven heavy and six light carriers, with accompanying fast battleships, cruisers, and destroyers. Vice Admiral Kelly Turner was again commander, Joint Expeditionary Force, an armada of some 1,300 ships carrying 182,000 assault troops of the Tenth Army. For the first time in the Pacific War, a British fast carrier force of twenty-two vessels aided the U.S. Navy.

The Tenth Army was made up of the III Amphibious Corps, Maj. Gen. Roy S. Geiger, USMC (1st, 2nd, and 6th Marine Divisions) and the XXIV Army Corps (7th, 96th, 77th, and 27th Army Divisions). Nimitz reclaimed the three army divisions loaned to MacArthur for the Leyte occupation, namely the 7th, 77th, and 96th. Interestingly enough, Nimitz's command used only ten divisions (six marine and four army) in his drive across the Central Pacific and move north, as envisioned by Plan Orange. Because army troops constituted a majority for the Okinawa operation, Lt. Gen. Simon Bolivar Buckner, U.S. Army, would command troops ashore. He had previously served four years in Alaska and the Aleutians and was the son of the Confederate general of the same name. A 28 March 1945 entry in Buckner's diary shows his awareness of this Southern heritage: "Finished reading the third volume of Freeman's *Lee's Lieutenants: Gettysburg to Appomattox*. A tragic epitaph to a nobly defended cause." [3]

This operation promised to be unique in that it was to be conducted for a prolonged period far from friendly bases. More than 200 service force vessels required for replenishing, salvage, and repair were placed under Rear Adm. Donald B. Beary's Service Squadron 6 in the forward area and Service Squadron 10 under Commodore Worrall R. Carter at Ulithi.

Okinawa is in easy fighter-plane range of Kyushu in Japan proper, Formosa, and China. It is ideally located as the advance base for the invasion of Japan proper. The Japanese High Command also recognized the vital importance of Okinawa. In accordance with the "Outline of Army and Navy Operations" approved by the emperor and promulgated 20 January 1945, Okinawa was designated as one of the key strongpoints to be developed.[4] The Japanese anticipated using the island as a delaying action. The high command said:

> When the enemy penetrates the defense zone, a campaign of attrition will be initiated to reduce his preponderance in ships, aircraft and men, to obstruct the establishment of advance bases, to undermine enemy morale, and thereby to seriously delay the final assault on Japan . . . Preparations for the decisive battle will be completed in Japan proper in the early fall of 1945.
>
> In general, Japanese air strength will be conserved until an enemy landing is actually underway on or within the defense sphere.[5]

The Joint Expeditionary Force to invade Okinawa assembled from all over the Pacific. It staged through Ulithi, Saipan, and Guam, with the three U.S. Army divisions loaned to MacArthur embarked from Leyte. On 14 March, Spruance's Fifth Fleet started from Ulithi with Spruance in strategic and Mitscher in tactical command for a strike on Kyushu. Attacks against enemy air bases met determined resistance plus effective counterattacks by the Japanese. Enemy planes damaged *Intrepid, Enterprise,* and the new *Yorktown, Wasp,* and the carrier *Franklin. Franklin* sustained more damage than any other ship in the war that did not sink. However, she somehow managed to sail 12,000 miles under her own power to the New York Navy Yard for repairs. She had lost 724 killed or missing and 265 wounded.[6] Spruance ordered all other damaged ships back to Ulithi for repair.

The Japanese navy, with only a few capital ships left, no longer posed a serious danger to Spruance's fleet. Enemy air power, especially kamikaze planes, presented the most hazardous threat. The kamikazes had first been employed against the Seventh Fleet in the Philippines in the fall of 1944 and again against the Fifth Fleet at Iwo Jima. The Fifth Fleet targeted Japanese planes in the air and on the ground prior to Landing Day, referred to most often as L-Day. Spruance's fleet destroyed an estimated 550 enemy planes in the air and on the ground prior to L-Day, yet he would learn there were many more left.

Vice Admiral Turner needed a nearby island for fueling and ammunition replenishment. The irregular-shaped islands known as the Kerama Retto seemed to fit this purpose. Water twenty to thirty-five fathoms deep lay between the largest island of the group and five smaller ones to the westward capable of accommodating seventy-five large ships. However, the islands themselves were unsuitable for airfields. Most navy officers opposed Turner's proposal beforehand, but the Iwo Jima operation accented the need of a sheltered anchorage for replenishment. Prior to the main assault on Okinawa, that is, on 26 March, the U.S. Army's 77th Infantry Division, commanded by Maj. Gen. A. D. Bruce, captured all principal islands except Kuba and Tokashiki by midafternoon. The rest of Kerama Retto was secured by the end of the next day, as there was very little Japanese opposition. On 27 March, Service Squadron 10 arrived from Ulithi. For the entire campaign it served as a floating base for replenishment and light repairs.[7]

At 4:06 A.M. on 1 April 1945, beneath still-darkened skies, Turner, aboard his flagship *Eldorado*, gave the expeditionary force commander's traditional order: "Land the landing force!" Forty-five minutes later with the break of dawn, the American bombardment force began firing, which drove the Japanese defenders deep inside their pre-arranged defenses.

Along eight miles of shoreline, two U.S. Marine and two U.S. Army divisions hit the Hagushi Beaches against no opposition. They called it "Love Day." Turner thought that the bombardment had ended all opposition. He reported to Nimitz: "I may be crazy, but it looks like the Japanese have quit the war, at least in this sector."

Back came the counter-message: "Delete all after 'crazy.' " [8]

Lieutenant General Mitsuru Ushijima commanded the Japanese ashore. He watched the preliminary bombing from Shuri Castle to the south. One of his staff officers later wrote that the flash and crash of this incredible bombardment was "a scene of unsurpassed grandeur." Ushijima could imagine the carnage if he had adhered to the old, discredited doctrine of "destruction at the water's edge." [9] Like the Japanese defense on Biak, Peleliu, and Iwo Jima, Ushijima erected deep underground fortifications with interlocking tunnels on the lower 20 percent of the island in his plan to maximize American casualties. The Japanese defense line faced north, "its points rested on the heights surrounding Shuri and Shuri Castle, the city and citadel of Okinawa's ancient kings." [10] The defense line reached the sea on each side. To the west lay Naha, Okinawa's largest city, and to the east lay Yonabaru Airfield. The Americans called Ushijima's defense positions the Naha-Shuri-Yonabaru line.

Altogether, General Buckner's seven combat divisions numbered 183,000 men, of whom 154,000 would be in assault on the Hagushi Beaches—half again as many as Ushijima's 110,000. Buckner planned to occupy the airfields, Yontan and Kadena, across from the landing beaches by L plus 3. Both were captured by midafternoon of the first day. American planes made emergency landings on 2 April. A U.S. Marine air group landed at Yontan the next day.

On the first two days, the U.S. Army's 7th and 96th Divisions raced across the island to reach the east coast. Turning south on 3 April, they met increasing resistance. By 8 April, these army units reached the outer works of Ushijima's Naha-Shuri-Yonabaru line, while U.S. fighters operated around the clock from both airfields. As yet, the 1st and 6th Marine Divisions had not encountered any significant resistance.

Marines of the 6th Division marched rapidly north, sweeping up both coasts, a regiment to either side. On 8 April, the tanks in the lead came to the mouth of the Motobu Peninsula, a headland jutting into the East China Sea on the left, or west of the marines. About 2,000 enemy soldiers occupied nearby Mount Yaetake. By 20 April, U.S. Marines secured the Motobu Peninsula while the 22nd Regiment, 6th Marine Division, reached Okinawa's northernmost point, marking the end of battle for the northern sector.

Marines of the 1st Division saw no serious fighting for the full month of April. Many of the division's battalions built bivouacs complete with gravel paths, showers, and mess halls.

Imperial Headquarters decided to defend Okinawa at every available cost. This included sending the battleship *Yamato* into the fight. Named for the clan generally credited with founding the Japanese nation, *Yamato* remained the most powerful battleship afloat. While hundreds of kamikazes roared down from the north in their first attack, *Yamato* came trailing afterward on 6 April.

She had survived the Battle of Leyte Gulf and could outshoot anything in the U.S. Navy. She had nine 18.1-inch guns firing a projectile weighing 3,200 pounds a distance of 45,000 yards, compared to the 2,700-pound shell and 42,000-yard range of the American 16-inchers. Before the crew departed, Vice Admiral Ozawa told them, "Render this operation the turning point of the war." [11] She now sortied out of the Inland Sea for Okinawa with only enough fuel for a one-way voyage, a planned suicide mission.

As *Yamato* moved south, the kamikazes struck American ships with full force. Both Spruance and Turner knew that a massive enemy aerial strike would arrive by reading messages in the broken Japanese code. To thwart the kamikazes, Turner deployed a wide circle of sixteen radar picket destroyers winding around Okinawa and its surrounding islands. Each picket destroyer could warn of an enemy attack but became a prime target for the kamikazes, especially those north of Okinawa. Kamikazes dove on the picket destroyers, sinking *Bush* and *Colhoun*. The ammunition ships *Logan Victory* and *Hobbs Victory* also went down, creating a temporary ordnance shortage for the Tenth Army. Nine other destroyers were damaged, as were four destroyer escorts and five mine vessels. Though they lost 135 planes, the kamikazes achieved an impressive day's work.

American planes were also busy. Hellcats and Avengers plunged from the skies to strike at the hapless *Yamato*. She died slowly. Explosions caused her own ammunition to blow up. In addition, *Yahagi, Isokaze, Hamakaze, Asashimo*, and *Kasumo* received deathblows and, like *Yamato*, all sank. Except for a small number of submarines, Japan no longer had a viable navy.

Without ships, Japan's military machine had to rely on ground troops, reduced air power, and desperation tactics such as human guided torpedoes and kamikaze attacks. More than 170 U.S. submarines operating in the Pacific now searched for a dwindling supply of targets. With only small tankers, freighters, and fishing boats available, 70 percent of U.S. submarine war patrols returned to home base without sinking a single ship. [12] Ferryboats transitioning the home islands now became prime targets. With its merchant marine decimated, Japan could no longer conduct offensive war in the Pacific.

As envisioned by Plan Orange, Japan had already lost the war. Emperor Hirohito recognized that defeat was imminent as early as January 1945 but could not say so publicly as the Japanese army controlled the government. Prince Konoe, the former premiere, stated bluntly that Japan faced certain defeat. He urged Hirohito to take positive action to end the war. [13] On 7 April, Hirohito appointed Baron Kantaro Suzuki the premiere with the understanding that he would work

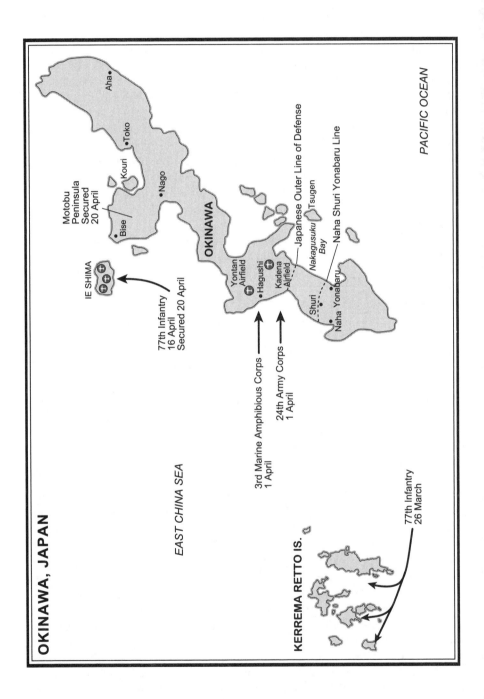

OKINAWA, JAPAN

PACIFIC OCEAN

EAST CHINA SEA

Aha

Toko

Kouri

Nago

Motobu
Peninsula
Secured
20 April

Bise

IE SHIMA

OKINAWA

Yontan
Airfield

Hagushi

Kadena
Airfield

Japanese Outer Line of Defense

Tsugen

Nakagusuku
Bay

Naha Shuri Yonabaru Line

Shuri

Naha Yonabaru

77th Infantry
16 April
Secured 20 April

3rd Marine Amphibious Corps
1 April

24th Army Corps
1 April

KERREMA RETTO IS.

77th Infantry
26 March

toward ending the war. However, because of the intransigence of the Japanese army, Japan's leaders needed more time to admit failure publicly. Indeed, intense fighting remained on Okinawa before the Americans could secure the island.

On 8 April, Maj. Gen. John Hodge, commanding the XXIV Army Corps, reported greatly increased resistance. His troops had reached the outer works of the Naha-Shuri-Yonabaru line known as Kakazu Ridge. For the next four days, frontal assaults failed to dislodge the Japanese occupying the reverse slope of the ridge. From 9 April through 12 April, the Americans assaulted the Japanese with heavy barrages from land, sea, and air, which failed to dislodge the enemy. Noting the American's failure, General Ushijima's second in command, Lt. Gen. Isamu Cho, prevailed upon his commander for a full-scale offensive against the American troops. Cho's plan called for massive infiltration of almost the entire east-west front of the U.S. 7th and 96th Divisions. Three battalions of the Japanese 24th Division would strike the U.S. 7th Division on the east, while three more from the Japanese 62nd Division would assault the battered American 96th. The Japanese planned to attack at night. Breaking through the advance American units, Japanese troops envisioned spreading out in their rear area four miles below Kadena Airfield. They planned the slaughter of the Tenth Army's rear-echelon troops on the morning of 13 April. The plan failed, partially because only two battalions instead of three engaged the 7th and 96th Divisions, but more importantly because U.S. soldiers held firm to their positions.

Meanwhile, Vice Adm. Matome Ugaki prepared his kamikazes for a second sally against Spruance's fleet. Ugaki realized the second attack would not equal the strength of the first because of previous losses. Due to their proximity to base, marine corsairs at Yontan and Kadena threatened his success. Nevertheless, the kamikazes again took a heavy toll.

On Friday the thirteenth, American troops were startled, then grief stricken, to hear the bullhorns of the ships offshore blaring, "Attention! Attention! All hands! President Roosevelt is dead. Repeat, our supreme commander, President Roosevelt, is dead." So many young soldiers and marines had known no president other than Franklin Delano Roosevelt. Some prayed in silence, then moved on. After the war, Gen. Dwight Eisenhower expressed the opinion of most senior officers when he wrote, "I knew him solely in his capacity as leader of a nation at war—and in that capacity he seemed to me to fulfill all that could possibly be expected of him." [14] Throughout the war, MacArthur on many occasions and to many people spoke disparagingly of Roosevelt. However, in his *Reminiscences*, he wrote of Roosevelt:

He became the leading liberal of the age. Whether his vision of economic and political freedom is within the realm of fruition, only future history can tell. That his means for accomplishment won him the almost idolatrous devotion of an immeasurable following is known to all. That they aroused bitterness and resentment in others is equally true. In my own case, whatever differences arose between us, it never sullied in slightest degree the warmth of my personal friendship for him.[15]

At once Harry S. Truman by authority of the U.S. Constitution became Commander in Chief, United States Armed Forces. After Truman's first meeting of the cabinet, 25 April 1945, Secretary Stimson spoke to the president privately. For the first time, the new president learned of the atomic bomb. Quoting from a prepared memorandum, Stimson said, "1) Within four months we shall in all probability have completed the most terrible weapon ever known in human history, one bomb of which could destroy a whole city." He also warned: "5) The world in its present state of moral advancement compared with its technical development would be eventually at the mercy of such a weapon. In other words, modern civilization might be completely destroyed." [16]

Shortly thereafter, Vannevar Bush, head of Scientific Research and Development, came to the White House and said in reference to the atomic bomb, "That is the biggest fool thing we have ever done . . . The bomb will never go off and I speak as an expert in explosives." [17] It is interesting to speculate the repercussions against Roosevelt had Bush been correct in his analysis. The atomic bomb development was by far the most expensive single project of World War II. Amazingly, Roosevelt kept its construction secret from all members of Congress.

A few days later, on 20 April, at the White House, Secretary Henry Morgenthau introduced Pfc. Rene A. Gagnon of Manchester, New Hampshire, Pharmacist's Mate John H. Bradley of Appleton, Wisconsin, and Pfc. Ira Hayes of the Pima Indian Reservation in Arizona to President Truman. These were the survivors of the American flag-raising on Mount Suribachi as shown in Joe Rosenthal's photograph. They would travel around the country to promote war bonds in the seventh War Loan campaign about to begin. The president told them that "the spirit they had displayed had been caught by the photographer and typified the greatness of those who wore their country's uniform." [18]

Because of the numerous ships either sunk or damaged, the Joint Chiefs of Staff ordered Maj. Gen. Curtis LeMay to hammer the kamikaze airfields on Kyushu from 16 April onward. LeMay objected. He appealed to Gen. Hap Arnold for permission to resume strategic bombing. Arnold turned him down because Nimitz had convinced him that the immediate short-range effects of destroying the suicide bases were more important than the long-range results of strategic bombing.

On 16 April, the 77th Infantry Division landed on the island of Ie Shima off the coast of the western tip of Motobu Peninsula. This island had three airstrips in relatively good condition. Air base construction plans called for an airdrome there large enough to support a B-29 group. After four days of savage fighting with the killing of 4,706 Japanese, the island with its completed airfields was secured. Unfortunately, the war correspondent, Ernie Pyle, often proclaimed the GI's favorite, was killed on April 18.

By 20 April, all but the southernmost portion of Okinawa lay in American hands. The 2nd Marine Division, in floating reserve, had been sent back to Guam on 9 April while still aboard ship. It was thought these marines would not be needed, and while aboard ship they were vulnerable to kamikaze attacks. During the remainder of April and into May, Ushijima's troops along the Naha-Shuri-Yonabaru line showed no signs of folding. Forward movement by the XXIV Army Corps was glacial at best. During this period, the GI's learned that the flamethrower, especially the tank flamethrower, was the best weapon to use against the entrenched Japanese.

For reasons known only to General Buckner, he allowed the two veteran marine divisions to stand idle, the 1st Division for almost a month and the 6th for nearly two weeks, instead of using them to relieve two badly battered U.S. Army divisions on the Naha-Shuri-Yonabaru line.

On 28 April, Buckner decided to put the marines into his renewed down-island offensive. The 7th Army Division would remain in place on the left, and the 77th Army Division would relieve the 96th Army Division. The 1st Marine Division would relieve the 27th Infantry Division on the 77th Army Division's right with the 6th Marine Division holding the western flank. Thus the line: 7th U.S. Army Division, 77th U.S. Army Division on the eastern front; 1st Marine Division, 6th Marine Division on the western front; XXIV Army Corps on the east; 3rd Marine Division in the west.

On 11 May a kamikaze scored a hit on Admiral Mitscher's flagship, *Bunker Hill*. It smashed through rows of planes on the flight deck to start fires before crashing overboard and exploding. Behind it came another diving straight down from astern. It hit armed planes refueling on the flight deck. A broken fuel line fed a roaring fire, which caused the planes to explode. Four hundred sailors were killed or missing and another 264 wounded. For five and a half hours, *Bunker Hill*'s crew fought the flames. Although Admiral Mitscher had to transfer his flag, *Bunker Hill* became the second-worst-hit ship in the navy to survive. Obviously, she would need many months for repair. On the next day, kamikazes hit only one ship, the destroyer *Bache*, on picket duty south of Okinawa. Forty-one sailors were killed when her power plant was knocked out.

The British carriers did not experience the same difficulty with the kamikazes as did the Americans. For the first time a British fleet supported the United States in the Pacific War. The metal flight decks on the British carriers made them far less vulnerable to catastrophic damage than the U.S. carriers, which had wooden flight decks.

On 11 May, Buckner speeded up his attack. The Tenth Army had four full divisions abreast. General Hodges' XXIV Army Corps was on the left, or east, with the 96th and 77th Divisions in that order; General Geiger's III Corps on the right, or west, with the 1st and 6th Marine Divisions. The 96th's objective was Conical Hill. The 77th would attack Shuri Castle. The 1st Marines would strike the complex guarding Shuri, and the 6th Marines, at Sugar Loaf Hill.

In the days ahead, the 6th Marine Division lost 2,662 killed and wounded in taking Sugar Loaf. Now it stood poised to drive down island into Naha. But friendly troops had to occupy Shuri Heights before the 6th could strike at Naha. To the east, the army's 96th Division moved against Conical Hill. In the ten days between 11 and 21 May, both sides locked into the worst fighting of the

Okinawa campaign.

In mid-May, Admiral Nimitz complained to Buckner about the slow progress being made, to which the latter took offense, stating that he wanted to reduce casualties. Nimitz reminded the general that he was losing an average of a ship and a half a day from kamikaze attacks by reason of the Tenth Army's failure to wind up the campaign. Nimitz again called on MacArthur to return the ships, which had been loaned the Southwest Pacific commander for the Leyte campaign. MacArthur refused because he had committed the vessels to his endeavor in the southern Philippines, an unnecessary military operation that continued until Japan surrendered.

By 27 May, the 6th Marine Division crossed the Asato River and was poised to break into Naha, which caused Ushijima to retreat south of the Yonabaru-Naha Valley. Shuri Castle, the key bastion of the Japanese defense, fell to the 1st Marines on 29 May. This placed the Japanese defenders in an untenable position. Now, only the Japanese air force could bleed the Americans.

Near the end of May, command of the Fifth Fleet passed to the Third Fleet. Shortly after taking command, Halsey's ships sailed into another typhoon. Although Halsey's fleet received substantial damage, no ships sank. The Board of Inquiry placed the full blame on Admiral Halsey. His retirement by Secretary of the Navy James Forrestal was blocked by Admirals King and Nimitz. They reasoned that Halsey posed too big a symbol to the sailors. His reputation with the American public approached that of MacArthur, who with many was bigger than life.

In the beginning, the kamikazes had been strictly volunteers, but as the Okinawa campaign continued, all Japanese sailors and soldiers were subject to suicide duty whether or not they wished it. On 3 June, the kamikazes made their ninth organized attack against American ships. Fewer than one hundred planes were engaged. Land-based marine corsairs had so sharply reduced their number that the kamikazes hit only one minelayer. The next day they dove again, but in almost negligible strength and without success.

In the meantime, after four months in Washington, Gen. Joseph Stilwell persuaded Marshall to allow him to travel to the Pacific in the hopes of securing a command for the invasion of Japan. Stilwell arrived at Okinawa on 3 June and had a long talk with Buckner that same day. In a matter of three days, he became disenchanted with Buckner. In his diary entry of 6 June, Stilwell sarcastically wrote: "Buckner is obviously playing the Navy. He recommended Geiger as army commander. Nimitz is perfect. His staff is perfectly balanced. Cooperation is magnificent. The Marine divisions are wonderful. In fact, everything is just dinky." [19]

In early June, Buckner redisposed his Tenth Army for the final surge of the war. On the west flank the marines' sector had been narrowed. The 6th Marine Division made a shore-to-shore amphibious assault on the Oroku Peninsula just south of Naha and advanced about a thousand yards against light resistance. [20] This obligated the 1st Marine Division with limited strength to cover the entire III Corps front.

The III Corps, in fact, was depleted. With the 2nd Marine Division sent back to Guam—rather than kept afloat as a kamikaze target—Major General Geiger had not been able to rest either his 1st or 6th Division. He had no reserve, and the divisions themselves had tried to maintain battle efficiency by resting one regiment while the other two attacked. The III Corps needed troops. Soon the 8th Regiment of the 2nd Marine Division was ordered into Okinawa for the relief. It had first to capture islands west of Okinawa to give Vice Admiral Turner long-range radar and fighter-director stations.

On the eastern flank, the 7th and 96th Infantry Divisions neared the southern coast. On 10 June, Lieutenant General Buckner made a surrender appeal to Ushijima. He dropped a letter behind the lines. It said:

> The forces under your command have fought bravely and well, and your infantry tactics have merited the respect of your opponents . . . Like myself, you are an infantry general long schooled and practiced in infantry warfare . . . I believe, therefore, that you understand as clearly as I, that the destruction of all Japanese resistance on the island is merely a matter of days.[21]

The letter reached Ushijima on 17 June. But a Samurai cannot surrender.

On the west flank, the 1st Marine Division battled through Kunishi Ridge while the 6th came into line on the right and was racing for Ara Point, the southernmost tip of Okinawa. In the east, the 96th Division finished off resistance in the Yaeju-Yuza Peaks, while 7th Division's soldiers closed in on the Japanese Thirty-second Army's headquarters.

On 18 June, Simon Bolivar Buckner came down to Mezado Ridge to see the fresh 8th Marine Regiment enter battle. The 8th had come to Okinawa on 15 June and was attached to the 1st Marine Division. While watching the marines, Buckner said, "Things are going so well here, I think I'll move on to another unit." [22] As he turned to leave, five Japanese shells exploded on Mezado Ridge nearby. A coral shard pierced Lieutenant General Buckner's chest. He died within ten minutes—knowing that his Tenth Army was winning. Command went to Maj. Gen. Roy Geiger, USMC, the senior officer, as he neared promotion to lieutenant general. On this same day, Stilwell met with MacArthur to discuss replacing Buckner as X Corps commander.[23]

On the night of 21 June—the day Major General Geiger declared the American victory on Okinawa—Ushijima and Cho realized the end had come. They took their own lives in the accepted Samurai ceremony. Five days later Gen. Joseph A. Stilwell relieved Geiger.

American casualties totaled 49,151, with U.S. Marine losses at 2,938 dead or missing and 13,708 wounded; the U.S. Army's at 4,675 dead or missing and 18,099 wounded; and the U.S. Navy's at 4,907 dead or missing and 4,824 wounded. In addition, there were more than 26,000 non-battle casualties. The United States Navy suffered 36 ships sunk and another 368 damaged, the heaviest losses in any Pacific battle—much larger than the campaign for Guadalcanal.[24]

After the war, records showed total Japanese losses, including those sustained in the area during the campaign, "amounted to almost 132,000 killed and 7,400 prisoners of war, sixteen naval ships sunk, and four damaged, and 7,830 aircraft destroyed." [25]

Major General Fred C. Wallace, USMC, became the military governor of Okinawa soon after the troops landed. Both army engineers and Seabees came under his command. In addition to taking care of the Okinawa civilians who had to be fed and sheltered, he conducted numerous construction projects on the island. By the end of June, he controlled 153,000 men of whom 95,000 were construction troops and Seabees. [26] With airfield construction, supply roads built, and seaport development, the face of the island changed dramatically. By mid-August, the Okinawa campaign had achieved its original purpose of being an excellent advance base for the invasion of Japan proper.

With the Pacific War nearing an end, inter-service jealousies were just as strong as ever. In his diary of 2 July, Stilwell spoke of visiting "Marine Corps Field (#2)—dirtiest I ever saw—bastard organization of Navy personnel, Army nurses, for Marine patients under Army command." [27] He then noted Maj. Gen. John R. Hodge's complaint of the marines hogging the show. Previously, on 30 June, Major General Hodge wrote, with some justification, a four-page memo to Stilwell:

> complaining that the press gave sole credit to the Marines for the success on Okinawa. "I read many clippings," he wrote, "giving outstanding exploits of the Marines on Okinawa, often crediting them with moves actually made by my own divisions." The disparity became even worse at the end of the battle: "I have been able to find but little mention of Army troops fighting their hearts out in the last twelve days of the 82-day battle. The big picture and the overall result is that the American public thinks the USMC are the only good troops in the Pacific area, that they do all the fighting and that no one else can execute amphibious landings. [28]

A review of newspaper clippings during the first and last months of the Okinawa campaign would lead the average reader to believe that the U.S. Marines, rather than the U.S. Army, were in the majority, which in reality was not the case. Marine infantry did have one advantage over army troops. The marines had better close air support. The Tactical Air Control Party (TACP) unit on the ground had a marine aviator who knew best how to communicate with the pilots in the air so that close air support could be brought in much closer to advancing troops without fear of inflicting harm on your own men.

After completion of the Okinawa campaign, Admiral Halsey's Third Fleet moved north from Ulithi to conduct a pre-invasion bombardment of the Japanese home islands. On 10 July, strikes were made against airfields and factories in and around Tokyo. He then moved on to blast targets in northern Honshu and southern Hokkaido on 14 and 15 July. On 17 July, the Third Fleet, in company with units of the British Pacific Fleet, combined to form the first U.S. and British bombardment of the Japanese home islands. Carrier planes attacked the Yokosuka Naval Base in Tokyo on 18 July; the Inland Sea area on 24, 25, and 28 July; and northern Honshu on 9 and 10 August. Except for continued sporadic fighting in northern Luzon and Mindanao in the Philippines, the Okinawa campaign marked the end of fighting for U.S. ground troops in the Pacific War.

Chapter 28
The Twentieth
Air Force

AFTER THE INVASION OF OKINAWA, the U.S. Navy—especially the submarine fleet—had the Japanese home islands cut off from the outside world. The key to Japan's final defeat now lay in the hands of the Twentieth Air Force, guided by Gen. Hap Arnold.

Admiral King regarded Arnold as a yes man for George Marshall, and with some justification. Arnold once told Ira Eaker, "If George Marshall ever took a position contrary to mine, I would know I was wrong." [1] But, Marshall had earned this respect. Although he outranked Arnold, he never pulled rank on him. In air matters, he gave Arnold virtual autonomy. In spite of King's opinion, Arnold's expansive knowledge of air power at all levels added a dimension to the Joint Chiefs of Staff that proved essential for the timely ending of the Pacific War. Admiral Leahy said, "He had a splendid appreciation of what the Air Force could do and was rarely in disagreement with the other chiefs. He knew the limitations of that arm of service. We generally accepted his views on air strategy as correct, and I cannot recall that he ever proposed a move that was not acceptable to the other chiefs." [2]

In 1939, Arnold prevailed upon Army Chief of Staff Gen. Marlin Craig to establish an air board to study the threat to the United States should the Axis powers obtain air bases in the Western Hemisphere. Charles A. Lindbergh, who had visited Germany and had been permitted by Herman Goring to fly several German fighters and bombers, reported to Arnold that the Germans had bombers capable of attacking the United States should it get bases on nearby islands, such as in the Caribbean. The air board recommended that medium and heavy bombers be developed to counter such a threat. Its report was delivered to Gen. George C. Marshall on 1 September, the day he became U.S. Army Chief of Staff. Marshall quickly endorsed the report's recommendations, saying, "This established for the first time a special mission for the Air Corps." [3]

Prior to the beginning of World War II, Arnold persuaded the U.S. government to develop the B-29, called the Superfort by its developer. Afterward, the U.S. proceeded to spend more money on its manufacture than on any other war project except the atomic bomb. But would it work?

On 21 September 1942, the first B-29 underwent its maiden test flight with Boeing's best test pilot, Edmund T. "Eddie" Allen, at the controls. He pronounced the plane a winner. The next day, Capt. Donald L. Putt, the army's project officer, confirmed Allen's finding by another test flight. He commented: "It's unbelievable for such a large plane to be so easy on the controls. It's easier to fly than the B-17." [4]

Five months later, on 18 February 1943, the second B-29 test airplane, with Eddie Allen at the controls, reported everything going normally. Then, at 12:21 P.M., Allen calmly requested landing clearance because his number one engine was on fire. He reported the engine's prop had feathered, but the trouble was not serious. The controller immediately warned other planes to leave the vicinity of Boeing Field and then gave Allen clearance for an emergency landing. The controller heard one of the crew members call, "Allen, better get this thing down in a hurry. The wing spar's burning badly." In an unhurried voice, Allen requested the tower to have fire equipment on hand: "I'm coming in with a wing on fire." [5] His voice was not heard again. The plane crashed into the fifth floor of the Fryer Packing Plant, killing all on board plus a number of employees and firemen.

All B-29 flight tests were suspended while Boeing engineers sought the source of trouble. They identified inadequate engine cooling as the culprit. Fixes were made but the problem was not resolved completely until after the B-29s were in combat. Engine fires continued to cause many operational losses during the early months of its use. Not until the middle of 1944 did the B-29 meet the requirements for which it was designed.

Previously, at the Casablanca Conference in January 1943, General Marshall expressed the view that Japanese industries were vulnerable to attack and that heavy, sustained attacks would drastically reduce Japan's war effort. Roosevelt agreed on the basis that limited bombing of Japan would have a great uplifting impact on the Chinese people. Marshall sounded a word of caution. He emphasized that supplying bombers in China would be terribly expensive, thus place a drain on transport aircraft needed elsewhere. Marshall later realized these fears.

After considerable debate among the Joint Chiefs concerning the establishment of a Headquarters Strategic Air Force, which would be administered by the Army Air Forces member of the Joint Chiefs, the Twentieth Air Force was activated in Washington on 4 April 1944 with Arnold as commander. Brigadier General Hayward S. Hansell, Jr., was named chief of staff with each member of Arnold's staff to perform his role for the Twentieth as well as the Army Air Forces. No public announcement was made at the time.

On 10 April 1944, the Joint Chiefs adopted a plan for the strategic bombing of Japan under the Joint Chiefs instead of the Combined Chiefs. The first B-29s were sent to the China-Burma-India theater with the activation of the Twentieth Bomber Command under the control of Brig. Gen. Kenneth B. Wolfe. In the third week of April, five B-29s crashed near Karachi because of overheated engines.[6] Wolfe grounded all B-29s. An investigation showed that overheating of the exhaust valves of the rear row of the cylinders caused engine failure. Major Victor Agather with members of a special group was sent to India to lend expertise. Afterward, modifications were made. On 8 September, Maj. Gen. Curtis E. LeMay replaced Wolfe. The same day, Maj. Gen. Hayward Hansell, Jr., was placed in command of the Twenty-first Bomber Command at Salina, Kansas, which had previously been activated.

Early in life, LeMay saw a future in flying and, unlike many of his peers, he developed a passion for navigation and instrument flying. His reputation for bluntness earned him the nickname "The Diplomat." As late as 1 January 1940, he was still a lieutenant with a dozen years of service who as yet had never commanded a squadron. Service with the Eighth Air Force in Europe ignited his rocket-like advance. His performance in the deadly skies over Germany made LeMay the youngest major general in the Army Air Forces by March 1944. He cultivated the free exchange of ideas with all ranks in his command. In the formulation of policy, "I never said *I*," he noted. "I always said *we*." [7]

From the start, the command organization in the China-Burma-India theater made operations difficult, as there existed two theaters, Mountbatten's and Stilwell's. In addition LeMay recognized a "major problem is supporting operations from India and China, thousands of miles from sources of supply in the United States." [8] He later said, "It quickly became apparent to me that no one is going to make a big mark with these B-29s from India and China against Japan. You just can't get the resources to do it. That's what I repeatedly tell Washington." [9] In addition, LeMay's problems with the B-29 multiplied because of the lack of spare parts. During three missions over Formosa, three losses were caused by engine and propeller failures. Others aborted because of malfunctioning engines.

Besides the B-29's mechanical and logistical difficulties, the Japanese army in China greatly curtailed their usefulness. Although Chennault was a master tactician, he was no match for Stilwell as a strategist. After the Fourteenth Air Force established a chain of airfields in eastern China astride the Hankow-Canton Railway to support Chinese armies and the B-29 base at Chengtu, the Japanese decided to eliminate them. Their armies easily threw back the Chinese. By mid-December 1944, the Japanese occupied all but two of the American airfields in eastern China and had created a threat to Kunming and Chungking. They now controlled all of China's large cities and its railroads and rivers. Chiang Kai-shek held a decreasing area in the south while Mao ZeDong increased his Communist control in the north. Supposedly, LeMay's B-29s would operate from the air base at Chengtu.

Early on, LeMay told Arnold that the few airfields in China badly needed resurfacing. Arnold replied that further expenditures on runways could not be justified. LeMay in return said that he hoped the Joint Chiefs would consider a Twentieth Bomber Command move to another theater. Because of logistical problems, the end of 1944 saw operation of the B-29s in China as more a liability than an asset. Of forty-nine missions flown from China, only nine dropped bombs and mines on or near Kyushu. These missions cost eighty-two B-29s plus those lost on supply and training flights, all to very little effect.

The Japanese capture of Liuchow and Nanning further curtailed B-29 operations in the Chengtu area. As a result, Lt. Gen. Albert C. Wedemeyer, who had replaced Stilwell, recommended on 12 January 1945 that the Twentieth Bomber Command be removed from China no later than the first week of February. He reasoned that with its displacement he could increase supplies for Chinese forces as well as augment the Fourteenth Air Force by units from India. The Joint Chiefs agreed on 15 January to withdraw the Twentieth Bomber Command to India for a planned move to the Marianas, the only logical place from which to bomb Japan.

LeMay had repeatedly reported to Washington that hauling supplies by air over the Hump made it virtually impossible to effectively use the B-29s in this theater. He explained that it took seven trips by B-29 tankers plus other cargo planes over the Hump just to get enough fuel for one mission over Kyushu.

In the meantime, the Twenty-first Bomber Command had been activated in contemplation of the navy's invasion and capture of the Marianas. Crews completed training in Colorado, Kansas, and Nebraska prior to leaving the United States. Unlike the Twentieth Bomber Command, which went overseas with a minimum of training, the Twenty-first had the advantage of knowing about the India-China experience, plus its airplanes had been modified so that their worst faults were largely eliminated.

Upon the completion of the Marianas campaign, two airfields large enough to accommodate the B-29s plus an air depot were constructed on Guam. Two airfields were built on Tinian and another on Saipan. Guam was designated the headquarters for the Twenty-first Bomber Command under Lt. Gen. Millard F. Harmon. Harmon previously had commanded U.S. Air Forces in the South Pacific. In keeping with the intent of the Joint Chiefs, the Twenty-first Bomber Command took orders only from Arnold. Harmon, its deputy commander, reported directly to Arnold rather than Nimitz.

Major General Haywood Hansell, Arnold's chief of staff, took the first crews of B-29s to Saipan in October 1944. He met with Admiral Nimitz en route. "I don't approve of this organization and command arrangement," Nimitz told him, "and if I had understood it more clearly I would have opposed it to Admiral King. But, since it is approved by the Joint Chiefs of Staff, I will go along with it. You may be assured that I will give you every help and support..." [10] Hansell found that Nimitz was as good as his word. Unlike in China, adequate supply was never a major problem.

Arnold directed Hansell to make his first attack against Nakajima's Musashino-Tama plant in the suburbs of northwest Tokyo because it produced almost half of all Japanese combat engines. Bad weather hampered this first military mission, but it did prove the feasibility of conducted daylight precision strikes against military targets in the Japanese home islands. When Arnold went to the White House to brief President Roosevelt, he said, "No part of the Japanese Empire is now out of range." [11]

A second mission to the same target was made on 27 November. The planes flew much too high to synchronize the bomb sites properly, thus the Musashino plant emerged unscathed. History shows that, despite Arnold's glowing reports to the president and the press, the B-29s could not have done a worse operational job. Unfortunately, poor results would continue through the end of 1944. From January until March 1945, the B-29s continued their daylight precision-bombing raids with disappointing results, even though Maj. Gen. Curtis LeMay assumed command of the Twenty-first Bomber Command on 19 January 1945.

Captain William Meador, U.S. Army Air Corps, a member of the 6th Bombardment Group, Twenty-first Bomber Command, also arrived at Tinian in January 1945. He was assigned to the B-29 *Jolly Roger*, which had a crew of eleven. In the months ahead he would fly thirty-five missions over Japan, and be awarded the Distinguished Flying Cross. He pointed out that North Field Air Base on Tinian was the largest in the world when completed. The Seabees constructed four runways running east to west with each runway being 8,500 feet in length. Upon completion of the the last runway, the Seabees had built an officers and servicman's club, a movie theater, and numerous Quonset huts for sleeping quarters.

On Meador's fourth mission, while traveling at 25,000 feet he ran into a strong, 180-knot headwind. Although Meador had been flying for five years prior to coming to the Pacific, this trip from Tinian to Japan was his first encounter with what is known today as the jet stream. Traveling at 25,000 to 30,000 feet above sea level, Meador admitted that he seldom landed his bombs on the intended target. Yet he encountered a large amount of flak on each mission. The round trip to Japan and back to Meador averaged fifteen hours and twenty minutes. On those occasions where his plane encountered a strong headwind, the round trip took in excess of sixteen hours, thus he often had to refuel at Iwo Jima before returning to Tinian.[12]

LeMay was particularly disappointed that only half of all planes on each January mission had bombed its primary target and with minimal results. In the months ahead, three factors would improve the results dramatically.

One of these was the seizure of Iwo Jima. When Iwo Jima's air base became operational, in LeMay's words, it was "used right up to the hilt." [13] Iwo Jima also denied Japanese bombers a base against attacks in the Marianas, as well as airfields for fighter protection for B-29 flights to Japan. In addition to saving many airmen's lives through emergency landings, Iwo Jima served as a base for the air-sea rescue program for B-29s operating out of the Marianas. Many B-29s in trouble were deliberately put down at sea in a process known to airmen as "ditching." An elaborate program for search and rescue at sea by the use of submarines and seaplanes saved many lives and improved moral among the B-29 crews. Cruise control techniques became refined so that crews could get to Japan and back with an adequate reserve of fuel.

Second, to get a better delivery of bombs, LeMay reduced the bombing altitude to 4,500 to 8,000 feet. Although LeMay had the nagging worry that such a dramatic change could be suicidal, he took the risk. Captain Meador explained that everyone was upset upon learning of this new order. "There was moaning and groaning throughout."

Captain Meador explained, however, that Japan's air defenses were strongest at high altitudes yet almost negligible at low and missle altitudes. This new bombing altitude turned out to be a blessing in disguise.

Third, LeMay decided to use incendiary bombs against Japan's congested industrial cities, which were constructed of wood. This change to incendiaries made a huge breakthrough in the effectiveness of strategic bombing. Unlike in Germany, many of the war supplies were produced in the Japanese home. In 1942, Gen. Francisco Aguilar, who had been Mexico's minister to Japan, advised that "manufacture of war material in Japan was largely accomplished at night in the residences of the workmen and that the destruction of almost any dwelling would directly affect the actual production of war material." [14]

On 4 February, sixty-nine B-29s dropped over 160 tons of incendiaries on Kobe.[15] Photoreconnaissance showed the results were devastating. In one daylight raid against Tokyo on 25 February, B-29s dropped over 450 tons of incendiaries. "The results exceeded all expectations with 27,970 buildings destroyed or damaged, and B-29 losses were minimal." [16] The Joint Chiefs now favored the bombing policy of incendiary attacks against urban industrial areas on a massive scale. On 7 March, before this new plan could be put into effect, Nimitz requested the Twenty-first Bomber Command to aid in the pre-invasion campaign of Okinawa.

In contemplation of this landing, some B-29s of the Twenty-first Bomber Command were diverted from industrial targets in Japan to strategic airfields in Kyushu plus mining of the Shimonoseki Strait, the approaches to Hiroshima, Kure, and Sasebo. This change did not prevent a previously planned raid on Tokyo as well as the follow-up bombing of other major cities.

On 6 March, LeMay told his public relations officer, Lt. Col. St. Clair McKelway: "This outfit has been getting a lot of publicity without really accomplishing a hell of a lot in bombing results." [17]

On 9 March, 324 B-29s bombed Tokyo with incendiaries.[18] "Japanese police records show that 267,171 buildings were destroyed, and that 1,008,005 persons were rendered homeless. The official total of casualties listed 83,793 dead and 40,918 wounded." [19] Radio Tokyo labeled the raids as "slaughter bombing." One broadcast reported that "the sea of flames which enclosed the residential and commercial sections of Tokyo was reminiscent of the holocaust of Rome, caused by the Emperor Nero." [20] Meador said he could never forget the sight of Tokyo burning. Looking below he could see only a sea of fire. Nowhere could he see the ground, the fire was so thick. He said American losses were not heavy.[21] Three more raids on major industrial cities followed in quick succession.

On 11 March, 313 B-29s attacked Nagoya, the Japanese aircraft center, with an estimated 1,790 tons of incendiaries.[22] The results were not as good as in the Tokyo raid because many bombs fell short of the target, but it still caused severe damage. Again, on 13 March, 274 B-29s dropped 1,644 tons of incendiary clusters on the industrial heart of Osaka. Fires throughout the city resulted in more than eight squares miles being burned out.[23]

On 16 March, 307 B-29s struck Kobe. Some 2,355 tons of combined oil and thermite clusters were dropped, destroying 65,951 houses. The entire eastern section of the business district and the industrial southeast including the submarine shipyards were gutted.[24]

In just eleven days, the Twenty-first Bomber Command flew 1,595 sorties against four of Japan's key industrial centers. Much greater damage lay yet in store. For the remainder of the war, Japan could not stop strategic air operations against her major cities, nor was she capable of taking the offensive in any theater due to the lack of oil.

Throughout the war, Japan needed between 6 and 7 million tons of petroleum per year, but her domestic production totaled only 250,000 tons. The oil fields of the Dutch East Indies and British Borneo, when captured, gave Japan the 7 million tons of oil per year needed for her war machine, provided the crude product could be moved to Japan's refineries, then returned to the war fronts. Thus, lack of transportation caused Japan's petroleum problem. American submarines had ravaged Japan's tanker fleet. No tanker reached Japan after March 1945. After the war, the U.S. Strategic Bombing Survey concluded that the lack of raw materials alone, especially oil, would have gradually reduced the output of Japanese industries to insignificance, even without the strategic bombing campaign. The noose around the home islands was drawn tighter by the invasion of Okinawa.

Nimitz called upon the Twenty-first Bomber Command to hit airfields in Honshu, Kyushu, and Shikoku in coordination with Seventh Fighter Command, now operating from airfields on Iwo Jima. LeMay again objected strongly to giving Nimitz this support because it slowed down his destruction of Japan's industrial might; however, the Joint Chiefs overruled him. From 16 April to 11 May, a large percentage of the Twenty-first Bomber Command's effort was directed to the support of the Okinawa campaign. On 11 May, when Nimitz released the Twenty-first Bomber Command from Okinawa operations, he stated he had a sufficient force of aircraft on the island itself.

In preparation for the invasion of Kyushu and Honshu, the Joint Chiefs planned a complete blockade of the home islands plus an intensive bombing campaign from Okinawa, Iwo Jima, and the Marianas. By June 1945, LeMay had carried his attack against many smaller cities of Japan. Before the first atomic bomb was dropped, sixty-six Japanese cities had been severely damaged by B-29s. In the fifth volume of *The Army Air Forces in World War II*, sixty-one of the smaller cities are listed as greatly damaged, some with populations as low as 40,000.[25]

General Arnold flew to the Marianas in early June. He met with LeMay and his staff, where he received a briefing on past operations and future plans. Near the end of the session, Arnold turned to LeMay. "I'm asking this question to everyone I see out here. When is the war going to be over?" LeMay replied, "We're too busy fighting to figure out a date but if you give me thirty minutes I'll give you an estimate." LeMay took several staff officers aside and said, "Go back and find out when we're going to run out of industrial areas as targets." A short time later, one of the officers handed LeMay a note. He told Arnold, "We'll run out of big strategic cities and targets by 1 October. I can't see the war going on much beyond that date." Arnold had always believed that Japan could be defeated by air power. He turned again to LeMay, "I want you to go back to Washington and give the briefing you've given me to the Joint Chiefs." [26] In sharp contrast to U.S. Army thinking, the top echelons of both the U.S. Navy and U.S. Army Air Force believed that Japan could be defeated without an invasion of the home islands.

Arnold, like LeMay, believed that Japan could now be defeated by air power and that LeMay could convince the Joint Chiefs to call off the planned invasion. The Joint Chiefs failed to be persuaded by LeMay's presentation. Upon his return to Guam, LeMay gave a briefing in which he said, "Japan has been defeated. It's merely a matter of time until they get their leadership to find a way to capitulate. They are totally defeated now. They must surrender. It's just a matter of time." [27]

However, the bombing tempo against Japan increased. By July, the tonnage dropped on the home islands had tripled that of March. Japanese production of war materials declined sharply. Oil refinery production decreased 83.5 percent; aircraft engine manufacture was down by 75 percent; airframes were down by 60 percent; and electronics equipment by more than 75 percent.[28]

In July, Gen. Carl Spaatz assumed command of the new United States Strategic Air Forces in the Pacific. This consisted of the Fifth, Seventh, Thirteenth, and Twentieth Air Forces, as well as the Twenty-first Bomber Command. Units of the Eighth Air Force in Europe were in the process of being redeployed to the Pacific theater. Spaatz decided to establish his headquarters at Guam.

The Twentieth Air Force headquarters officially moved to Harmon Field, Guam, with Twentieth Bomber Command inactivated and Twenty-first Bomber Command absorbed by HQ Twentieth Air Force. Major General Curtis LeMay assumed command of the reorganized air force.

On 20 July, the 509th Composite Group began a series of twelve precision attacks over Japan for familiarization purposes with tactics contemplated for scheduled atomic strikes. While the 509th practiced, seventy-five B-29s continued hitting the oil refinery and petroleum center at Kawasaki while another twenty-nine B-29s mined waters at Fushiki, Nanao, Pusan, Obama, and Sustin.

On 1 August, General Spaatz met with MacArthur and Kenney at Manila. Spaatz did not believe that a landing in the home islands would be necessary. He was so impressed with the efficiency of the Twentieth Air Force that on 2 August, he declared "that unless Japan desires to commit national suicide, they should quit immediately." [29]

"August 1 was Air Force Day and Arnold ordered a show of strength over the Empire. Seven hundred and sixty-two B-29s struck four cities and a petroleum center. Certainly a wing to each city was exorbitant but that wasn't the point. There were so few target cities remaining that LeMay didn't have a choice. After fire attacks against Hachioji, Nagasaki, Toyama, and Mito, and the destruction of Kawasaki Petroleum Center, Japanese radio broadcasts were frank in admitting terrible destruction and loss of life. Only one plane was lost and the crew was seen to bail out over Japan." [30]

In the month of July, B-29s made numerous mine-laying missions to the Korean ports of Rashin, Seshin, Gensan, and Fusad plus the Japanese ports of Fushiki, Nanao, and Niigata, all on the inland sea of Japan. Rashin missions proved to be the longest missions by any aircraft in World War II, as the minefields were 2,050 nautical miles from Tinian. A B-29 mission to Rashin (on July 11) flew the entire 4,100 miles nonstop, landing at North Field nineteen hours and forty minutes after takeoff. (Rashin is only sixty miles south of the Siberian port of Vladivostok.) This was undoubtedly the longest nonstop mission of the war. Most other B-29s stopped at Iwo Jima for refueling, either on the trip to Korean and Japanese ports or on the return flight back. [31]

The mining campaign complemented the bombing attacks by reducing Japan's essential supplies. United States Navy submarines sank 55 percent of all Japanese ships during the war, while the Twentieth Air Force accounted for 9.3 percent in four and a half months of mining operations. In congratulating LeMay, Nimitz said, "The planning and technical operation of aircraft mining on a scale never before attained has accomplished phenomenal results." [32]

During the last days of the war, the B-29s dropped leaflets in advance of attacks to warn the Japanese cities of their impending doom. [33] The finest tribute to LeMay and Arnold's faith in the B-29 came from Japanese leaders after the war. Prince Nauhiku Higashi-Kuni said, "The general conditions of the country began to show marked signs of impoverishment and exhaustion. So much so that in the days just preceding the termination of the war it seemed almost impossible to carry on modern warfare further for any long period of time." [34]

Prince Konoe said, "Fundamentally the thing that brought about the determination to make peace was the prolonged bombing by the B-29s." [35]

Premier Suzuki agreed. "It seemed to me unavoidable that, in the long run, Japan would be almost destroyed by air attack so that merely on the basis of the B-29s alone I was convinced that Japan should sue for peace." [36]

Prince Higashikuni said, "We had nothing in Japan that we could use against such a weapon. From the point of view of the Home Defense Command, we felt that the war was lost and said so. If the B-29s could come over Japan, there was nothing that could be done." [37]

The huge success of the Twentieth Air Force did not come about without exacting a substantial price. B-29 overseas losses totaled 512, while training losses in the States claimed another 260 Superforts. Some 576 fliers were killed, with another 2,400 missing in action. Most who bailed out over Japan were killed immediately by either the Japanese militia or civilians. This is understandable in view of the destruction and killing of Japanese civilians. However, it is interesting to note that 40 crewmen of the 6th Bombardment Group alone who bailed out over Japan were placed in prison camps and liberated after V-J Day.[38] Nevertheless, crew losses amounted to only 1.38 percent of all sorties.[39]

In reference to the defeat of Japan, the official Army Air Force history concluded that:

> In awarding credit for this victory, the extremely tough fighting that had fallen to the lot of the American ground soldier could not be ignored, but his task fundamentally had been to advance the bases from which air and naval forces operated. His role, in other words, had been a supporting one and the war had been won, despite the script, without his having to assume the lead. Something new had been added to America's experience with war—something that called for close study.
>
> It was evident enough that victory belonged primarily to air and sea power . . .[40]

It is interesting to note that Nimitz's command captured all bases from which the U.S. Army and naval air forces operated against the Japanese home islands.

Chapter 29
Japanese Surrender

AFTER THE FALL OF OKINAWA, Japan was clearly a defeated nation, but bringing about her surrender was the product of great dissension within the Imperial ranks. The question of how best to end the war also divided American forces.

The Joint Chiefs of Staff changed the command structure in the Pacific on 3 April 1945. The new Pacific Directive designated MacArthur commander in chief of U.S. Army Forces, Pacific. He was given control over all American army and army air force units except those in the inactive North and southeast Pacific areas and the Twentieth Air Force units in the Marianas, which remained under control of the Joint Chiefs. All naval resources in the Pacific except those in the southeast region came under the control of Admiral Nimitz. The change in command accelerated the acrimony between the U.S. Navy and U.S. Army.

Preliminary negotiations between Nimitz and MacArthur's Chief of Staff Sutherland aroused deep concern among the Joint Chiefs. Sutherland was reported to have advanced the view that all the Joint Chiefs' command arrangements had been unsatisfactory and that unity of command was an unworkable shibboleth. He noted further that, in the future, no army troops would be allowed to serve under an admiral.[1] So concerned was General Marshall that on 15 April 1945, he wrote a scathing letter to MacArthur in which he said, "It is very embarrassing for me to feel compelled to take up with you a question of the employment of your staff officer, but I seriously doubt the advisability of utilizing Sutherland in further negotiations with the Navy."[2]

In reference to his previous contacts with Sutherland, Marshall commented, "Unfortunately he appears utterly unaware of the effect of his methods but, to put it bluntly, his attitude in almost every case seems to have been that he knew it all and nobody else knew much of anything . . . The difficulty with the Navy in most of these cases lies with the feeling that Staff negotiations would present extraordinary difficulties if conducted for you by Sutherland."[3] A notation in General Marshall's file of correspondence with MacArthur states that this message was never sent.

As early as November 1944 the military staff in the Pentagon began working on Operation Downfall, the final assault on the programmed invasion of Japan. The Joint Chiefs tentatively approved the draft for Operation Olympic, the invasion of Kyushu, to begin on 1 September 1945, and Operation Coronet, the invasion of Honshu, on 1 December 1945. The actual campaigns on Leyte, Luzon, Iwo Jima, and Okinawa lasted longer than anticipated so that both Olympic and Coronet had to be postponed.

In April 1945, the Joint Chiefs considered the options for bringing about Japan's defeat. King proposed three alternatives to Nimitz, namely "1) encirclement, meaning blockade and bombardment; 2) invasion; and 3) both, pursuing encirclement while preparing fully for invasion." [4] Although Nimitz had pushed for the encirclement strategy at the beginning of the year, he now agreed to the invasion of Kyushu.[5] On 20 April, in response to a query by Marshall, MacArthur claimed that reliance on air and naval power would prolong the conflict indefinitely as he approved the assault on Kyushu in November and Honshu in March 1946.[6]

At no time could MacArthur bring himself to adopt the siege strategy of the prewar Plan Orange, even though this strategy had previously proved highly successful in use by the U.S. Army. For seven and a half decades after the close of the American Civil War, every West Point graduate knew or should have known how Ulysses S. Grant captured Vicksburg. After losing numerous soldiers by direct attack, with little damage to the enemy, Grant laid siege to the city. With nothing in and nothing out, coupled with forty-seven days of constant shelling, the Confederates surrendered on 4 July 1863. Thereafter, Grant became Abraham Lincoln's favorite general.

In mid-May, MacArthur and Nimitz reached agreement on Olympic and submitted their proposals to the Joint Chiefs on 25 May. The Kyushu invasion would be preceded by attacks of unprecedented magnitude by aircraft of the Far East Air Forces, the Twentieth Air Force, and Pacific Fleet carriers. Kruger's Sixth Army, consisting of eleven U.S. Army and three Marine Corps divisions, would lead the initial assault.

Wrangling over the location of a unified command headquarters began when General Arnold transmitted Admiral King's suggestion that MacArthur establish a command post with Admiral Nimitz at Guam. MacArthur wrote Marshall, ". . . this suggestion is impractical of accomplishment . . . Please tell Admiral King that I disagree totally with his concept that a long campaign experience has convinced me that if there is any one feature of a field commander that must be left to his sole judgment it is the location of his command post and the actual disposition of his own person." [7]

In General Arnold's diary of his meeting with MacArthur on 17 June, he noted the latter believed ". . . that bombing can do (a) lot to end the war but in final analysis doughboys will have to march into Tokyo . . . Can see no reason why we should not use gas right now against Japan proper. Any kind of gas.

Sees no reason for gassing Japs in by-passed areas . . . As far as moving his Headquarters to Guam for coordination and cooperation are concerned, the lid blew off—there was every reason why it should not be done, not one good reason for doing it." [8] Nevertheless, on 1 July 1945 Nimitz wrote MacArthur of the advantages to be gained by having him, Spaatz, and Nimitz together at Guam for frequent consultation. He stated, ". . . I hope that you will give consideration to establishing your advance headquarters on Guam well in advance of the coming operation. It is my feeling that this should take place not later than 1 September and as much earlier as your operations will permit. I believe that this arrangement will be most conducive to maximum success in the operations with which we are charged."

Nimitz pointed out that at Guam extensive communication installations necessary for the control of major operations had already been developed, that the headquarters now occupied by Admiral Spruance and his staff could be expanded to accommodate an echelon of MacArthur's headquarters staff, and that he would make available to MacArthur quarters identical with his own. He further noted that General Spaatz would have his headquarters on Guam. In closing, Nimitz noted that "In addition to the military advantage which would accrue, I would personally be most happy at your coming." [9] Nimitz's message made more sense when coupled with the fact that the primary bombing of the Japanese home islands would continue to originate from Saipan, Tinian, and Guam, joined by planes from Okinawa, and that Ulithi would remain as the U.S. Pacific Fleet's main staging base for the proposed invasion. Nevertheless, MacArthur did not change his mind.

Prior to the Joint Chiefs' directive of 3 April 1945, which changed the command structure in the Pacific, there existed a deep division between army and navy planners as to whether an invasion of Japan was desirable and necessary. As early as April 1944, the Operations Division of the War Department took the position that only invasion, not blockading and bombardment, could assure Japan's collapse. For many years, the U.S. Navy had taken the opposite view. The prewar Plan Orange envisioned Japan's defeat when it could no longer move materials and troops onto or off the home islands. Admirals Leahy, King, Halsey, and Spruance believed an invasion to be unnecessary, although King later agreed to such in order to make the decision of the Joint Chiefs unanimous. In late April, King's memorandum to the Joint Chiefs stated:

> It is clear that, if the invasion of Kyushu is to be undertaken on 1 November, a directive to that effect must be issued now in order that the necessary preparations can go forward. It is my belief that, if such a directive is issued and the operation is given top priority, the necessary resources can be assembled . . . If at a later date, such as August or September 1945, the Chiefs of Staff should decide against the Kyushu operation, they will then be in a position to exercise the choice.[10]

It is clear that British members of the Combined Chiefs of Staff did not feel that the Joint Chiefs had reached a final decision to invade Japan. As late as 24 May 1945 Field Marshal Alan F. Brooke wrote in his diary:

> . . . We want, if possible, to participate with all three Services in the attacks against Japan. It is, however, not easy to make plans as the Americans seem unable to decide between a policy of invasion as opposed to one of encirclement.[11]

Outside the Joint Chiefs of Staff, other high-ranking naval officers felt that an invasion of the Japanese home islands was unnecessary to win the war. After Okinawa, Spruance said:

> It was my opinion at the time, and I have never had any reason to change it, that landings in Japan proper, such as the planned Kyushu landings on 1 November 1945, were not necessary and would have been extremely costly. From our island positions around Japan, we had enough airfields for bombing objectives in Japan itself if further bombing attacks were needed. We controlled the sea approaches to Japan. Japan was cut off from the outside world, except to Korea and North China, and our submarines had been able to enter the Sea of Japan and operate there.
>
> In war the time element is often an important consideration. Sometimes time is working for the enemy and we ought then to push the fighting. In the case of World War II, towards the end, time was decidedly on our side. Japan was cut off and could well have been permitted to 'die on the vine' as we had done with the by-passed islands in the Pacific.[12]

Admiral Halsey held a similar opinion. He believed that preparations for the invasion of Japan were a waste of time and the dropping of atomic bombs was unnecessary. After the war, he quoted the statement of Adm. Soemu Toyoda, chief of the Japanese Naval General Staff:

> I do not think it would be accurate to look upon use of the atomic bomb and the entry and participation of Soviet Russia as direct causes of the termination of the war, but I think that those two factors did enable us to bring the war to a termination without creating too great chaos in Japan.[13]

Lieutenant General Holland Smith agreed with Halsey and Spruance. Upon his return to the United States on 5 July 1945, Smith held a press conference at the St. Francis Hotel in San Francisco. He told the newsmen that the war in the Pacific would be over by 1 September 1945.[14] He, too, believed that Japan had already been defeated and that an invasion of the home islands was unnecessary. Later, he wrote that at the time of his press conference he had no knowledge of the atomic bomb. He said, "The atom bomb did not win the war; it only completed the job already done and hastened surrender." [15]

The revelation of Japan's true economic situation soon after American troops occupied Japan appears to have justified Halsey, Spruance, and Smith's opinion. Japanese industrial production in September 1945 was only one-third of the 1934–36 levels. The shortage of food had reduced the average per capita intake to 1,500 calories daily.[16] The question arises, how long would the Japanese continue to resist had there been no atomic bomb? But more important, did the American public have the patience to continue the war without an invasion of the home islands? The best evidence indicates it did not. In a 1 June 1945 Gallup public opinion poll, Americans favored continuing the war rather than accepting a hypothetical peace offer with no occupation of Japan.[17]

On 25 May, one day after Sir Alan F. Brooke observed in his diary that the Americans could not decide between invasion or encirclement, the Joint Chiefs ordered preparations for the invasion of Japan. President Harry S. Truman did not readily agree that such action was necessary. On 17 June 1945, Truman wrote in his diary about his "hardest decision to date . . . I have to decide Japanese strategy. Shall we invade Japan proper or shall we bomb and blockade?" [18] The president was deeply concerned about the potential for staggering American losses. Iwo Jima and Okinawa seemed to foreshadow what the struggle for the Japanese homeland would be like. Former President Herbert Hoover sent a memorandum to Truman dated 30 May 1945, in which he recommended "that the Japanese retain Korea and Formosa as trustees under the world trustee system." [19] Hoover urged the abandonment of the unconditional surrender formula because he envisioned an invasion would cost between 500,000 and 1 million American fatalities.

At a White House meeting of the Joint Chiefs and the president on 18 June, Marshall noted that the impact of the Russian entry against the hopeless Japanese might well be the decisive action, causing them to capitulate at that time or shortly after the Americans landed in Japan. He quoted MacArthur:

> I believe the operation presents less hazards of excessive loss than any other that has been suggested and that its decisive effect will eventually save lives by eliminating wasteful operations of non-decisive character. I regard the operation as the most economical one in effort and lives that is possible. In this respect it must be remembered that the several preceding months will involve practically no losses in ground troops and that sooner or later a decisive ground attack must be made. The hazard and loss will be greatly lessened if an attack is launched from Siberia sufficiently ahead of our target date to commit the enemy to major combat. I most earnestly recommend no change in OLYMPIC. Additional subsidiary attacks will simply build up our final total casualties.[20]

Admiral King added his concurrence, as he believed that Kyushu would be vital to the air and sea blockade of Japan.

"The minutes record that Truman then commented that this "was practically creating another Okinawa closer to Japan," to which all the Chiefs of Staff agreed." [21] He now believed the Kyushu invasion should go forward, although he continued to receive reports that the Allies already had a stranglehold on Japan's ability to take the offensive. He was also aware that the United States home front was no longer unified to the extent it had been prior to V-E (Victory in Europe) Day. In the military service itself, no one wanted to be the last man or among the last to be killed in action. Mothers and wives of European veterans felt that their sons and husbands had experienced enough of war; it was now time to let somebody else do the fighting.

After Germany's defeat, military planners also recognized that a one-front war could not justify a force needed for a two-front war, and herein lay an explosive political situation. The American public demanded a partial demobilization. Individual servicemen feared it would be difficult to find jobs upon their return home.

As early as September 1944, the War Department issued a public plan that directed demobilization by individuals, not units. Individuals received points for length of service (one point for each month), overseas service (one point for each month), battle participation (five points for each campaign), decorations (five points for each), and dependents (twelve points per child for up to three children). Subject to involuntary retention under a military necessity clause, those with the highest scores would be discharged.[22]

"A poll showed seventy-two percent of Americans expected a partial demobilization while the rest wanted even more." [23] Fred Vinson, director of the Office of War Mobilization and Reconversion and later Chief Justice of the Supreme Court, warned the Joint Chiefs that he had never seen "the people in their present frame of mind. He was fearful of unrest in the country." [24]

On 12 May 1945, the War Department announced eighty-five as the magic number for immediate discharge. Thirty days were authorized for each command to accomplish personnel readjustment before European divisions moved for embarkation. Obviously, the battle-hardened and seasoned sergeants and corporals the unit commanders relied on in battle were redeployed home to the United States. General Dwight Eisenhower estimated it would take at least six months of further training to restore the European units to combat readiness. The profound difference in the character of fighting in the Pacific also mandated the retraining. In addition, the benefits offered by the GI Bill of Rights increased the desire of the veteran serviceman to return home rather than participate in the war against Japan.

The U.S. Navy and Marine Corps refused to embark on demobilization. Nimitz expressly recommended to King that all discharges and rotations be deferred until after Olympic. One can only guess whether the Navy Department would have been able to oppose public opinion through 1 November 1945.

Understanding the reality to end the Pacific War requires an examination of both MAGIC (diplomatic) and ULTRA (military) intercepts and the conditions inside Japan itself. Prior to mid-July, MAGIC had revealed a number of Japanese peace feelers in some European capitals. As early as May 1945, the Japanese Supreme War Direction Council began active discussion of ways and means to end the war, and talks were initiated with Soviet Russia seeking her intercession as mediator.[25] There was no diplomatic initiative by the Japanese government itself, with the exception of talks between former Premier Hirota and Soviet Ambassador Malik in Tokyo. These talks, aimed at opening Japanese negotiations with the Soviets, elicited no Soviet interest. ULTRA reports revealed that the Japanese army intended to fight to the finish, yet neither they nor most of the American top military were aware of the latest stage of development of the atomic bomb.

By the fall of 1944, the scientists of the Manhattan Project were absolutely confident that the atomic bomb could be produced by the summer of 1945. At a meeting with Stimson on December 1944, Roosevelt approved the production and testing of the bombs and the training of crews for their delivery. The B-29s were ordered not to bomb the cities where the atomic bomb might be dropped. The U.S. Air Force wanted some unspoiled targets for the new weapon. Stimson eliminated Kyoto from the list of cities presented by Gen. Hap Arnold. When Arnold argued that Kyoto was an important manufacturing center with a population of 743,000, Stimson countered that it was one of the holy cities of the world and had an outstanding religious significance. The four cities selected were Hiroshima, Niigata, Nagasaki, and Kokura. The War Department listed the four cities in its 24 July 1945 letter of instructions to U.S. Air Force Gen. Carl Spaatz.[26]

In mid-July, the Allies held a meeting to determine the final surrender offer to Japan. Representatives of the United States, Great Britain, China, and the Soviet Union met at Potsdam, on the outskirts of Berlin. President Harry Truman with his Secretary of State James Byrnes reached Potsdam on 15 July. Two days after his arrival, the president learned of the first successful explosion of the atomic bomb shortly before meeting with Churchill and Stalin. Truman's diary records his luncheon with Churchill the next day:

> Discussed Manhattan [the atomic bomb project] (it is a success). Decided to tell Stalin about it. Stalin had told [Churchill] of telegram from Jap Emperor asking for peace. Stalin read his answer to me. It was satisfactory. Believe Japs will fold up before Russia comes in. I am sure they will when Manhattan appears over their homeland. I shall inform Stalin about it at an opportune time.[27]

On 18 July the president wrote Bess Truman, "I'll say that we'll end the war a year sooner now, and think of the kids who won't be killed."[28]

On 25 July, Truman's diary notes his intention to use the "most terrible bomb in the history of the world," but to issue a warning first.[29]

On 26 July the United States, Great Britain, and China publicly released the Potsdam Declaration to give Japan an opportunity to end the war. The Soviet Union was still officially neutral. On this same day, the cruiser *Indianapolis* delivered the U-235 portion of an atomic bomb nicknamed "Little Boy" at the island of Tinian. After warning of the inevitable "utter devastation of the Japanese homeland" the declaration declared: "The following are our terms. We will not deviate from them. There are no alternatives. We shall brook no delay." [30] The declaration itemized, in part, dismissal " 'for all time the authority and influence of those who have deceived and misled the people of Japan into embarking on world conquest'; occupation of 'points' in Japan until the new order is established and 'convincing proof' is provided that war-making power has been destroyed; limitation of Japan's sovereignty to basically the home islands; and complete disarmament of Japanese military forces, after which the soldiers and sailors may 'return to their homes with the opportunity to lead peaceful and productive lives.' " [31]

If Japan agreed, the Allies guaranteed the establishment of freedom of speech, religion, and thought "as well as respect for the fundamental human rights." Japan would retain her industries, pay just reparations in kind, be granted access to raw materials, and gain eventual access to world trade relations. The Allies also promised that "the occupying forces of the Allies shall be withdrawn from Japan as soon as these objectives have been accomplished and there has been established in accordance with the freely expressed will of the Japanese people a peacefully inclined and responsible government." In the last paragraph the Allies called upon the government of Japan "to proclaim now the unconditional surrender of all Japanese armed forces." The document also ensured that the Allies did not intend the Japanese to "be enslaved as a race or destroyed as a nation . . . stern justice shall be meted out to war criminals." [32]

Australian External Affairs Minister Herbert Evatt protested that the terms proffered to Japan were "much more lenient than those imposed on Germany." [33]

In Japan, Foreign Minister Togo cautioned the Supreme Council on 27 July that it would be extremely impolite for Japan to reject the Potsdam Declaration. He secured agreement from the top ministers plus the cabinet not to discuss publicly the declaration but to pursue clarification through the Soviets. Because there could be no expectation that the Allies would not alert the Japanese public of the declaration by radio or leaflet, the newspapers received an expurgated version of the declaration. However, by the next morning, the Japanese media trumpeted the rejection of the Potsdam Declaration by Japan's rulers. By the afternoon, Prime Minister Suzuki stated to the press, "The government does not regard it (the Potsdam Declaration) as a thing of any value; the government will just ignore it. We will press forward resolutely to carry the war to a successful conclusion." [34] Nevertheless, at the 28 July meeting in Potsdam, Stalin announced that on 18 July Japan had requested him to mediate for them to end the war with the Allies. Japan would send a royal prince to Moscow as chief of the mission. Stalin turned down the Japanese proposal as being too vague to warrant his approval. He then said he had received another message from the Japanese this same day, "That the duty of the proposed mission was to try to avoid more bloodshed, to inform him of the policy that Japan would adopt toward Russia, and to make an offer of collaboration with Russia." Stalin said he would again turn them down. Stalin declared that the Soviets would enter the Far East war on 15 August. Admiral Leahy observed, "It was clearly evident that Stalin was at the time determined to enter the war against Japan which plainly was to the advantage of Russia now that Japan was certain to be defeated." [35]

At midnight on 29 July a Japanese submarine caused the sinking of the cruiser *Indianapolis* en route to Leyte. However, it was 3 August before the news of her sinking reached Guam. Her few survivors, after four days on rafts and in the water, had just been found. Admiral Nimitz promptly ordered a court of inquiry to convene at Guam to determine why the cruiser's failure to arrive at Leyte Gulf had not been reported. As a result, after the war a court-martial was ordered of Capt. Charles McVay. He "was charged with 1) hazarding the safety of his ship by neglecting to zigzag, and 2) failing to issue timely orders to abandon ship." [36] He was found not guilty of the latter charge but guilty of charge 1) even though Cmdr. Mochitsura Hashimoto, skipper of the Japanese submarine that sank the *Indianapolis*, testified that the *Indianapolis* could have been hit whether or not she had been zigzagging.[37] The members of the court-martial and judge advocate recommended Captain McVay to clemency. He was restored to duty.

On 30 July, Suzuki learned at a meeting of the Cabinet Advisory Council that the nation's leading businessmen had urged Japan to accept the Potsdam terms. He told the director of the Cabinet Information Bureau, "Precisely at a time like this, if we hold firm, they will yield before we do. Just because they have broadcast their Declaration, it is not necessary to stop fighting. You advisers may ask me to reconsider, but I don't think there is any need to stop (the war)." [38]

Truman, Byrnes, Stimson, Leahy, and Arnold reached a consensus at Potsdam that the atomic bomb should be used. Truman wrote: "I asked General Marshall what it would cost in lives to land on the Tokyo plain and other places in Japan. It was his opinion that such an invasion would cost at a minimum a quarter of a million American casualties . . ." Truman agreed and added, "I did not like the weapon." [39] Leahy did not agree that the bomb should be used, but to what extent he voiced his objection is not clear. He would write later:

> It is my opinion that the use of this barbarous weapon at Hiroshima and Nagasaki was of no material assistance in our war against Japan. The Japanese were already defeated and ready to surrender because of the effective sea blockade and the successful bombing with conventional weapons.[40]

Having reached the decision on the terms of surrender and the use of the bomb, what to do about the Japanese Emperor now became a major concern. Both the United States and Japan should be thankful that Joseph C. Grew became Undersecretary of State on 20 December 1944. He insisted that if Japan surrendered unconditionally, she should maintain her emperor. In late May, Grew called on President Truman, requesting that he explicitly state that Hirohito could retain his throne if Japan surrendered. Truman, though sympathetic, did not feel qualified to make so vital a policy decision without the advice of his military.[41] At Truman's request, Grew consulted General Marshall and Secretaries Forrestal and Stimson. They advised against making such assurances at the time.

To the end, Grew insisted that by maintaining the emperor both the Allies and the Japanese would be well served. It is fortunate that his view prevailed over public opinion. A Gallup poll in June 1945 showed that only 7 percent thought the emperor should be retained, even as a puppet. One-third of the people thought he should be executed as a war criminal.[42]

With no indication that Japanese surrender was in sight, a B-29 named "Enola Gay" dropped the first atomic bomb on Hiroshima on 5 August at 7:15 P.M. Washington time. The next day, at 11:00 A.M., President Truman issued the following message:

> Sixteen hours ago an American airplane dropped one bomb on Hiroshima . . . It is an atomic bomb. It is a harnessing of the basic power of the universe . . . We are now prepared to obliterate more rapidly and completely every productive enterprise the Japanese have above ground in any city. We shall destroy their docks, their factories, and their communications. Let there be no mistake; we shall completely destroy Japan's power to make war . . . If they do not now accept our terms they may expect a rain of ruin from the air, the like of which has never been seen on this earth. . .[43]

Feelings of relief swept the country among families with sons or husbands in the service. To those serving in the Pacific and others in Europe preparing to be sent, the news came as joyous relief. But many Americans felt great terror at the bomb's use. Hanson Baldwin in the *New York Times* expressed it best when he wrote, "Yesterday, we clinched victory in the Pacific, but we sowed the whirlwind."[44] For the next few days American newspapers speculated on the Japanese death toll together with the destruction. However, no news came from the emperor.

Both War and Navy Departments tried to influence Truman's selection of an officer to preside at the Japanese surrender ceremony. The U.S. Army won. On 8 August, Truman, a World War I captain of an army artillery unit in the Rainbow Division, made his decision in favor of MacArthur to head the Japanese occupation. When Admiral Nimitz heard of MacArthur's appointment over the radio, he was obviously annoyed as he exclaimed, "Well, this does it!"[45] He did not necessarily want to command the occupation, but "what he opposed was bringing an Army officer front and center when the Navy had born the brunt of the war against Japan."[46] Nimitz's command had sunk the Japanese navy, had caused its merchant's fleet to rest on the ocean's bottom, and had captured each and every island needed to destroy the Japanese manufacturing facilities. In contrast, to use prizefight language, MacArthur's command never laid a glove on the Japanese home islands. Because of American public opinion, the selection of MacArthur was an easy decision for Truman.

Even though Americans paid a heavy price for key territory, namely the Marianas, Iwo Jima, and Okinawa, American casualties sustained in the Pacific War were less that one-fourth of those experienced by the United States alone in the subjugation of Germany.[47] Admirals Ernest J. King and Chester W. Nimitz, plus Gen. Henry H. "Hap" Arnold, deserve the major credit for directing the American armed forces to victory at such a low cost in men and materials. Although he could never adopt the strategy responsible for Japan's defeat, Gen. Douglas A. MacArthur was awarded the grand prize, that is, supreme commander for the Allied powers in Japan. In his drive to liberate the Philippines, MacArthur received more favorable publicity in the United States than did any other field grade officer. A March 1945 survey conducted by the American Institute of Public Opinion found that the American public considered MacArthur to be the greatest American army general of World War II, substantially more popular than either Eisenhower or Patton, who came in second and third, respectively.[48] Clearly, in the eyes of the public, MacArthur's appointment received strong approval from most Americans.

Soviet Foreign Minister Vyacheslav M. Molotov lobbied U.S. Ambassador W. Averell Harriman for a Red Army marshal to serve jointly with MacArthur. Harriman would not yield. After all, the Soviet Union had just entered the conflict.[49] On 12 August, Truman received approval from British Minister Clement Attlee, Stalin, and Chiang Kai-shek to appoint MacArthur as supreme commander for the Allied powers in Japan.

On 9 August, six days before their scheduled entry into the war, newspapers reported a million Soviet troops had crossed into Manchuria. Obviously, Stalin feared that Japan might surrender before 15 August. If so, the Soviets would be left out of negotiations on the disposal of Japanese acquisitions. On this same day, the Americans dropped a second atomic bomb on the Japanese seaport Nagasaki. In his radio address Truman told the American people: "I realize the tragic significance of the atomic bomb." [50]

The U.S. armed services had scheduled a third atomic bomb to be dropped on Tokyo on 19 August. However, after Nagasaki, Truman ordered a holdup until further notice. Had an atomic bomb been dropped on Tokyo, in all likelihood it would have eliminated Emperor Hirohito from the scene, a tragedy of untold proportions. Winning a war militarily can be useless unless you can also win the peace. The latter would have been most difficult without the influence of Hirohito.

On the morning of the Nagasaki bombing, Japan's Supreme Council for the Direction of the War met in Prime Minister Suzuki's bomb shelter outside the Imperial Palace. The meeting deadlocked with three powerful military commanders (two generals and one admiral) arguing against surrender. General Anami, the war minister, called for one last great battle on Japanese soil, as demanded by the Japanese honor: "Would it not be wondrous for this whole nation to be destroyed like a beautiful flower?" [51] In less than twenty-four hours after the bombing of Nagasaki, Emperor Hirohito decided that Japan must "bear the unbearable" and surrender. In his Imperial Rescript, Hirohito spoke of a "new and most cruel bomb, the power of which to do damage is indeed incalculable, taking the toll of many innocent lives." [52] The Japanese government agreed to accept the Potsdam Declaration with the understanding that the emperor would remain sovereign.

Upon receipt of the message, Truman summoned Byrnes, Stimson, Leahy, and Forrestal for a meeting at the White House at 9:00 A.M. on 10 August. Stimson and Leahy agreed that the emperor should be allowed to stay. Byrnes wanted nothing less than unconditional surrender. He argued that the Big Three had called for unconditional surrender at Potsdam. He could not understand "why now we should go further than we were willing to go at Potsdam when we had no atomic bomb and Russia was not in the war." [53] Forrestal thought that with different words the Potsdam terms could be made acceptable, which appealed to Truman. The official reply stated that the emperor would remain, but subject to the supreme commander of the Allied powers. All Allies agreed except the Australians, who were adamantly opposed: "The Emperor should have no immunity from responsibility for Japan's acts of aggression." [54] Indeed, studies after the war showed that Hirohito was equally to blame with his war ministers for Japan's conduct both before and during the war.

By Saturday, 11 August, the Australians reluctantly agreed. Then the wait began. No word came on Sunday, 12 August, or Monday, 13 August. Then, at 4:05 P.M. on Tuesday, 14 August, news reached President Truman that Japan had surrendered. At 6:10 P.M. the Swiss chargé d'affaires in Washington presented the text of the emperor's proclamation to the Secretary of State:

> Accepting the terms set forth in the Declaration issued by the heads of the Governments of the United States, Great Britain and China on July 26, 1945, at Potsdam and subsequently adhered to by the Union of Soviet Socialist Republics, I have commanded the Japanese Imperial Government and the Japanese Imperial General Headquarters to sign on my behalf the instrument of surrender presented by the Supreme Commander for the Allied Powers and to issue General Orders to the Military and Naval forces in accordance with the direction of the Supreme Commander for the Allied Powers. I command all my people forthwith to cease hostilities, to lay down their arms and faithfully to carry out all the provisions of the instrument of surrender and the General Orders issued by the Japanese Imperial General Headquarters thereunder. [55]

In response to the emperor, President Harry Truman directed General MacArthur to assume his duties as supreme commander, Allied powers. This placed the emperor and the Japanese government subject to MacArthur's will in effectuating the surrender terms. An accompanying document, "Instrument of Surrender," called for the unconditional surrender of all Japanese forces wherever situated.

Immediate problems lay ahead in getting the Japanese military to peacefully lay down their arms. Unlike the war with Germany, the great mass of the

Japanese army had not been defeated. On 15 August, Japanese Gen. Lasuji Okamura, commander of the China Expeditionary Army, said:

> Such a disgrace as the surrender of several million troops without fighting is not paralleled in the world's military history, and it is absolutely impossible to submit to unconditional surrender of a million picked troops, in perfectly healthy shape, to the Chunking forces of defeated China.[56]

Okamura was not alone among Japanese army officers in his objections to surrender. This caused a delay in the signing of the surrender document so that Emperor Hirohito could send out envoys to the scattered Japanese troops requesting that they abide by his wishes.

On 2 September 1945, Gen. Douglas A. MacArthur and Adm. Chester W. Nimitz presided over the formal Japanese surrender ceremony onboard the battleship *Missouri*. Various admirals and generals were invited and in attendance, including Gen. Jonathan M. Wainwright and Gen. A. E. Percival. Lieutenant General Holland Smith, USMC, was left off the invitation list. Representatives of all governments who had fought against Japan were present for the signing. There was a tense atmosphere on the ship after the Japanese contingent came aboard.

Prior to the signing of the surrender document, MacArthur made a short speech, which concluded:

> It is my earnest hope—indeed the hope of all mankind—that from this solemn occasion a better world shall emerge out of the blood and carnage of the past, a world founded upon faith and understanding, a world dedicated to the dignity of man and the fulfillment of his most cherished wish for freedom, tolerance and justice.[57]

Mr. Toshikazu Kase, a member of the Japanese foreign office, recorded that the general's speech transformed the battleship's quarterdeck "into an altar of peace." [58]

Afterward, by order of Emperor Hirohito, 6,983,000 Japanese servicemen[59] peacefully laid down their arms and returned to their homes. Most came from bypassed islands and the continent of Asia. Only the emperor, revered by many in the military as a god, could have received such obeisance to orders. In the days and years ahead, Hirohito would take his place alongside Emperor Meiji "the Great" as the builder of modern Japan.

Chapter 30
Looking Back

MORE THAN SIX DECADES HAVE NOW PASSED since the end of the Pacific War. For a veteran looking back, one saddens when reflecting upon the numerous brave young men whose lives were cut short. After the war, Americans of all colors and creeds experienced far greater opportunities than ever before, opportunities not enjoyed by those who died in battle.

Before war's end, the president, Congress, and U.S. military leaders determined not to duplicate the mistakes of the past, especially those following the end of World War I. Yet, planning for the future is difficult when knowledge of the past remains blurred. Tight censorship, especially in the early years of the war, plus top-secret classification of intelligence information gleaned primarily from code breaking, made it impossible for political leaders and the public to see the ongoing true picture that led to Japan's defeat. Only in recent years can historians paint a clear picture of the Pacific War and the fortunes that changed that part of the globe.

Generations following the war owe a debt of gratitude to President Franklin D. Roosevelt for his handling of the nation's economy leading up to and during the war years. In spite of the tremendous cost of the nation's military machine, he left the country's financial house with an easily manageable national debt. In fiscal 1946, the interest of $4.747 billion on the debt was less than 2.5 percent of that year's gross national product of $212 plus billion.

The United States emerged from World War II as a country of unprecedented power. Its gross national product equaled that of all other nations combined. It had the strongest navy, a large, trained army, and was sole possessor of the atomic bomb. Then came the country's first big mistake. With the war over, parents and wives demanded that their sons and husbands be returned home. In response to this overwhelming public opinion, America's great military machine disbanded far too fast and too much in view of the nation's newly acquired position as world leader. This emasculation plus other political errors—both military and non-military—led directly to the U.S. involvement in the Korean War.

The nation's leaders did not visualize the danger caused by dividing Korea at the 38th parallel with the Soviet Union accepting the Japanese surrender in the north and the Americans the surrender in the south, although it is doubtful that this could have been prevented because Soviet troops then occupied the mainland of Asia and easily could have taken all of Korea at the surrender date.

On the positive side, unlike World War I's aftermath, the United States became a guiding member of the United Nations. In addition, Congress duly recognized its war veterans. Some 7.8 million servicemen availed themselves of the benefits under the GI Bill of Rights; 2.2 million veterans[1] earned a college education, most of whom previously could not have afforded it. This resulted in a wide broadening of America's middle class.

American military leaders and Congress recognized that inter-service rivalry had prevented the best planning for war as well as the most efficient execution of strategy. Congress decided to unify the armed services under the Department of Defense. The ensuing debate certified that old prejudices die hard. To make matters worse, the severe budget cuts pitted each service against the other.

Although much smaller in size than the U.S. Army and Navy, the U.S. Marine Corps received equal and oftentimes better press than either in the Pacific War. This favorable publicity did not help its cause in the political world, where its numbers were so heavily outweighed by army and navy veterans. Army generals, including Dwight D. Eisenhower, decided to eliminate the Marine Corps as a major fighting force. They claimed it should be the U.S. Navy's police force only. In memoranda, Eisenhower said no Marine Corps unit should be larger than a regiment. Later, Gen. Omar Bradley, chairman of the Joint Chiefs of Staff, testified against the need for the Marine Corps before the House Armed Services Committee. In October 1949, he said, "I also predict that large scale amphibious operations will never occur again." In response to U.S. Army objections and little support from the U.S. Navy, Congress reduced the U.S. Marine Corps to a shadow of its former self.

The National Security Act of 1947 institutionalized the Joint Chiefs of Staff as a permanent body. It separated the U.S. Air Force from the U.S. Army and placed the U.S. Army, U.S. Navy, and U.S. Air Force in a single Department of Defense. It established the Central Intelligence Agency and the National Security Council to ensure civilian-military coordination. This new establishment did not insulate the United States from error, nor did it put an end to inter-service rivalry. President Harry S. Truman appointed James Forrestal as the first U.S. Secretary of Defense. For two years, Forrestal presided over an agency filled with constant bickering among the military services. The mental strain and physical exhaustion caused him to resign in 1949, which resulted in his suicide on 22 May.

At war's end, the American public knew that Japan had been defeated primarily at the hands of the United States, but few knew how or why. The most comprehensive study of each nation's strategy, published 1 July 1946, received very little attention. With the war over, Americans were too busy thinking about the future to concern themselves with thinking about recent horrors of the past. A yearlong investigation by a distinguished civilian panel pinpointed the reasons the United States won the war of the Pacific in less than four years. This study came under the direction of the U.S. Strategic Bombing Survey. A panel was originally established pursuant to a directive from President Roosevelt on 3 November 1944. Its purpose was to conduct an impartial and expert study of aerial attacks on Germany. On 15 August 1945, President Truman requested the survey to conduct a similar examination on the effects of the air war against Japan. The president's select group's probe and analysis actually went much further.

The panel included Franklin D'Olier, Paul H. Nitze, Henry C. Alexander, Harry L. Bowman, J. Kenneth Galbraith, Rensis Likert, Frank A. McNamee, Jr., Fred Searls, Jr., Monroe E. Spaght, Dr. Louis R. Thompson, Theodore P. Wright, and Walter Wilds. With headquarters in Tokyo, the survey had satellite units in Nagoya, Osaka, Hiroshima, and Nagasaki. In addition, mobile teams visited other parts of Japan, the islands of the Pacific, and the Asiatic mainland. The survey's complement provided for 300 civilians, 350 officers, and 500 enlisted men. The U.S. Army composed 60 percent of the military segment; the U.S. Navy, 40 percent.

For nearly a year, interrogations were made of the top Japanese army and navy officers, government officials, industrialists, political leaders, and hundreds of subordinates. Commission members studied the principal surviving Japanese records, which included wartime military planning and execution, data on Japan's economy and war production, plus overall Japanese strategic plans and background of her entry. The report confirmed the wisdom of the prewar Plan Orange as it found that:

> Japan's geographical situation determined that the Pacific war should in large measure be a war for control of the sea, and to insure control of the sea, for control of the air over it. As a result, attacks against warships and merchant ships and amphibious operations for possession of island positions on which forward bases could be located were close to the heart of the struggle. Carrier task forces, surface ships to provide logistic support, and submarines therefore assumed roles of unusual importance.[2]

As shown by his diary entries of 23 February and 19 March 1942, Eisenhower correctly foresaw the danger of placing a greater emphasis on MacArthur's Southwest Pacific Command than militarily justified. The official Australian history accurately credits Nimitz's naval forces with their attendant infantry as the decisive factor in winning the Pacific War with operations under MacArthur's command and in Burma as being subordinate.[3] Because many army officers and enlisted men rightly take pride in their branch of service, they do not concede that liberation of the Philippines had little effect on the war's final outcome.

The U.S. Strategic Bombing Survey panel found that inside Japan, "Prior to the loss of Saipan confidence in eventual victory remained high in spite of exhausting work, poor nutrition and rising black market prices."[4] It also reported that after the fall of Saipan, which could not be kept from the Japanese people, Japanese morale began to decline; however, the psychological effect was much greater on the leaders and intellectuals than on the mass of the population.[5]

This finding received very little comment by the press or public in 1946. Maybe because it implied that dropping of the atomic bomb was unnecessary, President Truman, who created the commission and accepted its report, failed to mention either in his memoirs. After more than half a century, many Americans are again asking if the use of the atomic bomb should have been avoided. In answer to this supposition, consideration should be given to the overall picture at that time. The bomb did bring an abrupt end to the Pacific War. Had the war itself lasted until 31 December 1945 or even 1 November 1945, the Soviet Union would certainly have played a much greater role in the aftermath of the Japanese surrender. In all likelihood, the Soviets would have occupied all of Korea, and had they participated in the administration of the home islands after surrender, without question, Japan itself would not be the same as it is today.

Secretary Henry L. Stimson summed it up best when he wrote, "The decision to use the atomic bomb was a decision that brought death to over a hundred thousand Japanese. No explanation can change that fact and I do not wish to gloss over it. But this deliberate, premeditated destruction was our least abhorrent choice. The destruction of Hiroshima and Nagasaki put an end to the Japanese war. It stopped the fire raids, and the strangling blockade; it ended the ghastly specter of a clash of great land armies."[6] In view of the information presented to him at the time, together with all the attendant circumstances, President Truman's decision still seems justified.

The war permanently changed the political structure in Asia. Japan achieved one of its main objectives: the expulsion of the colonial powers' influence. North and South Korea achieved independence, and fighting escalated in Asia's heaviest populated country. With Japanese troops removed, Chiang Kai-shek and Mao ZeDong renewed hostilities for control of China. Stilwell's evaluation of the Generalissimo proved imminently correct, but with the U.S. public's limited information about the true picture inside China, U.S. Foreign Service officers who agreed with him would be vilified during the early 1950s, often referred to as the McCarthy Era.

Even though MacArthur achieved, yet failed to earn, the title supreme commander, Allied powers, most historians agree with biographer D. Clayton James' evaluation. He said, "I remain convinced at this stage of my research that in the long run MacArthur's most significant contributions were made when he served as an administrator during the Japanese occupation."[7] Prior to the formal signing of the surrender document aboard the USS *Missouri*, MacArthur stated that he "did not want to debase Hirohito in the eyes of his own people, as through him it will be possible to maintain a completely orderly government."[8]

Maintaining the emperor was a wise decision, which in itself assured a peaceful transition. In addition, MacArthur in most cases showed compassion for the Japanese people. For the most part, he followed the "Initial Post-surrender Policy for Japan" as prepared by the U.S. State Department and the Joints Chiefs of Staff plan titled "Basic Directive for Post-surrender Military Government in Japan Proper." However, he personalized the occupation so that the Japanese as well as the American public were led to believe that every decision was MacArthur's. His determination to take full credit rather than sharing it with others has been the cause of some criticism. Yet, as the supreme commander, Allied powers, for the most part, he deserves praise for a job well done.

Unfortunately, MacArthur could be very convincing, even when wrong. With his advice and full approval, the Departments of Defense and State placed South Korea outside future United States defense needs. Accordingly, MacArthur's penchant for publicity may have led the Soviets and North Korea to believe that the United States would not come to the aid of South Korea in case of attack by the north. On 2 March 1949, he told the *New York Times* that both Korea and Formosa were outside the United States' defense perimeter in the Pacific and Far East. To the London *Daily Mail*, he said:

Now the Pacific has become an Anglo-Saxon lake, and our line of defense runs through the chain of islands fringing the coast of Asia. It starts with the Philippines and continues through the Ryukyu Archipelago, which includes its main bastion, Okinawa. Then it bends back through Japan and the Aleutian Island chain to Alaska.

It is interesting to note that MacArthur's view on South Korea was deemed so unimportant at the time that it appeared at the end of an article headlined "MacArthur Pledges Defense of Japan" on page 22 of the *New York Times*. Nine months later, Secretary of State Dean Acheson expressed the MacArthur view on South Korea before the National Press Club in Washington. After the Korean War broke out, he was criticized severely by politicians who claimed his remarks invited the north to attack South Korea. No one censured the supreme commander, Allied powers in Japan for being the first to make this inauspicious announcement of what should have been classified information.

When the Korean War broke out, the United States was in poor condition to fight this first United Nations war. There seemed to be a feeling inside the country that since the United States had the atomic bomb, it could certainly meet any threat of lesser magnitude. Postwar U.S. Army troops were ill-prepared for conventional warfare.

Ironically, Gen. Douglas MacArthur unwittingly saved the U.S. Marine Corps. His demand for a full-strength marine division for the Inchon landing changed its fortunes. The outstanding performance of the 1st Marine Division throughout the Korean War impressed Congress and the nation. Only by the call-up of its reserves could the Marine Corps sustain a division in the field in Korea. In appreciation for its Korean service, Congress in 1952 enacted Public

Law 416, which fixed the organizational strength of the Marine Corps and made the commandant a member of the Joint Chiefs of Staff.

During the Pacific War, and into today, cryptanalysts never received due credit for the tremendous benefits they gave to the military. Failure to declassify some information shortly after the war, especially that relating to codes and code breaking, delayed recognition of many and fueled false information about others. It was not until 1969 that the nation first learned of the contributions of the Navajo code talkers, and these brave men did not receive full recognition for their service until 1982. That year, Congress passed a resolution designating 14 August, the thirty-seventh anniversary of the Japanese surrender, as National Navajo Code Talkers Day. President Ronald Reagan issued a proclamation in tribute to "all members of the Navajo Nation and to all Native Americans who gave their special talents and their lives so that others might live." [9]

The most persistent controversy about the Pacific War concerns the dismissal of Kimmel and Short as a result of the Pearl Harbor fiasco. Numerous books and papers have been written on the subject, many claiming that Roosevelt and other officials had prior knowledge of the attack on Pearl Harbor and this information was withheld from Kimmel and Short. Historians who have delved deeply refute this claim.

In his book *Battle of Wits: The Complete Story of Codebreaking in World War II*, Stephen Budiansky spells out the falsity of the conspiracy theory that U.S. Intelligence was reading the Japanese naval code and consequently had advance warning of the Japanese attack on Pearl Harbor.

As late as 1995, the Department of Defense conducted an independent examination of whether Admiral Kimmel and General Short should be advanced on the retired list to their highest wartime grades. Dr. Edwin Dorn, the Undersecretary of Defense, was chose to conduct the inquiry. The Dorn Commission concluded that the responsibility for the Pearl Harbor disaster should not fall solely on the shoulders of Admiral Kimmel and General Short, but they should not be promoted posthumously. It found no evidence to support the conspiracy theories. Among its findings were:

> e. Information-sharing and operational cooperation were hampered by bureaucratic rivalries. The Army and Navy were separate executive departments reporting directly to the President, and only the President could ensure that they were working together. Admiral Kimmel and General Short had cordial personal relations, but felt it inappropriate to inquire into one another's professional domains. This apparently was the standard at the time. . . .
>
> g. Resources were scarce. Washington didn't have enough cryptologists and linguists to decode all the Japanese message traffic, so the analysts gave priority to diplomatic [*sic*] traffic over military traffic. The Navy in Hawaii was short of planes and crews. The Army in Hawaii was short of munitions.

h. Finally, the Japanese attack was brilliantly conceived and flaw-lessly executed.[10]

Both Kimmel and Short were competent, well-liked officers, but it is part of the military tradition to hold top commanders accountable for disasters on their watch that could have been avoided. Admiral Nimitz appropriately stated, "It could have happened to anybody."

On the cover jacket of the book *Kimmel, Short and Pearl Harbor*, by Fred Borch and Daniel Martinez, which is an analysis of the Dorn report, Norman Polmer, a naval analyst and historian, states, "The authors have faithfully reported what should be the final investigation of the Kimmel-Short case. Their perceptions, coupled with the Dorn Report, should end all controversy on this issue . . . unfortunately, they won't."

Inside the United States, World War II had a lasting effect on women and minorities. At war's end, most women quit their jobs in defense industries and either married, returned to housekeeping, or went over to some other occupation. But never again would the women of America be satisfied with the very limited job opportunities that prevailed prior to the war.

The war instilled a fighting spirit inside the races who had been discriminated against, which in time would accelerate rather than go away. Citizens of color, particularly African Americans, determined to eliminate the legal stigma of second-class citizenship that occurred before, during, and after the end of hostilities. Through a series of legal attacks against the "separate but equal doctrine" that had been condoned by previous decisions of the U.S. Supreme Court, the Court in 1954 finally reversed the 1896 decision of *Plessy v. Ferguson*. It is ironic that Earl Warren, who in 1942 vocally called for the expulsion from the West Coast of all citizens of Japanese origin or descent, as Chief Justice of the U.S. Supreme Court would write the most important civil rights decision of the twentieth century. The Court unanimously adopted Justice Holland's previous line of thinking by the landmark case of *Brown v. Board of Education*.

After considerable delay, the nation attempted to rectify the injustice done to those of Japanese descent living in the United States. On 24 February 1983 the Commission on Wartime Relocation and Internment of Civilians found that "a long and ugly history of racism led to their internment in World War II." [11] Some compensation was awarded to the Japanese Americans who had been wronged but in most cases not enough to compensate them for their true losses. "In the last year of his presidency, Ronald Reagan signed the Civil Liberties Act of 1988 which officially declared the Japanese internment a grave injustice that was carried out without adequate security reasons and without any documented acts of espionage or sabotage." [12] In 1983 a federal judge vacated Fred Korematsu's conviction. "In January 1998, Korematsu received the Medal of Freedom from President Bill Clinton, who lauded [him] as 'a man of quiet bravery' who deserved the nation's 'respect and thanks for his patient pursuit to preserve the civil liberties we hold dear.' " [13]

One cannot ignore the positive effects of scientific research that bettered daily living. The use of antibiotics and whole blood alone lengthened the lifespan of the average person. The improvement in computers, air travel, and the peaceful use of atomic energy are among the numerous positive innovations obtained from wartime research. However, the progress in social reforms has lagged behind the fast pace of progress in scientific innovations. But what was the lasting effect of the war upon the defeated Japanese people?

At war's end, Japan found itself with its cities in ruins, idle factories, and millions of nameless refugees, truly an economic basket case. In the winter of 1945, thousands of tons of food had to be shipped in to prevent many from starving. The speedy trials of Japanese war criminals saw the conviction of former Premier Hideki Tojo and lesser-known officers who had ostensibly committed war crimes. They also saw the unjust conviction of Gen. Tomoyuki Yamashita, who was erroneously held accountable for the numerous civilian lives lost in Manila.

The war turned the intelligent and resilient Japanese people toward a different direction. Like the South of the American Civil War, Japan is a much better nation today than it would have been had it achieved military victory.

Notes

INTRODUCTION

1. Samuel Eliot Morison, *Coral Sea, Midway and Submarine Actions: May 1942–August 1942*, History of United States Naval Operations in World War II, vol. 4 (Boston: Little, Brown and Company, 1960), x.

CHAPTER 1

1. John Keegan, *Intelligence in War: Knowledge of the Enemy from Napoleon to al-Qaeda* (New York: Alfred P. Knopf, 2003), 184–185.
2. Edward S. Miller, *War Plan Orange: The U.S. Strategy to Defeat Japan, 1897–1945* (Annapolis: Naval Institute Press, 1991), 33.
3. Donald M. Goldstein and Katherine V. Dillon, eds., *The Pacific War Papers: Japanese Documents of World War II* (Washington, DC: Potomac Books, 2004), 71.
4. Dirk A. Ballendorf and Merrill L. Bartlett, *Pete Ellis: An Amphibious Warfare Prophet, 1880–1923* (Annapolis: Naval Institute Press, 1997), 1.
5. Ibid., 1–2.
6. James A. Cox, quoting John J. Reber, in "Pete Ellis: A Marine . . . raised on hay and whiskey," *Marine Corps League* 57, no. 3 (Autumn 2001), 42.

7. P. N. Pierce, "The Unsolved Mystery of Pete Ellis," *Marine Corps Gazette*, February 1962, 36.
8. Ibid.
9. Lionel Wigmore, *The Japanese Thrust*, Australia in the War of 1939–1945, Series One, Army, vol. 4 (Adelaide: The Griffin Press, 1957), 1–2.
10. Ibid., 2n.
11. Cox, "Pete Ellis: A Marine . . . raised on hay and whiskey," 46.
12. Ibid.
13. Miller, *War Plan Orange*, 124.
14. Henry G. Gole, *The Road to Rainbow: Army Planning for Global War, 1934–1940* (Annapolis: Naval Institute Press, 2003), 7.
15. Herbert P. Bix, *Hirohito and the Making of Modern Japan* (New York: HarperCollins Publishers, 2000), 155.
16. Ibid.

CHAPTER 2

1. Stephen Budiansky, *Battle of Wits: The Complete Story of Codebreaking in World War II* (New York: The Free Press, 2000), 27.
2. Ibid.
3. Alan Schom, *The Eagle and the Rising Sun: The Japanese-American War, 1941–1943* (New York: W. W. Norton and Company, 2004), 186.

4. D. Clayton James, *The Years of MacArthur, 1880-1941*, vol. 1 (Boston: Houghton Mifflin Company, 1970), 403-404.

5. James MacGregor Burns, *Roosevelt: The Lion and the Fox, 1882-1940* (New York: Harcourt, Brace and World, 1956), 163.

6. Ibid.

7. Henry G. Gole, *The Road to Rainbow*, 5.

8. Ibid.

9. Ibid., 39.

10. Burns, *Roosevelt*, 257.

11. Dudley McCarthy, *South-West Pacific Area—First Year: Kokoda to Wau*, Australia in the War of 1939-1945, Series One, Army, vol. 5 (Adelaide: The Griffin Press, 1959), 32.

12. John S. D. Eisenhower, *General Ike: A Personal Reminiscence* (New York: The Free Press, 2003), 23.

13. Ibid., 20.

14. James, *The Years of MacArthur*, 501-504.

15. Eisenhower, *General Ike*, 27.

16. Keegan, *Intelligence in War*, 187.

17. Burns, *Roosevelt*, 318.

18. Ibid., 318-319.

19. Thomas M. Coffey, *Hap: The Story of the U.S. Air Force and the Man Who Built It, General Henry H. "Hap" Arnold* (New York: Viking Press, 1982), 179-180.

20. Stephen R. Shalom, "VJ-Day: Remembering the Pacific War," *Z-Magazine*, July–August 1995, http://www.wpunj.edu/hmss/polisci/faculty/shalom/ssvjday.htm.

21. Leonard Mosley, *Marshall, Hero for Our Times* (New York: Hearst Books, 1982), 121-122.

22. Jon Meacham, *Franklin and Winston: An Intimate Portrait of an Epic Friendship* (New York: Random House, 2003), 43.

23. Jon T. Hoffman, *Chesty: The Story of Lieutenant General Lewis B. Puller, USMC* (New York: Random House, 2001), 85.

24. Ed Cray, *General of the Army: George C. Marshall, Soldier and Statesman* (New York: W. W. Norton and Co., 1990), 104-106.

25. Lewis B. "Chesty" Puller, conversation with author.

26. Ronald W. Clark, *Einstein: The Life and Times* (New York: World Publishing Company, 1971), 556-557.

27. Ibid., 558.

28. Gole, *The Road to Rainbow*, 107.

CHAPTER 3

1. Kenneth J. Clifford, *Progress and Purpose: A Developmental History of the United States Marine Corps, 1900-1970* (Washington, DC: History and Museums Division, 1973), 61.

2. Charles A. Beard, *President Roosevelt and the Coming of the War, 1941: A Study in Appearances and Realities* (New Haven, CN: Yale University Press, 1948), 3.

3. Ibid.

4. George C. Marshall, memorandum to Gen. Gerow, January 16, 1941, Microfilm Reel 32, Item 1303, Lexington, VA: George C. Marshall Museum.

5. Wigmore, *The Japanese Thrust*, 55, 93.

6. Henry C. Clausen and Bruce Lee, *Pearl Harbor: Final Judgment* (New York: Crown Publishers, Inc., 1992), 75; see also B. Mitchell Simpson, III, *Admiral Harold R. Stark: Architect of Victory, 1939-1945* (Columbia, SC: University of South Carolina Press, 1989).

7. Fred Borch and Daniel Martinez, *Kimmel, Short and Pearl Harbor: The Final Report Revealed* (Annapolis: Naval Institute Press, 2005), 50.

8. U.S. Congress, Joint Estimate of Army

and Navy Air Action, March 31, 1941, *Pearl Harbor Attack Hearings*, pt. 15, exhibit 44, p. 1437; U.S. Congress, Joint Committee on the Investigation of the Pearl Harbor Attack, Report, (Washington, DC: U.S. Government Printing Office, 1946), 83–84; Gen. George C. Marshall, personal letter to Gen. Maj. Short, February 7, 1941, WPD 4449-1.

9. Louis Morton, *Strategy and Command: The First Two Years*, United States Army in World War II: The War in the Pacific (1962; repr., Washington, DC: Office of the Chief of Military History, Department of the Army, 1962), 92.

10. Bix, *Hirohito and the Making of Modern Japan*, 397.

11. Wigmore, *The Japanese Thrust*, 190–210.

12. Ibid., 110.

13. Keith Wheeler, *War Under the Pacific* (Alexandria, VA: Time-Life Books, Inc., 1980), 97.

14. Ibid.

15. Gole, *The Road to Rainbow*, 88.

16. Dan van der Vat, *The Pacific Campaign: World War II, the U.S.-Japanese Naval War, 1941–1945* (New York: Simon and Schuster, 1991), 70.

17. Gole, *The Road to Rainbow*, 88.

18. Bradford Grethen Chynoweth, *Bellamy Park: Memoirs* (Hicksville, NY: Exposition Press, 1975), 194.

19. Wigmore, *The Japanese Thrust*, 93–94.

20. Memorandum, "Operations Plan R-5," to the Adjutant General, War Department, Washington, DC, October 1, 1941, Lexington, VA: George C. Marshall Museum.

CHAPTER 4

1. Bix, *Hirohito and the Making of Modern Japan*, 418.

2. Beard, *President Roosevelt and the Coming of the War, 1941*, 192.

3. George C. Marshall Museum, Lexington, VA, in correspondence file.

4. Simpson, *Admiral Harold R. Stark*, 110–111.

5. Borch and Martinez, *Kimmel, Short and Pearl Harbor*, 54.

6. Clausen and Lee, *Pearl Harbor*, 113.

7. Simpson, *Admiral Harold R. Stark*, 111.

8. Borch and Martinez, *Kimmel, Short and Pearl Harbor*, 61.

9. Doris Kearns Goodwin, *No Ordinary Time: Franklin and Eleanor Roosevelt: the home front in World War II* (New York: Simon and Schuster, 1995), 289.

10. Ibid., 290–291.

11. Ibid., 292.

12. Ibid.

13. Keegan, *Intelligence in War*, 191.

14. Borch and Martinez, *Kimmel, Short and Pearl Harbor*, 47.

15. Carl Boyd and Akihiko Yoshida, *The Japanese Submarine Force and World War II* (Annapolis: Naval Institute Press, 1995), 58.

16. Goodwin, *No Ordinary Time*, 295.

17. William H. Bartsch, *December 8, 1941: MacArthur's Pearl Harbor* (College Station, TX: Texas A&M University Press, 2003), 193.

18. Borch and Martinez, *Kimmel, Short and Pearl Harbor*, 40.

19. Clausen and Lee, *Pearl Harbor*, 74.

20. Morton, *Strategy and Command*, 114.

CHAPTER 5

1. David Bercuson and Holger Herwig, *One Christmas in Washington: The Secret Meeting between Roosevelt and Churchill that Changed the World* (Woodstock, NY: Overlook Press, 2005), 99.

2. Ibid., 100.

3. Ibid., 101.

4. Coffey, *HAP*, 239.

5. Mary H. Williams, comp., *Chronology 1941-1945*, United States Army in World War II, (Washington, DC: Office of the Chief of Military History, Department of the Army, 1960), 4-5.

6. *New York Times*, December 13, 1941, 6.

7. *Time Magazine*, December 29, 1941), 10.

8. James A. Cox, "The Wake Chronicles," *Marine Corps League*, Spring 2000, 44.

9. *Roanoke Times*, December 13, 1941.

10. Ibid., December 20, 1941.

11. Ibid.

12. Ibid., December 21, 1941.

13. Ibid., December 22, 1941.

14. Ibid., December 23, 1941.

15. Eisenhower, *General Ike*, 76.

16. E. B. Potter, *Nimitz* (Annapolis: Naval Institute Press, 1976), 17.

17. Hanson W. Baldwin, *The Crucial Years, 1939-1941: The World at War* (New York: Harper and Row, 1976), 438.

18. Bercuson and Herwig, *One Christmas in Washington*, 265.

CHAPTER 6

1. Barbara W. Tuchman, *Stilwell and the American Experience in China, 1911-1945* (New York: Macmillan, 1970), 250.

2. Ibid.

3. Michael Schaller, *Douglas MacArthur: The Far Eastern General* (New York: Oxford University Press, 1989), 59.

4. John Miller, Jr., *Guadalcanal: the First Offensive*, United States Army in World War II: The War in the Pacific (Washington, DC: Historical Division, Department of the Army, 1949), 257.

5. James, *The Years of MacArthur*, 36.

6. John Miller, Jr., *Guadalcanal: the First Offensive*, 535.

7. Schaller, *Douglas MacArthur*, 56, 57.

8. Ibid., 58.

9. Ibid.

10. Borch and Martinez, *Kimmel, Short and Pearl Harbor*, 81.

11. William D. Leahy, *I Was There: The Personal Story of the Chief of Staff to Presidents Roosevelt and Truman, Based on His Notes and Diaries Made at the Time* (New York: Whittlesey House, 1950), 94.

12. Coffey, *Hap*, 253.

13. Ibid.

14. Ibid.

15. Dan van der Vat, *The Pacific Campaign*, 147.

16. Robert H. Ferrell, ed., *The Eisenhower Diaries* (New York: Norton, 1981), 49.

17. Ibid., 50-51.

18. Morison, *Coral Sea, Midway and Submarine Actions*, 3.

19. Manny Lawton, *Some Survived* (Chapel Hill, NC: Algonquin Books of Chapel Hill, 1984), 5.

20. Ibid., 6.

21. Ferrell, *The Eisenhower Diaries*, 54.

22. Morison, *Coral Sea, Midway and Submarine Actions*, 6.

23. Leahy, *I Was There*, 103.

24. Ibid.

CHAPTER 7

1. Mark Harrison, "The Economics of World War II: An Overview," in Mark Harrison, ed., *The Economics of World War II: Six Great Powers in International Comparison* (Cambridge: Cambridge University Press, 1998), 3.

2. Robert Leckie, *Delivered from Evil: The Saga of World War II* (New York: Harper and Row, 1987), 311.

3. Eliot A. Cohen, *Supreme Command: Soldiers, Statesmen, and Leadership in Wartime* (New York: The Free Press, 2002), 50.

4. Goodwin, *No Ordinary Time*, 313-314.

5. John Kenneth Galbraith, *Name-*

Dropping: From F. D. R. On (Boston: Houghton Mifflin Company, 1999), 38.

6. Ibid.

7. *New York Times* June 10, 1942.

8. Doris Kearns Goodwin, *No Ordinary Time*, 357–58.

9. Ibid., 318–19.

10. *New York Times*, November 14, 1942, 1.

11. Greg Robinson, *By Order of the President: F. D. R. and the Internment of Japanese Americans* (Cambridge, MA: Harvard University Press, 2001), 77.

12. Ibid., 94.

13. Kyle Palmer, "Speedy Moving of Japs Urged," *Los Angeles Times*, January 31, 1942.

14. *New York Times*, February 15, 1942.

15. Greg Robinson, *By Order of the President*, 108.

16. *Los Angeles Times*, February 21, 1942.

17. Milton Eisenhower, letter to President Roosevelt, Container 2: War Relocation Authority: Misc. 1942–1944, Hyde Park, NY: The Franklin D. Roosevelt Library.

18. Ibid.

19. Geoffrey R. Stone, *Perilous Times: Free Speech in Wartime from the Sedition Act of 1798 to the War on Terrorism* (New York: W. W. Norton, 2004), 124.

20. Ibid.

21. Speech File, Box Container 66, Hyde Park, NY: The Franklin D. Roosevelt Library; see also*New York Times*, February 24, 1942.

22. *New York Times*, February 24, 1942.

23. Ibid.

24. Fireside Chat, Speech File, Box Container 66, February 23, 1942, Hyde Park, NY: The Franklin D. Roosevelt Library, 7.

25. Ibid., 10.

26. *New York Times*, February 24, 1942.

27. *Plessy v. Ferguson*, 163 US 537 (1896).

28. Goodwin, *No Ordinary Time*, 330.

29. Ibid., 328.

30. Ibid., 329.

31. Message to Congress, Speech File, Box Container 67, April 27, 1942, Hyde Park, NY: The Franklin D. Roosevelt Library, 4.

32. Fireside Chat, Speech File, Box Container 66, April 28, 1942, Hyde Park, NY: The Franklin D. Roosevelt Library, 5.

33. Ibid., April 28, 1942, Hyde Park, NY: The Franklin D. Roosevelt Library, 6–7.

34. Message to Congress, Speech File, Box Container 67, April 27, 1942, Hyde Park, NY: The Franklin D. Roosevelt Library, 4.

CHAPTER 8

1. Morison, *Coral Sea, Midway and Submarine Actions* 70.

2. Mitsuo Fuchida and Masatake Okumiya, *Midway: The Battle that Doomed Japan, The Japanese Navy's Story* (Annapolis: Naval Institute Press, 2001), 75.

3. Ibid.

4. Richard B. Frank, *Downfall: The End of the Imperial Japanese Empire* (New York: Random House, 1999), 5.

5. Fuchida and Okumiya, *Midway: The Battle that Doomed Japan*, 93.

6. Ibid.

7. Jack Gallaway, *The Odd Couple: Blamey and MacArthur at War*(Queensland, Australia: University of Queensland Press, 2000), 88.

8. Ibid.

9. Fuchida and Okumiya, *Midway: The Battle that Doomed Japan*, 97.

10. Boyd and Yoshida, *The Japanese*

Submarine Force and World War II,
114.

11. Gallaway, *The Odd Couple* , 90.

12. Ibid.

13. Ibid., 92.

14. Fuchida and Okumiya, *Midway: The Battle that Doomed Japan*, 133.

15. Keegan, *Intelligence in War*, 200.

16. Potter, *Nimitz*, 85.

17. Ibid., 79.

18. Ibid.,19; Fuchida and Okumiya, *Midway: The Battle that Doomed Japan*, 140.

20. Fuchida and Okumiya, *Midway: The Battle that Doomed Japan*, 157.

21. Potter, *Nimitz*, 87–91.

22. E. P. Forrestal, *Admiral Raymond A. Spruance, USN: A Study in Command* (Washington, DC: U.S. Government Printing Office, 1966), 41–42.

23. Paul S. Dull, *A Battle History of the Imperial Japanese Navy (1941-1945)* (Annapolis: Naval Institute Press, 1978), 146.

24. Morison, *Coral Sea, Midway and Submarine Actions* , 122; see also Gallaway, *The Odd Couple*, 99.

25. Edwin P. Hoyt, *Yamamoto: The Man Who Planned Pearl Harbor* (New York: McGraw-Hill, 1990), 164.

26. Forrestal, *Admiral Raymond A. Spruance, USN*, 49; see also Gallaway, *The Odd Couple*, 100.

27. Hoyt, *Yamamoto*, 165

28. Forrestal, *Admiral Raymond A. Spruance, USN*, 51–53.

29. Potter, *Nimitz*, 107.

30. Morison, *Coral Sea, Midway and Submarine Actions*,158.

31. *Time Magazine*, June 15, 1942, 16.

32. Ibid.

33. Ibid., 27.

34. Thomas B. Buell, *Master of Sea Power: A Biography of Fleet Admiral Ernest J. King* (Boston: Little, Brown and Co.,

1980), 336.

35. Fuchida and Okumiya, *Midway: The Battle that Doomed Japan*, 269.

36. Ibid., 289.

CHAPTER 9

1. A. B. Feuer, *Coast Watching in the Solomon Islands: The Bougainville reports, December 1941-July 1943* (New York: Praeger Publishers, 1992), xii.

2. Gallaway, *The Odd Couple*, 30.

3. Ibid.

4. Ibid., 83.

5. Ibid.

6. Douglas A. MacArthur, *Reminiscences* (New York: McGraw-Hill, 1964), 145.

7. Gallaway, *The Odd Couple*, 34.

8. MacArthur, *Reminiscences*, 145.

9. Gallaway, "Photo Gallery" in *The Odd Couple*.

10. David Jones and Peter Nunan, *U.S. Subs Down Under: Brisbane, 1942-1945* (Annapolis: Naval Institute Press, 2005), 8–10.

11. Theodore H. White, *In Search of History: A Personal Adventure* (New York: Harper and Row, 1978), 115–116.

12. Gallaway, *The Odd Couple*, 54.

13. Ibid., 5.

14. McCarthy, *South-West Pacific Area— First Year*, 29.

15. James, *The Years of MacArthur*, 186.

16. Gallaway, *The Odd Couple*, 111.

17. James, *The Years of MacArthur*, 197.

18. McCarthy, *South-West Pacific Area— First Year*, 33.

19. James, *The Years of MacArthu*, 202.

20. McCarthy, *South-West Pacific Area— First Year*, 33.

21. James, *The Years of MacArthur*, 203–204.

22. Ibid., 204.

23. McCarthy, *South-West Pacific Area—*

First Year, 330–331; see also James, *The Years of MacArthur*, 206.

24. McCarthy, *South-West Pacific Area—First Year*, 159.

25. Ibid., 158–161; see also James, *The Years of MacArthur*, 207.

26. James, *The Years of MacArthur*, 204–206.

27. Ibid., 207–208.

28. McCarthy, *South-West Pacific Area—First Year*, 186; see also James, *The Years of MacArthur*, 208–209.

29. James, *The Years of MacArthur*, 206.

30. McCarthy, *South-West Pacific Area—First Year*, 248.

31. James, *The Years of MacArthur*.

32. Ibid., 218.

33. Ibid., 234.

34. *Petersburg Plan*, October 31, 1942.

35. Ibid.

36. Ibid.

CHAPTER 10

1. Buell, *Master of Sea Power*, 215.

2. Ibid.

3. McCarthy, *South-West Pacific Area—First Year* (1959), 119.

4. Ibid.

5. Ibid., 152.

6. Ibid.

7. Ibid.

8. Martin Clemens, *Alone on Guadalcanal: A Coastwatcher's Story* (Annapolis: Naval Institute Press, 1998), 172.

9. Ibid, 22.

10. William Bradford Huie, *Can Do! The Story of the Seabees* (Annapolis: Naval Institute Press, 1997), 40.

11. Ibid.

12. Ibid., 43–44.

13. Richard B. Frank, *Guadalcanal* (New York: Random House, 1990), 233.

14. Eric Hammel, *Guadalcanal: Starvation Island* (New York: Crown

Publishers, 1987), 332, 241.

15. Coffey, *Hap*, 281–282.

16. Ibid.

17. Ibid.

18. Gen. Henry H. Arnold, "One Comdr for Pacific Theater April 3, 1942," memorandum to Gen. George C. Marshall, October 6, 1942.

19. Potter, *Nimitz*, 191.

20. Ibid., 193.

21. Dull, *A Battle History of the Imperial Japanese Navy (1941–1945)*, 223–224.

22. Deanne Durrett, *Unsung Heroes of World War II: The Story of the Navajo Code Talkers* (New York: Facts on File, 1998), 63.

23. Ibid., 36, 63.

24. Ibid., 63–64.

25. E. B. Potter, *Bull Halsey* (Annapolis: Naval Institute Press, 1985), 160.

26. Ibid.

27. Ibid., 162.

28. Ibid.

CHAPTER 11

1. Hammel, *Guadalcanal: Starvation Island*, 332.

2. Ibid., 352.

3. Ibid.

4. Hoyt, *Yamamoto*, 213.

5. Ibid., 216.

6. Ibid., 218.

7. Ibid., 219.

8. Ibid., 220.

9. Hammel, *Guadalcanal: Starvation Island*, 353.

10. Huie, *Can Do!*, 42.

11. Ibid.

12. Ibid.

13. Ibid., 41–42.

14. Alan Schom, *The Eagle and the Rising Sun: The Japanese-American War, 1941–1943* (New York: W. W. Norton, 2004), 407.

15. *Time Magazine,* November 30, 1942, 28; see also Schom, *The Eagle and the Rising Sun,* 407.

16. McCarthy, *South-West Pacific Area— First Year,* 342.

17. Potter, *Bull Halsey,* 180.

18. Hoyt, *Yamamoto,* 235.

19. Hammel, *Guadalcanal: Starvation Island,* 449–450; see also Hoyt, *Yamamoto,* 236.

20. Keegan, *Intelligence in War,* 189.

21. Durrett, *Unsung Heroes of World War II,* 94.

22. Hoffman, *Chesty,* 218.

23. Various Guadalcanal veterans, conversations with author, early 1943.

24. George C. Marshall, *Biennial Report of the Chief of Staff of the United States Army, 1939, to June 30, 1943, to the Secretary of War* (Lexington, VA: George C. Marshall Research Library, 1945).

CHAPTER 12

1. George C. Kenney, *General Kenney Reports: A Personal History of the Pacific War* (1949; repr., New York: Office of Air Force History, 1997), 136.

2. Messages, Colonel Sverdrup to General Casey, NO. 930, October 19, 1942, n.n., October 26, 1942, n.n.; October 27, 1942, No. 1686, October 29, 1941, No. RQ-902, October 30, 1942. All in 384, G-3 Files, GHQ SWPA, 114th Engineering Battalion (C). History Papuan Campaign; 32d Div AAR, Papuan Campaign.

3. Potter, *Bull Halsey,* 212.

4. Gallaway, *The Odd Couple,* 144.

5. Robert Lawrence Eichelberger Papers and Diaries, Durham, NC: Duke University Library, File 0CIII8.

6. General Blamey, letter to General MacArthur, December 27, 1942; see also Samuel Milner, *Victory in Papua,*

United States Army in World War II: The War in the Pacific (Washington, DC: U.S. Government Printing Office, 1957), 329.

7. Schaller, *Douglas MacArthur,* 72.

8. Ibid.

9. McCarthy, *South-West Pacific Area— First Year,* 531.

10. James, *The Years of MacArthur,* 274.

11. Ibid., 276.

12. Ibid., 276–277.

13. Jones and Nunan, *U.S. Subs Down Under,* 213.

14. Ibid., 259.

15. McCarthy, *South-West Pacific Area— First Year,* 531.

16. MacArthur, *Reminiscences,* 170.

17. David Dexter, *The New Guinea Offensive,* Australia in the War of 1939–1945, Series One, Army, vol. 6 (Canberra: Australia War Memorial, 1961), 55.

18. Milner, *Victory in Papua* (1957), 25.

19. James, *The Years of MacArthur,* 309.

20. Buell, *Master of Sea Power,* 358.

21. Leahy, *I Was There,* 263.

CHAPTER 13

1. Boyd and Yoshida, *The Japanese Submarine Force and World War II,* 114.

2. Ibid.

3. James, *The Years of MacArthur,* 295.

4. Ibid., 405.

5. Ibid.

6. Dexter, *The New Guinea Offensive,* 220.

7. Ibid., 57.

8. Ibid., 11.

9. Ibid., 57.

10. Ibid., 282.

11. Ibid., 28.

12. Ibid., 390.

13. Minutes of the Combined Chiefs of Staff, Quadrant Conference at Quebec, 17 August 1943.

14. Ibid.
15. Michael Howard, *Grand Strategy,* History of the Second World War, vol. 4 (London: Her Majesty's Stationery Office, 1970), 592.
16. Forrest C. Pogue, *George C. Marshall: Organizer of Victory, 1943–1945* (New York: Viking Press, 1973), 281.
17. James, *The Years of MacArthur,* 362.
18. Ibid., 363.
19. Gerald E. Wheeler, *Kinkaid of the Seventh Fleet: A Biography of Admiral Thomas C. Kinkaid, U.S. Navy* (Annapolis: Naval Institute Press, 1996), 344.
20. Ibid., 345.
21. McCarthy, South-West Pacific Area—First Year, 29.
22. Gerald Wheeler, *Kinkaid of the Seventh Fleet,* 348.
23. James, *The Years of MacArthur,* 336.
24. Ibid., 341.
25. Ibid., 344.
26. Gerald Wheeler, *Kinkaid of the Seventh Fleet,* 353.

CHAPTER 14

1. Brian Crozier, *The Man Who Lost China: The First Full Biography of Chiang Kai-Shek* (New York: Charles Scribner's Sons, 1976), 219.
2. Ibid.
3. Ibid.
4. Ibid., 236.
5. Ibid.
6. Ibid., 237.
7. Barbara Tuchman, *Stilwell and the American Experience in China, 1911–1945* (New York: McMillan, 1970), 222.
8. Ibid., 223.
9. Crozier, *The Man Who Lost China,* 216.
10. Leahy, *I Was There,* 157.
11. Kenneth S. Davis, *FDR, the War President, 1940–1943* (New York:

Random House, 2000), 412.
12. White, *In Search of History,* 115–116.
13. Tuchman, *Stilwell and the American Experience in China, 1911–1945,* 301.
14. Ibid., 303.
15. Ibid., 304.
16. Daniel Ford, *Flying Tigers: Claire Chennault and the American Volunteer Group* (Washington, DC: Smithsonian Institution Press, 1991), 245.
17. Ibid., 377.
18. Tuchman, *Stilwell and the American Experience in China, 1911–1945,* 337.
19. Ibid.
20. Ibid., 367.
21. Ibid.
22. Ibid., 371.

CHAPTER 15

1. Buell, *Master of Sea Power,* 336.
2. James, *The Years of MacArthur,* 307.
3. Buell, *Master of Sea Power,* 190.
4. Dexter, *The New Guinea Offensive,* 4.
5. Buell, *Master of Sea Power,* 279.
6. Frank, *Downfall,* 27.
7. James, *The Years of MacArthur,* 306.
8. Ibid.
9. Potter, *Bull Halsey,* 212–213.
10. Ibid., 216.
11. McCarthy, *South-West Pacific Area—First Year,* 590.
12. Buell, *Master of Sea Power,* 333.
13. Clay Blair, Jr., *Silent Victory: The U.S. Submarine War against Japan* (Philadelphia: J. B. Lippincott Co., 1975), 418.
14. Holland M. Smith and Percy Finch, *Coral and Brass* (Washington, DC: Zenger Publishing Co., 1979), 106.
15. James, *The Years of MacArthur,* 318.
16. Ibid., 319.
17. Outgoing classified message from Office Chief of Staff to Gen. D. MacArthur, July 14, 1943, Lexington,

VA: George C. Marshall Research
Library.

18. *Life*, October 1, 1945, 29.

CHAPTER 16

1. Edward Miller, *War Plan Orange*,
198–202.

2. Ibid., 202.

3. John Miller, Jr., *Cartwheel: The
Reduction of Rabaul*, United States
Army in World War II: The War in
the Pacific. (Washington, DC: Office
of the Chief of Military History,
Department of the Army, 1959), 235.

4. Ibid., 248.

5. Ibid., 351.

6. Ibid.

7. Ibid.

8. Ibid., 352.

9. Ibid., 377.

10. James, *The Years of MacArthur*, 387.

11. John Miller, Jr., *Cartwheel: The
Reduction of Rabaul*, 380.

12. Gavin Long, *The Final Campaigns*,
Australia in the War of 1939–1945,
Series One, Army, vol. 7 (Canberra:
Australian War Memorial, 1963), 557,
561.

13. Ibid., 557.

14. Ibid.

15. Ibid.

16. Ibid.

CHAPTER 17

1. Michael B. Graham, *Mantle of Heroism:
Tarawa and the Struggle for the
Gilberts, November 1943* (Novato, CA:
Presidio Press, 1993), 10–11.

2. Ibid.

3. Ibid., 62–65.

4. Ibid., 94.

5. Smith and Finch, *Coral and Brass*, 122.

6. Joseph H. Alexander, *Storm Landings:
Epic Amphibious Battles in the
Central Pacific* (Annapolis: Naval

Institute Press, 1997), 54.

7. Ibid., 258.

8. *Time Magazine*, December 6, 1943, 25.

9. Ibid., 22.

10. Ibid.

11. *Newsweek*, December 6, 1943, 112.

12. Forrestal, , *Admiral Raymond A.
Spruance, USN*, 98.

13. Alexander, *Storm Landings*, 49.

14. Graham, *Mantle of Heroism*, 311.

15. Forrestal, *Admiral Raymond A.
Spruance, USN*, 101.

16. Potter, *Nimitz*, 279.

17. Ibid., 280.

18. Ibid.

19. Ibid.

20. Ibid.

21. Jack Hawkins, as told to William B.
Hopkins, Sr.; see also William B.
Hopkins, *One Bugle, No Drums: The
Marines at Chosin Reservoir* (Chapel
Hill, NC: Algonquin Books, 1986).

22. Ibid.

23. Forrestal, *Admiral Raymond A.
Spruance, USN*, 111.

24. Potter, *Nimitz*, 278.

25. *Newsweek*, February 21, 1944, 26.

26. Ibid.

27. Forrestal, *Admiral Raymond A.
Spruance, USN*, 118.

CHAPTER 18

1. Keith Wheeler, *War Under the Pacific*,
29.

2. Blair, *Silent Victory*, 360.

3. Ibid., 381.

4. Ibid., 384.

5. Jones and Nunan, *U.S. Subs Down
Under*, 96.

6. Keith Wheeler, *War Under the Pacific*,
97.

7. Ibid., 98.

8. Ibid., 112.

9. Ibid., 114.

10. Boyd and Yoshida, *The Japanese*

Submarine Force and World War II, 161.

11. Ibid., xiii.

12. Jones and Nunan, *U.S. Subs Down Under*, 218.

13. Blair, *Silent Victory*, 768.

14. Ibid., 721.

15. Ibid., 337.

16. Ibid., 769.

17. Ibid., 816.

18. Keith Wheeler, *War Under the Pacific*, 23.

19. Ibid., 62.

CHAPTER 19

1. Gallaway, *The Odd Couple*, 170; Edward J. Drea, *MacArthur's ULTRA: Codebreaking and the War against Japan, 1942-1945* (Lawrence, KS: University Press of Kansas, 1992), 92-93.

2. Ibid., 170.

3. Douglas A. MacArthur, "Command organization in the southwest Pacific Area," memorandum to George C. Marshall, February 27, 1944, Lexington, VA: George C. Marshall Research Library.

4. Gallaway, *The Odd Couple*, 176.

5. Ibid., 178.

6. Gerald Wheeler, *Kinkaid of the Seventh Fleet*, 361.

7. Potter, *Bull Halsey*, 266; see also Gerald Wheeler, *Kinkaid of the Seventh Fleet*, 361.

8. Potter, *Bull Halsey*, 266.

9. Ibid.

10. Ibid.

11. Ibid.

12. James, *The Years of MacArthur*, 389; see also Gallaway, *The Odd Couple*, 182-183.

13. Gerald Wheeler, *Kinkaid of the Seventh Fleet*, 361.

14. Drea, *MacArthur's ULTRA*, 105.

15. Buell, *Master of Sea Power*, 444.

16. James, *The Years of MacArthur*, 334.

17. Ibid., 423.

18. Ibid., 430.

19. *Collier's*, February 12, 1944, 48-49.

20. James, *The Years of MacArthur*, 435.

21. Ibid., 434-435.

22. Ibid., 459.

23. Ibid., 463.

24. Ibid., 483.

CHAPTER 20

1. Smith and Finch, *Coral and Brass* , 181-82.

2. Edward Miller, *War Plan Orange*, 184.

3. Louis L. Snyder, *The War: A Concise History, 1939-1945* (New York: J. Messner, 1960), 324.

4. Ibid., 325.

5. Buell, *Master of Sea Power*, 440.

6. Ibid.

7. Ibid., 442.

8. Ibid.

9. Ibid., 444.

10. Forrestal, *Admiral Raymond A. Spruance, USN*, 123.

11. Ibid., 137.

12. Ibid., 140.

13. Ibid., 148.

14. James, *The Years of MacArthur*, 491.

15. Victor Brooks, *Hell Is Upon Us: D-Day in the Pacific—Saipan to Guam, June-August 1944* (Cambridge, MA: Da Capo Books, 2005), 310.

16. Smith and Finch, *Coral and Brass*, 9-10.

17. Forrestal, *Admiral Raymond A. Spruance, USN*, 152.

18. W. F. Craven and J. L. Cate, eds., *The Pacific: Matterhorn to Nagasaki, June 1944 to August 1945*, The Army Air Forces in World War II, vol. 5 (Chicago: University of Chicago Press, 1953), 577.

CHAPTER 21

1. Blair, *Silent Victory*, 693.
2. U.S. Strategic Bombing Survey, "Summary Report (Pacific War)," Washington, DC, July 1, 1946, 27.
3. Douglas MacArthur, "Formosa Campaign. G. C. Marshall Papers," memorandum to War Department, June 18, 1944, Lexington, VA: George C. Marshall Research Library.
4. George C. Marshall, memorandum to General MacArthur, G. C. Marshall Papers, Box 74, Folder 55, 24 June 1944, Lexington, VA: George C. Marshall Research Library.
5. Charles A. Willoughby, ed., *Reports of General MacArthur: The Campaigns of MacArthur in the Pacific*, vol. 1 (Washington, DC: U.S. Government Printing Office, 1966), 166.
6. James, *The Years of MacArthur*, 527.
7. Buell, *Master of Sea Power*, 467.
8. Leahy, *I Was There*, 345.
9. Potter, *Nimitz*, 291.
10. Ibid., 291–292.
11. Kenneth I. Friedman, *Afternoon of the Rising Sun: The Battle of Leyte Gulf* (Novato, CA: Presidio Press, 2001), 10.
12. Ibid., 14.
13. Weldon E. "Dusty" Rhoades, *Flying MacArthur to Victory* (College Station, TX: Texas A&M University Press, 1987), 260.
14. Ibid., 260.
15. *Honolulu Advertiser*, August 11, 1944.
16. Ibid., 1.
17. James, *The Years of MacArthur*, 540.
18. George C. Marshall, letter to General Douglas MacArthur enclosing *Time Magazine* August 21 article, September 8, 1944, Lexington, VA: George Marshall Library.
19. Memorandum, "MacArthur and His Command," to George C. Marshall,

February 16, 1944, Lexington, VA: George Marshall Library; *Harper's Magazine* was denied permission to publish this article.
20. Ibid.
21. Frank, *Downfall*, 30.
22. Ibid.
23. Leahy, *I Was There*, 245.
24. Buell, *Master of Sea Power*, 470.
25. James, *The Years of MacArthur*, 537.
26. Ibid., 538.
27. Potter, *Bull Halsey*, 249.
28. Gallaway, *The Odd Couple*, 260.

CHAPTER 22

1. Blair, *Silent Victory*, 691.
2. George C. Marshall, memorandum to Admiral King, G. C. Marshall Papers, Box 64, Folder 2, Lexington, VA: George C. Marshall Research Library.
3. Pogue, *George C. Marshall*, 365.
4. George C. Marshall, letter to Governor Dewey, G. C. Marshall Papers, Box 64, Folder 2, Lexington, VA: George C. Marshall Research Library.
5. Ibid.
6. Pogue, *George C. Marshall*, 472.
7. George C. Marshall, letter to Governor Dewey, G. C. Marshall Papers, Box 64, Folder 2, Lexington, VA: George C. Marshall Research Library.
8. Tuchman, *Stilwell and the American Experience in China, 1911–1945*, 489.
9. Ibid., 490.
10. Ibid., 493.
11. Ibid., 501.
12. Ibid., 499.
13. James, *The Years of MacArthur*, 489.
14. Joseph H. Alexander, "Surprise and Chagrin: The Navy's Battle for Peleliu," *Proceedings, U.S. Naval Institute* 130, no. 11: 69.
15. James, *The Years of MacArthur*, 491.
16. U.S. Bureau of Yards and Docks, *Building the Navy's Bases in World*

War II: History of the Bureau of Yards and Docks and the Civil Engineer Corps, 1940-1946 vol. 2 (Washington, DC: U.S. Government Printing Office, 1947), iii.

17. Samuel Eliot Morison, *Victory in the Pacific 1945*, History of United States Naval Operations in World War II, vol. 14 (Boston: Little, Brown and Co., 1960), 158.

CHAPTER 23

1. Friedman, *Afternoon of the Rising Sun*, 116.
2. Potter, *Bull Halsey*, 281.
3. Ibid., 282.
4. Ibid.
5. Ibid.
6. Ibid.
7. Ibid., 284.
8. Samuel E. Morison, *Leyte, June 1944–January 1945*, History of United States Naval Operations in World War II, vol. 12 (Boston: Little, Brown and Co., 1958), 113.
9. James, *The Years of MacArthur*, 547.
10. Ibid., 547-548.
11. Ibid., 557.
12. Ibid.
13. Ibid.
14. Ibid.
15. Potter, *Bull Halsey*, 286.
16. Friedman, *Afternoon of the Rising Sun*, 42-43.
17. Jones and Nunan, *U.S. Subs Down Under*, 223.
18. Blair, *Silent Victory*, 755.
19. Ibid., 46-50, 94-95.
20. Potter, *Bull Halsey*, 279.
21. Friedman, *Afternoon of the Rising Sun*, 254.
22. Evan Thomas, *Sea of Thunder: Four Commanders and the Last Great Naval Campaign, 1941-1945* (New York: Simon and Schuster, 2006),

205.
23. Ibid., 56.
24. Ibid.
25. Ibid., 270.
26. Ibid., 297.
27. James, *The Years of MacArthur*, 565.
28. Potter, *Bull Halsey*, 290.
29. Gerald Wheeler, *Kinkaid of the Seventh Fleet*, 404.

CHAPTER 24

1. Combined Chiefs of Staff, 175th Meeting, Octagon Conference, September 15, 1944, Lexington, VA: George Marshall Library, p. 2.
2. Ibid., 4.
3. James, *The Years of MacArthur*, 548.
4. Ibid., 568.
5. Potter, *Bull Halsey*, 308.
6. Ibid., 228.
7. James, *The Years of MacArthur*, 569.
8. *New York Times*, October 30, 1944.
9. James, *The Years of MacArthur*, 570.
10. Ibid., 580.
11. Ibid., 723.
12. Ibid., 602.
13. Robert L. Eichelberger, *Our Jungle Road to Tokyo* (New York: Viking Press, 1950), 181-82.
14. Potter, *Bull Halsey*, 320-321
15. William F. Halsey and J. Bryan, III, *Admiral Halsey's Story* (New York: Whittlesey House, 1947), 239; see also Potter, *Bull Halsey*, 322.
16. Potter, *Bull Halsey*, 323.
17. James, *The Years of MacArthur*, 609-610.
18. Ibid., 614.
19. Samuel E. Morison, *The Liberation of the Philippines: Luzon, Mindanao, the Visayas, 1944-1945*, History of United States Naval Operations in World War II, vol. 13 (Boston: Little, Brown and Co., 1959), 169.

CHAPTER 25

1. James, *The Years of MacArthur*, 592.
2. Ibid., 622.
3. Ibid., 625.
4. Morison, *The Liberation of the Philippines*, 183.
5. James, *The Years of MacArthur*, 630.
6. Morison, *The Liberation of the Philippines*, 183.
7. James, *The Years of MacArthur*, 631.
8. Ibid.
9. Ibid., 632.
10. Ibid., 637.
11. Ibid., 643.
12. Ibid., 647–648.
13. Tuchman, *Stilwell and the American Experience in China, 1911–1945*, 511.
14. Ibid.
15. MacArthur, *Reminiscences*, 261.
16. Schaller, *Douglas MacArthur*, 91.
17. Ibid.
18. Ibid.
19. James, *The Years of MacArthur*, 764.
20. Robert E. Sherwood, *Roosevelt and Hopkins, an Intimate History* (New York: Harper, 1948), 525–526.
21. Roger Mudd, *American Heritage Great Minds of History* (New York: John Wiley, 1999), 3, 188.
22. Boyd and Yoshida, *The Japanese Submarine Force and World War II*, 183–184.
23. Gerald Wheeler, *Kinkaid of the Seventh Fleet*, 426.
24. George C. Kenney, *General Kenney Reports: A Personal History of the Pacific War* (New York: Duell, Sloan and Pearce, 1949), 526–527.
25. Craven and Cate, *The Pacific: Matterhorn to Nagasaki, June 1944 to August 1945*, 470.
26. Morison, *The Liberation of the Philippines*, 214.
27. James, *The Years of MacArthur*, 738.
28. Ibid., 748–749.
29. Wilbur H. Morrison, *Point of No Return: The Story of the Twentieth Air Force* (New York: Times Books, 1979), 263.
30. Marshall. *Biennial Report of the Chief of Staff of the United States Army, July 1, 1943, to June 30, 1945, to the Secretary of War* (Lexington, VA: George C. Marshall Research Library, 1945), 83.
31. Roy Edgar Appleman and others, *Okinawa: The Last Battle*, United States Army in World War II: The War in the Pacific, (Washington, DC: Office of the Chief of Military History, Department of the Army, 1948), 652.
32. Halsey and Bryan, *Admiral Halsey's Story*, 255.
33. Long, *The Final Campaigns*, 584.

CHAPTER 26

1. Potter, *Nimitz*, 358; see also Forrestal, *Admiral Raymond A. Spruance, USN*, 168.
2. Richard F. Newcomb, *Iwo Jima* (1965; repr., New York: Bantam Books, 1995), 4–5.
3. Ibid.
4. Ibid., 8.
5. Ibid., 22.
6. Smith and Finch, *Coral and Brass*, 246.
7. *Time Magazine*, March 12, 1945; see also Morison, *Victory in the Pacific 1945*.
8. Potter, *Nimitz*, 358.
9. James Bradley with Ron Powers, *Flags of Our Fathers* (New York: Bantam Books, 2000), 165.
10. Ibid., 172.
11. Alexander Molnar, Jr., "Navajo Code Talkers: World War II Fact Sheet," Navy and Marine Corps WWII Commemorative Committee, August 12, 1997, http://www.history.navy.mil/faqs/faq61-2.htm.

12. Ibid.

13. Smith and Finch, *Coral and Brass*, 261.

14. Newcomb, *Iwo Jima*, 148.

15. Ibid.

16. Bradley and Powers, *Flags of Our Fathers*, 5.

17. Marshall, *Biennial Report of the Chief of Staff of the United States Army, July 1, 1943, to June 30, 1945, to the Secretary of War*, 106.

18. Neal Thompson, "Montford Point Marines," *Proceedings, U.S. Naval Institute* 131, no 11, 34.

19. Ibid.

20. Smith and Finch, *Coral and Brass*, 15.

21. Richard Wheeler, *Iwo* (1980; repr., Annapolis: Naval Institute Press, 1994), 13.

22. Newcomb, *Iwo Jima*, 240.

23. Ibid., 202.

24. Smith and Finch, *Coral and Brass*, 275.

25. Durrett, *Unsung Heroes of World War II*, 93.

26. Smith and Finch, *Coral and Brass*, 238.

CHAPTER 27

1. Forrestal, *Admiral Raymond A. Spruance, USN*, 164.

2. Ibid., 187.

3. Nicholas Evan Sarantakes, ed., *Seven Stars: The Okinawa Battle Diaries of Simon Bolivar Buckner, Jr., and Joseph Stilwell* (College Station, TX: Texas A&M University Press, 2004), 28.

4. Morison, *Victory in the Pacific 1945*, 92.

5. Ibid.

6. Forrestal, *Admiral Raymond A. Spruance, USN*, 194.

7. Potter, *Nimitz*, 369.

8. Robert Leckie, *Okinawa: The Last Battle of World War II* (New York:

Viking, 1995), 70.

9. Ibid., 69.

10. Ibid., 32.

11. Morison, *Victory in the Pacific 1945*, 203.

12. John Peter Stevenson, "A Submariner to Be Remembered," *Proceedings, U.S. Naval Institute* 126, no. 7, 92.

13. Morison, *Victory in the Pacific 1945*, 337.

14. Peter Lyon, *Eisenhower: Portrait of the Hero* (Boston: Little, Brown and Co., 1974), 339.

15. MacArthur, *Reminiscences*, 99–100.

16. Kai Bird and Lawrence Lifschultz, eds., *Hiroshima's Shadow: Writings on the Denial of History and the Smithsonian Controversy* (Stony Creek, CT: Pamphleteer's Press, 1996), 199–200.

17. Harry S. Truman, *Memoirs: Year of Decisions*, vol. 1 (Garden City, NY: Doubleday and Company, 1955).

18. Ibid., 67.

19. Sarantakes, *Seven Stars*, 75.

20. Ibid., 72.

21. Leckie, *Okinawa: The Last Battle of World War II*, 201.

22. Ibid., 200.

23. Sarantakes, *Seven Stars*, 71.

24. Leckie, *Okinawa: The Last Battle of World War II*, 202; see also Forrestal, *Admiral Raymond A. Spruance, USN*.

25. Forrestal, *Admiral Raymond A. Spruance, USN*, 218.

26. Morison, *Victory in the Pacific 1945*, 277.

27. Sarantakes, *Seven Stars*, 91.

28. Ibid., 91–92.

CHAPTER 28

1. Coffey, *Hap* (1982), 337.

2. Leahy, *I Was There*, 428.

3. Morison, *Point of No Return*, 9.

4. Ibid., 15.

5. Ibid., 19.
6. Ibid., 48.
7. Frank, *Downfall*, 51.
8. Morrison, *Point of No Return* , 90.
9. Ibid., 92.
10. Ibid., 157.
11. Ibid., 166.
12. William Meador, U.S. Army Air Corps, retired, personal DVD.
13. Morrison, *Point of No Return*, 92.
14. Leahy, *I Was There*, 79.
15. Morrison, *Point of No Return*, 185.
16. Ibid., 193.
17. Craven and Cate, *The Pacific: Matterhorn to Nagasaki, June 1944 to August 1945*, 608.
18. Morrison, *Point of No Return*, 198.
19. Craven and Cate, *The Pacific: Matterhorn to Nagasaki, June 1944 to August 1945*, 537.
20. Ibid., 617.
21. Meador, personal DVD.
22. Craven and Cate, *The Pacific: Matterhorn to Nagasaki, June 1944 to August 1945*, 618.
23. Ibid., 620.
24. Ibid., 622.
25. Ibid., 674–675.
26. Morrison, *Point of No Return*, 220–221.
27. Ibid., 221.
28. Thomas A. Siefring, *U.S. Air Force in World War II* (Secaucus, NJ: Chartwell Books Inc., 1977), 162–178.
29. Craven and Cate, *The Pacific: Matterhorn to Nagasaki, June 1944 to August 1945*, 731–732.
30. Morrison, *Point of No Return*, 263.
31. Ibid., 243.
32. Ibid.
33. Craven and Cate, *The Pacific: Matterhorn to Nagasaki, June 1944 to August 1945*, 731–732.
34. Morrison, *Point of No Return*, 243.
35. Ibid.
36. Ibid., 262.
37. Ibid., 183.
38. Ibid., 261.
39. Pirates Log, A History of 6th Bombardment Group, 13.
40. Craven and Cate, *The Pacific: Matterhorn to Nagasaki, June 1944 to August 1945*, 736.

CHAPTER 29

1. Potter, *Nimitz*, 379.
2. General Marshall, "Sutherland," memorandum to General MacArthur, April 15, 1945, Lexington, VA: George C. Marshall Research Library (not sent).
3. Ibid.
4. Frank, *Downfall*, 34.
5. Ibid.
6. James, *The Years of MacArthur*, 767.
7. Douglas MacArthur, "Command post at Guam," memorandum to General Marshall, June 19, 1945, Lexington, VA: George Marshall Library, Virginia Military Institute.
8. James, *The Years of MacArthur*, 729–730.
9. Chester Nimitz, "Headquarters at Guam," letter to MacArthur, July 1, 1945, Lexington, VA: George Marshall Library.
10. Frank, *Downfall*, 37.
11. Arthur Bryant, *Triumph in the West: A History of the War Years Based on the Diaries of Field-Marshal Lord Alanbrooke, Chief of the Imperial General Staff* (Bungay, Suffolk, UK: Richard Clay and Company Ltd., 1960), 363.
12. Forrestal, *Admiral Raymond A. Spruance, USN* (1966), 209.
13. Potter, *Bull Halsey*, 346.
14. Smith and Finch, *Coral and Brass*, 4.
15. Ibid., 5.
16. James, *The Years of MacArthur*, 6.
17. Leon V. Sigal, *Fighting to a Finish: The Politics of War Termination in the United States and Japan, 1945* (Ithaca: Cornell University Press, 1988), 95.

18. Frank, *Downfall*, 132.
19. Herbert Hoover, "Ending the Japanese War," memorandum to Truman, May 30, 1945.
20. Frank, *Downfall*, 141–142.
21. Ibid., 143.
22. Ibid., 124.
23. Ibid.
24. Ibid.
25. U.S. Strategic Bombing Survey, "Summary Report (Pacific War)," 26.
26. Ted Morgan, *FDR: A Biography* (New York: Simon and Schuster, 1985), 631.
27. Frank, *Downfall*, 242.
28. Ibid., 243.
29. David McCullough, *Truman* (New York: Simon and Schuster, 1992), 443.
30. Frank, *Downfall*, 232.
31. Ibid.
32. Ibid., 233.
33. Ibid.
34. Ibid., 234.
35. Leahy, *I Was There*, 420
36. Potter, *Nimitz*, 412.
37. Ibid.
38. Frank, *Downfall*, 235.
39. McCullough, *Truman*, 437.
40. Leahy, *I Was There*, 441.
41. Morison, *Victory in the Pacific 1945*, 339.
42. McCullough, *Truman*, 436.
43. Ibid., 455.
44. Ibid., 456.
45. Potter, *Nimitz*, 390.
46. Ibid.
47. Marshall, *Biennial Report of the Chief of Staff of the United States Army, July 1, 1943, to June 30, 1945, to the Secretary of War*, 107.
48. James, *The Years of MacArthur*, 408.
49. Ibid., 776.
50. Ibid., 458.
51. Ibid., 459.
52. Frank, *Downfall*, 346.
53. James, *The Years of MacArthur*, 459–460.

54. Ibid., 460.
55. Directive to the Supreme Commander for the Allied Powers and Instrument of Surrender – August 14, 1945, Lexington, VA: George C. Marshall Research Library.
56. Frank, *Downfall*, 328–329.
57. Morison, *Victory in the Pacific 1945*, 365.
58. Ibid.
59. MacArthur, *Reminiscences*, 285.

CHAPTER 30

1. *West's Encyclopedia of American Law*, vol. 5 (St. Paul, MN: West Publishing Company, 1998), 158.
2. U.S. Strategic Bombing Survey Summary Report (Pacific War) July 1, 1946, 27.
3. Long, *The Final Campaigns*, 584.
4. U.S. Strategic Bombing Survey, "Summary Report (Pacific War)," 21.
5. Ibid.
6. Bird and Lifschultz, *Hiroshima's Shadow* (1998), 210.
7. James, *The Years of MacArthur*, x.
8. Schaller, *Douglas MacArthur*, 118.
9. Durrett, *Unsung Heroes of World War II*, 106.
10. Borch and Martinez, *Kimmel, Short and Pearl Harbor*, 115–116.
11. *New York Times*, February 25, 1983.
12. Stone, *Perilous Times*, 307.
13. Peter Irons, review of *Wartime Hysteria: The Role of the Press in the Removal of 110,000 Persons of Japanese Ancestry During World War II* by the Japanese American Curriculum Project, *Washington Post*, September 30, 2001.

Bibliography

BOOKS

Alexander, Joseph H. *Storm Landings: Epic Amphibious Battles in the Central Pacific.* Annapolis: Naval Institute Press, 1997.

Appleman, Roy E., James M. Burns, Russell A. Gugeler, and John Stevens. *Okinawa: The Last Battle.* Washington, DC: Office of the Chief of Military History, Department of the Army, 1948.

Baldwin, Hanson W. *The Crucial Years, 1939-1941: The World at War.* New York: Harper and Row, 1970.

Ballard, Robert D., and Rick Archbold. *Return to Midway.* Washington, DC: National Geographic/Madison Press Book, 1999.

Ballendorf, Dirk A., and Merrill L. Bartlett. *Pete Ellis: An Amphibious Warfare Prophet, 1880-1923.* Annapolis: Naval Institute Press, 1997.

Barker, A. J. *Midway: The Turning Point.* New York: Galahad Books, 1981.

Bartlett, Merrill L. *Lejeune: A Marine's Life, 1867-1942.* Annapolis: Naval Institute Press, 1996.

Bartsch, William H. *December 8, 1941: MacArthur's Pearl Harbor.* College Station, TX: Texas A&M University Press, 2003.

Beard, Charles A. *President Roosevelt and the Coming of the War, 1941: A Study in Appearances and Realities .* New Haven, CN: Yale University Press, 1948.

Bercuson, David, and Holger Herwig. *One Christmas in Washington: The Secret Meeting between Roosevelt and Churchill that Changed the World.* Woodstock, NY: Overlook Press, 2005.

Bird, Kai, and Lawrence Lifschultz, eds. *Hiroshima's Shadow: Writings on the Denial of History and the Smithsonian Controversy.* Stony Creek, CT: Pamphleteer's Press, 1996.

Bix, Herbert P. *Hirohito and the Making of Modern Japan.* New York: HarperCollins Publishers, 2000.

Blair, Clay, Jr. *Silent Victory: The U.S. Submarine War against Japan.* Philadelphia: J. B. Lippincott Co., 1975.

Borch, Fred, and Daniel Martinez. *Kimmel, Short and Pearl Harbor: The Final Report Revealed.* Annapolis: Naval Institute Press. 2005.

Boyd, Carl, and Akihiko Yoshida. *The Japanese Submarine Force and World War II.* Annapolis: Naval Institute Press, 1995.

Bradley, James, with Ron Powers. *Flags of Our Fathers.* New York: Bantam Books, 2000.

Bradley, Omar N., and Clay Blair.

General's Life: An Autobiography. New York: Simon and Schuster, 1983.

Brooks, Victor. *Hell Is Upon Us: D-Day in the Pacific—Saipan to Guam, June-August 1944*. Cambridge, MA: Da Capo Books, 2005.

Browne, Courtney. *Tojo: The Last Banzai*. New York: Holt Rinehart and Winston, 1967.

Bryant, Arthur. *Triumph in the West: A History of the War Years Based on the Diaries of Field-Marshal Lord Alanbrooke, Chief of the Imperial General Staff*. Bungay, Suffolk, UK: Richard Clay and Company Ltd., 1960.

——. *The Turn of the Tide: A History of the War Years Based on the Diaries of Field-Marshal Lord Alanbrooke, Chief of the Imperial General Staff*. Garden City, NY: Doubleday and Company, 1957.

Budiansky, Stephen. *Battle of Wits: The Complete Story of Codebreaking in World War II*. New York: The Free Press, 2000.

Buell, Thomas B. *Master of Sea Power: A Biography of Fleet Admiral Ernest J. King*. Boston: Little, Brown and Company, 1980.

Burns, James MacGregor. *Roosevelt: The Lion and the Fox, 1882-1940*. New York: Harcourt, Brace and World, 1956.

Burns, Paul. *The Brisbane Line Controversy: Political Opportunism versus National Security, 1942-1945*. St. Leonards, NSW, Australia: Allen and Unwin, 1998.

Chambers, John Whiteclay II, ed. *The Oxford Companion to American Military History*. New York: Oxford University Press, 1999.

Chris, Henry. *Battle of the Coral Sea*. Great Naval Battles. Annapolis: Naval Institute Press, 2003.

Christianson, Stephen G. *Facts about the Congress*. New York: H. W. Wilson Company, 1996.

Chynoweth, Bradford Grethen. *Bellamy Park: Memoirs*. Hicksville, NY: Exposition Press, 1975.

Clark, Ronald W. *Einstein: The Life and Times*. New York: World Publishing Company, 1971.

Clausen, Henry C., and Bruce Lee. *Pearl Harbor: Final Judgment*. New York: Crown Publishers, Inc., 1992.

Clemens, Martin. *Alone on Guadalcanal: A Coastwatcher's Story*. Annapolis: Naval Institute Press, 1998.

Clifford, Kenneth J.. *Progress and Purpose: A Developmental History of the United States Marine Corps, 1900-1970*. Washington, DC: History and Museums Divisions, 1973.

Coffey, Thomas M. Hap: *The Story of the U.S. Air Force and the Man Who Built It, General Henry H. "Hap" Arnold*. New York: Viking Press, 1982.

Cohen, Eliot A. *Supreme Command: Soldiers, Statesmen and Leadership in Wartime*. New York: The Free Press, 2002.

Cohen, Eliot A., and John Gooch. *Military Misfortunes: The Anatomy of Failure in War*. New York: Vintage Books, 1990.

Connaughton, Richard. *Shrouded Secrets: Japan's War on Mainland Australia, 1942-1944*. London: Brassey's, 1994.

Costello, John. *The Pacific War*. New York: Rawson, Wade Publishers, Inc., 1981.

Cowley, Robert, ed. *No End Save Victory: Perspectives on World War II*. New York: G. P. Putnam's Sons, 2001.

Craven, W. F., and J. L. Cate, eds. *The Pacific: Matterhorn to Nagasaki, June 1944 to August 1945*. The Army Air Forces in World War II, vol. 5. Chicago: University of Chicago Press, 1953.

Cray, Ed. *General of the Army: George C.*

Marshall, Soldier and Statesman. New York: W. W. Norton and Co., 1990.

Crowl, Philip A., and Edmund G. Love. *Seizure of the Gilberts and Marshalls.* Washington, DC: Office of the Chief of Military History, Department of the Army, 1955.

Crozier, Brian. *The Man Who Lost China: The First Full Biography of Chiang Kai-Shek.* New York: Charles Scribner's Sons, 1976.

Daily, Robert. *The Code Talkers: American Indians in World War II.* New York: Franklin Watts, 1995.

Dallek, Robert. *Franklin D. Roosevelt and American Foreign Policy, 1932–1945.* New York: Oxford University Press, 1979.

Danchev, Alex, and Daniel Todman, eds. *War Diaries, 1939–1945: Field Marshal Lord Alanbrooke.* Berkeley: University of California Press, 2001.

Davis, Burke. *Marine! The Life of Lt. Gen. Lewis B. (Chesty) Puller, USMC (Ret.).* Boston: Little, Brown and Company, 1962.

Davis, Kenneth S. *FDR, the War President, 1940–1943.* New York: Random House, 2000.

Dexter, David. *The New Guinea Offensive.* Australia in the War of 1939–1945, Series One, Army, vol. 6. Canberra: Australia War Memorial, 1961.

Drea, Edward J. *MacArthur's ULTRA: Codebreaking and the War against Japan, 1942–1945.* Lawrence, KS: University Press of Kansas, 1992.

Dull, Paul S. *A Battle History of the Imperial Japanese Navy (1941–1945).* Annapolis: Naval Institute Press, 1978.

Durrett, Deanne. *Unsung Heroes of World War II: The Story of the Navajo Code Talkers.* New York: Facts on File, 1998.

Eichelberger, Robert L. *Our Jungle Road to Tokyo.* New York: Viking Press, 1950.

Eisenhower, John S. D., *General Ike: A Personal Reminiscence.* New York: The Free Press, 2003.

Ferrell, Robert H., ed. *The Eisenhower Diaries.* New York: Norton, 1981.

Feuer, A. B. *Coast Watching in the Solomon Islands: The Bougainville reports, December 1941–July 1943.* New York: Praeger Publishers, 1992.

Ford, Daniel. *Flying Tiger: Claire Chennault and the American Volunteer Group.* Washington, DC: Smithsonian Institution Press, 1991.

Forrestal, E. P. *Admiral Raymond A. Spruance, USN: A Study in Command.* Washington, DC: U.S. Government Printing Office, 1966.

Frank, Richard B. *Downfall: The End of the Imperial Japanese Empire.* New York: Random House, 1999.

———. *Guadalcanal.* New York: Random House, 1990.

Franzwa, Gregory M., and William J. Ely. *Leif Sverdrup. "engineer soldier at his best."* Gerald, MO: Patrice Press, 1980.

Friedman, Kenneth I. *Afternoon of the Rising Sun: The Battle of Leyte Gulf.* Novato, CA: Presidio Press, 2001.

Gailey, Harry A. *MacArthur Strikes Back: Decision at Buna, New Guinea, 1942–1943.* Novato, CA: Presidio Press, 2000.

Galbraith, John Kenneth. *Name-Dropping: From F.D.R. On.* Boston: Houghton Mifflin Company, 1999.

Gallaway, Jack. *The Odd Couple: Blamey and MacArthur at War.* Queensland, Australia: University of Queensland Press, 2000.

Goldstein, Donald M., and Katherine V. Dillon, eds. *The Pacific War Papers: Japanese Documents of World War II.* Washington, DC: Potomac Books, 2004.

Gole, Henry G. *The Road to Rainbow: Army Planning for Global War, 1934–*

1940. Annapolis: Naval Institute Press, 2003.

Goodwin, Doris Kearns. *No Ordinary Time: Franklin and Eleanor Roosevelt: the home front in World War II*. New York: Simon and Schuster, 1995.

Gordin, Michael D. *Five Days in August: How World War II Became a Nuclear War*. Princeton, NJ: Princeton University Press, 2007.

Gosnell, Harold F. *Truman's Crises: A Political Biography of Harry S. Truman*. Westport, CT: Greenwood Press, 1980.

Grace, James W. *The Naval Battle of Guadalcanal: Night Action, 13 November 1942*. Annapolis: Naval Institute Press, 1999.

Graham, Michael B. *Mantle of Heroism: Tarawa and the Struggle for the Gilberts, November 1943*. Novato, CA: Presidio Press, 1993.

Halsey, Willam F., and J. Bryan III. *Admiral Halsey's Story*. New York: Whittlesey House, 1947.

Hammel, Eric. *Guadalcanal: Starvation Island*. New York: Crown Publishers, 1987.

Hayes, Grace. The History of the Joint Chiefs of Staff in World War II: The War against Japan. Annapolis: Naval Institute Press, 1982.

Hoffman, Jon T. *Chesty: The Story of Lieutenant General Lewis B. Puller, USMC*. New York: Random House, 2001.

Holmes, W. J. *Double-Edged Secrets: U.S. Naval Intelligence Operations in the Pacific during World War II*. 1979. Reprint, Annapolis: Naval Institute Press, 1998.

Hopkins, William B. *One Bugle No Drums: The Marines at Chosin Reservoir*. Chapel Hill, NC: Algonquin Books, 1986.

Horner, D. M. *Crisis of Command: Australian Generalship and the Japanese Threat, 1941-1943*. Canberra, Australia: Australian National University Press, 1978.

Howard, Michael. *Grand Strategy* History of the Second World War, vol. 4. London: Her Majesty's Stationery Office, 1970.

Hoyt, Edwin P. *How They Won the War in the Pacific: Nimitz and His Admirals*. New York: Weybright and Talley, 1970.

———. *Submarines at War: The History of the American Silent Service*. New York: Stein and Day, 1983.

———. *Yamamoto: The Man Who Planned Pearl Harbor*. New York: McGraw-Hill Publishing Company, 1990.

Huie, William Bradford. *Can Do! The Story of the Seabees*. Annapolis: Naval Institute Press, 1997.

James, D. Clayton. *The Years of MacArthur*. 3 vols. Boston: Houghton Mifflin Company, 1970–1985.

Jones, David, and Peter Nunan. *U.S. Subs Down Under: Brisbane, 1942–1945*. Annapolis: Naval Institute Press, 2005.

Kahn, David. *The Codebreakers: The Story of Secret Writing*. New York: Scribner, 1996.

Keegan, John. *The Battle for History: Re-Fighting World War II*. New York: Vintage Books, 1996.

———. *Intelligence in War: Knowledge of the Enemy from Napoleon to al-Quaeda*. New York: Alfred A. Knopf, 2003.

Kenney, George C. *General Kenney Reports: A Personal History of the Pacific War*. New York: Duell, Sloan and Pearce, 1949.

Lane, Kerry. *Marine Pioneers: the Unsung*

Heroes of World War II. Atglen, PA: Schiffer Publishing, 1997.

Lawton, Manny. *Some Survived*. Chapel Hill, NC: Algonquin Books of Chapel Hill, 1984.

Leahy, William D. *I Was There: The Personal Story of the Chief of Staff to Presidents Roosevelt and Truman Based on His Notes and Diaries Made at the Time*. New York: Whittlesey House, 1950.

Leckie, Robert. *Delivered from Evil: The Saga of World War II*. New York: Harper and Row, 1987.

——. *Okinawa: The Last Battle of World War II*. New York: Viking, 1995.

Leffler, Melvyn P. *A Preponderance of Power: National Security, the Truman Administration, and the Cold War*. Stanford, CA: Stanford University Press, 1992.

Lejeune, John A. *The Reminiscences of a Marine*. Philadelphia: Dorrance and Co., 1930.

Levy, Leonard W., ed. *Encyclopedia of the American Constitution*. New York: MacMillan Publishing Company, 1986.

Long, Gavin. *The Final Campaigns*. Australia in the War of 1939–1945, Series One, Army, vol. 7. Canberra: Australian War Memorial, 1963.

Lowman, David D. *Magic: The Untold Story of U.S. Intelligence and the Evacuation of Japanese Residents from the West Coast during World War II*. Provo, Utah: Athena Press, 2001.

Lyon, Peter. *Eisenhower: Portrait of the Hero*. Boston: Little, Brown and Co., 1974.

MacArthur, Douglas A. *Reminiscences*. New York: McGraw-Hill, 1964.

Manchester, William. *American Caesar: Douglas MacArthur, 1880–1964*. Boston: Little, Brown and Co., 1978.

McCarthy, Dudley. *South-West Pacific Area—First Year: Kokoda to Wau*. Australia in the War of 1939–1945, Series One, Army, vol. 5. Adelaide: The Griffin Press,, 1959.

McCullough, David. *Truman*. New York: Simon and Schuster, 1992.

Meacham, Jon . *Franklin and Winston: An Intimate Portrait of an Epic Friendship*. New York: Random House, 2003.

Miller, Edward S. *War Plan Orange: The U.S. Strategy to Defeat Japan, 1897–1945*. Annapolis: Naval Institute Press, 1991.

Miller, John, Jr. *Guadalcanal: The First Offensive*. United States Army in World War II: The War in the Pacific. Washington, DC: Historical Division, Dept. of the Army, 1949.

——. *U.S. Army in World War II. The War in the Pacific. Cartwheel: The Reduction of Rabaul*. Washington, DC: Office of the Chief of Military History, 1959.

Millett, Allan R. *Semper Fidelis: The History of the United States Marine Corps*. New York: The Free Press, 1991.

Millis, Walter, ed. *The Forrestal Diaries*. In collaboration by E. S. Duffield. New York: Viking Press, 1951.

Milner, Samuel. *Victory in Papua*. United States Army in World War II: The War in the Pacific. Washington, DC: U.S. Government Printing Office, 1957.

Mitsuo, Fuchida, and Masatake Okumiya. *Midway: The Battle that Doomed Japan, The Japanese Navy's Story*. 1955. Reprint, Annapolis: Naval Institute Press, 2001.

Morgan, Ted. *FDR: A Biography*. New York: Simon and Schuster, 1985.

Morison, Samuel E. *The Rising Sun in the Pacific, 1931–April 1942*. Vol. 3 (1948).

Coral Sea, Midway and Submarine Actions: May 1942–August 1942. Vol. 4 (1960). The Struggle for Guadalcanal: August 1942–February 1943. Vol. 5 (1949). Breaking the Bismarcks Barrier: 22 July 1942–1 May 1944. Vol. 6 (1950). Aleutians, Gilberts and Marshalls: June 1942–April 1944. Vol. 7 (1951). New Guinea and the Marianas: March 1944–August 1944. Vol. 8 (1953). Leyte, June 1944–January 1945. Vol. 12 (1958). The Liberation of the Philippines: Luzon, Mindanao, the Visayas, 1944–1945. Vol. 13 (1959). Victory in the Pacific 1945. Vol. 13 (1960). Supplement and General Index. Vol. 15. History of United States Naval Operations in World War II. New York: Little, Brown and Co., 1948–1962.

Morrison, Wilbur H. Point of No Return: The Story of the Twentieth Air Force. New York: Times Books, 1979.

Morton, Louis. Strategy and Command: The First Two Years. United States Army in World War II. The War in the Pacific. 1962. Reprint, Washington, DC: Office of the Chief of Military History, Department of the Army, 1978.

Mosley, Leonard. Hirohito, Emperor of Japan. Englewood Cliffs, NJ: Prentice-Hall, 1966.

———. Marshall, Hero for Our Times. New York: Hearst Books, 1982.

Muller, Eric L. Free To Die for Their Country: The Story of the Japanese American Draft Resisters in World War II. Chicago: The University of Chicago Press, 2001.

Nardo, Don. The War in the Pacific. San Diego, CA: Lucent Books, 1991.

Nelson, Craig. The First Heroes: The Extraordinary Story of the Doolittle Raid—America's First World War II Victory. New York: Viking, 2002.

Newcomb, Richard F. Iwo Jima. 1965. Reprint, New York: Bantam Books, 1995.

Pitt, Barrie, and Frances Pitt. The Month-by-Month Atlas of World War II. New York: Summit Books, 1989.

Pogue, Forrest C. George C. Marshall: Organizer of Victory, 1943–1945 New York: Viking Press, 1973.

Polmar, Norman, and Thomas B. Allen. World War II: America at War, 1941–1945. New York: Random House, 1991.

Potter, E. B. Bull Halsey. Annapolis: Naval Institute Press, 1985.

———. Nimitz. Annapolis: Naval Institute Press, 1976.

Powell, Alan. The Shadow's Edge: Australia's Northern War. Carlton, VC, Australia: Melbourne University Press, 1988.

Rhoades, Weldon E.. Flying MacArthur to Victory. College Station, TX: Texas A&M University Press, 1987.

Robinson, Greg. By Order of the President: F. D. R. and the Internment of Japanese Americans. Cambridge, MA: Harvard University Press, 2001.

Ross, John A., ed. International Encyclopedia of Population. Vol. 1. New York: The Free Press, 1982.

Sandler, Stanley, ed. World War II in the Pacific: An Encyclopedia. New York: Garland Publishing, 2001.

Sarantakes, Nicholas Evan, ed. Seven Stars: The Okinawa Battle Diaries of Simon Bolivar Buckner, Jr., and Jospeh Stilwell. College Station, TX: Texas A&M University Press, 2004.

Schaller, Michael. Douglas MacArthur: The Far Eastern General. New York: Oxford University Press, 1989.

Schom, Alan. The Eagle and the Rising Sun: The Japanese-American War, 1941–1943. New York: W. W. Norton, New York, 2004.

Shepherd, Peter J. Three Days to Pearl: Incredible Encounter on the Eve of War. Annapolis: Naval Institute Press, 2000.

Sherwood, Robert E. *Roosevelt and Hopkins, an intimate history.* New York: Harper, 1948.

Sides, Hampton. *Ghost Soldiers: The Forgotten Epic Story of World War II's Most Dramatic Mission.* New York: Doubleday, 2001.

Siefring, Thomas A. *U.S. Air Force in World War II.* Secaucus, NJ: Chartwell Books Inc., 1977.

Sigal, Leon V. *Fighting to a Finish: The Politics of War Termination in the United States and Japan, 1945.* Ithaca: Cornell University Press, 1988.

Simpson, B. Mitchell III. *Admiral Harold R. Stark: Architect of Victory, 1939–1945.* Columbia, SC: University of South Carolina Press, 1989.

Smith, George W. *Carlson's Raid: The Daring Marine Assault on Makin.* Novato, CA: Presidio Press, 2001.

Smith, Holland M., and Percy Finch. *Coral and Brass.* Washington, DC: Zenger Publishing Co., 1979.

Smith, Robert Ross. *Triumph in the Philippines.* Washington, DC: Office of the Chief of Military History, Department of the Army, 1963.

Snyder, Louis L. *The War: A Concise History 1939–1945.* New York: J. Messner, 1960.

Spector, Ronald H. *Eagle against the Sun: The American War with Japan.* New York: The Free Press, 1985.

St. John, Philip A. *USS Enterprise (CV-6).* Paducah, KY: ers, 1997.

Stoler, Mark A. *Allies and Adversaries: The Joint Chiefs of Staff, the Grand Alliance, and U.S. Strategy in World War II.* Chapel Hill, NC: The University of North Carolina Press, 2000.

———. *George C. Marshall: Soldier-Statesman of the American Century.* Boston: Twayne Publishers, 1989.

Stone, Geoffrey R. *Perilous Times: Free Speech in Wartime from the Sedition Act of 1798 to the War on Terrorism.* New York: W. W. Norton, 2004.

Thomas, Evan. *Sea of Thunder: Four Commanders and the Last Great Naval Campaign, 1941–1945.* New York: Simon and Schuster, 2006.

Toland, John. *The Rising Sun: The Decline and Fall of the Japanese Empire, 1936–1945.* New York: Random House, 1970.

———. *Infamy: Pearl Harbor and Its Aftermath.* Garden City, NY: Doubleday, 1982.

Truman, Harry S. *Memoirs.* 2 vols. Garden City, NY: Doubleday, 1955–1956.

Tuchman, Barbara W. *Stilwell and the American Experience in China, 1911–1945.* New York: Macmillan, 1970.

U.S. Bureau of Yards and Docks. *Building the Navy's Bases in World War II: History of the Bureau of Yards and Docks and the Civil Engineer Corps, 1940–1946* vol. 2. Washington, DC: U.S. Government Printing Office, 1947.

U.S. Marine Corps. *Third Marine Division's Two Score and Ten History.* Paducah, KY: Turner Publishers, 1992.

U.S. Strategic Bombing Survey. *The Fifth Air Force in the War against Japan.* Washington, DC: Military Analysis Division, 1947.

Van der Vat, Dan. *The Pacific Campaign: World War II, the U.S.-Japanese Naval War, 1941–1945.* New York: Simon and Schuster, 1991.

West's Encyclopedia of American Law. Volume 5. St. Paul, MN: West Publishing Company, 1998.

Wheeler, Gerald E. *Kinkaid of the Seventh Fleet: A Biography of Admiral Thomas C. Kinkaid, U.S. Navy.* Annapolis: Naval Institute Press, 1996.

Wheeler, Keith. *War Under the Pacific.* Chicago: Time-Life Books, Inc., 1980.

Wheeler, Richard. *Iwo*. 1980. Reprint, Annapolis: Naval Institute Press, 1994).

White, Theodore H. *In Search of History: A Personal Adventure*. New York: Harper and Row, 1978.

Wigmore, Lionel. *The Japanese Thrust*. Australia in the War of 1939–1945, Series One, Army, vol. 4. Canberra: Australian War Memorial, 1957.

Williams, Mary L., comp. *Chronology 1941–1945*. United States Army in World War II. Washington, DC: Office of the Chief of Military History, Department of the Army, 1960.

Willmott, H. P. *Grave of a Dozen Schemes: British Naval Planning and the War against Japan, 1943–1945*. Annapolis: Naval Institute Press, 1996.

Willoughby, Charles A., ed. *Reports of General MacArthur: The Campaigns of MacArthur in the Pacific*, vol. 1, and *MacArthur in Japan. The Occupation: Military Phase*, vol. 1. Supplement. Washington, DC: U.S. Government Printing Office, 1966.

PAPERS

Arnold, Henry H. "October 6, 1942, re: One Comdr for Pacific Theater". Memorandum to Gen. George C. Marshall. Operations Division of the War Department General Staff File 384 (4-3-42).

Combined Chiefs of Staff. Minutes 1942–1945. Lexington, VA: George C. Marshall Research Library.

Combined Chiefs of Staff. Minutes of 175th Meeting of the Octagon Conference, September 15, 1944, at 10:30 a.m .

"Directive to the Supreme Commander for the Allied Powers and Instrument of Surrender." August 14, 1945. Lexington, VA: George C. Marshall Research Library.

Doolittle Raiders Bomb Tokyo, May 15, 1995. Assistant Navy Secretary Bernard D. Rostker's remarks to Task Force 16 as three navy citations awarded at the Pentagon.

Eisenhower, Milton. Letter to President Roosevelt. Container 2: War Relocation Authority: Misc. 1942-1944. Hyde Park, NY: The Franklin D. Roosevelt Library.

"February 16, 1944, re: MacArthur and His Command," Memorandum to Gen. George C. Marshall. Article *Harper's Magazine* was denied permission to publish. Lexington, VA: George C. Marshall Research Library.

Hoover, Herbert. "Ending the Japanese War." Memorandum to Truman, May 30, 1945.

Joint Chiefs of Staff. Minutes 1942–1945. Lexington, VA: George C. Marshall Research Library.

MacArthur, Douglas A. "February 27, 1944, re: command organization in the southwest Pacific Area." Memorandum to Gen. George C. Marshall. Lexington, VA: George C. Marshall Research Library.

———. "June 18, 1944, re: Formosa campaign." Memorandum to War Department. George C. Marshall Papers. Lexington, VA: George C. Marshall Research Library.

———. "June 19, 1945, Re: command post at Guam." Memorandum to General Marshall. Lexington, VA: George C. Marshall Research Library.

Marshall, George C. "April 15, 1945, re: Sutherland." Letter to Gen. Douglas A. MacArthur. Never sent. Lexington, VA: George C. Marshall Research Library.

———. January 16, 1941. Memorandum to Gen. Gerow, Microfilm Reel 32, Item 1303, Lexington, VA: George C. Marshall Museum.

———. June 24, 1944. Memorandum to

General MacArthur. Box 74, Folder 55, G. C. Marshall Papers. Lexington, VA: George C. Marshall Research Library.
———. September 8, 1944, letter enclosing August 21 *Time Magazine* article. Lexington, VA: George C. Marshall Library.
———. Letter to Governor Dewey, G. C. Marshall Papers, Box 64, Folder 2, Lexington, VA: George C. Marshall Research Library.
———. Memorandum to Admiral King, G. C. Marshall Papers, Box 64, Folder 2, Lexington, VA: George C. Marshall Research Library.
———. Personal letter to Gen. Maj. Short, February 7, 1941, WPD 4449-1.
Memorandum, "Operations Plan R-5," to the Adjutant General, War Department, Washington, DC, October 1, 1941, Lexington, VA: George C. Marshall Museum.
Nimitz, Chester A. "July 1, 1945, re: headquarters at Guam." Letter to General Douglas A. MacArthur. Lexington, VA: George C. Marshall Research Library.
Office Chief of Staff. Outgoing classified message to General Douglas MacArthur, July 14, 1943. Lexington, VA: George C. Marshall Research Library.
Petersburg Plan. October 31, 1942. General Headquarters, Southwest Pacific Area. Carlisle, PA: U.S. Army Military History Institute.
Roosevelt, Franklin D. Fireside Chat Transcripts, Speech Files, Box Container 66, Hyde Park, NY: The Franklin D. Roosevelt Library.
———. Message to Congress, Speech File, Box Container 67, April 27, 1942, Hyde Park, NY: The Franklin D. Roosevelt Library.
Secret War Department Document MID

000.7 Great Britain.
U.S. Strategic Bombing Survey, "Summary Report (Pacific War)." Washington, DC, July 1, 1946.

PERIODICALS

Alexander, Joseph H. "Surprise and Chagrin: The Navy's Battle for Peleliu." *Proceedings, U.S. Naval Institute* 130, no. 11: 68-72.
Collier's. February 12, 1944; April 1, 1944.
Cox, James A. "Pete Ellis: A Marine . . . raised on hay and whiskey." *Marine Corps League* 57, no. 3 (Autumn 2001).
———. "The Wake Chronicles." *Marine Corps League* 56, no. 1 (Spring 2000).
Honolulu Advertiser. Friday, August 11, 1944.
Peter Irons, review of *Wartime Hysteria: The Role of the Press in the Removal of 110,000 Persons of Japanese Ancestry During World War II* by the Japanese American Curriculum Project, *Washington Post,* September 30, 2001.
Life, October 1, 1945, 29–31.
Los Angeles Times, various, 1941–45.
Newsweek, various, 1941–1945.
New York Times, various, 1941–1945.
Odyssey 8, January 1999, p. 16.
Palmer, Kyle. "Speedy Moving of Japs Urged." *Los Angeles Times,* January 31, 1942.
Pierce, P. N. "The Unsolved Mystery of Pete Ellis." *Marine Corps Gazette.* February 1962, 36.
Reber, John J. "Pete Ellis: Amphibious Warfare Prophet." *Proceedings, U.S. Naval Institute* 103, no. 11: 53–64.
Roanoke Times and World News. 1941–1945.
Skanchy, T. C. "Not at the Iwo Jima Memorial." *Old Breed News* 1, no. 2 (April 2000).
Stevenson, John Peter. "A Submariner to Be Remembered." *Proceedings, U.S.*

Naval Institute 126, no.7 (July 2000), 92.
Thompson, Neal. "Montford Point Marines,"
Proceedings, U.S. Naval Institute 131, no.
11 (November 2005), 34.
Time Magazine. 1941–1945.

REPORTS

George C. Marshall, *Biennial Report
of the Chief of Staff of the United States
Army, July 1, 1943 to June 30, 1945, to
the Secretary of War* (Washington, 1945).
Historical Statistics of the U.S. Pt. 1. U.S.
Department of Commerce, 1975.
U.S. Congress, Joint Committee on
the Investigation of the Pearl Harbor
Attack, *Report,* (Washington, DC: U.S.
Government Printing Office, 1946).
U.S. Congress, Joint Estimate of Army
and Navy Air Action, March 31, 1941,
Pearl Harbor Attack Hearings, pt. 15,
exhibit 44.
U.S. War Department General Staff,
*Biennial reports of the Chief of Staff of
the United States Army to the Secretary
of War: 1 July 1939–30 June 1945*
(Washington, DC: Center of Military
History, 1996).

WEBSITES

www.marauder.org/marauder.htm—
Merrill's Marauders 5307 Composite
Unit Provisional. Unit History.
www.history.navy.mil/faqs/faq10-3.
htm—"Vice President Bush Calls World
War II Experience 'Sobering.'" Research
by JO2 Timothy J. Christmann, *Naval
Aviation News* 67 (March–April 1985):
12-15. Department of the Navy, Naval
Historical Center, 805 Kidder Breese SE,
Washington Navy Yard, Washington, DC
20374-5060.
www.history.navy.mil/faqs/faq61-2.htm—
"Navajo Code Talkers: World
War II Fact Sheet." Research by
Alexander Molnar, Jr., U.S. Marine
Corps/U.S. Army (Ret.). Department
of the Navy, Naval Historical Center,
805 Kidder Breese SE, Washington
Navy Yard, Washington,
DC 20374-5060.
www.wpunj.edu/hmss/polisci/faculty/
shalom/ssvjday.htm—Stephen R.
Shalom, "Dollar Diplomacy: V-J Day:
Remembering the Pacific War."
Z Magazine.

Index

Yap, 245, 246, 253, 256, 258, 259
Yardley, Herbert, 15, 16
Yat-sen, Dr. Sun, 159
Yellow River, 161, 162, 234
Ying, Hsiang, 161
Yogaki plan, 186
Yokohama, 84
Yokosuka Naval Base, 315
Yokoyama, Lt. Gen. Shizuo, 280

Yonabaru, 306, 309, 311, 312
Yontan Airfield, 306, 309
Yoshida, Maj., 232

Z
ZeDong, Mao, 159, 160, 162, 284, 319, 344
"Zero Hour," 181
Zhukov, Gen., 161

MILITARY UNITS
American
I Corps, 220, 279
1st Battleship Division, 57
1st Cavalry Division, 183, 215, 265, 281, 282
1st Marine Amphibious Corps, 134
1st Marine Division, 105, 107, 114, 116, 119, 123, 131, 134, 143, 156, 168, 175, 154, 254, 306, 307, 310, 312, 345
8th Marine Regiment, 313
1st Marine Parachute Battalion, 107, 112, 116, 180
1st Marine Raider Battalion, 107, 110
2nd Engineer Special Brigade, 156
2nd Marine Division, 7, 107, 131, 174, 186, 187, 189, 192, 194, 227, 229, 234, 311, 313
3rd Battalion, 192
8th Regiment, 313
2nd Marine Raider Battalion, 114
2nd Provisional Marine Raider Battalion, 180
III Amphibious Corps, 232, 304
3rd Infantry Brigade, 7
3rd Marine Defense Battalion, 107, 180, 182
3rd Marine Division, 1, 134, 177, 180–182, 186, 232, 296, 299, 311
9th Regiment, 299
21st Regiment, 296
3rd Special Base Defense Force, 187
4th Marine Brigade, 7
4th Marine Division, 227, 295, 296, 298
4th Marine Regiment, 183
V Amphibious Corps, 187, 301
5th Marine Division, 295, 296, 298, 301
2nd Battalion, 28th Regiment, 296
5th Marine Regiment, 107

6th Bombardment Group, 321, 325
6th Infantry Division, 280
6th Marine Defense Battalion, 89
6th Marine Division, 279, 304, 306, 311–313
22nd Marine Regiment, 306
6th Marine Regiment, 89, 191, 192
1st Battalion, 192
2nd Battalion, 192
6th Ranger Battalion, 262, 263
6th Seabees Battalion, 115
7th Amphibious Force, 219
7th Army Division, 174, 196, 197, 253, 263, 304, 306, 309, 311, 313
7th Marine Division, 1st Battalion, 124
7th Marine Regiment, 107, 116, 124
2nd Battalion, 124
8th Marine Division, 1st Battalion, 192
X Corps, 265, 313
XI Corps, 253, 281
11th Airborne Division, 281, 282
11th Marine Regiment, 124
XIV Corps, 175, 182, 183, 279
19th Regimental Combat Team, 24th Division, 275
XX Corps, 265
XXI Corps, 253
21st Infantry Division, 265
21st Marine Division
1st Battalion, 180
2nd Battalion, 180
3rd Battalion, 180, 295, 298
L Company, 298
22nd Marine Regiment, 198, 306
XXIV Corps, 263, 265, 304, 309, 311
24th Infantry Division, 265
27th Army Division, 186, 187, 189, 198, 200, 229, 230, 304, 311
28th Marine Regiment, 295, 296

SHIPS AND OTHER VESSELS
American and Allied